D1593596

Conceptual Foundations for Multidisciplinary Thinking

Conceptual Foundations for Multidisciplinary Thinking

Stephen Jay Kline

Stanford University Press
Stanford, California

Stanford University Press
Stanford, California

© 1995 by the Board of Trustees of the
Leland Stanford Junior University

Printed in the United States of America

CIP data are at the end of the book

Stanford University Press publications
are distributed exclusively by Stanford
University Press in the United States,
Canada, Mexico, and Central America;
they are distributed exclusively by
Cambridge University Press throughout
the rest of the world.

To Naomi and my other intimates who provide the love and acceptance that allow me to be myself, help me stay connected and honest, and thus make life worth living;

and

To our children and our children's children, to whom we elders owe an explanation of the world that is understandable, realistic, forward-looking, and whole.

Acknowledgments

Institutional

The Program in Science, Technology and Society at Stanford University has for more than twenty years maintained a discourse among scholars and researchers from more than a dozen disciplines. These ongoing discussions have provided a background that was essential to the shaping of these materials both in overall form and in many of the details. For these inputs I am grateful not only to the STS Program and the individuals in it but also to Stanford University and the successive provosts and members of the provost's staff for supporting programs of this breadth.

Three successive deans of the School of Engineering and four successive chairmen of the Department of Mechanical Engineering, which has paid my salary, have been exceedingly generous in granting me time to teach and do research in a program that passes far beyond the normal boundaries of the department and the school.

Individuals

The faculty members of the Program in Values, Technology, Science, and Society, past and present, via numerous discussions, have contributed to this work in ways too numerous to list. Among the VTSS faculty particular thanks are due: Walter Vincenti, who has read and made insightful comments on the papers that underlie Chapters 4 through 11 and on the complete manuscript; Robert McGinn, for innumerable enlightening conversations on many topics; Barry Katz, for much useful information and detailed comments on Chapters 15 and 16; Cliff Barnett, Ray Clayton, William Clebsch, Ted Good, Alex Inkeles,

Philip Rhinelander, Nathan Rosenberg, Bernie Siegel, and Robert Textor, for suggesting many papers and texts of important value to constructing these materials. Virginia Mann, the secretary of VTSS for its first fifteen years, provided not only cheerful and efficient assistance, but personal support and an atmosphere that significantly aided cooperative work. Al Eaton made important comments about the relation between the concepts of control and design.

A score of individuals volunteered to read the complete manuscript in the third draft and made constructive comments: Robert Anderson, Peter Bradshaw, W. Bliss Carnochan, Al Eaton, Alex Inkeles, Don Kash, David Kline, Pierre Noyes, Norris Pope, David Robb, Steve Robinson, M. R. Showalter, Robert Textor, and Walter Vincenti. Their comments resulted in many improvements in the final draft.

Provocative conversations with John McCarthy and Joel Ferziger have stimulated considerable thought. Moses Abramovitz of Economics has been particularly supportive on concepts of innovation. Dan Okimoto, Tom Rohlen, and James Raphael of Asian Studies have provided much information on developments in the Far East. Nashad Forbes supplied information about what has occurred in India since the end of the colonial era as it relates to these materials. Peter Galison provided information about the current state of work in the history and philosophy of science. Harold Bacon of Mathematics contributed much wisdom during many luncheon conversations about the underlying issues and suggested the metaphor of the map that is used at several points in the book.

My friends Robert H. Simmons, Lauren Oliver, Chuck Adams, Ed Eisen, David Robb, Rob Sauer, Norm Shea, and Bill Turner contributed a great deal over the years, not only through a deeper understanding of the issues involved in creating cooperative groups and workplaces and about the nature of projections, but also on the ways human thought processes can become tangled by personal background and by strong emotions.

In the Provost's Office, the efforts of William Miller and James Gibbs in helping form Program objectives and clarifying goals for VTSS are particularly noteworthy.

Individuals at other institutions who have provided both input and encouragement include: Rustum Roy, William F. Williams of Penn State, Steve Goldman of Lehigh, Caroline Whitbeck of MIT, Edward Constant of Carnegie-Mellon, Ed Layton of Minnesota, Robert M. White of the National Academy of Engineering, Don Kash of George Mason University, Thomas Park Hughes of the University of Pennsylvania, Gino Sovran of General Motors Research, Ed Wells and Jerry Paynter of the Boeing Company, Walt Robb of General Electric, Harvey Brooks and Lewis Branscomb of Harvard, Fumio Kodama of Tokyo University and NIST, and Yoshiaki Yahagi of Toyota Motors. Dennis Bushnell of NASA-Langley Research Center and James McMichael of AFOSR provided input about the relation of innovation models in military applications. Amitai Etzioni supplied information on the need for value-based economics through several papers.

Both my son, David M. Kline, and my friend Robert Showalter have many times discussed issues concerning the underlying logic of Chapters 4 through 12 as has another friend, David Robb. David Kline helped improve the bet for economists in Appendix B. Bob Benjamin and Peter Denning provided insight about the issues discussed in Chapters 4 and 5. Alexandre Favre of Marseilles commented on the paper underlying Chapters 6 and 7. Bliss Carnochan, as Director of the Stanford Center for the Humanities, and as co-teacher in one quarter of a VTSS class, gave both useful suggestions and moral support for the work. Harry Rowen stimulated work on innovation by his long-continued interest in U.S. productivity and its slowing pace after 1970. William Durham and Carolyn Kline were both helpful in discussing materials and suggesting references about genetics, behavioral biology, and paleoanthropology.

Very able secretarial support has been supplied by Cyndi Mortensen, Cherie Scott, Ditter Peschcke-Koedt, and Starr Russell. Preparation of the final manuscript was done by Lee Vorobyoff and Stanley R. Jacob, whose conscientious attention to many matters and cheerful assistance are gratefully acknowledged. A special thanks is due Ditter Peschcke-Koedt, who coordinated all aspects of the manuscript preparation with Stanford University Press and whose skills at word processing, layout, formatting, and manuscript organization are without parallel in my experience.

Successive generations of students in VTSS (now STS) classes have made many contributions through questions and suggestions. In particular, the students in VTSS 106 during Spring 1992 read the entire second draft of the book and made detailed comments on errata and points that were hard to follow as well as on substance. Members of this class included: Scott Crosby, Alan Daly, Deepa Francis, Eric Fleckten, Rafael Furst, Edward Garcia, Robert Jackson, Colleen Kirk, Patric McGowan, Jeremy Myers, Jacqueline Nerney, Courtney Newman, David T. Proefke, Kevin Rugg, Kathleen Wilds, and Jeffrey Wrona.

Since the background of this work has continued for twenty years, and the final form was only shaped in the past four years, I have no doubt forgotten some conversations that were important, and apologize in advance to any individuals who may have been overlooked.

Finally, many results in this work are iconoclastic, and hence I need to be particularly clear that the author is the only one responsible for the views expressed. Neither the institutions nor the individuals mentioned in the Acknowledgments are in any way responsible for the results and viewpoints expressed.

S.J.K.

Contents

Preface   *xiii*

1. Introduction   *1*

PART 1. THE SYSTEM CONCEPT

2. Systems, Domains, and Truth Assertions   *15*

3. Sysreps and the Human Mind   *30*

PART 2. COMPLEXITY

4. An Index for Complexity   *49*

5. Thinking About Complex Systems   *69*

6. Feedback as a Source of Complexity   *80*

PART 3. STRUCTURE

7. Hierarchy as a Structural Feature: The Hierarchy
    of Constitution   *101*

8. Interfaces of Mutual Constraint and Levels of Control:
    Polanyi's Principle   *110*

9. The Theory of Dimensions   *122*

10.   Integrated Control Information   *129*

11.   Disciplines at One Level: Disciplines and the Human Design Process   *137*

12.   Consistency as a Primary Criterion: The Limits of Reductionism and Synoptism   *143*

13.   Operational Procedures in Forming Sysreps for Complex Systems   *156*

14.   Examples of Multidisciplinary Analysis   *171*

15.   The Evolution of Disciplines, 1500–1900   *194*

16.   Relations Among the Disciplines in the Twentieth Century: Similarities and Differences   *213*

PART 4. FALLACIES OF PROJECTION

17.   Fallacies of Projection: Illustrations   *235*

18.   Fallacies of Projection: Possible Sources   *244*

PART 5. CONCLUSIONS

19.   What Have We Learned? A Summary of Results and Conclusions   *263*

20.   What Have We Learned? Implications and Inferences   *276*

Appendix A.   Implications for Education   *295*

Appendix B.   Two Standing Bets   *301*

Appendix C.   Hypotheses, Guidelines, Dicta, and Queries   *311*

Appendix D.   Glossary   *315*

References   *319*

Index   *331*

Preface

This work is intended for anyone interested in the human intellectual enterprise as a whole or in the non-major part of university education. Why is this work intended for such a broad audience of scholars?

The intellectual system developed largely in the Western world since the Reformation has become enormously powerful and productive as a means for understanding ourselves and our world. At the same time, our intellectual system is severely fragmented and lacks views of the whole. The lack of overviews creates two difficulties. We have no basis for understanding the relationship between our special area of expertise and the complete intellectual enterprise. There is no viewpoint we can use to understand the appropriate relationships among the various disciplines of knowledge. This book accordingly addresses such questions as:

- Can we erect overviews of our intellectual enterprise?
- Do we need them?
- Are there systems so complex that we cannot provide analytic or computer solutions for the entire systems in full detail? (If so, can we create and manage such systems?)
- Do the limitations of the human mind affect the way we have done and do scholarship?
- Has the absence of intellectual overviews created significant difficulties in our theories and practices?

In order to discuss these and other related questions, the materials within the book evolve through three stages: (1) Erection of appropriate definitions and concepts; (2) Creation of various kinds of conclusions built on (1); and (3) Emergence of several further results from combining elements of (2). By the end of the work, it is shown the answer to all five questions above is Yes! In addition, many other results emerge. A good many of these results are apparently new, and some contradict current wisdom within particular disciplines. Among the results are:

- A quantitative index for estimating the complexity of any system.
- Three overviews of the intellectual territory for the disciplines of knowledge that deal with truth assertions.
- Discussion from several viewpoints of why the principles of the human sciences necessarily differ in fundamental ways from the principles that apply to inert, naturally-occurring objects.
- Concepts and tools that help make more operational our tests of the appropriateness of models for real systems.
- Three independent demonstrations that neither the reductionist nor its opposing (synoptist) view is sufficient to treat all the problems of vital concern to humans, and delineation of what is needed to move beyond these two quarreling positions.

When one looks back over the material of this book, what it seems to be is a beginning, a first treatment, of a new area of discourse. I will call this area "multidisciplinary discourse." Multidisciplinary discourse is not what we usually mean by interdisciplinary study. There is some overlap, but the two are largely distinct approaches. Chapter 1 defines the area studied by multidisciplinary discourse.

Because the materials of this book build through several stages and use a number of words in newly defined ways, a typical précis would not be of much value at this point. For this reason, two kinds of summaries are given in Chapters 19 and 20. Also the appendixes include a glossary of new terms and a restatement of hypotheses, guidelines, and dicta.

The emergence of many new results in what we had thought was old terrain, and also of what appears to be a new area of discourse, is surprising. It is not what I had expected when I began this work in 1970. Hence, a brief history of the sources of this work may help the reader understand how this book came to be.

In 1970, I was one of four faculty members at Stanford who founded what is now called the Program in Science, Technology and Society (STS). The others were P. Rhinelander of Philosophy, W. C. Clebsch of Humanities Special Programs, and W. G. Vincenti of Aero/Astronautical Engineering. Professor Vincenti was interested in the history of the interaction of technology and society. My interests centered on basic concepts and their uses in providing clearer explanations for significant and largely unexplained areas. Neither a good supply of case studies nor sound basic concepts seemed to be available at that time for the STS field. Hence Professor Vincenti and I agreed that he would do case studies, and I would work on foundation concepts. Since the two types of studies need to inform each other, he and I have read the drafts of nearly all of each other's papers during the intervening twenty-odd years.

The field of Science, Technology and Society requires the use of ideas and results from many conventional disciplines. Consequently, foundation concepts need to be very broad. Over about fifteen years, nearly two books of materials of two different kinds emerged in the form of two volumes of syllabus. This work proceeded in the usual way, that is, continuing study punctuated yearly by the need for preparation of class materials. A number of published papers resulted. These papers are the basis for most of Chapters 2, 4, 6, and 7 through 12. This work was in large part made possible by an active STS forum among faculty members from a dozen or more disciplines at any given time, with some members entering and leaving during the years.

About 1989, I realized that the two separate volumes of syllabus could be unified and made more powerful if the focus of the work was shifted from concepts for the field of Science, Technology and Society to concepts for what I am now calling multidisciplinary discourse. Since 1989 several drafts of this book have been prepared under various titles, and comments received from scholars in a wide variety of fields. The large majority of these comments have been incorporated here. This process of integrating and rounding out the materials into a more unified whole has led to further emergent results that are the primary bases of Chapters 3, 5, 15, 16, 18, and 20. One result that emerged very late in the work (early 1993) is the realization of how much the limitations of the human mind affect our scholarly work. This result has a number of significant implications, and seems underdeveloped. References will therefore be appreciated.

The work in this book is as free from presuppositions as I have been able to make it. There are, however, two matters on which my position needs to be clear to the reader at the outset. These concern the reality of the world and the existence of a supreme being. This book does not attempt to settle either issue, but handles the two issues in different ways.

For the purposes of this book, I will assume that the world is real and, to a considerable (but not complete) extent, can be understood by human observation, human reasoning, and accumulated human knowledge and wisdom. I make these assumptions for several important pragmatic reasons. First, if we consider that the world is not real, that all we observe is no more than shadows dancing on the wall of Plato's cave, the position leads us toward hedonism, nihilism, and fatalism. It thereby augments the very human tendency to avoid the hard responsibilities we all encounter. Denial of what is too hard for us to face is a part of the human condition, but denial seldom leads to the solution of problems. Moreover, if the world is not real, why should we be serious about it? If we believe that the world is not real, then we may conclude that any view is as good as any other. And, if we accept that conclusion, we are more likely to end our existence by annihilating each other via wars or pollution of the earth to a point where we can no longer survive.

Moreover, the entire weight of science, including its enormous successes in facilitating human understanding of the world around us, assumes that human observations can be made reliable up to some limit of uncertainty. And in many areas this scientific knowledge is more profound, more detailed, and more reliable than prior types of human knowledge. In some (but not all) problem areas scientific knowledge allows us to generalize the observations into reliable predictive principles. We all need to delineate the areas for which fixed, reliable predictive principles can be erected and those for which they cannot. However, clear discussion of this matter needs some of the tools and concepts developed in the body of the book, and is therefore postponed.

Regarding the existence of a supreme being, I will not take a position. I will instead at a few places, where it becomes important, look at the question from each of the scientific and the religious views in order to include what each view shows.

Conceptual Foundations for Multidisciplinary Thinking

CHAPTER 1

Introduction

The intellectual system erected largely in the Western world since the Reformation is enormously powerful and productive. Although we have much yet to learn, the scientific approach to knowledge since the time of Galileo has provided the human race with a far better understanding of our world and of ourselves than was available to any previous society. This gain in understanding has arisen primarily from two sources. We have adopted what we loosely call "scientific methods," and we have broken the intellectual enterprise into a larger and larger number of parts (disciplines and research programs). We have created working groups of scholars who study each of the parts in as "scientific" a method as they can bring to bear. However, there is a near total absence of overviews of the intellectual terrain.

The lack of overviews of the intellectual terrain causes several difficulties. We have no means for understanding the relationship of our individual area of expertise to the larger intellectual enterprise. We have no viewpoint from which we can look objectively at the relations among the various disciplines. We tend to see science as a single method (usually based on physics), and thereby underestimate the differences in the methods and natures of various fields dealing with truth assertions. It seems past due that we begin to see if we can rectify these difficulties. That is the primary purpose of this book.

This book deals with questions such as the following:

- Can we erect overviews of the intellectual domain dealing with truth assertions about physical, biological, and social nature?
- Are such overviews important?
- What is the appropriate nature of the "principles" for various disciplines?

Are these the same for all fields, or are they necessarily in part different for different "domains of knowledge"?

- Is the dominant (reductionist) view of science sufficient? Or do we need other views to augment it?

In this book we will call the discussion of these and other related questions "multidisciplinary discourse." More specifically, multidisciplinary discourse will denote the study of two topics: (1) the relationships of the disciplines of knowledge to each other; and (2) the relationships of a given discipline to human knowledge about the world and ourselves as a whole.

Multidisciplinary discourse is not the same as what we usually call interdisciplinary study. Interdisciplinary study generally denotes the combining of knowledge from two (or sometimes more) disciplines to create syntheses that are more appropriate for certain problem areas. Multidisciplinary study examines the appropriate relationships of the disciplines to each other and to the larger intellectual terrain. There is some overlap between interdisciplinary and multidisciplinary study, but for the most part they are different areas.

The remainder of this chapter sets out the preliminary groundwork. It lists the topics that multidisciplinary discourse needs to cover, defines the terrain we will examine, and sets out some hypotheses we need to begin the discussion. Chapter 2 begins the discussion of the first overview of the terrain.

Multidisciplinary discourse needs to cover at least the following four topics:

1. The description of several overall frameworks that exhibit the place of the disciplines of knowledge with respect to each other.

2. The delineation of what a given discipline can (and cannot) represent in the world. The word "represent" here includes such things as descriptions, taxonomies, understanding, and possibly predictions.

3. The development of insight into the similarities and differences of the disciplines in matters such as the complexity of paradigmatic systems, the invariance of (or variation in) behaviors and principles over time, and the typical variables used in analyses.

4. The study of the following:

    (a) How the disciplines ought to constrain each other when applied to problems that inherently require knowledge from many disciplines, including examples or specific difficulties that have arisen from lack of this kind of discussion.

    (b) Some ways in which scholars can judge when subfields, or research programs, have drifted into error, nonproductive triviality, or approaches that inherently cannot produce the results sought.

    (c) Application of (a) and (b) to at least a few important historical and current examples.

(d) Implications of (a) and (b) for methodology in various disciplines, and in our total intellectual system.

This book examines elements of all four items above and other related topics.

Our discussion will focus on those disciplines of knowledge that deal with truth assertions about our world. The word "discipline" is not given a tight definition. Since we will want to examine carefully the differences between disciplines, a tight a priori definition might overconstrain our study. It is enough at this point to say, "a discipline" can be understood as the subject of study of a university department (or major sector of a department) in a late-twentieth-century university. This implies that a discipline possesses a specific area of study, a literature, and a working community of paid scholars and/or practitioners.

The operative verb about this discussion of multidisciplinarity is "to begin," for several reasons. For at least a century, there has been no community of scholars concerned with multidisciplinarity, and therefore no continuing discourse. As a result, there has been relatively little opportunity for the sort of ongoing discussions with colleagues that so often provide aid in testing and improving conceptual work. Many valuable and insightful suggestions for improvements have been made by reviewers, as the Acknowledgments note, but these do not entirely replace discussion within an ongoing, mature body of scholars.

Moreover, no work known to the writer covers all of the four topics listed above, or any part of item 4. These gaps further reinforce the idea that we have neglected the area of multidisciplinary study.

We will make no initial assumption concerning the question of the importance of multidisciplinary discourse. However, beginning at this point, I will start to build a case for its importance. This will allow us to draw conclusions concerning its importance in later chapters.

Several reasons why a discourse on multidisciplinarity is potentially important can be seen even at this starting point. First, the inability to perceive human knowledge as a whole, as a complete pattern, is one of the sources of pervasive anxiety in our times. In the face of a plethora of experts, whose specialized languages form a tower of Babel, we tend to feel uninformed, helpless, and lacking in control over our own lives. Even a modest amelioration of these feelings of anxiety would in itself justify the discourse. This is not to suggest that multidisciplinary activity is a way to solve all problems. On the contrary, I will argue that multidisciplinary discourse needs to be an additive to, not a replacement for, disciplinary work. To put this in different words, I will construct reasons why multidisciplinary discourse is needed not only to solve some problems but also to help disciplinary experts better understand the connection of their own field to the whole of human knowledge.

Another reason we need multidisciplinary discourse is the existence of "emergent properties." Systems constructed from qualitatively disparate parts often exhibit emergent properties (also called "holism"). To put this differently, systems made of qualitatively different kinds of parts, when hooked together and wired up, often can do things which precisely the same parts cannot do when they are unconnected. Even systems with homogeneous composition sometimes exhibit emergent properties, although far less commonly. These new properties of the whole system "emerge" from the interactions of the parts within the specific structure. Therefore the emergent properties exist only when the system structure is complete in an appropriate sense. For example, if you lay out all the bits and pieces of your car in your driveway, the bits and pieces will no longer carry out the main function of a car — to move and thereby "transport" passengers and their belongings. The "transport" function of a car is a characteristic of the structure of the systemic nature of the whole system; the transport function is not possessed by the unconnected individual parts of an automobile. A second example is a manufacturing corporation, let's say General Electric. The corporation is made up of people, plants, offices, and various forms of machinery. But no one person or machine can, by itself, do all the things General Electric does. It is only when the appropriate pieces are connected that refrigerators or jet engines or other devices can be manufactured and sold.

The concept of emergent properties is far from new, and emergent properties are common in systems of many kinds we see every day. We have acted, nevertheless, as if the concept of emergent properties did not apply to the realm of ideas. We have done so even though we often have experiences in which new and improved ideas emerge from the discussion of a problem or analysis in more than one conceptual framework. The process of arguing out the U.S. Constitution plus the Bill of Rights is a notable historical example.

There is also a pragmatic reason why multidisciplinary concepts are potentially useful for business, government bodies, and other enterprises that routinely deal with inherently multidisciplinary problems. We have usually treated such problems by assembling working groups containing all the relevant kinds of experts. But these experts often have trouble understanding each other; as a result only a small amount of information can then be fused into an improved or reframed solution to the problem at hand. There is a good likelihood that if all experts understood the relationship of their particular disciplines to other disciplines and to the totality of human knowledge more clearly, the problems of mutual communication and understanding would be ameliorated. As Gene Bouchard, a member of the group called the "skunk works" at Lockheed Aircraft, said to me recently, "It is not enough to assemble a multidisciplinary group; the individual people must themselves be multidisciplinary or willing to become so." Since the Lockheed skunk works is both multidisciplinary and noted for repeatedly producing successful and unusual advanced aircraft designs, Bouchard's remark brings relevant experience to the point under discussion.

For at least a century, we have acted as if the uncollected major fragments of our knowledge, which we call disciplines, could by themselves give understanding of the emergent ideas that come from putting the concepts and results together. It is much as if we tried to understand and teach the geography of the 48 contiguous states of the United States by handing out maps of the 48 states, but never took the trouble to assemble a map of the country. No one questions the importance of the map of the country even when state maps exist. Nor do people question our ability to assemble a map of the country as a whole. We do not question our ability to form the map of the whole because we know a map of the country fulfills two conditions: first, it does not contain all the details that 48 maps of the 48 states provide; and second, we make sure that the overall map does not do violence to the symbols, boundaries, or details of the 48 state maps. Does this metaphor of the map provide a useful way of thinking about the relation between disciplines and also between each of the disciplines and overviews of our total knowledge about truth assertions? Used with caution it seems to. Overviews, whether in the form of maps or in some other forms, necessarily suppress some detail if they are to be understandable. Despite this necessary loss of detail, we know that overviews are important. In the metaphor of the U.S. map, the overall map allows us to deal with the relation of the states to each other, which the individual maps do not. The view of the country as a whole, in one piece, also has value for a variety of other purposes.

Also in the metaphor of the map, we insist that the state maps be consistent not only with each other but also with the map of the whole. But in recent decades we have not insisted that the results from various disciplines be consistent when they are applied to a single problem; there has been no common discourse that could insist upon and strive toward such consistency. We will see some important difficulties that have arisen in our intellectual system as a result of the failure to seek consistent results when more than one discipline is applied to the same problem. In one illustration, we will see an important problem where six disciplines each created a model of the same system; all six models were discipline-bound and therefore oversimple, and there was little if any awareness within each of the six fields that the other five models existed.

Moreover, if we extend the map metaphor a little further, we might say, "In the scholarly world we have not authorized or paid anyone to try to assemble a map of the country of ideas and knowledge. We have instead usually discouraged volunteers, not only because we have seen the task as impossible or 'fuzzy,' but also because we have envisaged the disciplines as the only route to sure knowledge."

It is not much of an exaggeration to say that in our late-twentieth-century universities we have acted as if there were a "First Commandment of Academe" which reads, "Thou shalt not transgress thy disciplinary boundary." A caution is needed here: the discussion here and above, and throughout the rest of this book, is not an argument against disciplinary knowledge. As already stated, the division of intellectual labor into various disciplines has been a major factor in the accelerating accumulation of relatively well-grounded human knowledge. The argument in this discussion is for disciplinary knowledge and, in addition, for a discourse on multidisciplinarity so that both specialists and students can better understand the connections of the fragments to each other and to the whole.

The map metaphor also helps clarify what a multidisciplinary discourse should not be. The discourse should not deal with all the content of various disciplines; that vast amount of knowledge does seem impossible to contain in a single book or a single mind (see particularly Chapter 3). In the map metaphor we need to deal with how the state maps go together and their relation to the whole, not with all the details contained within the finer-scale maps except as they affect relationships to the whole. This is why multidisciplinary discourse is, for the most part, a different topic than the knowledge content within disciplines.

Potentially, it seems that a discourse on multidisciplinarity can help us overcome several kinds of difficulties that have arisen from viewing the world of knowledge as an assortment of fragments without "maps" of the whole.

Let's begin the task of creating multidisciplinary discourse by stating three hypotheses. A number of other hypotheses and guidelines will emerge later in the discussion. All of the hypotheses and guidelines are restated at the end of the book for ready reference.

Three Starting Hypotheses

Hypothesis I: *The Possibility of Multidisciplinary Discourse.* Meaningful multidisciplinary discourse is possible.

Hypothesis II: *Honor All Credible Data.* In multidisciplinary work, we need to honor all credible data from wherever they arise. (This includes not only data from various disciplines and from our laboratories, but also from the world itself, since we have no labs from which we can obtain data for many important purposes.)

Hypothesis III: *The Absence of Universal Approaches.* There is no one view, no one methodology, no one discipline, no one set of principles, no one set of equations that provides understanding of all matters vital to human concerns.

If we are to go to the trouble of creating a multidisciplinary discourse, Hypothesis I is a necessary initial belief. The results we find will in themselves confirm or disconfirm Hypothesis I.

Hypothesis II is also a necessary starting point since, by construction, a multidisciplinary discourse must draw on data from many fields and from the world itself. It must not restrict itself to the data or the contexts (and assumptions) of any one discipline, or only to data that emerge from laboratories. Are there credible data outside of carefully erected disciplinary knowledge? Yes! As an example, we can establish the existence of objects, processes, and organisms merely by pointing at them and saying "There they are!" even when we cannot provide double-blind data or do not understand why the objects or species exist.

If we want to establish the existence of that odd-looking animal the giraffe, all we need do is locate some and say, "There is one, and over there is a whole herd of them, the animals we call giraffes." We need not be skilled zoologists to do this. To establish the existence of automobiles we need only point at a few types and look at what they do. We need not be skilled automotive engineers to do this. So long as we believe that the world is real, these observations are sufficient. We will call such directly verifiable facts that can be observed by lay people, and that do not need laboratory research or elaborate protocols in order to be credible, "barefoot data" in order to have a name for them.

In thinking about the credibility of data and processes it is useful to hold in mind what I will call Heaviside's Query. When mathematicians complained of some of his methods, Oliver Heaviside asked, "Shall I refuse to eat my breakfast because I do not understand the process of digestion?" As Heaviside reminds us, digestion exists, even though we may or may not understand the details of how the process works. The mathematicians were right about some of the details of his methods, and Heaviside was wrong. Nevertheless, by moving ahead to solve problems, Heaviside forged a set of methods that later were adopted by mathematicians and are still widely used.

The key word in Hypothesis III is "one." Over and over, we will see that the distinction between "one" or "some" on the one hand, and "all" on the other, is critical in multidisciplinary discourse. Moreover, we will see this obvious point of logic has been ignored in many different guises and locations within the intellectual world as it stands in the 1990's. We will also examine why these lapses in logic seem to have occurred.

Hypothesis III is a central idea in multidisciplinary discourse. Though not necessary as a beginning statement, Hypothesis III seems useful to state at the outset so the reader can look back and check its verity as we develop materials.

About the Domain of Truth Assertions

The phrase "truth assertions" throughout this book denotes "statements that we assert (that is, claim) describe accurately some portion of physical, biological, or social nature." The words "physical," "biological," and "social" in the previous sentence all should be understood in a very broad sense.

The domain of truth assertions about physical, biological, and social nature includes what we call science in the late twentieth century. Over the past three centuries, science has become so powerful in helping us understand and control our world that in some quarters of the Western world a number of people tend to believe that truth covers all the matters of vital concern to human beings. Since the domain (or system) to be discussed in this book focuses on truth assertions, it is vital that we be clear at the outset about the domain that truth assertions cover and do not cover. If we take for examination the assertion, "Truth assertions can cover all matters of vital concern to humans," we can proceed by what we will call negative inference. That is, we search for examples that disconfirm the assertion. Logically one counterexample is enough to destroy a hypothesis; however, we will often give two or three to make the demonstrations robust. In this case, we ask, "What areas of human life, if any, cannot be understood through truth assertions?"

Many philosophers and others agree that on this kind of question the ancient Greeks were thoughtful and wise. Therefore, a good place to start looking for areas that may lie outside the domain of truth assertions is the taxonomy used by the ancient Greek philosophers to describe what they saw as the total range of human concerns. The ancient Greeks divided the areas of vital concern to humans into four categories: truth, beauty, happiness, and the good. As Phenix (1964) has delineated for us, we need to add at least two more areas for completeness: communications and values.

Why did Phenix need to add these two other categories? Communications are important because they are necessary for all the other areas of human life, and communications are not covered within the ancient Greek taxonomy. We add values because they include more territory than "the good" as the compiled literature of cultural anthropology (ethnology) shows us. The literature of ethnology now covers all of the known ethnic groups on earth, a total of 2,000– 3,000 depending on how we count. This literature indicates that many values of particular human cultures are neither good nor bad; they are simply inherent in things members of a given culture believe or do. These other values are by no means trivial; they constrain, and sometimes even control, much of what the people in any culture do and do not do. Moreover, the values vary enormously from one culture to another. This huge variation in beliefs and behaviors across human cultures is a point we will meet at many places in our discussion. Because anthropology has been created since the late nineteenth century, we ought not be surprised that the ancient Greeks did not understand all that the data of that field imply.

As we have already noted, this work will deal primarily with truth assertions. However, we will need to discuss some aspects of communications and values because they affect how we create and understand truth assertions. This work also has some discussion of happiness (belongingness, self-esteem, and self-fulfillment) and of their relation to truth assertions. It has little to say about beauty (aesthetics) or the good (ethics and moral actions). It is important that these omissions be clear from the beginning.

Ethics and aesthetics are not omitted because they are unimportant, but rather because I do not presently know how to integrate them successfully with the other parts of this work. They still seem to stand aside as largely separate from the domain of truth assertions. Integration of these other areas remains as an undone task for further discussions. This is another reason why this work is a beginning toward construction of a discourse on multidisciplinarity.

We will see, within the domain of truth assertions, clear reasons why human ethical choices are, first, unavoidable; second, are in some cases of great significance to the human race and our planet; and third, often are not susceptible to decision by science alone. The philosophers and the religious sages have long been clear on the third point in the previous sentence. They have told us many times that one cannot get "oughts" (ethical decisions, if you like) from "izzes." By far the best way we have for confirming, or disconfirming, truth assertions about nature is what we call "science." Not all truth assertions are, or are ever likely to be, science. We know many things about the world besides what we normally call science. However, science is so much better than any other method we have for testing truth assertions that, as Vince Lombardi said in another context, "There is nothing else in second place." In this volume we will, therefore, define science by its goals — that is, we will take science to be "A group of methods for the purpose of discovering, creating, confirming, disconfirming, reorganizing, and disseminating truth assertions about nature."

What we call "science" can provide us with the best available facts that can act as critical information for making ethical decisions in many cases. However, in the end we humans must make the decisions involving ethical issues. The buck stops with us.

The first formal body of scientists knew what the previous paragraph says. The founding document of the Royal Society of London says, "We will not deal with matters of religion and personal preferences." Since that time, science has been so successful that there is a temptation to believe that science will ultimately solve all our problems.

Am I creating a straw man here? I don't think so! Not many years ago, a particularly able interpreter of science wrote an essay with the central theme, "Science is the source of all human values," thus assuming that we can and should get "oughts" from "izzes."

I have not named the "particularly able interpreter of science" in the preceding paragraph because my intention is to attack ideas where I think error has occurred, but, whenever possible, not to demean living individuals. I will follow this course throughout this work, but please be assured that when I do so, I am at no point making up illustrations. Citations can be produced should they become necessary. I take this course because we will be more successful in multidisciplinary discourse to the extent that we can reach consensus and avoid long-running "feuds" between groups with fixed positions. Blaming individuals for errors tends toward feuds.

Truth, then, does not encompass "the good." Nor does truth tell us much, if anything, about what things are beautiful, and thereby add amenity to our lives. Surely most of us would feel our lives to be less rich than they are without the paintings many individuals have created in a variety of styles, our many forms of music, our great storehouse of published fiction, objets d'art of many types, embellishments in our clothing, buildings, and rooms, and many other forms of artistic expression. Nevertheless, as Phenix (1964) has explicated for us in detail, "beauty" is essentially a different "realm of meaning" from truth, and truth tells us little about the realm of beauty. The poet Rilke told us the same thing decades ago when he reminded us that analysis of the chemistry of paints and colors is not a viable route to apprehending the impact of a painting.

There is still another important reason why the domain of truth assertions does not cover all matters of vital concern to humans. This is the area of intimate personal relations. In dealing with our intimate others, we may quite possibly use our very personal "truth" as a hostile weapon. If we become angry enough, we may use truth as a form of "character assassination," thereby diminishing the self-esteem of our intimate others, perhaps seriously, and also damaging the relationship (see Gottman et al. [1976] for examples). Unless we take care to listen to other people's views of what constitutes truth to them, and also their feelings and thoughts, we cannot build cooperative long-lasting relations.

A common example of this kind of problem is the married couple who arrive in a therapist's office with a pattern in which the man discounts the woman for being overemotional, and thus "not rational." The wife reacts by being even more emotional in the attempt to make her feelings known to the husband. The husband reacts with more discounting, and so on ad nauseam. This repeated overemoting played off against overrationality creates a vicious cycle that can escalate into divorce or even physical violence. The sexes can be reversed in this problem, of course, but reversal is rare in the United States. In either case, the pattern cannot be broken, nor domestic harmony restored, solely by considera-tion of the truth, since truth statements by the "rational" member of the couple will continue to squeeze out the emotions that need to be recognized and re-spected in order to resolve the difficulties. The feelings, whether truth-based or not, are real, and they must be dealt with as real in order to reach satisfactory resolution and the restoration of positive regard of the couple for each other. (For some details on good processes for reaching resolution, see Gottman et al. [1976] and Simmons [1981]). This illustration shows that to believe one can deal with all interpersonal problems "rationally" is irrational. There are many other exam-ples that illustrate the same point in the arena of intimate relations, but this is enough for our purposes.

In sum, the areas of values, beauty, and intimate personal relations (and hence also happiness) cannot be understood or handled well in our lives based on truth assertions, or science, alone. Thus it seems the ancient Greek philosophers were on the right track in noting that there are important areas of human concern that lie outside and beyond the domain of truth assertions.

Even in this starting stage, we see the emergence of the primary lesson of multidisciplinarity. There is no one approach, no one method, no one viewpoint that is adequate for understanding and coping with the complex systems — including humans — that play a very large role in our lives.

Many readers will, by this point, probably have recognized two things about this work: first, the writer cannot be (and indeed is not) expert in all the disciplines that will be discussed; and second, a number of the conclusions that will be reached go beyond the merely controversial and directly contradict certain claims long held as typical wisdom within some disciplines, particularly concerning what emerges from this beginning multidisciplinary discussion. The author will therefore appreciate constructive suggestions (particularly when specific references are provided) on how such matters can be improved in future multidisciplinary discourse. Such improvements can aid in making sure multidisciplinary discourse is properly articulated to disciplinary knowledges.

PART I

The System Concept

CHAPTER 2

Systems, Domains, and Truth Assertions

The system concept forms the basis for the first overview of how the disciplines of knowledge are formed and how they relate to each other. As we will see, the system concept has many uses and is closely related to the ideas of domains and truth assertions.

The system concept is the single concept that most sharply differentiates ancient from post-Newtonian modes of science. The concept (sometimes with different names, such as the client, the control volume, the free body diagram, the market, the culture, and so forth) is utilized in setting up the basis for essentially every branch of science. In some, but not all, fields of science, the system concept is used explicitly at the beginning of every problem analysis. The system concept provides a window through which the non-technical person can understand both the power and the limitations of what we call science. The technical worker in science and engineering needs to understand the limits of the system concept in order to understand how her or his discipline connects to the larger ideas and problems of the world.

Let us begin to elaborate the system concept in sufficient detail so it can serve these purposes. We can start by looking at the usages given in standard dictionaries. *Webster's Unabridged Dictionary* (1946 edition) lists eighteen meanings for the word "system"; the *Random House Unabridged* (1966 edition) lists thirteen. Surprisingly, none of the meanings given in either dictionary corresponds with the way the system concept is used as a basis for science. Since it is clear from many entries in both dictionaries that the editors were well aware of the importance of science in the twentieth century, this extraordinary omission highlights what C. P. Snow some decades ago dubbed "the Culture Gap." Snow (1969) discussed the difficulties scientists and literati have in communicating with each other. However, in the late twentieth century many other gaps in communications exist between each type of specialist and everyone else who lacks the specialist's specific background and working experiences. My hope is that this overview, and the others that follow, will act to some degree as mental bridges across these culture gaps.

What, then, do we mean by the word "system" as it is used in science and as it will be used in this book? There are in fact two related scientific meanings that are critical to our discussion; we will need to differentiate them from each other. There is also a widespread third use of the word "system" which we will need to retain.

In the technical world, we have used the word "system" to denote:

1. "The object of study, what we want to discuss, define, analyze, think about, write about, and so forth"; I will call this the **system**. When I intend to denote an accurate and appropriate definition of a particular system (or class of systems) for a specified study, I will use the word **system** in boldface type as illustrated in this and the prior sentence.

2. A picture, equation, mental image, conceptual model, word description, etc., which represents the entity we want to discuss, analyze, think about, write about, I will call the "sysrep."

Since we normally intend the sysrep to represent the **system** accurately, we have often used the same word for both. But we cannot do that in this discussion because the relation between the **system** and the sysrep is a key concept in this chapter and many other matters that follow in this book. Thus to use the same word would confound and confuse our discussion. However, the association between the two words is close and critical, and thus I have chosen to retain the first three letters "sys" in the word sysrep so that we are continually reminded of the relationship.

The third use of the word "system" will denote an integrated entity of heterogeneous parts which acts in a coordinated way. For this usage of "system" (or "systemic"), I will use ordinary type or the word "systemic" where that fits. Thus we might talk about the systemic properties of the air transport of the United States or the educational system of New York City. We need this third usage because we will need to talk of the behaviors of complete systems, which are often qualitatively different from the behaviors of the parts as the result of emergent behaviors at the level of the complete entity (system). Indeed, in many cases, the reason we put human-made systems together is to utilize the emergent behaviors of the complete system.

Making up new words (like sysrep) is a troublesome process for readers, and I do so here only because it seems conceptually essential for much of what follows. I promise the reader not to introduce other new words in the book. For the other words we will need to understand with precision, I will refine the definitions of some existing words and phrases so they fit our needs in the way it is done in nearly every field of twentieth-century scholarship. Let us turn, then, to delineating more fully the meaning of the two words **"system"** and "sysrep."

The first thing we must understand about the use of the concept of a **system** is that in a given analysis our **system** can be anything we choose, but we must choose. The choice is wholly and absolutely at the discretion of the person doing the analysis, writing, thinking, or whatever. Thus you, or I, or someone else doing a study can choose the **system** of study to be an idea, a factory for making semiconductors, a range of mathematical processes, a branch of philosophy, a novel, a class of individuals who work at a given trade, a nation, a rifle, an institution, a total vacuum, or anything else we choose. This very wide ability to choose may look like a weakness, but turns out to be a great strength.

Thus the definition of a **system** is much like the view of words expressed by Humpty Dumpty in Lewis Carroll's *Through the Looking Glass* when he said, "When I use a word, it means what I choose it to mean — neither more nor less." So it is with the **system**; it is just what you, or I, or anyone else doing a study says the **system** is. This flexibility provides great power for the analyst and very little restriction.

The second thing we must understand about the concept of a **system** is that this total power to decide, like most power, carries with it a burden, if the power is to be used effectively and responsibly. To be effective in our thinking within the terrain of truth assertions, we must be entirely clear about what **system** we intend to think about, write about, analyze. To be responsible, we must make that intent clear to the reader or listener. If we fail in the first task, we will muddy our own thinking, perhaps hopelessly. If we fail in the second, we will at best be misunderstood and at worst mislead our audience. We will see why this is so, via many examples.

The third thing we need to understand about the concept of a **system** is we need to hold tight and clear two distinctions: between what is inside the **system** and what is outside the **system**, and between the parts of the **system** and the **system** as a whole. For the first we need to draw a boundary around the **system** in some way so that we are entirely clear about what is inside and what is outside, and in many cases we also need to be clear about what sorts of things can and cannot cross the boundaries and thus pass into or out of the **system** as we are defining it. This does not mean that the **system** must be all in one piece physically or conceptually; it only means that we have to be clear about what is inside regardless of how many pieces there are. All this is just as true about ideas as it is about material bodies. When the **system** is a material body, we will assume it does or can exist in a real world, for reasons discussed in the Preface.

Let us turn to the concept of the sysrep. All the remarks in the four preceding paragraphs about **system** (the entity) apply equally to the concept of sysrep (the model, simulation, image, schema, or other representation of the entity). The sysrep can be a word description, a picture, a sketch, a perspective rendering, a map, a formal drawing with dimensions and instructions for manufacturing, a set of concepts, a set of equations, a computer program, or combinations of these forms of representation. However, all these forms and others like them rest on three basic types of representation: words, pictures, and mathematics. We create sysreps so frequently and for so many purposes that English contains more than one hundred synonyms for what we will call a "sysrep," but the synonyms are not precise enough for our purposes. Nor do we want one hundred terms. For clarity we need one word adequately defined.

The second thing we need to know about the relationship is that the sysrep does not equal the **system**. As Alfred Korzibski (1948) so aptly put it, "The map is not the territory." For short, I will call this statement Korzibski's Dictum.

The **system** and the sysrep cannot be the same whenever we are trying to study a piece of the world using a sysrep. However, Korzibski's Dictum does not apply to what are usually called "formal systems," such as a branch of mathematics. When we are analyzing formal systems, the sysrep is the **system** of ideas by definition. A sysrep may represent a piece of the real world, but it also may represent a set of ideas.

An interesting example of the confusion that arises when the distinction between sysrep and **system** is not held clear occurs in some tribes that lack a written language. In some of these pre-literate tribes, many people make no distinction between a person and a picture or drawing of the person, and thus believe one can hurt an individual by hurting a picture of him or her. Those of us who understand the distinction between a real entity and a picture (one form of sysrep) of the entity regard this belief as what ethnologists call "magic." The word "magic" as used by ethnologists denotes an assumed causal connection that is not correct — here between the picture (sysrep) and the person (**system**).

To put this distinction another way, we can say that when we are studying a **system** that is a piece of the real world, we are usually doing experimental work; when we are studying the sysrep, we are doing analysis, theory, computation, conceptual modeling, or some other form of essentially mental activity.

The third thing we need to understand about the relations between **system** and sysrep is our goal in creating a sysrep. What we want to do whenever we are attempting to create a truth assertion about a piece of the world is to make the sysrep a perfect mirror of the characteristics of the **system**. By "perfect mirror" we mean not only that the sysrep will fully represent each and every characteristic of the **system** with total accuracy, but also that it will represent nothing more. The clause stating "nothing more" is important, for we do not want our analysis based on the sysrep to tell us that the **system** will do things of which it is not capable any more than we want the sysrep in its mirroring to omit things the **system** can do. This perfect mirroring is, of course, an ideal, a goal we can only approach, not a reality (except when our **system** is a set of well-defined ideas). However, there is a continuum of appropriate representation stretching from sysreps that mirror the characteristics of the **systems** we want to study very well, almost perfectly, to sysreps that mirror the characteristics of the **system** very weakly, almost not at all. We will see illustrations of both very accurate and very weak sysreps, and many cases that lie in between. Moreover, it is far easier to approach the "perfect" end of the scale in some disciplines than in others, for reasons we will see. It thus becomes important to understand where a given sysrep lies on this continuum from very accurate to very weak. It is incorrect to insist that all sysreps lie near either one end or the other as disciplinary experts sometimes do. Not surprisingly, when this occurs, we find the expert is usually talking about the sysreps that characterize his or her own area of expertise.

When the mirroring is weak, we need to be very cautious about using analyses of the sysrep to predict how the **system** will behave. This is not to suggest that the exercise of such caution is either obvious or easy. On the contrary, we will see that it is often both subtle and difficult. These difficulties and subtleties have been a primary source of some of the overclaims we will examine in this book.

Why do we need sysreps at all? Why not merely interrogate **systems**? There are many reasons. When the mirroring of the **system** by the sysrep is adequate, we can understand and often predict the behavior of the **system** very accurately by analyzing the sysrep. This greatly adds to our power to understand the world, for we can often study the sysrep far faster, in more detail and depth, and more easily than we can interrogate the **system** directly. We may also be able to predict behavior for configurations and cases that do not yet exist. In some instances, for ethical or other reasons, we cannot study a particular **system** in the way we need to, and must therefore turn to a sysrep to study the problem at hand. When we are designing a new type of object, one never before seen, we must first make a sysrep in our head, and then usually also on paper, in order to work out the details of the object. Thus the use of some form of sysrep is critical to what we will call the "design process." In addition, by creating analytical models we can often generalize the results for an entire class of **systems**, which provides us with important principles for organizing and improving our thinking about a sector of the world. Moreover, if we want to understand the world, this generalizing is not avoidable because of the limitations of the human mind, as we will see in the next chapter. In sum, sysreps are mental tools of great power for humans.

The three preceding paragraphs suggest that we can learn a great deal about truth assertions by studying how we can tell when the sysrep is strong and when it is weak, and this will turn out to be the case. In fact, how the sysrep is checked against data (mirrored) in a given field plays a large role in how accurate analytical, computational, and conceptual work in the field will be as a predictor of what will occur in the world. The nature of the mirroring, and the rapidity with which the mirroring is checked against data, also plays an important role in how fast the field will advance. An important example of how method affects both the speed of advance and the reliability of a field is given in the essay by John Platt called "Strong Inference" (1966). We already used part of Platt's ideas when we applied negative inference to disconfirm the idea that truth assertions cover all matters of vital interest to humans (in Chapter 1). The basic power of the method of negative inference lies in the fact that negative inference often reaches closure; it can settle issues. This is unlike the more common methodology of listing examples and then drawing conclusions inductively. Inductive reasoning does not close. Using more and more examples in inductive logic merely makes the conclusion more and more probable, as logicians and mathematicians have been telling us for a long time.

Complete reasons for using the word "sysrep" (and not an existing word) will not be evident until Chapters 13, 15, 16, and 17, when we can utilize the materials of Chapters 3–12.

Domains and Truth Assertions

Before we give examples to make clearer how we use the relations between **systems** and sysreps, we need to lay out the relation between what we will call "the domain" and the definition of the **system**.

Any particular truth assertion seems to apply to some **systems**, but not to others. I hope you will check this for yourself by trying out at least a few truth assertions you consider the most general you know. You can do this in the following way. Set down the truth assertion, and then look for some **system** that does not obey that particular assertion; apply negative inference. I think you will find that you can nearly always bring to mind rather quickly and easily one or more **systems** that do not obey any truth assertion you choose to examine. If your own testing discloses some truth assertion(s) that are universal in the sense that they apply to all possible **systems**, please let me know. Any hypothesis that is truly universal is probably important, not only because of its generality, but also for any discussion of multidisciplinarity.

I have repeated the test just suggested, for some years. I have also done the exercise with groups of doctoral students. I have in this way convinced myself that there are very few if any universal truth assertions that apply to any and all **systems**, provided only that we exclude tautologies such as $A = A$. There is also strong support for the result of the previous sentence in both Bertrand Russell's Theory of Types (see, for example, Watzlawick, Beavans, and Jackson [1967]) and what I will call the Theory of Dimensions (see Chapter 9). This result is so important that I set it off as a hypothesis:

Hypothesis IV: *The Necessity of System Definition.* Each particular truth assertion about nature applies only to some **systems** (and not to all).

What then do we imply when we speak of "general theory"? As Corning (1983) has remarked, in effect, "General Theory is some general remarks about a specific class of systems." Here again we see the vital need to specify (define) the class of **systems**, otherwise we do not know to what classes of **systems** the "general theory" applies. If Hypothesis IV is true, then it follows that we must always state the domain (that is, the class of systems) over which a given truth assertion applies, for if we do not, our assertion will be in part untrue. We will be making a claim of universality, implicitly, and there will then be some systems where we are asserting that our claim holds where in fact it does not. Thus our statement is not what we intended it to be, an assertion of the truth and nothing but the truth. There is an aphorism that plays off the witness' oath and summarizes this set of ideas: "Science tells the truth, nothing but the truth, but never the whole truth." Science does not tell the whole truth precisely because each branch of science is set up to deal with a specific class of **systems** (but not all possible **systems**). This "setting up" is the definition of the paradigmatic class(es) of systems that the given branch of science will study. This idea is sufficiently important that I will label it Hypothesis IV, Corollary A:

Hypothesis IV, Corollary A. No truth assertion about nature is complete without a statement of the domain of applicability.

Hypothesis IV rests on experience. It is an inductive generalization, and as such it needs continuous testing against further experiences. We may someday find a truth assertion that does apply to all possible systems even though we do not seem to have found any so far. A question thus arises about Corollary A to Hypothesis IV: Would it still be an appropriate statement if there were some truth assertions that were universal in the sense that there are no known exceptions for any system? The answer to this question is Yes! It will help our discussion to examine why.

For ease of discussion let's say our total stock of important truth assertions numbers 5,000. Let's further suppose, contrary to fact, that of these 5,000 important truth assertions, 10 have universal applicability. Would we then still need to describe the domain to which each applied? If we want to be clear and accurate about our truth assertions, Yes we would. For the 4,990 assertions that are not universal we would need to be clear about the domain to which each applies and does not apply. Even for the remaining 10 "universal" truth assertions, we would need to state that they were universal. This is equivalent to stating that the domain to which they apply is the largest possible domain.

It is usually desirable to define the domain for a given truth assertion as having three pieces (rather than two). More specifically we can define: (1) a domain or region where we are quite sure the assertion is true or at least a very good approximation; (2) a domain where the assertion may be true, or is partly true, and may have some utility; (3) a domain where the assertion is wholly or almost wholly untrue (see Figure 2-1).

The three-part-domain picture in Figure 2-1 allows us to test the proper domain of the given statement that we intend to be an assertion of truth about a piece of the world. The three-part picture helps us see how far the given truth assertion can be used with some utility, and where, on the contrary, we need to give it up entirely and make some other kinds of truth assertions.

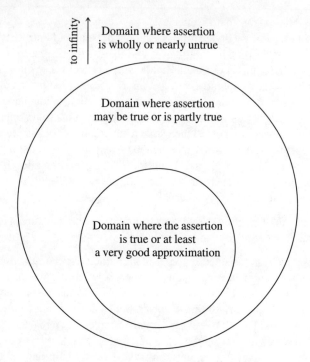

Figure 2-1. Three-Part Domain for Truth Assertions.

Examples of the Use of the System Concept

Let us turn to some examples of how these ideas about the system concept work. We consider, first, two quite different examples where the system concept has worked spectacularly well. They both concern relatively simple inert, naturally-occurring physical **systems.**

In the nineteenth century several physicists, particularly Max Planck, defined a **system** as consisting of a vacuum. That is, the **system** contains nothing at all. To do this they had to be clear that air is not a vacuum and that vacuums do not contain some mysterious substance called "ether" (which had for a long time been thought to be true). The resulting analysis forms a key part of the theory of heat transfer and also of electromagnetic propagation of energy, as we understand those nearly ubiquitous phenomena today. The understanding of the propagation of electromagnetic energy is a foundation stone for radio, TV, and many other devices. So this **system** of nothing at all turns out to be important and useful both in understanding the world and in practical applications.

In another instance, J. W. Gibbs in the 1870's began with a very simple **system** — a unit of mass of one pure chemical substance in equilibrium. We can think of it as the water in a glass, for example. In doing this, Gibbs listed eight other conditions that all had to be fulfilled in order to define the sysrep fully for the problems he had in mind. He noted, for example, that there had to be an absence of the effects of motion, electricity, and five other classes of physical phenomena. A ridiculously simple system; one thinks, why bother with this **system** and all these picky details? When one follows Gibbs's work up through his famous third paper, the answer to why we bother becomes very clear. As he moves on, Gibbs relaxes some of these nine conditions one by one. In his third paper Gibbs establishes virtually a whole science that had not existed before. He erects a complete theory of chemical equilibrium, and thus the basis of modern chemistry and chemical engineering, as we know them in the twentieth century. This tour de force by Gibbs stands unaltered in the late twentieth century. To date no one has found errors in Gibbs's work. And the central trick in this astounding solo virtuosity was extreme clarity about just what the **system** is and what it is allowed to do at each step in the analysis.

Like many other conceptual ideals, a complete and accurate sysrep is a rarely reached goal. I have described Gibbs's work on chemical equilibrium as an example because it approaches this ideal about as closely as any example I know. The example of Gibbs's work on chemical equilibrium will be useful, not only because it approaches the ideal for careful use of sysreps, but also as a point of reference for the relationships between sysreps and the human mind.

One can proliferate these examples of successful use of sysreps in the physical sciences and engineering, that is, in the inert physical world, almost endlessly. In each and nearly every part of the modern disciplines in the technical world, one begins with a very simple **system**, very carefully defined, and then erects a superstructure of sysreps that unfolds into the entire field by gradual relaxation of the restrictions on the system definition, but always with care at each step to define the **system** under analysis at that step. Gibbs's work stands as an early classic example of this process.

It is important for our purposes to emphasize that these successes in the physical sciences deal with relatively simple systems (a fact we will make quantitative in Chapter 4). That does not imply that analyses like those by Planck and Gibbs (1872) are easy or that the selection of the systems with which to begin was obvious in the various areas of physical science, for neither is true. Historically, in many cases, the system definitions were at first not clear, and the analysis in a given field was often at first muddled or even wrong. However, bit by bit, the systems became better chosen, and the analyses were improved through repeated trials, often with much heated debate among many workers.

It is also important to note that the behaviors of each kind of system studied in the physical sciences are invariant over time and space. This means that workers can repeat tests over long periods of time, in many laboratories, and compare the results, thus providing a process for converging on more and more accurate sysreps for adequately defined systems. The sysreps for this kind of **system** therefore tend to lie toward the perfect end of the continuum of accuracy of sysrep mirroring relative to many other classes of systems. This point will play an important role when we come to discuss the differences and similarities between the various disciplines that deal with truth assertions.

Let us look next at one example that was difficult, and was done wrong several times, but has been around long enough so that gradually, over about two centuries, it has been worked out correctly. This example will help us see the deep subtlety that can sometimes occur in the problem of mirroring a **system** by a sysrep even in a relatively simple class of systems.

The problem concerns the forces that a gas or a liquid exerts on a solid body as the fluid flows past the body. We will consider the particular kind of body we know as airfoils, the cross-section shape of wings on aircraft. It is quite easy to get very bad answers with what looks like a good sysrep in this problem.

Jean d'Alembert already encountered this difficulty in the eighteenth century. D'Alembert used the only equations then available, those derived by Leonhard Euler from Newton's mechanics for an "ideal fluid," that is, one without friction. D'Alembert used the theory to predict the two important forces a fluid exerts on an airfoil, the lift (the upward force that balances gravity) and the drag (the force that retards the movement of the wing through the air). D'Alembert found both the lift and the drag were exactly and precisely zero for any wing shape at all (indeed for any body). But this is all wrong, and d'Alembert knew it. Hence it seemed to be a paradox — what seems like good theory gives nonsensical, qualitatively wrong answers. We still call this result d'Alembert's Paradox.

You know d'Alembert's result is wrong from flying in airplanes; the wing does give the lift that holds you and the airplane up. If you want, you can test the fact more directly for yourself by putting your hand out a car window at, say, 40 miles per hour. With your fingers pointing ahead, lift the tips of your fingers gradually. You can easily feel the reality of both the lift and the drag on your hand. (If you did this in water at the same speed, you would injure your arm; the forces are not small.) So d'Alembert's result is very wide of the mark. What went wrong in d'Alembert's calculation? It was not his mathematics, which were elegant.

A more complete sysrep than that of Euler was developed by the middle of the nineteenth century for the airfoil problem and other problems in fluid flow. A Frenchman (M. Navier) and an Englishman (Stokes) created a sysrep in the form of a set of differential equations for the motion of the common types of gases and liquids which included the effects of viscous action. However, the equations they created, the Navier-Stokes equations, are very hard to solve analytically for anything other than a handful of exceptionally simple cases. As a result, a number of theoretical scientists throughout the nineteenth century simplified the sysrep so they could find solutions. These scientists argued as follows: the effects of friction are very small compared to the forces the momentum of the flowing fluid exerts on a body whenever the flow is reasonably fast. For ordinary air this is any speed over about two miles per hour. So the nineteenth-century scientists said, let us drop the small friction terms from the Navier-Stokes equations. They then noted that if they assumed that the flow had no rotation, as air at rest into which an airplane flies does not, then they could simplify the sysrep still further. Using the assumptions of both no friction and no rotation in the fluid, the equations collapse without further assumptions to a much simpler form, in particular to what is known as Laplace's equation. This form of the sysrep was given the name "ideal fluid flow" or "perfect fluid flow" and formed the basis for what is still called "ideal fluid theory." Since Laplace's equation is relatively easy to solve analytically via a number of sophisticated mathematical methods, this led to lots of solutions. Some of these solutions are still used today. However, some of the solutions produced by ideal fluid theory were very bad, as the airfoil illustrates. For an airfoil, ideal fluid flow theory provides the same answers d'Alembert obtained. Thus no explanation for d'Alembert's Paradox occurred during the entire nineteenth century. As a result, there was a long and bitter feud between practical workers who built systems for handling fluids such as pumps, dams, and so forth, and the theoreticians, with each side demeaning the other.

Since those developmental geniuses the Wright brothers were bicycle mechanics by background, they apparently did not read d'Alembert's paper or those by the nineteenth-century theoreticians who used ideal flow theory. D'Alembert's result does not seem to have held back the invention of the airplane. However, this history leaves us with a question that is important for our discussion. What went wrong in analyses by d'Alembert and the nineteenth-century theoreticians?

It is quite true that the forces of friction are small compared to the forces the momentum of the flow exerts on bodies at anything beyond very low speeds. Indeed for a typical airfoil at flight speeds the friction forces per unit area are tens of times less than the forces arising from the momentum of the flow. It is also true that air at rest into which an airplane flies usually has no rotation.

As we already said, d'Alembert's mathematics were correct and elegant. Where, then, is the trouble? It lies in the fact that the sysrep created when we drop the effects of viscosity from the equations no longer fits the **system** well for some important problems. The reasons why, and what to do about it, were worked out by Ludwig Prandtl in 1904 in a paper now generally considered the genesis of modern fluid mechanics. What Prandtl's paper shows is that the small effects of friction grossly alter the flow pattern very close to the wing from that which is predicted by the ideal fluid flow, and this remains true no matter how small the friction forces become. We therefore cannot use d'Alembert's sysrep for this problem; we must use a different sysrep formulated by Prandtl, as aerodynamicists now all do. For details, see Schlichting (1968).

The point for our discussion is that this sysrep problem was subtle enough that many good theoreticians failed to see the answer for more than a century, and it required what many see as an act of genius for Prandtl to provide the explanation. The assumptions of the nineteenth-century theoreticians look quite reasonable; they were accepted by many able researchers for decades. The difficulty in this problem was only identified by comparing the results with data for the systems of concern. Careful comparison showed that ideal fluid flow can be used for some parts of some flow fields but not others. Ideal fluid flow must be supplemented to find complete answers. Essentially all sysreps involve some assumptions that deviate from the precise reality. The best test we have for establishing whether a sysrep is appropriate is to compare results from the sysrep with the **system** it was created to represent under the relevant conditions. Historically, when we have failed to make the comparisons with real systems we have encountered difficulties often enough that a clear warning is evident. We will return to this point in Chapter 13.*

Let us look next at an example that occurred in more complex systems, humans. In the "human sciences" an overnarrow system view that dominated thought for decades in many groups of scholars has in part been corrected by later work. Before we look at the example, let's define what the phrase "human sciences" will denote in this discussion, since we will need it often. Following a suggestion by Professor Robert Anderson of Mills College, I will use "human sciences" to include six disciplines: anthropology, sociology, psychology, economics, political science, and history. I will also include in this area related professional practices such as psychotherapy and policy studies. The common feature of these areas of study is a focus on human behaviors and human-made systems. As the term will be used, human sciences do not include the biological sciences and the related professions of human physiology and medicine. The first three of the six disciplines (anthropology, sociology, and psychology) I will sometimes call the "newer human sciences" and the other three (economics, political science, and history) the "older human sciences," since they have much earlier historical roots as explicit areas of study.

In the work of Freud, and that of his followers up until about the middle of the twentieth century, the object of concern and study, in the language of this book the **system**, was an individual human being and his or her intrapsychic world. By the 1950's some therapists (particularly Harry Stack Sullivan and his student Don Jackson) had begun to observe that treating patients from the view of Freud's **system** definition was inadequate in some cases where there were strong family ties. The client would improve, and then be pulled back to the old behavior by what were homeostatic family dynamics. They therefore defined a new **system**, namely, the family as a whole. This new perspective, that is, the new definition of the **system** being studied, led to very important increases in understanding human behavior. It is now widely accepted that some problems that arrive in the psychotherapist's office are primarily family problems. Hence, the system to be treated must be the family as a whole and may require some

---

*A remark about references is appropriate at this point. Since we are concerned with the relations between the disciplines rather than with detailed contents of disciplines, we do not need the exhaustive references normally provided in specialized papers. The references in this volume are therefore intended only to be highly relevant to the points in question and where possible to include further references for interested readers.

participation of all members if the work is to be effective. This approach has come to be a recognized branch of psychotherapy. It is often called "family system" work. By the 1980's, therapists using a family system approach constituted an entire branch of the field with their own methods of practice, journals, special knowledge, and viewpoint. The family approach is seen by many as much more effective, in such matters as the relationship in marriage, than the approach of treating individuals one by one. Many family system workers emphasize that the family system as a whole possesses properties (in this case behaviors) that the individual members may not exhibit alone or in contexts outside the family. Of course, there may be a need for both couple and individual therapy. We do not need the details in this discussion. The points for us are: this shift in **system** definition brings increased insight, and has vast consequences for therapeutic processes; and adequate system definition is just as important in the human sciences as in the physical and biological sciences.

A few years ago I had an interesting experience concerning the need for **system** definition that enlightens this discussion. I was reading a book by a well-known social scientist that had been recommended by a colleague. It did have some ideas I found useful. However, at one point I read a page and, on reaching the bottom, found I had not comprehended it. Thinking my attention had wandered, I read it again. I still did not understand it. I read it a third time with the same result. Since the material was not of a basically dense kind, this gave me pause, and I studied the page carefully, sentence by sentence. What I found was that the author had shifted the implied **system** — what he was writing about — a dozen times on one page without ever saying so. All meaning simply vanished. There was no way to understand the author's intent, nor could there be when the need for deciding what one is talking about is so grossly disregarded.

It is easy to proliferate these examples of where a failure to take care about the **system** definition has caused confusion. But the examples given are enough for the purposes of our present discussion. The point is clear. When we want to be rational, to analyze logically, to plan effectively, we need to make sure we are entirely and sufficiently clear about what we are analyzing or planning. We must use a **system** definition that is clear and appropriate. What this entails is determined case by case, and thus may often need more than one discipline to get the problems worked out appropriately. What history tells us, with extraordinary clarity, is that if we do not define clear and appropriate **systems**, we will very probably end in confusion. Moreover, this is true over the entire range of truth assertions we make about the world, that is, for the biological and the human sciences fully as much as the physical sciences.

The Limits of the System Concept

The system concept is the central idea we use to formulate, confirm, and disconfirm truth assertions about nature. The system concept is thus the idea (not the method) that most clearly distinguishes what we call modern science in the twentieth century from older modes of human thought. This tool is particularly powerful when we are careful about how we define our sysreps and check the sysreps frequently against the **systems** we are trying to study to see how well they mirror the **system**. To put this differently, the domain over which the system concept is useful is more or less the same as the domain of truth assertions. However, as we have already seen in Chapter 1, truth assertions are not sufficient to cover all important areas of human concern.

Moreover, since truth assertions are the major focus of work in the physical sciences and in engineering analyses, the use of the system concept becomes ingrained in technical workers. Individuals working in these fields know well from long training and practice that they must define their **systems** and sysreps carefully. This experience is ever-present for such individuals working in these areas. As a result, they may come, after a while, to believe the system concept and its handmaiden, rationality, are enough for solving all problems of the world. But this is not true. If you have any doubts on this score, look back again at the examples in Chapter 1 which delineate several important areas that lie outside the domain of truth assertions.

Moreover, the importance of the system concept led a few workers to create what is sometimes called "systems theory." Please distinguish here between the system concept on the one hand and systems theory on the other. This paragraph applies only to system theory. System theory is at bottom based on two ideas: (1) we need to pay attention to the careful definition of the **system** whenever we are stating truth assertions; (2) **systems** have holistic properties. Up to this point, the ideas are both important and sound. However, a few overenthusiastic workers in systems theory, following the lead of Korzibski (1948), have made claims that go far beyond these basic points. In the most extreme forms, some workers have suggested that systems theory is a method that could in itself solve all the problems of the world. There are two fundamental difficulties with this claim. First, as we have seen, the system concept is useful for more or less the same domain as truth assertions, and that domain fails by a wide margin to cover all problems of human concern. Second, the notion that the methodology that defines a sysrep can solve problems without specific knowledge from within the class of **system** under study is wrong. It is wrong precisely because we need to check the accuracy of the sysrep by looking at how well it mirrors the **system**. This demands that we understand and have data about the **system**, and that is just what this extreme form of systems theory denies. We will call this sort of over-claiming a "universalism" or sometimes a "unibloc approach," depending on the application.

In this chapter, we have looked at the use of the system concept in a rational way. We have seen some examples where the ideal of total clarity and perfect mirroring of our **system** by our sysrep has been very closely approximated and some others where a failure to take care in system definition or sysrep formation has led to errors. We have not yet looked at the way in which the human mind modulates and constrains the kind of sysreps we can work with effectively. That is the task of the next chapter.

Conclusions for Chapter 2

If we hope to establish correct and verifiable truth assertions about nature we need to formulate and carefully check appropriate sysreps for well-defined systems. Use of the combined system/sysrep idea is the central concept that distinguishes ancient from twentieth-century science.

When either the sysrep or the domain is not appropriately defined, we can and have created long-standing misconceptions and errors. Nevertheless, the system concept has distinct limitations; it is not a tool for all occasions and all seasons.

What workers on the two sides of Snow's culture gap need to learn about the system concept is quite different. Workers in the non-technical disciplines, on the average, need to learn the importance of and more careful use of systems and sysreps. Workers in the technical disciplines need to learn that the system concept, powerful though it is, cannot solve all problems.

CHAPTER 3

Sysreps and the Human Mind

As we saw in Chapter 2, the central concept for creating truth assertions in twentieth-century science is the system/sysrep idea. We define a **system** carefully, and then make a sysrep that mirrors the **system** as accurately as is feasible for the problems of interest. However, before any sysrep can be set down, it must first be created in a human mind.

In this chapter, we will examine the question, Are there limitations of the human mind that constrain and modulate the way we create and use sysreps? We will find the answer is Yes! There are several we know in the 1990's, even though our knowledge of how the human mind works is still far from complete. Moreover, the impact of the limitations we already know is important in scholarship but has had little if any discussion. Notice that while we do not yet understand how the human mind works, limitations of the mind can be directly tested, and we do have some clear ideas about them.

The bulk of what researchers know about how the human mind forms and uses mental representations of the world is less than two generations old. We are now quite clear, however, that each human mind does construct mental representations, and we are beginning to know the general scope and limitations of the nature of these representations. We will call these mental representations "schemata."

A number of different words have been used for mental representations. Kenneth Boulding, for example, called them "images." In a short and readable book, *The Image*, Boulding (1969) elaborates on many of their impacts on our thoughts and behaviors. He shows that the formation of images affects nearly everything we do in some way because our "pictures" of "how things work" and "the way people are" govern to a very large degree how we perceive the world and how we react to given circumstances. The word "pictures" is put in quotes because it must include not only literal pictures but also concepts, feelings, and so forth. We will not repeat all the things Boulding says. We only note that *The Image* is a good source with which to start on an understanding of how many things our mental pictures of the world affect for the reader who wants to explore in more detail. We will combine the idea of the importance of mental images with more specific results from recent studies.

A word of caution: in his final chapter Boulding goes a bit too far, in my view, and as a result creates a universalism. He suggests that the study of what he calls images can be a universal approach to all problems of human concern. Like other uni-bloc approaches, Boulding's idea falls short because it only includes how we form sysreps, and thus excludes the empirical information we must also have in order to verify or disconfirm given sysreps for given domains or classes of systems. Boulding's book has been widely cited, but the suggestions of his last chapter have not taken root nor diffused.

Moreover, even Boulding's concept of images is a narrower class than what we will call schemata in this volume. In particular, Boulding's examples do not include solution processes or the indexing systems that are necessary for utilizing complex schemata. However, these are matters we need to examine, since no doctor could practice medicine without them, nor could an engineer design a device, or a master play chess.

If the word schemata is more than "pictures" or "images," what does it denote? We will use the term "schemata" to denote all the ideas in a person's head which are used to represent and interact with the world. Some of our human schemata are simple, some moderately complex, and some relatively very complex.

Words are an example of simple schemata. In whatever language we speak and write, words are a primary way we apprehend and think about the world. If you doubt this, try to plan your schedule for tomorrow without thinking or writing any words in some language you know well.

Unlike other animals, humans use words to describe classes of actions, objects, and shades of refinement of meaning for actions and objects. We also use sentences built on agreed syntax to extend the meaning of words. For example, "You hit a ball" does not equal "A ball hit you." Other animals do not seem to use words for classes of things or actions, nor do they use syntax in the sense just illustrated (except perhaps dolphins). Even these schemata, which are relatively simple for humans, pass beyond what most or all other animals can do in forming mental representations of the world. But words are only one class of human schemata among many others.

We also have in our heads many repertoires of relational ideas (interconnected matrices, if you like) that help us do the things we do every day. Some of these relational repertoires are moderately complex; others are as complex as anything humans seem to be able to do or think about.

Moderately complex schemata (or relatively simple repertoires, if you like) include the things you do every morning in getting up, bathing, dressing, eating breakfast, and preparing for work. This set of acts is not difficult for a normal adult human; we do it more or less on "autopilot," because the routines it requires are well learned and have become "automatic," or nearly so. But neither a young human child nor any other animal can accomplish a repertoire this complex. Other animals seem not to have a mental apparatus that can construct schemata this complex, and young human children have not yet constructed them; they lack the experiences from which the human mind organizes schemata. This already suggests that while the ability to form relatively complex schemata is inherited genetically by humans, the details and the structure of the information within the relatively complex schemata are at least mostly learned.

Relatively complex schemata seem to be the basis for all kinds of expertise wherever the question has been tested. This has been documented for chess playing (de Groot [1946/1965], Chase and Simon [1973]); solving physics problems (Larkin et al. [1980]); solving math problems (Qin and Simon [1990]). Qin and Simon also include simple engineering analyses. Although there do not seem to be formal studies, oral reports and analyses of creative work in science and many other areas suggest creativity is also rooted in, and built upon, complex schemata.

Complex schemata constitute the basis for a doctor in diagnosing illness, for a musician in playing his or her instrument, for an engineer designing a device, and so forth. These more complex schemata are not merely a string of information but, rather, form complex relational networks that are acquired by and only by long experience and usually also focused study. The engineer cannot diagnose illnesses with either the speed or the accuracy of the physician—if she or he can do it at all—but to the extent we can measure, the innate intelligence of engineers is at least as great as that of physicians. Neither the musician nor the physician can design a computer, with the speed and finesse of the engineer—if they can do it at all. What makes the difference in problem-solving skills and performance of the physician, the engineer, and the musician is complex, particular schemata acquired from long periods of learning. It seems reasonable then to assume, for our discussion, that all disciplinary knowledge is based on relatively complex, learned schemata in our minds and often also in our muscular system, as in the case of musicians and surgeons. Heaviside's Query seems to apply here and ought to be used, at least until we have more data.

We need, then, to look in more depth at what we now know, collectively, about schemata. We will start with a simpler idea by Miller, and then take up the work of de Groot and others who followed him on the matter of human schemata that form complex repertoires.

To avoid misunderstanding, this paragraph repeats what was already said in Chapter 2 about references. In many instances the references given are not exhaustive. They are instead intended to be directly relevant to the point in question and when possible to include further references that will aid readers who want to dig deeper on a given topic.

A very important fact for our discussion was documented by George Miller (1956). Miller showed that the human mind can hold only about 7 bits of information in short-term memory at a given instant. The word "about" indicates for most people the number is 7 plus or minus 2. If we try to hold more bits in short-term memory, we will lose some of them. I will call this fact "Miller's 7-Bit-Rule" so we have a name for it.

The semantics of this area remain loose, and many words are used for the human short-term memory (for example: awareness, focus of attention, consciousness, working memory, and so on). We will follow Simon and his associates, and use the term "working memory," since that phrase has what seems to be the appropriate connotation for the part of the human mind that is actively working on data, ideas, designs, etc. The working memory is roughly analogous to the central processor in a computer; it is the part of the brain that "works" on things in contrast to holding them passively within memory.

To understand Miller's 7-Bit-Rule we need to know what a "bit" is. A bit is a single unitary fact or idea, such as the picture of a letter or a number, or the population of the United States. The word bit comes from computer usage: a bit is either a one or a zero in a given storage cell of the computer memory. Miller's 7-Bit-Rule tells us we cannot think about (process, if you like) more than seven or so uncorrelated bits (or facts) at a given moment. To think about more than 7 (plus or minus 2) bits we must observe them again or bring them into our working memory from long-term memory. This is not to deny that we sometimes solve problems at a deeper level in the mind; it is only to say that what we ordinarily call "thought" has distinct limitations in the number of items we can consciously "think about" at a given moment.

How do we think about more complex matters? We use two methods, the first wholly within the mind and the second largely outside. Inside the mind we arrange important bits into "chunks" of several bits, not more than ten and usually about four or five. A chunk can then be defined as a set of bits that have become connected to each other from repeated associations, and hence are recognized as a single unit in the mind.

Words are chunks made up of sounds or letters, depending on whether they are spoken or written. How many words do you know with more than ten letters or sounds? Your home telephone number is probably one chunk to you, but probably not to many other people. The critical point about chunks is that each chunk is known as a unitary item in your mind, and not as a string of uncorrelated bits. The arrangement of your local street or neighborhood, with the location of stores and so on, is probably contained in one or a few chunks in your memory as a picture. Familiar faces also seem to be held in the mind as one chunk: the mind has a special place for storing faces, probably because the distinction between friend (our tribe) and enemies (other tribes) was important for survival in most pre-literate societies.

What I am saying is that bits we focus on, or use over and over in a pattern, after a while become "chunks" in our minds. If we consciously want to form, say, six bits into a chunk so we can remember and use the chunk as a whole rather than deal with the six bits each time we need them, we must do two things. First, we must focus on the chunk for roughly eight seconds, according to Simon and his co-workers, or we must use the chunk over and over within a reasonable time span. This gets the chunk into long-term memory. Second, we must "index" the chunk in some way so that we can recall it readily. Thus the words "home phone" may index your seven-digit telephone number, and "neighborhood" may act as an index to many things you know about the area near your home. The process seems to be much like what we do when we make an index to a book or for a filing cabinet, but we usually do the indexing in our mind without much conscious attention. Indexing is something the human mind seems to do naturally.

Simon and his co-workers suggest that we can process about four chunks in our working memory at an instant in time. Since 4 chunks may be 28 bits (7 times 4) or even more, the ability to form chunks allows us to think about more things in a domain we know well than in an area unfamiliar to us.

When we need to think about more things than we can handle at one time, even in chunks, we have to move the focus of our minds, our working memory, from one set of items to another and back again to cover the entire terrain. In many cases we need to do this over and over. One of the reasons why writing is so important to the advance of human knowledge is that we can record many bits and/or chunks and index them so we can go back and forth not only between chunks but also between levels of aggregation in a given system, and between carrying out tasks and longer-term goals we are holding in "background" (in software language).

The relational repertoires included in our more complex schemata need to do several different kinds of things. They need to form bits of data into chunks in order to increase the number of bits we can handle in working memory. They apparently need to attach solution routines (processes) to sets of facts and also to possible output actions. They need to tell us when to move between possible solutions, or bits of solutions, and when to move back to solving. And they must somewhere contain criteria for the complete solution of the current problem, bringing the criteria from background as needed so we can see where we are along the road to a solution.

Simon and his co-workers suggest that an expert in a given professional area, such as physics or mathematics, will have learned from experience something like 50,000 chunks covering patterns of facts, solutions, actions, and so forth, in her or his area of expertise. They also note that to learn this many chunks at the rate normal for university classes would take about ten years. We know from experience that this is about the right gestation period for experts in complex areas like medicine, physics, linguistics, and so on, so the result seems reasonable. A university-educated person also will typically have a vocabulary of something like 50,000 words. The data so far appear consistent.

It is important to distinguish clearly between working memory and long-term memory in the human mind, since they are quite different in capacity. Working memory can hold about 7 bits or 4 chunks; long-term memory can hold 50,000 bits or related chunks for a single area. Since many of us know not only an area of expertise but also have vocabulary and information about other areas, an experienced and intelligent human mind must have hundreds of thousands of total bits or chunks in long-term memory.

A variety of tests has also shown that observing a new fact in the world and focusing on it within working memory takes something like two seconds. Sorting through our index system and bringing an item from long-term into working memory takes less than one-tenth that long. This recall process seems to become slower or develop short-term blockages when we grow old. Given these various facts we have just summarized, the importance of indexing is obvious.

Dennett (1991) makes one important further point. He suggests that our working memory is a serial or linear processor. This means that one thought after another flows through the working memory in a serial fashion. You can check for yourself if this is what occurs in your working memory, the stream of things that runs through your mind. Also ask yourself, What happens when I try to think about three or even two things at once? You will probably find the mind gets confused. Dennett also suggests that there is at least one lower, not consciously accessible level within the mind. According to Dennett, this lower level contains multiple processors (parallel processors, in computer language) that attend to various functions such as sight, finding solutions, recalling memories, body feelings, and so on. Dennett hypothesizes that these parallel processors throw up multiple drafts — that is, possible solutions — and working memory then chooses which one to follow. Dennett's data on multiple possible drafts of a solution are persuasive. However, we do not seem to know, in the early 1990's, how the choice between drafts gets made.

What is the level of assurance about the things we have been saying about working memory? Since we have no comprehensive theory of the human mind, we must depend on empirical data to assess this question.

Miller's 7-Bit-Rule has been checked and rechecked by many researchers in many areas of mental activity. It is established empirically beyond reasonable doubt. The "7-bit-limitation" on the human working memory, imposed by Miller's 7-Bit-Rule, is probably the most important single constraint on the human mind in regard to how we form sysreps.

The way we form chunks and the limit on the number of chunks we can hold in working memory are not yet thoroughly documented, but four or so chunks appear very reasonable on the basis of available data.

You can check Miller's 7-Bit-Rule for yourself using telephone numbers. The old "Ma Bell" system, bless her dear departed soul, knew the rule. Local phone numbers in the United States are 7 bits long, and they are expressed as one string of three numbers and one of four. Many of us can look up a 7-digit phone number and then dial it from memory. However, when we come to a number with 17 digits (a telephone number with area code plus a 7-digit access code), we can no longer hold the whole set of numbers in mind; we have to write them down unless they are numbers we have used over and over so that they are stored in long-term memory as a few chunks. For example, the first three digits of the local exchanges, which you use over and over, may be one chunk in your mind.

Let's try an exercise to fix these ideas. Please study the set of keyboard characters on the line that follows this sentence for five seconds, and then see if you can write the line down correctly without looking back at this page.

$$R\#29CG\&*4P@2DL6B \qquad (3\text{-}1)$$

If you do not get all the characters from line (3-1) reproduced, please do not be discouraged; essentially no humans can do this except individuals with a peculiar and rare kind of mind. But now please try the same experiment with the next line.

$$\text{The Cat is in the Hat} \qquad (3\text{-}2)$$

Probably you succeeded in reproducing line (3-2) correctly, even if you looked at it for less than 5 seconds. Each of the lines, (3-1) and (3-2), has sixteen characters. Why then the difference? First in writing line (3-1), I chose sixteen characters so the number is not huge, but is significantly more than seven plus two. Also, I chose the characters in line (3-1) so they would be uncorrelated for most readers, that is, it would be unlikely that a given person could associate any two successive characters in the string of line (3-1) with an already-known sequence, a chunk. In the sentence about the cat on line (3-2), I did several things differently. The expression has the data broken into short strings, less than seven bits each. Perhaps even more important, each string is likely to be a known chunk (word) that most readers of English have stored in their minds as a unitary item. Also the entire line (3-2) has a simple meaning that can be grasped and stored. Beyond all that, the line (3-2) has a meaning similar to a book title that many people know, one of the Dr. Seuss books. And if you know those books, some images or feelings associated with reading to children may have been revivified. Thus line (3-2) will tie to known schemata for many readers at several levels: letters, words, images of objects (cats, hats, and so on), the entire message or meaning, and for some readers memorable experiences and attached emotions.

Please pause and think about the implications of what was just said about the phrase "the Cat is in the Hat." The phrase not only illustrates Miller's 7-Bit-Rule. It also shows that other images, including facts, pictures, and emotions, may be attached to the "bare facts" through a schema (the singular of schemata) in a human mind. Notice also that this schema about cats and hats is implicit in our minds, yours and mine. We did not say to ourselves, "I am going to store this sentence along with the known words 'cat' and 'hat' and the emotions attached to reading to children as one schema in my head labeled 'The cat in the hat schema.' " However, our minds did store this as a schema at a non-conscious level.

The Cat in the Hat example shows us that the human mind does not store all the details we observe, nor usually the exact words we read or hear, unless we spend time and energy memorizing them exactly. Instead when the mind puts something into long-term memory so we can recall and use the fact or idea later, it stores the gist of the message as a whole. Moreover, it attaches that gist (the core of the message) to related facts, feelings, images, or ideas that are already stored in the mind, and puts them away as chunks or schemata under one or more labels (indexes) for later possible recall. We also see that schemata are often made up of more than one chunk (for example, the words in line [3-2] and the asssociated pictures and emotions). For a summary of data on the fact the mind stores the gist of messages and not the precise details, see Riley (1963). This attachment of the context and emotions to the facts stored in the mind seems to help us recall the fact or idea or feeling later when we need to do so by tracing along lines of association. This is not a simple one-on-one association, or tracing, nor is it as simple as stimulus and response, which is pushed so strongly by radical behaviorists (see Chapter 6). On the contrary, if the data we have been reviewing provide even a roughly correct picture of the human mind, then there are at least four categories in stored memory, and these four categories seem to be arranged into hierarchical levels. These categories are: facts, chunks, schemata, and finally goals and long-term strategy. There may be more than four levels, but it is hard to see how there can be less.

This attachment process is simultaneously a vital part of human thought and the source of some difficulties in the way we think. We cannot think about complex matters without our schemata. You might test this by trying to think about nothing at all. You might test the idea further by observing the steps you go through in solving any problem in an area in which you have significant expertise. Schemata are vital to human thought, but at the same time, the particular schemata we know may and often do distort our ideas. This distortion is sometimes slight, but it may be strong. It may be strong, because the mind attaches new data to old schemata and sometimes seems to overlay (or mix) the new ideas with parts of older schemata. This attachment of new data to old schemata seems useful for indexing and also for building up knowledge about related problems and situations. However, the old schemata may carry a lot of extra baggage in terms not only of facts but also attitudes, emotions, viewpoints, and solutions suggested. Because this attachment process is subtle and relatively little studied, we often tend to underestimate its impact on our thoughts, attitudes, and emotional reactions. The distortion process operates with particular force in two kinds of cases: (1) when we come to think about new domains and carry known schemata from the domain they were learned for into areas that have a quite different character; (2) when there exists strong trauma from past experiences, as in post-traumatic stress syndrome (see Herman [1992]).

We do not seem to understand at present the ways these attachment processes work, but there is ample data to be sure they do exist. Some of these are carefully controlled laboratory data. See, for example, Bower (1981). However, most of them are "barefoot data." As we already noted, such data are sufficient to establish existence even when we do not fully understand the processes involved. Non-conscious formation and storage of schemata with other associated schemata are like Heaviside's digestion, real but not well understood.

The non-conscious process of attaching schemata to observations and then storing the gist of the idea with the attached schemata has profound implications regarding the way we think about the world. The word "non-conscious" does not denote unconscious in Freud's sense. The unconscious described by Freud refers to memories that are so hurtful and distressing that they are repressed, that is, walled-off in a separate part of the mind, and not normally available to recall into the working memory. For examples of the reality of repression, see Dennett (1991) or Briere (1989) concerning the etiology of multiple personality disorder. But Freud's repressed — that is, inaccessible — memories are not what we are discussing here. Non-conscious, as used here, denotes a process the mind does without explicit directions from our conscious thought processes. The materials created by non-conscious processes are recallable from memory at will. Non-conscious is the opposite in this sense of "deliberate." We can get some idea of the power and importance of the non-conscious formation of schemata in the mind from the details of the work of A. de Groot (1946/1965) on chess players.

De Groot set up two series of tests of memory with regard to chess pieces on a chess board. In one series of tests de Groot set 25 normal chess pieces on a chess board in arrangements from actual, partly played chess games among master players. He had a grand master, a master, a class A player, and a class B player each examine the arrangement for five to ten seconds, and then try to reproduce the arrangement of pieces on a blank chess board without referring back to the original board. None of these players were novices; the least skilled was a past champion of the city of Utrecht. De Groot used carefully developed protocols and repeated the tests for several arrangements on the board. The grand masters often reproduced 100 percent of the placements of the pieces; the masters reproduced about 90 percent; the class A player about 60 percent. The class B player seldom reproduced the positions of more than 8 or 10 of the 25 pieces correctly. "Aha!" one thinks. "The masters are individuals with enormous and quick powers of memory retention; that is why they are masters." However, this thought turns out to be entirely wrong, as de Groot's second series of tests showed.

In a second series of tests, de Groot again set 25 normal chess pieces on a chess board, but this time in random arrangements not related to chess games. He then had the same players take the same test. In this second series of tests there were no differences between the grand masters, the masters, and the less-skilled players. None of the groups got more than 8 or 10 of the 25 pieces, on average, placed correctly. In other words, everyone was reduced to the level of the least-experienced player in the first series of tests. De Groot ran several variations on these tests, but this one example is enough for our purposes.

Because these results are so important in terms of understanding how the human mind works, the tests have been repeated in more depth and with more detailed protocols by Simon and his co-workers (see references above). Simon and co-workers fully confirmed de Groot's results, and added some additional ideas including the ideas about chunks we have discussed above.

What do these results by de Groot and Simon et al. imply? The results are very strong evidence for the fact that the masters and grand masters could reproduce the boards 90 to 100 percent correctly owing to the fact that they had stored in their minds schemata relating to a wide variety of actual chess games. They did this by holding in their minds chunks representing certain positions and strategies rather than individual pieces. Simon and his colleagues show that each chunk the masters knew included only a few pieces, and almost always the pieces in a given chunk were related in some way, such as proximity, color, and/or as standard parts of game play in chess. By repeated glances of short duration, the grand masters could thus reproduce the whole board from a few parts of a chess game, just as you or I can reproduce the picture of a tree from a few leaves and branches or the picture of a house from seeing a front door and porch. Simon et al. have demonstrated that the same processes operate in several other areas of problem solving, including mathematics, science, and engineering.

De Groot's conclusion from his long and seminal work expresses particularly well the central result we need. Speaking of the repertoire that grand masters and masters use in playing chess, de Groot says, "The master knows from experience an enormously large number of playing methods — strategic goals, means, standard procedures in certain positions, combinatorial gimmicks in position A — which the weaker, less effectual player does not have available. What the master on looking over a situation 'actualizes,' just by routine, a weaker less experienced player has to build from the ground up — if such a thing is possible at all." De Groot goes on to say, "The crucial question remains: Is it really experience that makes achievements of the master so much better? This question is not difficult to answer; there are a host of reproductive factors at work and they are of decisive importance." De Groot then explains that these "reproductive factors" are not merely memory, nor other forms of innate intelligence, nor are they the number of moves the player looks forward; the masters look forward no farther than the others. The reproductive factors are, rather, grounded in and built from experience, and they are relational nets, often very deep nets, not simple forms of association such as 4 follows 3 or elephants are big mammals. In short de Groot is describing what we are calling complex schemata in this discussion.

It seems, then, that expert knowledge is primarily learned, and it apparently is learned by making bits into chunks; storing the chunks together with processes for solving problems; keeping track of the steps, of how far along the road we have come toward a satisfactory solution (our goal); and finally using some kind of labeling process so that the entire relational network, the schema, can be quickly recalled from long-term into working memory when needed. So far, these ideas seem to apply to all expertise, that is, to all the areas for which a person has effective working skills for complex situations and problems. We have a lot to learn about these processes still, but this much has a reasonable amount of documentation and seems to be consistent with our own experiences.

How does learning of expertise come about? What are the steps? Here the work of Dreyfus and Dreyfus (1986) gives us useful information. The Dreyfus brothers have shown that we do not become experts merely by learning the rules of the game; they show fixed rules constitute only a primitive level of knowledge about complex systems. The Dreyfus brothers described four higher levels all above the level of rules, and they argue that only the fifth (highest) level is true expertise. The fifth level, in their examples, involves (in our words) accumulating and storing schemata in the form of relational networks from many experiences.

The Dreyfus brothers use the examples of driving a car and of playing chess as typical. We can see the major implications of their work by thinking briefly about driving.

The necessary rules for operating a modern car with an automatic transmission are simple; once the engine is on, there are only three: push or let up on the accelerator to go faster or slower, step on the brake to stop, and turn the wheel to change direction. Anyone can learn these rules the first day. When you had learned those three rules and no more, were you a good or even an adequate driver? Obviously not! You need also a lot of schemata about what to do under various conditions, not only in your mind, but also in integrated neuromuscular reactions. This is particularly true in emergency conditions. Experienced drivers invoke what psychologists call "ballistic reactions" under emergency conditions. Using ballistic reactions, we do not stop and take thought. Instead we invoke a well-learned response, stored in the muscles, which once set off continues ballistically, that is, without feedback, to its end point. Experienced musicians do the same with well-known musical pieces. As we already noted, Simon et al. demonstrated empirically that to begin to think about a new piece of information coming from the outside in working memory takes about two seconds, and to store it in long-term memory about eight seconds of concentration. However, recalling a chunk of information from long-term memory takes only about one-fifth of a second. To be effective, a musician must have put how to play his or her instrument into well-learned schemata. For formal concerts, the particular selections played also need to have been stored, each as a series of chunks within a schema.

As we have already noted, schemata are vital, but they can also distort. However, for many of us the distortion idea is a foreign concept (and for intellectuals perhaps a distasteful one). Hence I will elaborate with a little more discussion and some examples.

Schemata can distort more strongly than "blinders" that narrow vision. Schemata are more like filters that can brighten some portions of what we see while dulling or blacking out other portions. Schemata can also distort our stored understanding and thus also our memory in many ways. This is particularly true when strong emotions are aroused. If you doubt this, ask a husband and wife, each separately, to tell you what happened in the same recent fight. Often you will hear stories that seem to be about different events. Strong emotions and ego defenses often distort memory. In this sense, ego defenses form a subtle but very powerful part of our schemata. A classic depiction of this phenomenon in literature is the story called *Rashomon*, in which several participants tell very different versions of the same events.

An instructive example of how we use schemata is given by Hirsch (1988). Hirsch says in effect, "Looking out the window of my office I see some oval-shaped, flat, green objects attached to tan-colored things of tubular shape and various sizes." It may help understanding to ask yourself, "What is Hirsch talking about?" before you continue reading.

Hirsch then says, "When I ask people 'what [do you] see outside my window?' they all say, 'a tree.' " Hirsch is, in fact, describing a few leaves and branches. How do the visitors know that these few bits of green and tan objects are part of a tree? They know it because they have already stored in their minds a relatively simple schema, namely, the idea of a tree and pictures of many kinds of trees. The mind fills in the missing details and the total context from the known "schema" for trees. Moreover, this process seems to be general; the human mind seems to do this "filling in" to the stored gist of what is observed, read, or heard whenever there are relevant, or what seem to be relevant, pre-existing experiences in the mind and there are no strongly contradicting data. The process seems similar to what is called extrapolation in mathematics. Dennett (1991) gives several other examples illustrating that this "filling in," in the absence of contradictory data, is apparently natural to the human mind.

In another famous example from ethnology, an anthropologist leads a member of a tribe of forest-living African pygmies to the edge of the forest where they see a group of lions some distance away across the savannah. The anthropologist points to the lions and says, "Lions!" The pygmy says, "No! Ants!" The anthropologist insists, "Lions!" The pygmy becomes indignant and accuses the anthropologist of lying. Why does the pygmy do this? It is because he has lived all his life in a dense forest where there are no distant objects; everything he has seen during his life has been within a short distance. Hence the pygmy has no schema in his mind which tells him how distance affects the apparent size of objects. I have chosen this example because it emphasizes how strong the need for schemata is. The illustration is on the borderline of "hard to believe." Indeed, some students who read drafts of this book found this incident unbelievable and asked if I had made it up. The incident was, however, reported to me by anthropologists. For an even more striking example about vision, see Oliver Sacks's report (1993) about a man who had been blind from childhood and was enabled to see via operations on his eyes during his fifties, but could not integrate vision successfully.

These are only a few examples of how we think with schemata and how we cannot think about complex matters without them. You can check both these ideas for yourself by thinking about what a doctor, an engineer, and an accountant can each do in her or his own field as compared to what each can do in the other two fields.

Current research is relatively rapidly pushing forward what we know about how the mind works. It is likely that we will know a lot more in a few decades than we do now. However, this seems to be about as much as we can say that has a direct impact on our discussion of multidisciplinarity based on available data.

How do these known results affect this work? We can see one significant implication by reminding ourselves of what we would do to answer Hirsch's question about what is outside his window. We would construct (integrate) the whole picture of a tree by attaching what we see to a schema we call "a tree," a schema nearly all of us know well. There are three aspects of this process that we will need in discussing the structure of knowledge about systems in later chapters. We can illustrate them by thinking about trees a bit more.

We understand trees by examining their parts. This is a three-step process: (1) we disassemble the tree into its parts; (2) we study the parts so we can understand how leaves, the cambium layer, roots, and the other parts work; and (3) we reassemble the parts to understand the whole. It is the way we come to understand structure. We must use this three-step process because Miller's 7-Bit-Rule forces us to disassemble information into strings of a size we can understand completely in order to get the full details right. However, this three-step process creates a hazard to full understanding which arises from the process of disassembly. There is often a temptation to let the interesting nature of the details prevent us from doing step 3, the reassembly. We can get engrossed in some aspect of the details and lose sight of the meaning of the whole. If we remain engrossed in the details long enough, after a while we may even claim that the details are all we need to understand the whole tree.

Moreover, even a simple schema like that for a tree can mislead us. How could this happen? If what we saw outside Hirsch's window was in fact only some newly cut branches, the schema "tree" in our mind could fool us into the false belief that a whole tree was actually out there, by filling in the missing details that are not actually present. Schemata can mislead us — and often have, when we have not been careful.

The different schemata that experts from disparate disciplines bring to the discussion of a common problem is a major source of what creates the culture gap. Differing schemata can also be a major impediment to multidisciplinary discourse; recall Bouchard's remark from Chapter 1 about the need for multi-disciplinary people in creating an integrated work team.

What is the relation of a sysrep to schemata in the mind? A sysrep is a particular kind of schemata, a very special class of the totality of the schemata we construct in our minds. A sysrep is a special subclass of schemata because it is deliberately and carefully formed for specific purposes and deliberately named and stored in the mind (and often in writing) for future recall and use. A few examples will help clarify the distinction between deliberately formed sysreps, on the one hand, and the far more common non-consciously formed and typically more "fuzzy" schemata in our minds, on the other.

The word "rocks" is a relatively straightforward concept in English. When you read the word "rocks," probably some pictures of various kinds of rocks you have encountered came into your mind. However, unless you are a geologist you probably did not consciously or deliberately form this set of images of "rocks" in your head in an organized way. For example, you probably did not earlier say to yourself, I am going to file this set of rocks under the label "rocks from the Jurassic period" or some equivalent. This deliberate formation of organized schema about rocks by a geologist is a major part of the sysreps of his or her profession. Most of the rest of us merely accumulated and added together various experiences with objects that we think of as rocks without much deliberate thought. Moreover, the set of rocks in my head is very probably different from the set in your head because our personal experiences with and of rocks has not been the same. For these reasons, geologists can talk to each other about rocks in a more precise, deeper, and faster manner than you and I can. Moreover, since rocks are representations of reality, and not formal systems, neither the rocks in my head nor the ones in yours are real. At least we both hope they are schemata, and we do not really have "rocks in our heads." Korzibski's Dictum applies.

The same remarks apply to most nouns, verbs, and their modifiers that we use in everyday language. For example: the verbs swimming, bicycling, eating; the nouns books, telephones, and rifles; and the adjectives beautiful, fast, and low each bring up many images for most of us. Each is a schema that our mind has formed and holds. Some non-consciously formed schemata, such as the words "books" and "telephone," are relatively unambiguous. However, others are quite ambiguous—for example, "fast" has at least four qualitatively different meanings in English. (Consider the phrases: run fast; stick fast; go on a fast; and he or she is a fast person.) Language as we ordinarily use it is highly ambiguous and evocative. This is largely because, first, the bits we each attach to given words as we form schemata vary for each of us; and, second, many schemata have enormous and even self-contradictory connotational baggage intimately tied to them as part of the "bundle" that forms each chunk and each schema. These ambiguities have important utility for us when we want to be descriptive or leave open possibilities for the imagination (as in reading fiction and in creative activities). However, when we want to be accurate about truth assertions that we use to represent pieces of the world, we must be precise about what our schemata are.

In short, to form reliable truth assertions about the world, we must deliberately and carefully form sysreps for well-defined domains. A near ideal example of this process is the work of Gibbs, described in Chapter 2. In many cases, when this has not been done, severe scholarly difficulties have ensued. We will see a good many examples before the end of this book, in addition to those already noted in Chapter 2. This distinction between tightly and deliberately formulated sysreps on the one hand and non-consciously formed "fuzzy" chunks and schemata on the other is what makes the linked ideas system/sysrep a critical (and central) concept of twentieth-century science. We will elaborate this idea in Chapters 13, 16, 17, and 18.

As a final section for this chapter we will look at one more process the human mind commonly uses in formulating sysreps, the process Sigmund Freud labeled "projection." What is a projection in Freud's sense?

Projection in Freud's sense is the idea that we tend to believe that others know what we know, think in the way we do, and have the same feelings we do about a given situation. For our purposes, we can define "projection" more broadly as the attribution of what we know about ourselves to other people, and of what we know about systems very familiar to us to other systems about which we know far less. In mathematical operations, we call projection "extrapolation."

Projection is a very natural, and often useful, human mental process. The results we obtain in this way are often correct; however, they are also often wrong. Let me illustrate. Suppose you and I are sitting together in a room, and I feel somewhat chilly. My natural assumption is that you will be feeling somewhat chilly too, and this may be correct. However, you may be wearing thermal underwear, out of sight under your clothes, and therefore be feeling hot instead. In terms of disciplines, it is learned schemata that tend to make engineers see problems as questions that can be answered by appropriate hardware; economists to see a very wide variety of problems as things that can be solved by the free market alone; lawyers to see situations as legal problems, and so on. In each case, this is sometimes a "projection" from a domain the individual knows well to larger areas or other domains in the world. The ideas and processes familiar to us (our schemata) may be correct in domains not familiar to us, but they may also mislead us.

Is the process of projection common? From experience, anyone who has observed the matter closely knows that it is very common. Projection is far more common and has much more impact than we are likely to think it does, unless we have understood the concept and watched how it operates carefully for a considerable time. A very large fraction of personal advice is wholly or partly projections.

Is there a known basis for the process of projection? Yes! As we already noted above, Dennett (1991) gives a number of examples that show in summary that in the absence of contradictory data the mind fills in what we cannot "see" directly by means of something like extrapolation. This is true even in matters of simple vision, as Dennett shows. There is nothing wrong in this process. Indeed, in the absence of contradictory data, it is the logical and economical way to think and believe. What we need to carry forward is the idea that projections are often correct, are invaluable as hints, but also are often incorrect. As a result we need to recognize projections for what they are, and examine them carefully if we are to claim that we are doing careful scholarship in the domain of truth assertions.

Conclusions for Chapter 3

What ideas from this brief survey of how the human mind works are important for our multidisciplinary discussion?

Probably the most important, and also the best documented, is Miller's 7-Bit-Rule because it is a strong constraint on what the human mind can do. Because we cannot keep more than 7 (plus or minus 2) bits of information in our working memory, we form small numbers of connected bits into chunks. This augments our working memory, making it more powerful than it would be if we thought only in terms of bits by themselves. However, there are still strong constraints, since we seem to be able to hold only about 4 chunks in working memory at a given instant. As a result, we store our accumulated chunks of information in long-term memory and form schemata of many chunks (apparently up to 50,000) to help us do complex tasks and solve complex problems.

Because of these constraints on the way the human mind comprehends and stores information, it is necessary for us to break down complex systems into comprehensible chunks, study the chunks individually, and finally to reassemble the chunks into the whole and study the whole once again. The mind also needs connectional matrices (representational repertoires, if you like) in our schemata so we can call a chunk from long-term into working memory as needed, and also hold in background solution routines, strategies, and goals to be used when needed.

Thus our schemata are central to how we think, particularly about complex systems and problems. Without our schemata we cannot think about complex matters effectively, if at all. At the same time, our schemata can distort our thinking when we take already-known schemata from one area and project them onto an unfamiliar and quite different kind of problem or domain. Since the uses of schemata and of projection are subtle, powerful, and very common, the combined distorting effects can be strong; in the limit the distortions can create and have created outright errors.

These effects taken together give additional strong reasons why we need to use explicit, appropriate sysreps for carefully defined domains when we want to create truth assertions about physical nature. The relatively "fuzzy" schemata the human mind naturally forms at a non-conscious level are often not precise enough for the task. As noted above, we will elaborate this idea in Chapters 13, 16, 17, and 18.

Except for a few illustrations, the limitations of the human mind have been stated in isolation in this chapter. However, we will find these limitations important at many later places.

PART TWO

Complexity

An Index for Complexity

Now that we have a rough picture of the limitations of the human mind and know how the mind works, we can ask, How do the limitations compare to the complexity of the systems we study? Although complexity is a much-discussed subject, we have not had a numerical measure of complexity for various types of systems (except for computer programs). In this chapter we will construct a complexity index, which can provide an estimate of complexity for any system or class of systems. We will then examine the complexity of some typical classes of systems in order to see what the values tell us about the nature of various systems and thus the disciplines that describe them.

An Index for Complexity

We will define a complexity index — denoted C — in terms of three other quantities:

V = the number of independent *Variables* needed to describe the state of the system;

P = the number of independent *Parameters* needed to distinguish the system from other systems in the same class;

L = the number of control *feedback Loops* both within the system and connnecting the system to the surroundings.

Since the use of the words "variables" and "parameters" varies from one discipline to another, we will use a simple example of a class of systems to help clarify how we will use them in this discussion. Figure 4-1 shows what I will call a "rectangular room" **system**. It is a room with all right-angle corners, of length

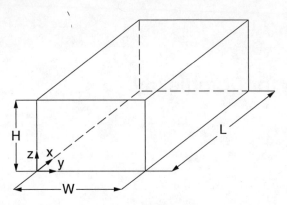

Figure 4-1. The Rectangular Room **System**.

B, width W, and height H. Let's agree to locate points in the rectangular room by measuring (or stating) values of x, y, and z from one corner on the floor, as shown in Figure 4-1.

The three quantities B, W, and H are the parameters of the **system** shown in Figure 4-1; they define the **system** in terms of its characteristics. When we set each of the three parameters B, H, and W, we define a particular room in this class of rooms. If we change the value of any one of the three parameters, we move in our "design space" to another room in this class of rectangular rooms.

We locate points in the space inside the room, the "operating space," by the variables x, y, and z. If we change the value of any one of x, y, or z, we move from one point in the operating space to another, but we do not change to another room.

When we change, add, or remove an item in the complete list of parameters and/or variables, we change the class of system under study. Thus a change in value of one of the variables or the parameters implies a process fundamentally different from changing the nature or the number of one or more parameters or variables. More specifically, changing values moves us around inside a class of systems; changing the number or the nature of an item in the list of variables and parameters changes the class of systems we are describing.

As an illustration, let's alter the rectangular room in Figure 4-1. As shown, the room has no feedback loops. But let us suppose, momentarily, that the **system** is a new room, a room in a house that has a thermostat hooked to an air conditioner/furnace for controlling temperature. Then the value of L will be 1; there is one feedback control loop. The room with the thermostat and air conditioner/furnace is a significantly more complex and variable system than without. With the feedback control system the room can keep us comfortable in winter and summer with the mere setting of the desired temperature on the thermostat control.

Suppose the furnace in our modified rectangular room pushes hot air in near the floor and then shuts off. For some time, the temperature in various parts of the room will vary over both space and time. If we wanted to describe the temperature throughout the room during this time, we would need two additional variables, temperature T, and time t. Our system has gotten more complicated because we now have five variables, and they describe not only lengths but other kinds of **system** characteristics. Thus a variable can be any relevant characteristic that describes the operating "space" of the **system** of concern. Thus the word "space" here takes on a generalized meaning that goes beyond the geometric.

Let us next modify the design of the room by adding a door and some windows. To describe the new room we would now need some additional parameters describing the sizes, types, and placements of the door and windows. The increased complexity of the room is indicated by the need for additional parameters to describe it.

The example of the original rectangular room **system** is peculiarly simple in two ways: first, all the variables and parameters are simple lengths that can be visualized as straight lines; second, the variables are orthogonal to each other, and the parameters are orthogonal to each other. Orthogonal is used in the mathematical sense to denote a generalization of the idea of perpendicular. When variables are orthogonal, whether geometric or of other kinds, changing the value of any one variable entails no change in the value of the others. For example, in the rectangular room, changing x causes no change in y or z. Similarly, changing H entails no change in B or L.

This simplicity and geometric nature of the rectangular room system provides a good starting point, since it allows a way to visualize relatively easily the concepts we need. However, we will need to generalize the concepts of both parameters and variables so that we can discuss a wider variety of cases. We saw above how we need to generalize the idea of variables, in the example of the temperature at various points in the rectangular room over time. Parameters might involve quantities like the thermal or electrical conductivity of a system; that is, parameters are not limited to geometric quantities.

We are now ready to define an index of complexity. Using · to denote multiplication, we can provide upper and lower bounds for a complexity index, C, in terms of V, P, and L, as follows:

$$V + P + L < C < V \cdot P \cdot L \qquad (4\text{-}1)$$

For a particular system, the location of the value of C between the lower and upper bounds of equation (4-1) will depend on the degree of "connectedness" within the structure of the **system** and between the **system** and its surroundings.

We need to note two idiosyncrasies that occur for very low values of C in equation (4-1). First, in many systems L = 0. Second, when each of V and P is 1 or 2, the left-hand side of equation (4-1) may exceed the right-hand side. As a reader of a draft, Peter Bradshaw, pointed out, it is possible to repair these idiosyncrasies by a slightly more complex definition of the upper and lower bounds of C. I will not do that because we will be very little concerned with values of C below 3. And thus I retain the definition of equation (4-1) for ease of understanding. When L = 0, or V and P both have low values, we can take C to be V + P + L.

We will usually not try to make exact estimates of C. We will instead usually make rather crude one-sided estimates of C, using inequalities. This strategy makes the task much simpler than it would otherwise be. Fortunately, the crude estimates will be adequate for our purposes because the gap in the value of the index C between the simple systems consisting of inert, naturally-occurring objects and the very complex systems that contain human social and learning elements is so great that we will not need to refine the estimates.

Let us then estimate the value of C for some broad classes of common systems.

Class A: Paradigmatic Systems of Physics, Chemistry, and Simple Engineering Analyses

The typical systems analyzed in classes in physics, chemistry, and in analytic problems in beginning engineering classes have no control feedback loops; so L = 0. Initially, in such beginning problems we nearly always fix the values of the parameters and study a particular case. For these systems, typically V = 1, 2, or 3; thus we can write:

$$C_A < 5 \qquad\qquad (4\text{-}2)$$

Class A systems include, for example, deflection of simple structural members; the motion of pieces of matter under prescribed forces; the properties of chemical solutions; the path of light rays through gases or transparent solids; behavior of simple semiconductors, and many other systems consisting of inert, naturally-occurring matter and energy in the sense of physics. Since equation (4-2) gives values for a variety of systems, it should be read not as indicating precise values but only as an indicator of order of magnitude for comparison with the other classes of systems discussed below.

In discussing this work with a number of other individuals over the past few years, I have found two ideas that are not familiar to many people, even some highly educated and bright people: (1) L = 0 in inert naturally-occurring objects; (2) there is more than one kind of information. Since both these ideas will be important at many places in this book, the ideas are elaborated before we go on to estimate C for other classes of systems.

Four Types of Information in the World

There seem to be in the world four qualitatively distinct classes of information, which are listed in order of their appearance on earth:

1. Information inherent in the structure of inert, naturally-occurring objects;
2. Information encoded in DNA;
3. Information in the brains of animals (we will look primarily at information in the brains of humans);
4. Information recorded by humans on inert matter, as, for example, in pictures, writing, or equations.

We have called all four classes by one name, information, and assigned no recognized names to the subclasses. Has this caused difficulties? Let's consider a different case to see the potential for difficulty. Suppose we called all of lake water, rain, ice, snow, and steam by one name, "Water stuff," and had no names for the various forms of water. All these forms have the same chemical formula, H_2O, but that does not diminish the need for names of the subclasses. If we had only one name for rain, ice, steam, and so forth, we would be in severe confusion when we wanted to think or describe weather, electric steam power plants, or many other matters. Has this kind of confusion occurred because we have used one word for all four types of information? We will see that it has caused both confusion and major difficulties in many places. Let's therefore examine each type of information and give each a name so we will be clear when the issue comes up in our discussion.

The information inherent in inert, naturally-occurring objects concerns the structure of the material as in rocks, air, oceans, and so on. The rocks and the air are not aware that they contain information. Inert, naturally-occurring objects have neither awareness nor information-processing capacity of any kind. We will call this class (1, above) "information inherent in the structure of inert, naturally-occurring objects" or, for short sometimes, "the information in rocks."

DNA (class 2, above) appeared on earth far later than the rocks, the oceans, and so forth. DNA codes information in a precise chemical form. DNA can replicate itself. However, the replication is blind; it seems to have no teleological aim other than to replicate itself, as explained at length by Dawkins (1987). Except for "rare mistakes," a few of which may be successful mutations and become embodied in living plants or animals, DNA does not alter; it only replicates itself. The "urge" to replicate, if we can call it an urge, is strong, as evidenced not only by the tenacity and variety of living forms on earth but also by the strength of sexual impulses in all their variety. We will call information carried in DNA "genetic information."

Information in animal brains (class 3, above) is of a quite different character from information in DNA. It has a different physical structure (neurons and axons, for example, not the double helix of DNA). Some of the information in animal brains is learned in many (but not all) animals. As we saw in Chapter 3, the information in the human brain typically forms complex relational repertoires (schemata) among a large number of bits and chunks of information. Schemata are a key to thinking. Schemata probably exist in other forms of animals, which do have an ability to learn and demonstrate complex behaviors, but are probably simpler than schemata that humans routinely create and use. We will call this class "human information" or "animal information," as appropriate. Rothschild (1990) estimates that human information embodied in "technology and economic systems" has changed at a rate one million times higher than DNA over the past 35,000 years. In Chapter 14, I will argue that human information is a separate pathway for using information in addition to, but interacting over time with, genetic information; I will call this Durham's Hypothesis.

Humans, and only humans, record information from their brains on matter (class 4, above). Thus far we have no record of any animal, other than the human, drawing pictures equivalent to the earliest pictures drawn by our ancestors in caves. As both de Solla Price (1962) and Rothschild (1990) have elaborated, without this fourth type of information, science could not have developed. Indeed, both make the point that it was not possible to create science until after Gutenberg had invented movable type, because only then were humans able to disseminate information with the speed, accuracy, and low cost that science requires. Moreover, most children in industrial societies have already learned how to read and do some arithmetic when they finish elementary school. This critical information for civilization passes beyond what any member of a preliterate tribe will learn about this kind of thought. The recording of information is thus a critical portion of what humans have learned to do. We will call this "recorded human information." As we have elaborated ways to record human information, we have begun to study the information-carrying capacity of given forms of inert objects. We can consider this type of information as a subclass of recorded human information.

Now that we have these types of information sorted out, can we see why they need to be distinct? Examples of the need are easy to find. Surely we do not want to confuse the information about the carrying capacity of a telegraph line with the message containing human information we send over the line. Consider the two messages, "Thanks, Mom. I love you! Come see me" and "I hate you, Mom! Get out of my life!" The messages are roughly the same length; the telegraph wire does not care about the difference between them; but mom almost certainly does. Surely also we do not want to confuse the information transfer from mother to child via DNA, which ends at conception, with either the information including antigens carried through the umbilical cord or messages between mother and child, like the telegraph messages (above). Are these other forms of information exchange important? The antigens will shape what immunities the child acquires. Affectional (or hostile) word messages from mom (and dad) will to a significant degree shape the character of the child. (See, for example, Spitz [1965], Stern [1985], Alice Miller [1983, 1984], and Whitfield [1989].)

Is this kind of distinction peculiar to information, or is the need for distinctions general in some sense?

Let's look at a very simple case — apples and oranges. Suppose we called them both "orples," and had no other word for either. Observations would then show us that, first, "orples" grow on deciduous trees and need a hard frost to grow well; and second, "orples" grow on evergreen trees only in climates where there is no or, at most, mild frost.

Given both observations, we would no longer know how to grow apples and oranges reliably. Such distinctions are important in understanding the world even on very simple matters. If we lack "needful" distinctions, we will probably find it difficult to understand almost anything.

Before we return to our discussion of the complexity of inert, naturally-occurring objects, one more comment is needed. Precise representations of systems (sysreps) used for analysis arise only in human brains, as far as we know. These transformations of information into sysreps, and the recordation of the sysreps, carry with them the possibility for many kinds of imperfectly mirroring the systems concerned, including outright errors. This is the reason why such close attention needs to be paid to how we form sysreps, how we use them, and how they are influenced by the limitations of the human mind.

We are now ready to continue the discussion of the complexity of inert, naturally-occurring objects and to consider the use of information in feedback loops. Inert, naturally-occurring objects do exhibit what we can call "relaxation to equilibrium"; that is, they can move or change under the effect of external prodding (forces, in a general sense) of many kinds. Thus inert, naturally-occurring systems can and often do change over time. Information can be recorded in or on inert systems. What inert, naturally-occurring systems do not do is create, read, or process messages. Hence inert, naturally-occurring systems do not and cannot use information to control themselves. More specifically, inert, naturally-occurring systems do not do any of the following: (1) sense information; (2) transform that information; (3) given this transformed information, compare their condition (state) to a desired end condition; or (4) modify themselves in such a way that they ultimately reach a desired end condition. The processes (1) through (4) are exactly those of a control feedback loop. We will take these four steps as a definition of what the words "control feedback loop" will denote in this volume.

Norbert Wiener (1948) made feedback processes a part of the common knowledge of many people by naming them "cybernetic" and pointing to the importance of cybernetic processes in many systems, including human-designed systems. Nearly all organisms and ecologies have control feedback loops. Even plants and single-cell animals use them to some degree. The human body has more than 1,000 feedback loops, according to physicians.

Humans now often design control feedback loops into systems we build. Thus some human-built inert systems differ qualitatively from naturally-occurring inert objects. Feedback control and how it operates are very familiar in some disciplines, but not in others. So I include a short description of how feedback control loops operate.

Perhaps the most widely known control feedback loop in human-built hardware is the thermostat with the air conditioner / furnace system for a room (or building), which we already mentioned. Let's look at the four steps for the common type of temperature control by a feedback loop. (1) The thermostat senses temperature by the heating or cooling of a bimetallic strip; (2) the bimetallic strip transforms the "sensed" signal (by bending); (3) when the strip bends enough, owing to temperature change so that it passes a preset point (controlled by your setting of the room temperature on the dial), it closes an electric circuit generating an electric signal; (4) the electric signal activates the heating (or cooling) equipment. The equipment then remains on until the room reaches the desired temperature range. At this point the bimetallic strip opens the circuit, and the air conditioner / furnace goes off.

The car you drive probably has several such control feedback loops controlling engine spark, fuel/air ratio, and other variables within the engine. You don't need to know that these feedback loops are present in order to drive your car; but they are important in making your car run under a wide range of conditions, smoothly, and with a minimum of polluting emissions.

Several points needed to be extracted from the examples in the preceding paragraphs for later reference. First, nearly all biological systems, and some systems designed and created by humans, handle information. As far as we know, inert, naturally-occurring systems do not and cannot handle information (even though information can be recorded on them). This is a fundamental difference in the character of the systems that affects not only their behaviors but also the way "rules" can be applied to their behaviors, as we will see.

Second, the example of the thermostat, as the paradigmatic example of feedback control, has been widely used in psychology, particularly in the form of psychotherapy known as family therapy, as a model of human feedback processes. Unfortunately, it is not a good example for these purposes because the thermostat uses only the simplest kind of feedback, and there are a number of other, more complex types of feedback that humans routinely use in communicating with each other. These more complex modes often include such elements as multiplying feedback signals to amplify them, and using higher-level comments within secondary loops. The use of oversimple sysreps of feedback modes has caused serious misunderstandings on some issues in psychology and other areas. We will return to the details of this issue in Chapter 6.

The Pathway of Physical Sciences and Engineering for Studying Class A Systems

The central pathway for predicting behaviors in both the physical sciences and engineering (historically and in practice) is designed to solve simple problems first — that is, problems with low values of C — and then gradually increase the complexity of systems studied. Over the past few centuries this strategy has succeeded brilliantly for problems in the domain of inert systems. It has provided humans with knowledge sufficient to design many successful types of systems with functions that were beyond human imagination only two centuries ago. We think immediately of airplanes, telephones, computers, CAT scanners, atom bombs, lasers, printers, and compact disc players, to mention only a few.

The procedures include a number of mathematical tricks for reducing the value of C for given classes of sysreps both in the physical sciences and in designs of hardware. Scientists and engineers have been at some pains to create these tricks precisely because they have learned well how hard it is to analyze in full detail sysreps where C is not small, and because an increase of even one in C usually brings a large addition of difficulty in creating solutions. We need not deal with those tricks here. The interested reader can find many of them elaborated in Kline (1965, 1986).

An easy way to picture the effect of increasing C is via the magnitude of the data required to set down a table of results. For V = 1, we need a line to record the data; for V = 2, a page; for V = 3, a book; V = 4, a library. It will be useful for later comparison to illustrate the nature of a solution in one problem where C = 4.

In turbulent flow of gases or liquids usually L = 0, and if we fix the values of the parameters, then we are in the operating space, and C = V = 4. A complete detailed computer solution of one such problem in turbulent flow in 1990, even of the simplest sort, required about two man-years of very skilled programming and threee to six months' running time in the largest supercomputers then available. Complete solutions of any problem in this class were not possible until the 1980's because we had no computers large enough for the task. Moreover, in 1990 each solution, of the simplest problems in this class, cost more than $250,000 in computer time alone, even at the lowest going rates. It is thus not surprising that turbulence has often been called "the hardest problem in classical physics." Thus, for our discussion, C = 4 locates in a rough way the boundary between simple systems for which we could accurately predict all details of behavior and complex systems for which we could not in 1990.

Class B: Systems of Human-Designed Hardware

Analyses of hardware are nearly always built up out of analysis of the sysreps for the paradigmatic systems described in class A (above) by joining them together to create more complex behaviors as required to meet design goals. The criteria for joining two pieces seldom contain more than a few items, and thus the criteria are seldom of high complexity. By building up systems in this way, we can analyze and make predictions about systems of considerable complexity; however, most of this complexity is characterized by the number of parameters, P; the number of independent variables for both the parts and the joining criteria typically remains small. We note for later reference, however, that the design goals cannot be found in this way; design goals are set by humans and thus involve the complexity of the human mind; see the section "Class C" below. See also Chapter 6.

In short, the whole design process for hardware can proceed based on low values of C in each part of the analyses employed, but only after the goals have been set. Despite this, it will be useful to provide an estimate of C for complete hardware systems for comparison with other types of systems. The systems may involve feedback loops. If feedback loops exist, and are connected to many parts, the value for C will become higher as indicated by equation (4-1). However, in 1990 we would consider as many as six control feedback loops a large number for one human-designed hardware system. Hence, we can use the number of parameters as a first estimate of the values of C. We can take the number of specifications on the manufacturing drawings of the hardware as a measure of the number of parameters in the system, P.

For very complex hardware systems such as an automobile, an airplane, or a computer, P may be in the 1,000s, 10,000s, or even 100,000s, and we can write:

$$C_B < 10^6 \qquad\qquad (4\text{-}3)$$

It is important for later discussion to note that in 1990 analytic and/or computer procedures that provide the bases for the solutions described cover only some systems in class B. In 1990 there still remained some systems in class B for which analyses cannot be carried out even at these relatively low levels of complexity. Examples of inadequate analyses or computer models include any combustion system, automobiles, most machine tools, most shop-floor manufacturing processes, and many other systems. In such cases, we design from past experience, add perhaps some modifications, and then test the results for performance and reliability. This may include systematic testing over a range of parameters in order to optimize designs. Good examples are given by Vincenti (1989) and by Kline (1991a). Because unpredictable elements exist in designs of complex hardware, successful developmental practice usually holds many elements constant while varying a few to produce new models. Thus, in mature industries, last year's models become "technological paradigms" from which practice evolves, as Edward Constant (1980) has described with particular clarity. Indeed, the phrase "technological paradigm" seems to have been created by Constant.

Class C: A Single Human Being

The number of neurons in the normal adult human brain is typically taken as between 10^{10} and 10^{12}. As a conservative estimate, we can take 10 percent of the lower value as "programmable" via learning for an individual over time. This assumes that the remaining 90 percent of the brain serves to mind the body, and to interact with muscles and with signals from the external world through the senses. Since each neuron can take on various values, the programmable neurons need to be counted as independent variables, and thus we can write, as a first estimate, for the human brain:

$$C_C > 10^9 \qquad\qquad (4\text{-}4)$$

The greater-than sign is used to indicate that equation (4-4) provides a significant underestimate because we are considering only the brain, not a complete human being. Since we have considered only the brain and have given a lower bound, equation (4-4) can also be used for a complete human being. This is a very crude estimate of the value of the complexity index for a human being. It is, nevertheless, a useful estimate for the purposes of this discussion, and will be important in much of what follows. Since the estimate is important, and questions can be raised about how it has been formed, a somewhat more detailed justification for equation (4-4) is given in an addendum to this chapter. It reconfirms equation (4-4) on different grounds.

If we had to deal with the full complexity of the internal workings of the human brain whenever we dealt with other humans, our situation would be hopeless for any planning or rational action in social systems. Fortunately, we do not have to do that. We don't have to because the number of emergent properties that humans exhibit and react to is far smaller than the number of variables in the brain. Moreover, we do not know how to describe the behaviors of humans in terms of neurons. Shakespeare had no knowledge of neurons, but he still was able to write plays that many see as deeply insightful about human nature.

Is this difference in the number and the nature of variables from one level of aggregation to another in a structure unique to humans? Indeed not. It is the typical case, and we will encounter it again and again. Let's examine one more example here to fix the idea.

Consider what the chemists call one "mol" of a particular gas in a bottle under the nine provisos listed by Gibbs. We can call this a "Gibbs simple **system**." A mol of gas always has the same number of particles (atoms or molecules), $6.02 \cdot 10^{23}$, more than a thousand billion billion. Each of these billions and billions and billions of particles follows its own trajectory in moving through the operating space within the bottle. However, as we already saw in Chapter 2, we can represent the condition (or state, as scientists call it) of the gas in the bottle as a whole by only two variables, pressure and temperature. For at least some purposes, we do not need to deal with each of the $6.02 \cdot 10^{23}$ molecules.

So the problem of the complexity of humans is not as bad as we might think at first glance. Nevertheless, the complexity of humans lies far beyond that of the gas in a bottle (just discussed), and this fact will affect many of the results we will find. An example occurs in the next section.

Class D: Human Social Systems

Let us assume for discussion purposes that each of the 10^9 programmable neurons can be connected to any of the 1,000 neurons within the nearest 10 percent of the volume of the human brain; a fact that we now believe is roughly correct. With this assumption, the possible number of configurations of all possible human brains becomes of the order of $10^{8,000}$, a number so enormous that it is hard to imagine or even write out in the ordinary arithmetic form. "There are perhaps one hundred billion neurons, or nerve cells, in the brain, and the number of possible connections between these cells is *greater than the number of atoms in the universe*" (emphasis added).

This begins to make clear the enormous complexity of the human brain and hence the basis for the enormous number of observed variations in human behaviors in individuals, in human cultures, and in complex human-operated systems. However, if we are concerned with human social systems, $10^{8,000}$ is too large a number because it describes the states of neurons and not the smaller number of emergent properties humans use when they interact with each other. However, we can make an estimate for C_D in a different way. Let's suppose we have 100 or more humans in the **system**, the V for the collection of humans will be at least 100 times 10^9; hence we can write for typical human social systems:

$$C_D > 10^{11} \tag{4-5}$$

where we again adopt the strategy of using a significant underestimate of C that is sufficient for this discussion.

Class E: Ecologies Containing Humans

For these systems, C cannot be less than that for human social systems. Hence, for this discussion, we can again accept the estimate:

$$C_E > 10^{11} \tag{4-6}$$

In thinking about equation (4-6), we need to recognize that once again we have omitted many sources of complexity and that complex ecologies, such as a rain forest with mammals, even without humans, may have values of C well above 10^{11}. We can leave more careful estimates to ecologists.

Class F: Sociotechnical Systems

The term "sociotechnical systems" is used to denote complete systems of coupled social and technical parts which humans erect and operate primarily to control our environment and perform tasks we cannot do without such systems. The human powers created by such systems have increased via innovations at an accelerating pace for roughly the past two million years (see Chapter 14). Over the past two centuries, the powers of these human sociotechnical systems have become so great that we humans, for many purposes, have become the lords of the planet. Four types of sociotechnical systems are common: manufacturing enterprises (Boeing, General Electric, Sony, Rolls Royce), systems of use (aircraft transport, newspapers and TV networks, households, orchestras and bands, armies), systems of distribution (Sears, Takashima, Harrods), and systems of research and development for creating new or modified sociotechnical systems.

Sociotechnical systems are pervasive in human affairs, and it is important for us to have an estimate of their complexity.

In 1990 many large sociotechnical systems involved thousands of humans, very complex hardware of many kinds, and feedback loops circling the planet. It is difficult to make accurate estimates of the value of C for such systems. However, for the present discussion it will again be sufficient to take a significant underestimate. Since sociotechnical systems involve not only a number of humans but also complex hardware and many feedback loops both within the system and to the world, we can take this estimate as:

$$C_F > 10^{13} \qquad (4\text{-}7)$$

Equation (4-7) will be an underestimate for any sociotechnical system involving, say, ten or more people, social arrangements, and the use of several kinds of hardware. Actual values of C for such systems can easily exceed 10^{15} or 10^{20}.

What type of systems are the most complex? Scanning the values of C given in this chapter for the various classes of systems — inert, naturally-occurring systems (including the subatomic and the astronomical); biologic systems, human-made hardware systems; communication systems; value systems; and sociotechnical systems — leads to the conclusion that sociotechnical systems are the most complex class of systems we know. This ought not surprise us, since sociotechnical systems include all the other classes of systems and depend on interactions among them. Thus, bigger does not always imply more complex.

We also see, from comparison of equations (4-3) through (4-7), that most of this complexity comes from the existence of human beings and other forms of life in the system, and not from hardware, even in the cases of the most complex hardware available in the late twentieth century. Thus, we might say that the systems in class A are simple, those of class B are often complex, and those of classes C, D, E, and F are typically very complex.

When we compare the values of C in the systems of classes A through F, the striking feature is the range in the values of C. Not only is C for inert, naturally-occurring systems typically very small, but C for sociotechnical systems is astoundingly large. This disparity of many orders of magnitude raises obvious questions concerning the applications of the methods that work so well for analysis of systems in class A to the systems discussed in classes C, D, E, and F. We will begin to explore these questions in this chapter and continue the discussions in Chapters 5 and 6.

As the example of turbulent flows in class A shows us, systems with V as large as 4 are often very difficult to analyze completely by any available analytic theory or computer program. Indeed, in the physical sciences and engineering, a problem with $V = 6$ is generally considered too complex to be analyzed in complete detail. When $V > 5$, even when $L = 0$ and we hold the values of parameters fixed, we begin to seek simpler models that will help us analyze some components of the system or some aspects of the complete system.

What, then, can we say about systems were C is greater than a billion? We already saw a hint about this question when we mentioned human design process. With the values of C given by equations (4-2) through (4-7), we can now expand on that remark.

Let us first continue the discussion about design, as contrasted with analysis, of hardware systems. As we saw in discussing systems in class B, when we cannot carry out analyses, we proceed by using experience and testing. We usually call this process "development." We do not need all the details of the processes of development at this point.

What is important here is the relation between probable incompleteness of the sysrep and system complexity. If the system (or the component of the system) of concern is too complex for full analysis via analytical or computer processes, we cannot construct adequate sysreps for the entire system. Under these circumstances, we have no recourse but to design, build, and test when we want to make innovations. For such systems, "developmental" process is thus a matter not of choice but, rather, of necessity. This is nearly always the case when $C > 5$ for entire systems and sometimes even when C has a lower value. It thus seems absurd to believe that we can create adequate sysreps for the entire system when $C > 10^9$, which includes all systems containing humans, that is, all human social systems, all sociotechnical systems, and at least many ecologies. Recognition of this limitation on what we can do via explicit analysis of entire systems, and hence via reliable prior predictions, is a critical first step toward understanding how we construct, operate, and improve very complex systems. We will therefore set it off as a guideline for emphasis, and so we have a name for it. We will use the term "guideline" to indicate an idea that is important and true most of the time, hence worth keeping in mind.

Guideline for Complex Systems

In very complex systems, such as sociotechnical systems, we have no theory for entire systems, and must therefore create, operate, and improve such systems via feedback: that is, repeated cycles of human observations plus trials of envisaged improvements in the real systems. In such very complex systems, data from a wide variety of cases therefore become the primary basis for understanding and judgments, and should take precedence over results from theory based on cuts through the hyperspace (called "the primacy of data").

We will examine what this means in Chapter 5.

At this point, we can begin to see conjunctions in method between human design of hardware systems and the far more complex systems involving human beings. One conjunction arises from the fact that design criteria for hardware systems utilize the full complexity of human beings, since these criteria represent, in capsule form, the expressed (or presumptive) desires and needs of individual humans and human institutions. A second conjunction arises from the need for "developmental" processes in innovations not only for complex hardware but also in social and sociotechnical systems of all kinds as a matter of necessity, not of choice. To be more specific, we construct and operate such systems based on prior experiences, and we innovate in them by the human design feedback mode. The human design feedback mode denotes the following: first, we look at the system and ask ourselves, How can we do it better?; second, we make some change and observe the system to see if our expectation of "better" is fulfilled; third, we repeat this cycle of improvements over and over. This process is used in designs, in developments, in research, and in innovations. This cyclic, human design feedback mode has also been called "learning-by-doing," "learning-by-using," "trial and error," and even "muddling through" or "barefoot empiricism." By whatever name, it is the only available process for managing and improving very complex systems. This same point is made on quite different grounds by Braybrooke and Lindblom (1963) in discussing policy decisions.

We have used the phrase "human design feedback mode" because we need to distinguish at least three kinds of feedback. Let's now list them and give them specific names to clarify discussion. (1) We will use "autonomic control" to denote feedback of fixed character which operates without external inputs (in either living systems or systems designed by humans); (2) we will call human-in-the-loop control (of a given system) "human control"; (3) we will call human-in-the-loop design "human design" (this term will apply to a new system or re-design of an old system, including research developments and innovations). The operation of a speed governor on a motor is an example of autonomic control feedback. Driving a car requires human control feedback. Designing a car requires human design feedback.

There seems to have been no single name that connotes any prestige for the essential method of human design feedback in the twentieth-century Western world. In Japan, it is part of the process called "kaizen," and has high prestige. Human design process can be quite rational or largely intuitive, but by whatever name, and however rational or intuitive, it is an important process not only in design but also in research, development, and technical and social innovations because it is often the only method available.

Expertise and Ethics Surpass "Rules"

Similar remarks apply to questions of both expertise and ethics. In discussing their five-level hierarchy of how human expertise develops, Herbert Dreyfus and Stuart Dreyfus (1986) make the point that only the lowest of these five levels can be adequately captured by formal rules. More specifically, the expert has gone far beyond formal rules and utilizes a flexible and deep relational network in solving problems, as we saw in Chapter 3. She or he will not only know the rules but will also have looked at the subject many times and probably from at least several views; solved many problems in the area; developed a relevant repertoire of both schemata and skills which can be brought to bear quickly in solving problems; had some failures as well as successes; and built a network of colleagues and others who supply consulting and supporting functions when needed. As a result of these experiences, the expert will have an armamentarium of schemata that she or he can bring to bear on problem solution within the area of expertise.

Essentially all the computers we have in the early 1990's are constructed with what is called "von Neumann architecture" (after John von Neumann, who suggested the basic arrangement of functions of the major components). Computers built with von Neumann architecture are "rule bound"; that is, the programmer must put in a set of rules that directs the computation precisely, step by step, before a computer can execute a program. As a result, such computers cannot solve problems for entire systems of very high complexity. In 1990, computers had moved our ability to compute results for complex systems up only a little in the value of C (roughly from 3 to 4). For good reasons we consider this an important gain in problem-solving ability. However, we remain, as the twentieth century draws to a close, a long way from being able to do accurate computations for complete systems with $C > 10^9$. Since other types of computers were under study in 1990 in many places, this limitation may change, but it remains the situation in the early 1990's. Moreover, as Eric Drexler (1992) has pointed out, it is possible to have a system that does all the things the human mind does within a space about one cubic foot in size; we have five billion of them walking around in human heads.

Caroline Whitbeck (1992) recently made a similar comment about the use of ethics in day-to-day living. Whitbeck points to the fact that many ethical questions cannot be decided appropriately by using fixed rules. She emphasizes that ethical decisions often constitute a "design" problem in which a suitable solution that balances benefits and costs for all stakeholders needs to be constructed, that is, designed, on a case-by-case basis. If that is so, then follow-up to see if further improvements are needed via the human design process should be part of the process.

We must not let the conjunctions in method between complex hardware and the social aspects of the systems described in the preceding paragraphs confuse us into thinking there are not important differences. The differences between physical and social systems are not only qualitative and very important, they also seem to have been underestimated for a long time in much scholarship. To help us discuss very complex systems, we will examine some tools for the task in the next chapter.

Policy Analysis and Decision Theory

An important application of the guideline for complex systems occurs in policy analysis and decision theory. Since this work deals with conceptual foundations, we will not pursue details of policy analysis or decision theory in this book except to see if what we have found is consistent with results in those fields.

Since policy analysis and decision theory usually deal with very complex systems, the guideline for complex systems applies. This implies two things. First, we need data; history matters. Second, we do not have complete theories for the entire system, so it is therefore risky to make large changes all at once. Since we cannot tell in advance what will happen, we may provoke many kinds of unforeseen difficulties, even disasters. Incrementalism of some form is strongly suggested. Using incrementalism, we can accomplish large changes over time, and we can also use feedback to guide the process. Using feedback reduces risks and, in the end, usually produces better results as well. This agrees with the widely known and highly regarded results of Braybrooke and Lindblom (1963). After a far more detailed analysis of the problems of decision making in complex systems than is given in this discussion, Braybrooke and Lindblom conclude that large changes are dangerous, and recommend what they call disjointed incrementalism, which they elaborate in some detail. They also note that optimizing processes based on top-down views in complex systems seem appealing but cannot in fact be carried out. They conclude that incrementalism is not only safer than "grand theory" but also the only pragmatic course as well. Incrementalism is what policy makers therefore actually do, despite various so-called ideal approaches. Braybrooke and Lindblom base their conclusions on essentially different grounds than we have used in this chapter, although there is some overlap in the reasoning. In addition, Braybrooke and Lindblom discuss only the areas of policy analysis and decision theory. This chapter shows that the results apply to all kinds of very complex systems. In sum, the results of this chapter and Braybrooke and Lindblom are in agreement where they overlap, and supplement each other in several ways.

The results of Braybrooke and Lindblom also provide strong, independent confirmation of the importance of the limitations of the human mind in scholarship. They cite useful data. We have space for only a few of these data in simplified form. Readers desiring the full results should see Braybrooke and Lindblom.

In a study of what methods are successful in hypothesis formation, the researchers laid out a deck of fifty-two playing cards face up. They then asked subjects to find a selection criterion for a subset (for example, all even-numbered spades) using the following protocol. Subjects could pick up cards one by one, and were told if the card was in the selected set. Subjects who thought up criteria in advance (grand theory) and then tested to see if their assumed criterion was right were unable to find the criterion of the set. These subjects often complained of "brain drain." On the other hand, subjects who picked up cards and accumulated information incrementally, without prior ideas about the "set," were usually able to find the criterion without difficulty. As Braybrooke and Lindblom state, the subjects who thought up criteria failed because the hyperspace of all possible criteria is too large for the human mind.

To put this differently, if we ask the mind to use processes it cannot accomplish, we will not get the task done. However, we may be able to complete the same task by incremental learning, the formation of chunks and ultimately the appropriate schemata.

We can conclude two things. Braybrooke and Lindblom give strong, independent confirmation of the importance of the limitations of the mind on scholarship, even on relatively simple problems. Their results provide another reason for the primacy of data in understanding complex systems.

Conclusions for Chapter 4

The index of complexity gives a rough but useful estimate of the complexity of various types of systems. The values of the index show an enormous variation. The values run from $C < 5$ at the low end for the systems we study in the physical sciences, to $C > 10^{13}$ at the high end for sociotechnical systems. This enormous range leads to a question we will need to discuss in more depth: Are the methods and type of "rules" that are appropriate to inert, naturally-occurring systems also appropriate for human social and sociotechnical systems?

In very complex systems, we do not have and cannot expect to have (at least in the near future) adequate theories for the entire systems. We must therefore create, operate, and improve such systems by what we are calling human design feedback. Moreover, since we lack adequate theory for the entire system, for such systems there is what we will call a "primacy of data." That is, where theory is necessarily incomplete, and the theory conflicts with data for a variety of systems of the type we are thinking about, we need to give priority to the data. We will examine what "incomplete" implies in this sense in the next chapter.

Addendum to Chapter 4

Alternate Estimates of C for a Human Being

A few readers of a draft of the paper on which this chapter is based (Kline [1991a]) asked, "Why should we take each neuron as independent when we don't treat each molecule in, say, a fluid field in this way?" The reasons for this different treatment are grounded in the different nature of a neuron as part of a brain and a molecule as part of inert field of flow.

The state of each neuron in a given brain has evolved over time owing to genetic and experiential history, and is not determined by the boundary values on the brain at a given instant in time (as fluid particles are determined). Moreover, the individual neurons can take on different values of electrochemical potential over time as the result of further experiences. Thus when we reexperience a situation we have met before, we may act differently from our behavior in prior episodes. If this were not true, we would never learn to speak new words, improve our tennis game, or learn to follow new forms of reasoning, to mention only a few matters. Nor would strong, long-term reactions to certain situations arise from earlier experiences involving strong emotions, as illustrated in post-traumatic stress syndrome. Rape often causes significant changes in a woman's personality, as battle experiences do in soldiers. This is part of what is implied by the word "history," as used above.

Inert, naturally-occurring systems do not behave in these ways. When a given system of this type meets a given situation, the individual molecules in it will respond in the same way time after time. Moreover, in a fluid field, typically we need specify only a limited amount of boundary-value information to completely determine what each particle will do. Even in chaotic systems, this is true of the average performance. It is not remotely true of human behavior. We can make this idea memorable by noting that when two molecules collide they do not say "ouch," nor do molecules hold grudges as a result of the collision, as humans are prone to do. Molecules merely collide, and they react in predictable ways. The outcome of the collision of two humans is not predictable; they may pass over the pain lightly or they may sue each other.

Moreover, each neuron in a human brain can take on a range of values and hence is more complex than a memory element in a current digital computer that can have only the values zero and one. Thus the behavior of neurons seems to be like that of independent variables and not like dependent parts of inert systems (for example, molecules in a fluid field). Nevertheless, it is possible that we ought to use a higher level of aggregation than neurons to assess the complexity index of the brain. The estimate of the complexity index for a single human is so important in what follows in our discourse that we need to be sure that equation (4-4) is justified. For this reason the rest of this Addendum provides a wholly different basis for equation (4-4).

A highly educated, middle-aged human being will typically know the meaning of and be able to use fifty thousand words or more in her or his native language. Many of these words, when brought into the active attention of a human, will activate pictures of a number of different items. Consider the number of images that each of the following words brings into your mind: "rocks," "houses," "women/men," "fruit," "pictures," "stories," "tools," "faces," "dresses," "jewelry," "playing," "boating." Since some words imply only a few images and others hundreds, let us assume, as an estimate, that the average for such multiple images attached to each word is twenty. Thus at the level of storable and reprogrammable items the brain must certainly be able to hold the order of 10^6 definable and distinguishable pictures and ideas. In addition to these 10^6 items, the brain can also form them into thoughts, sentences, and patterns for actions. A human brain can invent new, never-before-seen ideas. Moreover, the brain can do all of this while simultaneously choosing among and partly attending to one or two of five sense channels, two of which (sight and hearing) have quite wide bands. Thus we ought not to take a value less than 10^6 for the complexity index of the brain even if we want a very conservative lower bound at a level of aggregation of ideas and actions. This result is consistent with the statement of Simon that the expert will know something like 50,000 chunks and hold them in relational networks within her/his domain of expertise, as we noted in Chapter 3. If we take such a conservative estimate for the brain, then we need to estimate the complexity of at least some of the remaining parts of the human to obtain a lower bound for the complexity of a complete human being. We make estimates of some other human parts next.

In addition to the brain, the human animal contains about 2,000 muscles, more than 1,000 chemical feedback loops, 5 sensing channels with sensors and transducers that relay information to the brain, apparatus for very complex speech, hundreds of bones, a cardiovascular system, a pulmonary system, a reproductive system, an endocrine system, a digestive and excretory system, and many other parts. Moreover, the human structure is strongly coupled so that an appropriate value for the complexity index will lie closer to the upper limit than the lower limit of equation (4-1) with regard to many components. The coupling of the brain to the muscles must be very close; if it were not, we could not pick up a strange object. We also know that many of the chemical feedback loops in the body are connected to the brain, although we do not yet seem to understand those connections well. We need to assign at least one independent parameter for the mass of each muscle when we differentiate between humans, and at least one independent variable for the tension of each muscle when we consider postures and motions. We need to count at least some of the chemical feedback loops as strongly coupled. If we take $C = 100$ for the coupled feedback loops, and $P = 2,000$ for the description of muscles, the estimate from equation (4-1) in product form is:

$$C^C > 10^6 \cdot 100 \cdot 2000 = 2 \cdot 10^{11} \qquad (4\text{-}8)$$

Equation (4-8) does not take into account the effects of the quite complex speech and sensing systems, or a number of other body systems mentioned above. Hence the $>$ sign in equation (4-8) is justified, and we can see that the estimate of equation (4-4) is justified even when we take a very low estimate of complexity for the brain. Thus we can safely conclude that the complexity index for a single human is far greater than 10^9.

Thinking About Complex Systems

Chapter 4 shows that we cannot create analytic or computer solutions for all the details of a complete solution for complex systems. This leaves us with a question: How can we think about such systems? We can reframe this question by asking, What can we do when we cannot find complete answers for a class of problems?

First, we will look at some methods we have developed over the past few centuries for describing inert, naturally-occurring systems in cases where we cannot find complete solutions. Then we will look at what happens when we apply the same kind of methods to very complex systems.

Let's take as our **system** the class of simple rectangular rooms as shown in Figure 4-1. We can choose a particular room from this class by setting values for three parameters, the length B, the width W, and the height H, in the design space. We can delineate the operating space using three variables x, y, and z, as we saw in Chapter 4. We can write these two sets of facts in a functional form as follows:

$$R_1 = f(x,y,z; B,W,H) \text{ and no more} \tag{5-1}$$

In functional equations, like equation (5-1), we will regularly show the variables first in lower case and then show the parameters in caps after a semicolon, except when a variable like temperature is normally capitalized.

Once we choose the values of B, W, and H we can write:

$$R_2 = f(x,y,z) \text{ and no more} \tag{5-2}$$

The words "and no more" are important in both equations (5-1) and (5-2). They tell us that we have a complete description in each case. Equation (5-1) delineates all the variables needed to describe the operating space, and also all the parameters needed to define the design space. Equation (5-2) delineates all the variables in the operating space.

Mathematicians, scientists, and engineers nearly always leave off the words "and no more." Nevertheless, the words are understood to be there for anyone who comprehends the meaning of functional equations like (5-1) and (5-2).

Equation (5-1) is what I will call "a functional representation of a complete hyperspace." A complete hyperspace has two parts, the operating space and the design space, and we can examine each independently or the two together.

Equations (5-1) and (5-2) are specific to our class of rectangular rooms. Our next task is to generalize the concepts involved. The two concepts "function" and "hyperspace" are common parlance in some disciplines, but not others. Hence we need to explain them briefly. Let's begin by setting down what equations (5-1) and (5-2) say in words.

Equation (5-1) reads, "The dependent variable (or result), R_1, for rectangular rooms is a function of (is determined by) the variables x,y,z, and the parameters B,W,H, and no more variables or parameters." Equation (5-2) reads, "The location of a point in the operating space of a given rectangular room, R_2, is a function of x,y,z, and no more." These sentences illustrate and define what the word "function" means in this kind of mathematical (functional) language. Alternative words for function are "relational dependence on."

How about the word "hyperspace"? What does it denote? The word hyperspace is a metaphorical extension of what we mean by ordinary — that is, geometric — "space." Ordinary, geometric space is three-dimensional, that is, it has three independent space dimensions, as our rectangular rooms illustrate. However, our functional representation of the complete hyperspace for the room has six items in it, three geometric variables and three parameters. If we think of the sysrep of equation (5-1) as a space, it has six dimensions in it: x,y,z and B,W,H. So the prefix "hyper" is used in mathematical language to indicate a "space" with more than three dimensions. Since nearly all the spaces we will examine in this work have more than three dimensions, I will use the words "complete hyperspace" to denote "the metaphorically extended idea of the 'space' of all the appropriate variables and parameters, regardless of the number of variables and parameters or their types."

In the example of the rectangular rooms, the operating space has three independent variables, and the design space has more independent parameters. We could represent either space geometrically, using three axes. However, in complex systems such as a human being or an automobile, the operating space has far more than three variables and the design space far more than these parameters. In such cases, the operating space and the design space can each be thought of geometrically as a "hyperspace." Hence the combination of the operating and design spaces will be called the "complete hyperspace."

In the example of the temperature in a rectangular room in Chapter 4, we found that for a time after the furnace shuts off for a given room we needed two new variables, temperature T and time t. Our functional representation for the complete hyperspace would then read:

$$R = f(x,y,z,T,t; B,W,H) \qquad (5\text{-}3)$$

We can then say "the dimensionality" of the hyperspace is eight. This illustrates what we will denote as "dimensionality" of a "hyperspace." Dimensionality is the number of independent variables and parameters needed to describe the result (dependent variable) for the class of problem of interest. To put this in more detail: The dimensionality of the operating space equals the number of independent variables; the dimensionality of the design space equals the number of independent parameters; and the dimensionality of the complete hyperspace is the number of independent variables plus the number of independent parameters. In some descriptions the variables and parameters do not separate neatly, but we will leave discussion of various cases to technical experts.

The word "dimension" has three distinct meanings that we need to distinguish. In architecture "dimension" denotes the value of a length. We say, for example, the dimensions of a room are 10 ft. × 20 ft. × 8 ft. Physical scientists usually call these values, like the sizes of a room, the magnitude; they reserve the word "dimensions" to denote the character (or nature) of the variables and/or parameters of the class of system under study (length, for example, or temperature, or . . .). However, it is rare for variables and parameters to be distinguished as carefully as is done above. We will follow the scientific nomenclature, and in addition distinguish variables from parameters in the way described above, because it aids clarity in many issues we will discuss.

Since the idea may seem strange for some readers, it bears repeating: the variables and the parameters in a hyperspace need not have any relation to what we ordinarily mean by space; that is, they need not be lengths in the geometric sense. Let's look at one more example.

If we examine the Gibbs simple **system** of Chapter 2, the water in a glass with the nine provisos Gibbs listed, then the functional representation of the energy in the water per unit mass is

$$e = f(T,p) \qquad \text{[and no more]} \qquad (5\text{-}4)$$

where T is the temperature, p the pressure, and e the energy per unit mass of the water. Equation (5-4) is written for water; however, Gibbs took the dimensionality to be two, for any Gibbs simple **system** whatsoever. Gibbs did this based on data; his idea is an empirical generalization. So far we have not found exceptions to Gibbs's generalization; it appears to be an invariant "rule." Equation (5-4) implies a dimensionality of two, but this important fact has often been left implicit, and sometimes totally forgotten. Thus the operating space of the Gibbs simple **systems** in equation (5-4) has a dimensionality of two, but neither of the dimensions is a geometric length. The hyperspace for the Gibbs simple **system** includes in addition one parameter, the mass of the system:

$$E = f(T,p; M) \tag{5-5}$$

where M is the mass of water and E the energy of the total system.

We are now ready to begin exploiting the concept of the functional representation of operating, design, and complete hyperspaces.

Notice that writing an equation in functional form, like equations (5-1), (5-2), (5-3), or (5-4), does not require that we know the solution to the problem, that is, we do not demand an explicit known form for the function f. For example, equation (5-4) does not tell us the value of energy per unit mass for the water; it merely says that the energy per unit mass is determined by the temperature and the pressure. For some substances, we could get the value of the energy per unit mass from a theory founded on physics. However, to get the energy per unit mass of liquid water, we would have to go to tables of recorded data on water, because we have no theory for the energy of water even in this very simple system. When we went to the tables, we could look up the value of energy under the appropriate temperature and pressure; we would find that these two variables are enough. Equation (5-4) is a useful sysrep for the Gibbs simple **system**. Thus, if we run into a substance where we don't have tables, we know what must be fixed, and what varied, to get the data we need. We also know that we should not try to fix more than two variables independently, since that would very probably create contradictions. Thus, when we know the hyperspace, we already have significant information about the system even when we do not have the complete solution that would provide numbers. Indeed Gibbs's "rule" for the dimensionality of systems that contain more than one chemical substance, called "the phase rule," is not only very famous in science but also a foundation principle in such fields as chemistry and metallurgy.

An important use of the concept of a functional representation of a hyperspace in multidisciplinary discussion is to examine the question, Is a given functional representation of the hyperspace complete in the sense that all the variables and parameters needed to get a complete solution have been listed? This question is particularly important for very complex systems where we cannot find solutions for the entire system. We can see the importance by looking at the situation the other way around. If we start with an incomplete list of variables and/or parameters in what we use as the hyperspace in our sysrep, then no later mathematical manipulations will get us a complete solution. Any solution we find will be seriously incomplete and probably will mislead us in at least some if not all the problems we want to study.

Let's see what this kind of incompleteness does in the case of our simple rectangular rooms. Figure 5-1 shows a rectangular room with a plane parallel to the floor cutting through the room higher up.

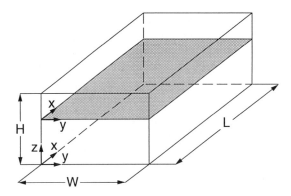

Figure 5-1. The Rectangular Room **System** with Midplane.

What would happen if we try to describe the operating space of the room by two of the three dimensions? Suppose we start at the bottom corner from which we measure x, y , and z, but only allow x and y to vary. We can reach any point on the floor this way, but we cannot reach any point higher up. We might also look at a plane halfway between floor and ceiling, as shown in Figure 5-1. We could then explore this midplane by varying x and y, but could not reach either the ceiling or the floor or points in between. Thus what we can find by varying x and y (but not z) is what we will call a "cut through the operating space" (or a cut through the complete hyperspace, when appropriate).

Suppose, then, that we examine data for fixed z and try to find the variation of temperature through the room in a situation when temperature varies from point to point as expressed by equation (5-3). What we will find is some of the variation but not all. The idea of the preceding sentence will be of critical importance in many places in our discussion. To put this more memorably, if we try to study temperature throughout the room, using only x and y, starting from our reference corner, our exploration will never get off the floor.

The same comments apply to assuming that there are fewer than three parameters in the design space of rectangular rooms. If we assume that the only parameters are B and W, we get a cut through the design space that allows us to choose rooms of only one height. The Greeks had a name for such a process; they called it Procrustean after a tyrant who chopped off the legs of his guests to fit his beds.

Thus we see that the need to represent the system by an appropriate and complete set of variables and parameters is fundamental and unavoidable. The idea applies just as much to complex human systems as to simple physical systems.

Moreover, a knowledge of the functional representation of the hyperspace must precede doing any analysis or adequate data taking. This remains true whether or not the functional representation is made explicit or is left implicit in the mind. It is also true regardless of whether the system characteristics are deterministic, probabilistic, or chaotic. In all these cases, we must know what variables and parameters we need to study before we can do the study. If you think about various cases, I believe you will see that if we do not use a complete and appropriate set of variables and parameters, we cannot expect to get solutions that are complete and appropriate for all the problems in the class we are considering. At best, we will get incomplete answers for some problems; at worst, we will get trivial and/or misleading answers for the entire domain. Typically we will get a mixture of useful and misleading results, and have difficulty distinguishing one from the other.

Given the preceding paragraph, it makes sense, as a precaution, to examine a functional representation of the hyperspace of the domain of interest as a means for explicit study of the completeness and appropriateness of the equations and data we will obtain. The relevant hyperspace may be an operating space, a design space, or a complete hyperspace, depending on the problem. Such an examination is a useful tool for multidisciplinary analysis because, without solving problems completely, we can study the state of knowledge under various initial assumptions to see what the functional representation of the hyperspace can yield, what domain can be covered. In many cases, this step can show us at once that the space is incomplete, and we can then take steps to fix the difficulty, or at least explicitly recognize that the solutions we will get will be short of complete predictive capability.

Does this imply that we should not use a cut through a hyperspace as the basis for models and analysis of real-world systems? No! Given the limitations of the human mind (discussed in Chapter 3), we cannot avoid using cuts through the complete hyperspace of very complex systems. It does imply several other things, however. First, we must not accept the idea that results derived from cuts through the hyperspace of the real system are more accurate than data on the same class of systems. In such cases we must respect the primacy of data and, whenever possible, use data from a variety of cases to guide decision making. Second, when we do use cuts through a hyperspace for analysis, we need to examine what fraction of the variance the variables we use cover in the hyperspace. We need to seek variables that cover as much of the variance as we can find. Third, we must keep in mind that variables used in a given "cut" may be appropriate for some problems or some cases within the complete hyperspace but not for other problems.

Another way we can deal with complex systems is to suppress details at levels for sizes smaller than the level where our problem lies. We will see more about how this should (and should not) be done in Chapters 7 through 13. Still another way to deal with very complex systems is to create a taxonomy of various cases in a form that lets us use different hyperspaces for different cases. Many human designs or devices are done this way. The subdivisions of medicine accomplish this in part, as do the subdivisions of the sciences. In the physical sciences the subdivisions often separate cleanly so we can reduce the dimensionality of our study without entailing serious hazards; see, for example, the description of the work of Gibbs, Maxwell, and Newton in Chapter 2.

In the human sciences, we encounter more difficulties when we use subdivisions based on a taxonomy of disciplines because the problems do not separate cleanly. As a result, we entail more hazards when we reduce the dimensionality of our analyses and data taking. Disciplines that deal with sociotechnical systems such as economics, political science, and sociology are at particular risk in their analyses for this reason. We will begin to look at this problem further in the next section.

Degrees of Freedom

For another view that we will find useful, let's think about what happens in the operating space when we fix z, but still allow x and y to vary in the rectangular room **system** of Figure 5-1 in a new way. We can think of fixing z as a constraint on the system. Where we had "three degrees of freedom," that is, three different ways to make changes in location in the operating space, when we fix z, we have only two. Notice also that by applying one constraint we have reduced the dimensionality of the space from 3 to 2. We could still study all three dimensions, by treating z as a parameter, that is, by looking at a series of planes, each at a different value of z, one by one. This parametric examination will sometimes give complete data, but in other cases it will be inadequate. For example, when the elements we are concerned with in our result are intrinsically connected over significant spans of z, and also vary over time, we will usually be unable to get complete information with a series of cuts through the hyperspace taken at different times. The details of this situation pass beyond what we need in this discussion.

This use of the phrase "degrees of freedom" is a third way (or mode) for denoting the number of independent variables or the dimensionality of the space.

Let's review these three modes. "Independent variables" is an analytic, mathematical mode of description that allows us to bring what we know about formal systems to bear. "Dimensionality" and "spaces" refer to a geometric mode that helps us visualize the situation even when the dimensionality is high. "Degrees of freedom" is a physical mode of description that is useful in thinking about effects of design changes and questions concerning control of the system.

We will normally take the number of degrees of freedom to be equal to the number of independent variables (and/or parameters) and also equal to the dimensionality of the relevant space. This means that we will ignore some special cases, leaving them to appropriate specialists. We will do this because we are concerned primarily with the common cases, rather than the pathological ones, and also because moving back and forth among all three of these modes of thinking is a useful tool for multidisciplinary discussions.

We are now ready to see what these ideas can do when we examine a complex system, a single human being. We will assume that each human is in some ways different from any other. This seems to be true, since fingerprints do not seem to duplicate, nor does the totality of a person's DNA, or a detailed map of any two human brains.

We ask, first, how many parameters do we need to fully specify (determine) one human and differentiate her or him from all other humans? I cannot answer this question, but surely it is a very big number. Let's see why. To begin, we would have to specify the sizes and chemical descriptions of each of thousands of muscles; hundreds of bones; the nature of the cells in the skin, finger- and toenails, hair, and so on; the geometry of many facial features; the sizes and compositions of various internal organs; and the many thousands of elements in the eye system. (See, for example, van Essen, Anderson, and Fellemon [1992].) And this is only to begin. The list just given omitted the lungs, the vascular system, the endocrine system, and other body parts. Surely no 3 (or even 100) parameters will fully determine a human being. To determine a human, even physiologically, requires a space of huge dimensionality. This is precisely why the complexity index for any system containing humans is so large. When we also consider the variables in the mental state of the brain, and the hookups of the brain to muscles that make it possible for us to be skilled piano players, lathe operators, or pilots, the number becomes even more enormous. It is the variations in mental states and brains that are of most concern in this discussion, because, whatever their source, they create enormous differences in the way individual humans behave under any particular set of circumstances.

If people are so different in so many ways, how do we recognize people we know and differentiate them from others we do not know? Usually we do this by looking at faces. Since it was probably a matter of survival for our biological ancestors to be able to tell friend (our clan, our tribe) from foe (all others), the brain has a special section devoted to assimilating and remembering faces (but not names). We assimilate and store "pictures" of faces remarkably quickly. Hence we often say, "I can see the face, but can't recall the name." Does this recognition of faces tell us all there is, or even all we often need to know, about other people? Of course not! Often we need to know much more for many reasons. In this sense, recognition of a face is a cut through a hyperspace of much larger dimensionality. We can also often identify individuals by voice quality or gestures, but the same remark applies. Voice quality or gestures are each a cut through a hyperspace of much larger dimensionality that would be needed to determine a complete human being. Indeed, there are two difficulties here which we need to note. First, the dimensionality of any hyperspace that would describe a single human completely is huge. Second, we do not know how to set down a list of all the variables, parameters, and feedback loops that would be needed to fully describe the hyperspace for a single human being. To put this in different words, there is no way we know to write a functional representation of the hyperspace needed for describing a human in the full sense we described the location in the rectangular room **system** or the state of the Gibbs simple **system**. It is not only that we don't know the function, there is an even more fundamental difficulty; we cannot provide a sufficient list of the variables and/or parameters.

These difficulties in describing a single human carry over into descriptions of human social and human sociotechnical systems and other systems of very high complexity. Since we cannot effectively think about all the dimensions of such a huge hyperspace, we try to simplify by making models based on fewer dimensions (that is, variables and parameters). In *Limits to Growth*, for example, Meadows et al. (1972) tried to model the entire world system with only five variables. In many of the equations of economics, we find only two "primary variables" (money and the interest rate). Indeed, it is common when we use what we call "models" as sysreps that the models have fewer independent variables and/or parameters than the complete system we are attempting to represent.

It follows that models often describe a cut through a larger hyperspace that is needed to represent the full system. Why do we do this? As already noted, we do it in order to make analyses possible by the human mind, given the limitations discussed in Chapter 3. However, having created cuts through the hyperspace, we ought to expect these models to produce some of the results characteristic of the system we are modeling, but not all. As constructed, such models cannot explore the entire "territory," that is, the full hyperspace. This is a fundamental limitation on disciplines which we will need to hold in mind for later discussion.

Open Degrees of Freedom, Constraints

Let's call the sum of the number of variables and the number of parameters in a given hyperspace N, "the total number of degrees of freedom" in a particular space. We will distinguish the total number of degrees of freedom, N, from what we will call the number of open degrees of freedom, O. In counting N, we do not need to include L, the number of feedback loops, because they are described by the parameters of the system (even though adding one feedback mode usually increases the complexity significantly more than one more parameter, such as a length).

The difference between N and O is the number of independent constraints operating on the system, M. When we are thinking in terms of functional representation of a hyperspace, M is the number of variables and/or parameters that are constrained. For example, in our rectangular room **system**, $N = 3$ in the design space. If we decide to make the height of the room 8 feet, then this is one constraint, and the number of open degrees of freedom is reduced to 2 within the design space. The general relation is

$$O = N - M \qquad (5\text{-}6)$$

There are some special cases (exceptions) that mathematicians have worked out about equation (5-6) which depend on the specific equations defining the result. However, the exceptions are not common in practice and seldom change results much for complex systems. We will therefore ignore the exceptions and think only about the common case, since that will be enough for this discussion.

Similar remarks apply to operating spaces and complete hyperspaces. If we have N variables in an operating space, there are N ways we can move. If we fix M of the variables, we reduce the space to a dimensionality $O = N - M$. Fixing one or more variables may be the result of an equation that the system must satisfy. Let's use the rectangular room system to illustrate.

Suppose we are thinking of the design space of a rectangular room. Suppose also that we decide the room must have a certain floor area $A = 300$ square feet. Then the equation $A = B \cdot W = 300$ acts as a constraint. If we demand this floor area, then only one of B and W can still be set. The condition, floor area equals a constant, acts as a relatively tight mutual constraint between B and W, but does not fully determine either one. Under these circumstances if we try to set both B and W independently, we will very probably create a contradiction. More generally, if we try to set more constraints than there are degrees of freedom in either an operating space or a design space, we will usually create contradictions; something will not work as we had intended.

In a slightly more complex case, we might decide for reasons of cost to limit the area of a one-story house to 2,400 square feet. If the floor plan has seven rooms, then we can choose the area of only six of the rooms independently. Since there are still many possible room plans, this is a looser constraint on the rooms than the case where we set the floor area of one room.

The distinction between "constraint" and "determination" is an important logical distinction; it does not seem to be understood as widely as it should be. This distinction is crucial to many matters we will discuss in this book. Let's therefore define "constraint" and "determination."

Constraint denotes "limits to within a range of values." Variations may occur within the range, and the range may be small or large. Determination denotes "to fix so that no variation is possible," in whatever is specified. We might say we need a rod between 1 and 2 feet long (constraint). We might alternatively say we need a rod 1.50 feet long (determination).

Suppose we have a dog confined to a fenced back yard, and the dog cannot get through, under, or over the fence. The dog's location is constrained, we know that the animal is within the yard. The yard may be small, 20 feet by 20 feet, or as large as 10 acres. To determine the dog's location, we must peg down all four of its feet.

The rod compares constraint and determination in one dimension. The dog in the yard compares for two dimensions. The concepts apply for any number of dimensions and to lengths or other types of variables and/or parameters.

Typically, then, for every open parameter we must choose one value to get a design. If there were no "open" parameters, there would be only one design, a very rare condition. For our purposes, it is important to turn this statement around, and say, "If there are open parameters, then human choices about the design exist." Equation (5-6) tells us this explicitly:

$$\text{If } O > \text{zero, then } N > M.$$

This implies that the design of such things as rooms is not determined by the laws of physics, but is only constrained either loosely or tightly. As we all know, we exercise lots of degrees of freedom in designing many kinds of devices and systems for various tasks that humans want to accomplish. This remark is important in understanding biology as well. If there is a "God the creator," she obviously exercised lots of degrees of freedom in the "design" of the millions of species of plants and animals on earth. The same is true if species arose through some form of evolution. If the "laws" of physics and biology fully determined biological structure, only one species would have arisen. The laws of physics and chemistry leave many open choices in biological systems; they only constrain and do not determine species.

Constraints can arise from many different sources: the "rules" of physics or biology; the inherent linking of either variables or parameters owing to the structure of the system; choices we make; laws of the land, social mores, aesthetic choices, and so on.

Several points from these illustrations will be needed later in our discussion. One or more constraints can limit the choices in a design space, an operating space, or a complete hyperspace, but still leave many other choices open. Constraints can be either direct or shared among a number of parameters or variables (be mutual). There are many possible sources for constraints on both variables and parameters of given systems. When there are open degrees of freedom in a hyperspace, it is prima facie evidence that the system is not determined by the laws of physics, biology, or other disciplines. Given the idea of the preceding sentence, an uncountable number of barefoot data tell us beyond reasonable doubt that the principles of physics and chemistry do not determine either human designs or biological species; they only constrain them.

CHAPTER 6

Feedback as a Source
of Complexity

The very large gap in values of the complexity index between inert, naturally-occurring objects on the one hand and social and sociotechnical systems on the other suggests a question, Do the two kinds of systems have qualitatively distinct behaviors, and thus perhaps require different kinds of "rules"? In this chapter we will examine the question from two views: first, via invariance and variation; second via the kinds of feedback various classes of systems can utilize.

In looking at principles that we assert describe a class of systems, we need to ask, Is the principle general in the sense that all systems in the class of systems under study obey the principle? To deal with this question we will use two definitions.

> An Entire Paradigm will denote: a principle that applies to every system in the class, without known exceptions.

> An Entire Invariant Paradigm will denote: a paradigm that predicts that all systems in the class will have the same behavior, in detail, for all times and in all places.

For what classes of systems are Entire Invariant Paradigms appropriate? There is one class where we know such paradigms are often appropriate, based on the empirical testing of many, many cases: the class of inert, naturally-occurring objects, the systems studied in physics, chemistry, and the other physical sciences.

To be more specific, under a given set of forces (in a general sense), in many classes of inert, naturally-occurring objects the system will react in the same way in one observation after another, again and again, whether the behavior is static or includes changes over time. Since the behaviors of these classes of systems are invariant, they can be described by "rules" that are invariant over time and space — that is, by fixed principles or, if you like, "iron laws." We had, by 1990, created Entire Invariant Paradigms for most but not all classes of inert, naturally-occurring systems.

Classes of systems for which we now have what appear to be well-tested Entire Invariant Paradigms include, but are not limited to, the equations set down by J. Clerk Maxwell in the late nineteenth century, which seem to describe all electrical and magnetic effects (including propagation of light and radio/TV signals); the three great principles of thermodynamics for all systems of human and planetary size in equilibrium states, which seem to describe both energy transformations and the dimensionality of states of substances; Newtonian principles of classical mechanics for the motions of ordinary-sized bodies at reasonable speeds; the attraction of bodies for each other that we call gravity. And, it bears repeating, this is not an exhaustive list.

In many cases we have been able to express these Entire Invariant Paradigms in detailed mathematical form, as in Maxwell's equations. When we have detailed mathematical forms of the paradigms, we can make detailed predictions with extraordinary accuracy about systems in the domain the paradigm covers. In some instances we have even been able to predict a phenomenon we have never seen, and then later confirm the existence of the phenomenon by experiments. It seems hard to think of a more critical test of the appropriateness of a sysrep.

Because of all this, many physical scientists and engineers have come to believe that the behaviors of inert, naturally-occurring objects and human-designed hardware are invariant even when we do not have explicit detailed mathematical paradigms for the given class of systems. In some cases this invariance involves fluctuations over time, but even those fluctuations appear the same, on the average, under a constant set of conditions.

The advent of the large digital computer has vastly enhanced the range over which we can use appropriate Entire Invariant Paradigms to make predictions about inert physical nature and thus also about systems of human-designed hardware. It seems fair to say that our ability to make such predictions and the design capacities this knowledge provides twentieth-century engineers, is one of the seven wonders of the late-twentieth-century world. These abilities are a large part of the knowledge that underlies the flow of new "hi-tech" devices that have profoundly altered the daily lives of many of us.

A caution is needed here. We can never be 100 percent sure we have reached the goal of an Entire Invariant Paradigm for a given class of systems. In fact, historically, we have often not gotten the principles or the equations right the first time, even for quite simple inert, naturally-occurring systems. Nevertheless, provided only that we have been careful about defining the domain to which the particular paradigm applies, in the sense discussed in Chapter 2, we have learned more and more about inert, naturally-occurring objects over the past three centuries, and so the equations we use as sysreps for these kinds of systems in many cases have more and more closely approached Entire Invariant Paradigms.

One of the reasons we believe that the Entire Invariant Paradigms we have created for inert, naturally-occurring systems are relatively well-grounded knowledge comes directly from their invariant behaviors. Different individuals, in different places and at different times, can repeat the critical data and thereby check the results independently. Thus when we repeat Galileo's experiments on falling bodies anywhere in the world today, we find we get the same results within a small uncertainty in the data owing to instrumental techniques, even though Galileo's experiments were done from the Leaning Tower of Pisa centuries ago.

Astronomy gives further strong evidence of invariance in the inert, naturally-occurring world. If the governing equations for inert, naturally-occurring objects were not invariant over time and space, astronomy would be nonsense, since the whole field rests on the assumption that the properties of light, and the principles describing these properties, are the same now as they have been throughout several billion years over the entire observable universe. Moreover, the appropriateness of our sysreps for many features of astronomy has been critically tested by the correct prediction of the course of space vehicles.

In sum, there are strong reasons for believing that Entire Invariant Paradigms exist for many (perhaps all) systems consisting of inert, naturally-occurring objects and processes. We know this is so about as firmly as we know anything.

If you want to try out for yourself how invariant such behaviors are, you can do the following. Go to a window on the second floor of a building, and drop a tennis ball from the same spot 100 times onto some markings so you can see where it hits. If you want, you can also use a stopwatch to see how long the fall takes. I need hardly add that the ball will land in the same spot and take the same time to fall, within the relatively small uncertainty owing to instrumental techniques (provided only that a sudden strong wind or some other unusual change does not alter the test conditions). For easy reference, I will call this procedure the "second-floor tennis-ball test."

Let's now compare the picture we have just been describing for inert, naturally-occurring systems with the picture for very complex systems. We can take a single human being, a central element in these social and sociotechnical systems, to see the differences clearly.

When we look at the human sciences, we see that considerable numbers of Entire Paradigms have been erected. For example, all tribes we have found on earth have a religion; all use the family as the primary social unit; all have an explanation for how the earth and the human species came to be. (The word "all" implies we do not know of exceptions.) However, none of these things are done in the same way in each tribe or society. Almost any place we look, the details vary from one tribe to the next, and the variations over the full range of human societies are enormous. The structures of families and the cosmogenic "stories" both vary widely from one ethnic group to another. Moreover, the social forms and "stories" that underlie and hold in place the culture in any one society have often changed when observations are made over many generations. See Cohen (1968), Tuan (1974).

In later chapters we will see a good many Entire Paradigms in the human sciences, but no Invariant Paradigms. If any reader knows of a paradigm within the human sciences that is both Entire and Invariant, please let me (and the world) know, with reference to the relevant data. If it can be confirmed, such a paradigm is important in principle, as well as for multidisciplinary discourse, even if it covers only a small range of behaviors.

Another way to clarify the differences between the physical and the human science is to ask, What are the key questions researchers ask colleagues about new results? In the physical sciences, the key question is often about the uncertainty of results. As in the second-floor tennis-ball test, this question implies that we expect the results to be the same, over and over, and are looking to see if the scatter in the data can be explained by the limits (residual uncertainties) arising from the instrumental procedures. The experienced researcher in the human sciences asks a different question, How much of the variance do your variables explain? This question implies essentially the opposite view from the question asked by physical scientists. The question of the human scientist assumes that variations in behavior exist, are to be expected, and need to be accounted for. To put this in the language of Chapter 5, the question is, To what extent have the variables used covered the complete "space" in the functional representation of the relevant hyperspace? Given the values of the complexity index for typical systems, this is the crucial question. Thus the key questions we ask assume invariance of behaviors in the physical sciences and, on the contrary, large variations of behaviors in the human sciences. Let's look at some specific examples.

It is particularly instructive to look at the broad history of the study of human cultures within ethnology. When the anthropologists began ethnographic studies near the end of the nineteenth century, a major declared goal of the dominant founders, particularly Franz Boas and his many influential students, was to study and document all human cultures on earth in order to find what was "universal" in human behaviors. But this is not what has been found. Ethnologists tell of repeated occurrences at their annual meetings over the decades, along the following lines. A scholar would rise to formally report, "I have been studying the 'Zoramberalls' of the wilds of New Guinea [or Africa, or Brazil] and I have found they all do 'A.' I suggest that 'A' is a universal trait of human nature." Whereupon a colleague would rise during the discussion and say, in effect, "But in my tribe, the 'Ambergonians,' everyone does just the opposite of 'A.' "

It is true that members of all tribes that survive eat, drink water, sleep, reproduce and raise children. However, the ways in which they do each of these things are so variable that we have thus far found precious few things that one can reasonably call invariant behavior for human activities. Nearly all of us fear falling; nearly all of us jump when someone pops a paper bag behind our head. But these residual instincts are few in number for humans and do not, as far as we know, extend to human social systems.

It is also true that all humans perforce grapple with the great existential uncertainties surrounding death, intimacy, freedom, meaning, and sexuality/ birth. Essentially all of the several thousand tribes on earth have now been studied in some detail, and each one has an explanation for these great existential problems, beliefs about how they are to be viewed, and behaviors that surround these questions.

Since all peoples face these same great issues, many of the beliefs have similar elements, as Joseph Campbell (1968) and others have documented. Nevertheless, the details vary greatly from tribe to tribe. For example, every tribe has an explanation of how the earth and humans came to be. But when we look at the details — for example, as given to us by Tuan in *Topofilia* (1974) — we find virtually nothing that can be called invariant. Each tribe has a belief system tied in some way to its local environments and local needs, but the details vary enormously. In the end the compiled ethnographic data show the "rule" in human social systems and human social behaviors is not invariance; it is variation. Indeed, the variations in both behaviors and values are so wide that no one came close to imagining the full scope of the variations before the ethnologists had begun to document them. The full scope was literally unimaginable. For a summary, see, for example, Cohen (1968).

Moreover, the ethnographic studies show that changes in social behaviors occur over time in nearly all societies. Changes have occurred even in the few societies where a ghost-bound belief system seems to make changes in beliefs and behaviors, if not impossible, at least very difficult (see, for example, the study of the Yir Yoront, in Sharp [1967]). The "rules" governing falling bodies are just as Galileo described them centuries ago, but the sociopolitical system of the Italian peninsula has, since Galileo's time, changed from a set of warring principalities and dukedoms to a single, modern industrial state; the operative political rules have changed.

Let's next look at some typical statements of the paradigms we have found within the human sciences. Here are five of twelve principles of communications given by John W. Riley (in Berelson [1963], p. 245).

> That messages are typically more effective when there is discussion among the audience.
>
> That one-way communication in a group tends to lower morale. [This includes imperative hierarchies.]
>
> That mass communications are passed on in patterned ways through opinion leaders.
>
> That voters or buyers or readers who are under social cross pressures tend to vacillate and often to withdraw from decision making.
>
> That recipients of messages do not hear or see the total message, rather they perceive what they want or need, and this is known as selective perception.

I quoted the first four principles above in the order given by Riley so as not to bias his results. I include the last item because it reinforces what we have been saying about schemata and mental images since Chapter 3, and it also indicates once again the highly individualistic nature of human responses. Of the twelve statements given by Riley, only one uses a form of the verb "to be," the third one quoted above (without a qualifier). Even in this instance, Riley weakens the impact of that verb. In short, Riley is not willing to make any statement that is unqualified, that is invariant. Seven of the twelve principles use the verb "tends to." Riley does not tell us what "tends to" denotes in terms of probabilities of outcomes.

In sum, these results from observations of human communications reinforce what we have been saying about the lack of Entire Invariant Paradigms in the human sciences. "Tends to" is not a verb we use to describe an Entire Invariant Paradigm, or even an Entire Paradigm. Despite this, it seems evident that principles of the sort Riley gives contain very useful information.

Let's look at one more example. Grimm's "Law" has been said to be one of the firmest principles in the human sciences. It concerns the rate of drift of language in non-literate societies. Use of Grimm's "Law" allowed Joseph Greenberg to work out a taxonomy of the "descent with variations" of languages which covers most known languages worldwide. This has become important for advancing ethnology, for documenting that cultures do indeed "evolve" in something like a Darwinian sense; it is also important as a separate means for dating human migrations, which is useful in paleoanthropology and other areas of study. In his article in Berelson (1963), Greenberg states Grimm's Law as "of 100 commonly used terms (like those for body parts), 86% will remain stable for 1000 years with an error of 6.5% at the 50% confidence level."

The word error in Greenberg's statement does not have the usual meaning; it is, rather, a statistical measure providing an estimate of what is called "uncertainty" above. The uncertainty meters the expected range of deviations between one case and the next. (For a discussion of the distinction between error and uncertainty, see Airy [1879]; Kline and McClintock [1953].) Thus Grimm's Law, this "firmest" principle, does not describe invariant behavior; it states a statistical average and provides a measure of typical deviation from the average. It is not an "iron law" that dictates precisely the same result every time. Indeed, given the current state of worldwide communications, one wonders if the rate of shift of language will remain the same as that which occurred in the relatively isolated tribes that constituted most past societies. Not enough time has passed for us to tell.

Nothing I have just said or will say anywhere below is intended as, or should be read to imply, a negative comment on the human sciences. Nor is there any implication that the human sciences are less important than the physical sciences. All of this and what follows is intended as a comment on the inherent nature of the fields, and no more. Indeed, I believe, as many others have and do, that in many ways the human sciences are more important to the future welfare of humans than the physical sciences. Whether or not that is true, it is clear, from the results described in Chapter 4, that the systems studied by the human sciences are nearly infinitely more complex than those studied in the physical sciences. This complexity inevitably makes the tasks of scholarship harder. Those who would denigrate the human sciences because they do not produce "hard results" in terms of "hard variables" are, in my own view, not only displaying ignorance about the relative complexity of systems, but also coupling that ignorance with an appeal to intellectual snobbery.

Let's now ask a somewhat different question. Have changes in human social systems over time been great enough so that the "rules" needed to describe the behaviors have altered over time? Let's consider as a first example *economics*. Have the "rules" needed to describe behaviors in human economic systems changed over time? Indeed, they have!

The invention of money occurred more than two millennia ago. As soon as money became widely accepted as a form of exchange, the nature of the marketplace was radically altered and reshaped. Thus the "rules" governing business were radically altered in many nations in ancient times.

The invention of the legal fiction of a corporation as a person of limited liability at law, a few centuries ago, again altered the "rules" under which business can be carried on. The partnership form of enterprise, which was all that was known earlier, is quite unsuited to large-scale businesses because it leaves all partners liable for all eventualities. Hence this shift in the "rules" (laws, in this instance) was an important factor in creating large-scale manufacturing industries and international trade as we know them in the twentieth century.

In 1898, J. P. Morgan created the idea of underwriting the sale of shares of corporate stock by investment bankers to raise funds for Procter and Gamble. Over the next few decades, underwriting not only created new markets for equities, it also freed businesses from the need to raise capital locally, and diffused ownership of corporations far more widely.

As soon as nations began to act on the observation by John Maynard Keynes (after about 1930) that it is possible to affect the course of national economies by creating feedback loops on interest rates and bank reserve levels, the "rules" of macro-economics were fundamentally altered. Some people argue that these powers are not effective. However, when the interest rate went above 18 percent in the early 1980's in the United States, construction and some other forms of industry there essentially ceased. The power to affect the economy certainly exists, although we do not seem to understand the effects with much precision.

This list of changes in the "rules" of economics is not exhaustive. Consider pension plans, the federal insurance system for the banks, options markets, and other relatively recent financial inventions. There are many other examples. Nor is this process of change completed. In the past decade the advent of computers, FAX machines, and telecommunication networks has restructured the way businesses operate and hence to some degree economics worldwide.

In *politics*, we date from the time of Hammurabi the idea of written laws that constrain the ways people behave. These laws also change over time, often bringing major changes in the rules of a society. Indeed, in the United States, every year brings new laws that to greater or lesser degree alter social forms and political behaviors. "Attack journalism" has altered the unwritten rules of the behaviors allowable for politicians over the past decade. The writers of the U.S. Constitution adapted, adopted, and invented a number of political forms in order to create a new kind of government, for example, the idea of a government under laws, not men; the retention by the states and the people of all powers not explicitly granted the federal government; the separation of church and state; and the balance of powers among branches of government. These sociopolitical innovations provided new "rules" that have opened a door to new and, in my view, better forms of government for a large fraction of the planet. Consider also the Bill of Rights, the Emancipation Proclamation, women's suffrage, and the various additional measures on civil rights that we have adopted in the twentieth century. We have changed the "rules" over and over, and continue to do so. These changes, like those in economics, also continue; see, for example, Steinem (1992).

It is easy to proliferate these examples. Consider the changes in styles of Western art, music, and architecture since the Middle Ages. Compare Asian art, music, and architecture with Western.

Top-level values also change in some cases. The decision by the leaders of the Muslim clergy (in the middle of the Middle Ages of Christendom) to the effect that what is important are the things of the spirit, and not the material goods of the world nor their production altered the top-level values ("rules") of Muslim society that had existed until that time. According to many historians, this shift in the top-level "rules" of the society seems to have played a major role in the gradual loss of the lead the Muslim community had held for several centuries over the Western world in mathematics, the sciences, and the production of goods. For details, see, for example, William McNeill's *The Rise of the West* (1963).

These examples make clear that at least some of the "rules" of social systems can and do change over time. These changes have affected economics, politics, aesthetics, and values in the examples just listed. Even then the list is far from exhaustive. But all this is still not the whole story as it affects multidisciplinary discourse.

The pursuit of and false belief in oversimple rules that were (and sometimes still are) taken to be Entire Invariant Paradigms for systems of very high complexity may be even worse than merely a waste of time. They can have serious negative effects. The process holds the potential for great harm via a triumph of one-dimensional ideology over skills and knowledge gained by experiences and innovations created through human control and human design processes. And this is not merely theorizing, as an example will show.

In the political arena, communism forms an example of a sysrep for society based on a one-dimensional view transformed into ideology. The one-dimensional view is Karl Marx's theory of surplus value. This theory assumes, at bottom, that the hyperspace of a national polity has a dimensionality of one. Marx himself had deep empathy for humans and their needs. However, in the implicit sysrep for governments taken from Marx's writings by many of his followers, all actions of humans are seen as flowing from economic values. Other human motivations, such as self-esteem, desire for social support from others, and aesthetic considerations, are omitted from the model. Beyond that, in the sysrep implied by Marx's followers, Lenin and Stalin, economics is largely collapsed to an ideology that deals with one problem — the inequities of the owner/worker system of western Europe in the nineteenth century. There seems to be no reason to doubt that the owner/worker relations in Marx's time in Europe were iniquitous (indeed, often brutal and abusive); that is not the point. The point is, rather, that Marx's sysrep, and the analysis his followers based on it, focuses on one and only one idea. Thus Lenin and Stalin created an economic **system** run by top-down planning coupled with imperial control in order to avoid the "evils of capitalism." Such a **system** neglects, in my view, at least three matters of signal importance in human sociotechnical systems: (1) the need for feedback among the parts of large sociotechnical systems, including information flow not only from the top down but also from the bottom up, laterally through-out the system, and to and from the environment; (2) the need for competition between productive units as a spur to efficiency; and (3) the need to keep the desires and needs of the individual human coupled closely to the social welfare, that is, to the good of the economic system as a whole and to other elements of the system.

By 1991, after seven decades of experiences, the disastrous results of this one-dimensional ideological position as the basis for economics had become abundantly clear. No country using pure Marxian ideology as a basis for the economy, and many have tried it, has yet been able to create an economy strong enough to provide acceptable amounts and quality of food, clothing, and con-sumer goods for its people. Thus in the late 1980's and early 1990's we have seen country after country abandoning this oversimple model of economics as a basis for governance. This is not to argue that the capitalist economic system is per-fect, only that it seems to be the best we have devised thus far.

Moreover, the theoretical arguments between communist and capitalist econ-omists never closed. In the end, communist economic theory has been overtaken and largely demolished by observation of its results. Marx's theory of surplus value, then, provides an example that supports the idea we are calling "the primacy of data for very complex systems" — in systems for which theories are of necessity cut through a hyperspace of much larger dimensionality, we need to give data priority over theoretical predictions.

Other oversimple sysreps have also caused serious difficulties in fields such as sociology, psychology, philosophy, and in the theory of innovation. For exam-ples, see Etzioni (1988); the discussion of radical behaviorism, later in this chapter; and the discussion of innovation, in Chapter 14.

In sum, we have seen a number of examples that show three things about systems where the complexity index exceeds a billion, that is, the domain studied by the human sciences:

1. There are Entire Paradigms for the systems studied by the human sciences. Since Entire Paradigms apply to all known human societies, they are important virtually by definition. They help us understand ourselves, our societies, and our systems, and thus to plan for the future more effectively.

2. There appear to be no Entire Invariant Paradigms for human social and sociotechnical systems.

3. The application of what were assumed to be Entire Invariant Paradigms for social and sociotechnical systems can and have caused both misunderstandings and misguided actions.

Nevertheless, the examples we have seen leave a residual question because our process thus far has been inductive. We have only given a finite list of examples which is far from exhaustive. And we must not mistake some for all, since that is a fundamental logical error. Thus, at this point in our discussion, we have shown that Entire Paradigms exist, but we have not excluded the possibility of finding Entire Invariant Paradigms in some region or other of the domain of the human sciences or in value systems. Since we saw in Chapter 4 that we cannot expect to erect complete theories for systems of very high complexity, we need to continue our exploration along a different route. We will look underneath the examples to see if we can find inherent systematic differences between systems of inert, naturally-occurring objects on the one hand and those of human social and sociotechnical systems on the other. We will ask specifically, Are there inherent characteristics within social and sociotechnical systems that differ qualitatively from the characteristics of inert, naturally-occurring systems; and that can allow both behaviors and the "rules" describing the behaviors to change over time? If Yes! is the answer to both questions, it will put the conclusions just stated on a much firmer basis.

Categorization of Systems via Use of Feedback

To answer the question at the end of the preceding section, we need only examine the capacities of systems for utilizing information purposefully, in goal-directed activities including feedback loops of various sorts. Figure 6-1 provides one such categorization.

Figure 6-1 constitutes a hierarchy, a set of five levels that are distinct from one another. The breaks between the levels in this hierarchy are not all clean. There are some gray cases where systems lie on the border between two adjacent levels, particularly between levels 3 and 4. However, this lack of cleanness among the hierarchical levels is not important for the purposes of this section because we will be primarily concerned with the differences between systems at

Type of system	Feedback modes and source of goals	Examples
1. Inert, naturally-occurring	None of any kind; no goals	Rocks, mountains, oceans, atmosphere
2. Human-made inert — without controls	None, but with purposes designed-in by humans	Tools, rifles, pianos, furniture
3. Human-made inert — with controls	Autonomic control mode usually of a few variables; cannot by themselves change set points of variables	Air conditioner / furnace with thermostat, automobile motor, target-seeking missile, electric motor with speed control
4. Learning	Human control mode. Humans in system can learn and improve operations; systems can themselves change set points since they contain humans	Automobile with driver, chess set and players, piano with player, plane and pilot, tractor and operator, tank and driver, lathe and operator
5. Self-restructuring	Human design mode. Humans can look at system and decide to restructure both social and hardware elements via designs	Human social systems, human sociotechnical systems: household, rock band, symphony, manufacturing plant, corporation, army

Figure 6-1. A Hierarchy of Systems Classified by Complexity of Feedback Modes.

levels 1 and 2 on the one hand and those at levels 4 and 5 on the other. Between these two sets of levels the differences in information-handling capacity are distinct and qualitative.

The repertoire of functions that the system can do is different in each level from all the others; this is what makes Figure 6-1 a hierarchy. In each higher level the systems typically have a wider repertoire of accessible feedback modes than in the repertoire at any lower level. The foundation for these differences is the complexity of information-handling capability the systems possess.

The increase in information-handling capacities that appears at higher levels in Figure 6-1 arises primarily from three sources: first, the use of information in feedback loops increases the number of modalities of possible actions; second, systems in the higher levels typically have more layers of hierarchy in their structure than those in lower levels; third, "jumper connections," which operate within feedback loops, often exist between non-adjacent levels in the structure of more complex systems; these "jumper feedback loops" allow higher levels to create actions at lower levels that would not otherwise occur. See, for example, van Essen, Anderson, and Fellemon (1992) concerning primate vision. We will develop this point further when we discuss the structure of systems (Chapters 7–13). So we can put the details of structure at various levels aside for the moment. The key feature we need to focus on here is the difference in capacity for use of information in feedback loops.

Systems at level 1 have no information capacity, feedback loops, or goals, insofar as we humans know, as we already noted. Some religious individuals may argue that God has created purposes for such systems. However, we do not know God's intentions, and thus this possibility is covered by the words "insofar as we humans know."

Systems at level 2 have purposes built in via use of human design capacity, but have no feedback loops. A timber saw has wood-cutting capacity built in by the human design process, but has no information-handling capacity within itself.

Systems at level 3 have autonomic controls created via human design capacities. As a result these systems have a capacity for self-adjustment of one or more variables (in Norbert Wiener's language, cybernetic behaviors become part of the repertoire). As we have seen, the controller for the air conditioner / furnace has been taken as exemplary of human feedback by some in psychology and psychotherapy, but it is not. We will now examine the reasons why it is not and compare the repertoire of accessible behaviors of systems at level 3 with those of levels 4 and 5 in Figure 6-1.

Let's look again at a typical air conditioner / furnace with thermostat as an example of a **system** that lies at level 3 in Figure 6-1. Such a system can keep the control variable (temperature) near a given "set-point value." However, the set-point value of the control variable (in this case, temperature) is selected by human choice. You or I move a control to set the value of temperature we want. The hardware cannot choose the value of temperature for the set point. Also notice that in the air conditioner / furnace **system**, no variable other than temperature is controllable within the **system**. All other parts of the system were arranged and created by the human designer(s) and builder(s), and cannot be redesigned without further human thought and work. This **system** has a one-variable, autonomic control.

Systems at level 4 typically have a much wider repertoire of variables that the system can control through human control processes than is the case in the air conditioner / furnace **system**. Level 4 systems can learn from experience or from immediate feedback from the environment, and then readjust their behaviors. Even a micro-organism as simple as the one-celled Stentor can do this; see, for example, Rothschild (1990). Micro-organisms often can do this adjusting for a considerable number of variables. Using this kind of feedback loop, humans learn to drive cars, write, ride horseback, operate machine tools, shoot rifles, paint, and so on. At level 4, feedbacks can control the system within its operating space, but they do not restructure the system within the design space. This level includes the human-control feedback mode.

Systems at level 5 have still more extended capacities for employing feedback loops. In particular, systems at level 5 have the capacity to restructure many of their own internal arrangements using the human-design feedback mode when they choose to do so. Let's look at a few examples.

Christian missionaries and other Western people in the South Seas had over the course of some decades a large effect in creating new values among the natives in many locations. In some places these changes have been large enough that the activities that occur on one day out of seven (Sunday on the Christian calendar) have been nearly completely altered; the dress arrangements have altered; and the Gods seen as creating and controlling human life have greatly changed in both number and character. See, for example, Mead (1956). And these are only a few matters from a much longer list. In sum, over time, both basic belief systems and social life have been rearranged significantly by human choices, and this has occurred again and again in most of the societies on earth. For present purposes, we need not argue whether these results were "good" or "bad." We need only note they changed the "rules" of the society, and that to do that we had to have the power to envisage and create changes in the design space of the social systems we employ.

In another example, the new chief executive officer of a company may decide that the company has become too large, too bureaucratic, and too authoritatively controlled. She or he therefore chooses to "reorganize" the company by delegating authority for most operations to profit centers. The CEO also decides (by choice, using human design capabilities) that there should be more input from all levels of the company in decision making, and therefore sets in place a system of consensus decision-making of the sort used in many Japanese companies (see Nakane [1971, 1973]). These two changes may cause enormous rearrangements in the structure and the "culture" of the company. They may alter the basic social forms used by many if not all of the workers. They probably will have a significant impact on the happiness and morale of employees.

In these two cases, the choices are goal directed and arise from opportunities for creating structural changes within the system which humans think are likely to be improvements. Each involves human-design feedback loops in which the system is studied and then potential improvements visualized, implemented, and later observed with regard to their effects. As we know, humans can stand outside our systems and view them in a largely detached way; we also have human design powers to consider improvements. The bases of the changes we make may be spiritual, economic, or institutional. And these cases are merely illustrations from a much larger set of situations of this type. Even when such changes are impelled by force of arms, they are still human choices that are imposed by the winners on the losers. I have emphasized the verb "to choose" because it tells us explicitly that there are significant open degrees of freedom about choices that can be made by humans in such systems, for the reasons we saw in Chapter 5.

To put this differently, there are constraints on human social and sociotechnical systems which must be kept in view if the systems are to survive; however, these constraints are not sufficient in number and kind to fully determine outcomes. A significant range of choices remains open to humans in our social and sociotechnical systems. This existence of choices, that is, open degrees of freedom, implies that there are no Entire Invariant Paradigms that determine how all the choices in these systems must be made; they are not deterministic systems. Since we are suggesting not that all imaginable changes can occur in such systems, but that only some can, the examples we have seen are sufficient for the demonstration. Figure 6-1 thus answers the questions about the lack of Entire Invariant Paradigms for human social and sociotechnical systems. Since we can ourselves redesign human social and sociotechnical systems in significant ways, we cannot also expect to find "iron laws" that are invariant over time and space and that determine all behaviors in these systems. Some behaviors may be determined, but some remain open.

In an excellent and extensive discussion of these matters, Corning (1983) calls systems at levels 4 and 5 in Figure 6-1 "teleonomic," meaning self-steering. I have chosen to separate classes 4 and 5 and to use words that are more self-defining in terms of ordinary English usage. I have separated classes 4 and 5 because systems at level 5 in the figure have significant feedback capacities that pass beyond the "cybernetic." Moreover, the differences are critical. Systems at level 3 are already cybernetic in Wiener's sense. That is, they do use built-in, closed-loop autonomtic feedback control to bring the system to set points, but they do not have the capacity to readjust their set points. Systems at level 5 have qualitatively more powerful feedback modes; such systems can set goals and change both the nature of their own regulators and the set-point values on some of those regulators. Moreover, human design capacity is needed to create autonomic controls in hardware.

If you have residual doubts about the idea that we humans make social inventions, and thus alter the "rules" in our social and sociotechnical systems as we go along, or if you want to see a more complete list of social inventions, Conger (1973) provides an extensive compendium of social inventions.

What are the key capacities that allow us to restructure our social and sociotechnical systems? There seem to be two. First, in the structure of level-5 systems the "units" that carry out actions are usually much less tightly coupled to each other than the components of systems at lower levels. A biological organism can only change internal structure a little and still survive. Social systems can often change internal structure quite a lot and survive; indeed, at times institutions may need to restructure in order to survive. Second, some of the "subassemblies" of social and sociotechnical systems are themselves level-4 systems, that is, humans. As a result, the "units" of action can learn to alter their behaviors individually in ways the physical subassemblies of level-4 systems cannot. Moreover, people can talk back if they don't like what is going on; machines can only break down or malfunction. The abilities to learn, talk back, and to set goals independently within the opreating units of social systems (that is, by individual people) make level-5 systems much more flexible and thus much more adaptable than systems at lower levels. To put this memorably, if you can talk back to the doctor, you're alive.

An Example of the Use of the Ideas in Figure 6-1

Let's use what we have been saying about the distinctions in feedback modes between different levels in Figure 6-1 to see what we can learn about what psychologists call "behaviorism" in order to show the utility of the concepts we have been developing. We will look at an extreme form and, using the words of de Groot (1946) call it "radical behaviorism." I include the modifier "radical" to distinguish this form from more complex models of behaviorism which suffer far less from the difficulties we will examine.

Put simply, radical behaviorism is the idea that human behavior depends only on "conditioning" from experience. The idea of conditioning was first put forward by Pavlov, using his experiments in which dogs were taught behavior by a system of rewards and punishment.

Radical behaviorism became a powerful school of psychology in the United States in the 1920's, a status that lasted through the 1960's. The key datum cited as support for radical behaviorism can be called the "Skinner box" — an apparatus used by the Harvard psychologist B. F. Skinner. Skinner became a particularly influential advocate of radical behaviorism. He and others argued that all human behavior could be understood through no more than what they called "operant conditioning."

Radical behaviorism hypothesized that experiments such as those done in a Skinner box are a sufficient basis for a theory describing all human behaviors. However, when we look at those experiments in terms of the information in Figure 6-1, we see that the hypothesis is not sustainable. The experiments most often concerned the behaviors of rats running in mazes. If we use Figure 6-1, that is, the feedback loop capabilities tested, we can see that rats running in mazes or selecting various levers will exhibit some but not all human behaviors. Why is this so?

In the Skinner box, the rats have no means for talking back. All the constraints on the system, including the choice of experiments, lie in the hands of the human experimenters. In human social systems, there always remains the ability of humans not only to learn lessons from the environment but also to set their own individual goals and to talk back. The rats running the mazes have no such choices available. The rats cannot reflect on the system and then try to improve it for their own purposes even if we grant, for this discussion, that rats have such capacities. The rats can only push levers or run through passages; they cannot rearrange the levers or the partitions. The rat-in-a-box system is at most a level-4 system, not a level-5 system, in the terms of Figure 6-1. Is the difference important? We have seen the importance of the human ability to talk back, to decide goals individually. History offers many other examples — the direct confrontation against tanks in Beijing only a few years ago, and the events in a number of Eastern European and Baltic countries recently. We can also cite the Magna Carta in England, the Boston Tea Party, and the fall of the Bastille in France. Anyone who has studied marital communications also knows that they are not adequate when they are a one-way street; good communications require that each spouse not only speak but also listen attentively. Good human communications demand the use of a higher level of feedback modes and thus of information-handling capacity than can be achieved by the rat-in-a-box system. We need not continue these examples. We have the central point: the distinction in levels of feedback can help us clarify matters that otherwise may remain confused.

Did confusion arising from radical behaviorism cause difficulties in the world? It is probably impossible to trace all the effects. I will, however, mention one instance of deleterious effects on many children. J. B. Watson, Skinner's predecessor as the leading radical behaviorist, advised mothers to be careful with the amount of "mother love" given to infants because "too much love" seemed to conflict with the theory of radical behaviorism. Later data by Spitz (1953), Stern (1985), Harlow and Harlow (1962), and many others have shown us that this was extremely bad advice, which must have adversely affected many infants whose mothers followed the suggestions, as some did.

By the 1990's, radical behaviorism had been abandoned by many research psychologists owing to results in linguistics and in computer sciences. Researchers in six fields concerned with the human brain formed a coalition and their work, called cognitive sciences, has replaced radical behaviorism in leading research institutions. Despite this, radical behaviorism is still taught as the basis for psychology in many U.S. universities in the late twentieth century.

In sum, radical behaviorism is an example of a case in which clarity about levels of feedback could have told us directly and easily what we learned only at great cost over a long time. Radical behaviorism is also an example of an area where oversimple theory was allowed to take precedence over much barefoot data, and as a result gave a lot of information, but also did significant harm.

Figure 6-1 tells us still more that is useful for our multidisciplinary discourse. A fully adequate sysrep must represent all behaviors the system can actuate; and not represent, suggest, or predict behaviors the system cannot actually carry out. All five levels of systems in Figure 6-1 have systems that contain mass. Therefore what we know about matter (that is, the principles and data of physics, chemistry and the other physical sciences) gives some relevant information for all five classes of systems in Figure 6-1. The word "some" in the preceding sentence is the operative word because those principles can never be complete sysreps for any class of system above level 1 in Figure 6-1. This follows because systems lying in all higher levels have access to behaviors that are qualitatively distinct from and cannot occur in systems at level 1. This difference is particularly great for systems at level 5. The converse is also true. That is, any general principles that are adequate sysreps for complete systems in level 5 will not be a correct sysrep for systems in level 1. This must be so because the principles for level 5 must allow for the ability to create goals and restructure the systems internally in order to meet those goals, and no system at level 1 has such a capacity. We will see several additional, independent, reasons why the principles in the physical and the social sciences have a different character, in Chapters 7 through 12. The dangers inherent in not recognizing these differences are considerable, as the example of radical behaviorism illustrates. Moreover, this one example provides only an illustration; it by no means exhausts the list of such cases that have already occurred.

At this point, we can also relate the results of the discussion to the disciplines in a relatively general way. We need only note that the physical sciences are sysreps for systems at level 1 of Figure 6-1, and only level 1. On the other hand, the human sciences (ethnology, sociology, psychology, history, economics, and political science) are sysreps for systems at levels 4 and 5.

Conclusions for Chapter 6

The complexity index given by equation (4-1) plus the discussion in this chapter provide a means for gaining increased perspective about the great disparity in complexity between the systems studied in the physical sciences and those studied in the human sciences. This increased perspective leads to several conclusions.

For systems of very high complexity, that is, social and sociotechnical systems, we have no means for creating analyses of the full details for entire systems either by formal mathematics or by computer models. Nor are we likely to in the near future. We have only the ability to do analysis for some components of such systems.

As a result, we create, manage, and attempt to improve very complex systems using the human-design feedback mode. That is, we observe the system; ask how we might change the system to make it meet our goals more closely; try the changes; observe again; and keep on keeping on. Thus human design feedback is an important mode of research, and we forget that at our own peril in many important situations.

Many examples verify the fact that, to a significant degree, we make up the "rules" of social and sociotechnical systems as we go along. As a result, not only the behaviors but also some of the "rules" in each society change over time. This has two important consequences: first, the underlying characteristic that typifies social and sociotechnical systems is not invariance but variation; second, since some of the "rules" change over time, we cannot expect to find Entire Invariant Paradigms for entire social and sociotechnical systems, only for some of their parts. And, thus far, we seem not to have found any for entire systems. (Once again, if you know any, please let me and the world know.) This result is supported not only by many examples from a number of distinct areas, but also by careful examination of the capacity for utilizing information, including feedback modes and goal-directed activities summarized in Figure 6-1. Since Entire Invariant Paradigms do exist for a wide variety (probably all) inert, naturally-occurring objects, the "rules" for such systems are inherently different from those for social and sociotechnical systems.

PART THREE

Structure

CHAPTER 7

Hierarchy as a Structural Feature

The Hierarchy of Constitution

This chapter begins the discussion of a third overview of the intellectual terrain based on study of the structure of systems. As used in this and succeeding chapters, the word "structure" will denote how systems are put together, how the pieces are joined to constitute the whole.

Hierarchy as a structural feature characterizes most parts of the world we know. There are two particularly common forms of hierarchical structure: trees and ladders. Sometimes we find mixtures of the two forms or other forms such as matrices that include hierarchy.

Hierarchy is an essential concept for organizing our knowledge of the world. Without the concept of hierarchy we lose almost entirely the bases of biology, chemistry, geology, and other sciences.

Nevertheless, dislike and distrust of hierarchy are both common and understandable. Imperative hierarchies in social institutions are often an evil. The mere idea of top-down social hierarchies brings thoughts of the Roman legions, Genghis Khan, the Spanish Inquisition, and Hitler's storm troopers. For many individuals the idea of hierarchy also revivifies traumatic experiences within autocratic modern corporations or authoritarian families. We like to think of social forms that are fair and egalitarian, rare as they may be. But regardless of what we prefer, all documented societies have some degree of social hierarchy.

We begin ostensively, pointing at examples of hierarchical structure in a wide variety of systems. I will give quite a few examples in order to emphasize how widespread hierarchical structures are and to indicate that social hierarchy is only one of many examples.

Hierarchy of Human Speech (tree structure):

5	Message
4	Style
3	Grammar
2	Words
I	Noises

In this hierarchy of human speech, I have put arbitrary numbers at the left, and have used indents to indicate the 5 levels (or layers) of the structure. In the examples of tree-structured hierarchies that follow, I will indent to indicate layers and omit the numbers.

In the hierarchy of speech, notice that each higher layer tends to have fewer elements than the next lower level; hence the name "tree structure."

Hierarchy of Human Structure (tree structure):

Complete Human Organism

Major systems of organism
- brain (control level; has complex internal hierarchical structure)
- cardiovascular
- neuromuscular
  Cells
      Macro-molecules
          Atoms
              Subatomic particles
- digestive
- . . . . .

In this hierarchy of human structure, and in some of the examples that follow, subelements of a given layer will sometimes be listed following "bullets." Five dots are used to indicate when the list of subelements is incomplete.

The use of the word "tree" as a form of hierarchy reminds us that plants also have hierarchical structure. If we look, we see that essentially all living organisms have hierarchical structure. What we call "complex" organisms, such as mammals, typically have more layers of hierarchical structure than simpler organisms.

Hierarchy of a Mountain (tree structure):

Mountain
    Strata (or rock layers)
        Rocks
            Molecules and atoms
            Subatomic particles

Continents, oceans, the atmosphere, and so forth, have similar hierarchical structure.

Hierarchy of Undergraduate Students (ladder structure):

Senior
Junior
Sophomore
First-year student

Ladder hierarchies have the same (or nearly the same) number of elements at each level, and often therefore describe human cohorts that move through time — babies, children, parents, grandparents, and so on.

Hierarchy of a Typical Book (tree structure):

Book
    Chapters
        Pages
            Paragraphs
                Sentences
                    Words
                        Letters

Without hierarchical structure most scientific documents and essays would be unorganized and, at best, hard to comprehend.

Hierarchy of Human Needs (Maslow ladder):

Self-fulfillment of potential
Self-esteem
Belongingness (love and affection, community)
Security (economic needs)
Survival (physiological needs)

There are many lists of human needs; the Maslow ladder is a widely used and useful one in part because it does not violate Miller's 7-Bit-Rule. From the bottom, the levels in the Maslow ladder indicate the priority in which individual needs are typically fulfilled. The priorities are even stronger for a democratic society than for an individual because of the effects of averaging. An individual can choose to invert some of the levels; voters often constrain democracies from doing so.

Hierarchy of a Machine (automobile; tree structure):

Automobile

Main assemblies
- frame
- engine and power train
    Subassemblies (engine illustrated)
      - carburetor
      - distributor
      - crankshaft

Parts (distributor illustrated)
rotor
cam
. . . . .
- Molecules and Atoms
- Subatomic Particles
- body
- other assemblies . . . . .

Since airplanes, TV's, washing machines, artillery, computers, and so on, have similar hierarchical structure, we can use the automobile as typical of the structure of hardware devices.

Hierarchy of Concepts (mixed tree-ladder structure):

Concepts for building "rules"
Rules for deciding validity of "principles"
Principles Predicting Behavior in Class of Concern
Taxonomy of observations, concepts, and/or items
Observations

This mixed tree-ladder hierarchy of concepts shows tree relations indented and ladder relations aligned vertically.

The necessity of hierarchy in both concepts and communications is well known. Bertrand Russell asserted, "If we mix concepts from different levels in a hierarchy of concepts, we will create paradox." This idea is formalized in Russell's Dictum and is familiar to logicians. (See, for example, Kneebone [1963].) We will give only one example here to illustrate the reality, since the details pass beyond what we need. If we mix up the rules of arithmetic and the numbers, we will end in confusion. Suppose, for example, that we take the numbers as usual up through 4, but then use the symbol 5 to indicate both the number 5 and also the commutative rule for numbers (for example, that $3 \cdot 4 = 4 \cdot 3$). When we then try to understand the question What does $4 + 1$ equal? we have an ambiguity and a paradox. We don't know whether 5 is a number or a rule about numbers. Our whole arithmetic is upset whenever we happen to need the number 5. The rules of arithmetic must be held separate from the numbers; we usually say the rules lie at a higher level of concepts, but the choice of higher or lower in this case is arbitrary; the important point is that they be set off as a distinct "class of concepts."

Paul Watzlawick and his colleagues (1967) have shown that clear human communication often requires hierarchical structure. We will give only one example to illustrate this idea. Suppose that you are on the witness stand in a court under oath. Suppose also that the opposing attorney turns to you and says, "Have you stopped beating your spouse yet? Answer yes or no." What do you do? Either a yes or a no question is an admission that you have not only committed a crime, but are a cruel person. The way out of this "communicative trap" is to turn to the judge and say, "Your honor, do I have to answer that question?" If it is a U.S. court, the judge will reply something like, "No. That is a leading question. Strike it from the record." He will then presumably admonish the opposing attorney not to ask more questions of this kind. This legal cliché illustrates forcibly why we sometimes need to comment on a question or statement instead of replying at the same of concepts. Watzlawick and colleagues call this a "meta-communication." Metacommunications are necessary to straighten out unclarities in many forms of human communication. For other examples about both Russell's Antinomy and metacommunications, see Watzlawick, Beavin, and Jackson (1967), Gottman et al. (1976).

In some of the examples of hierarchy given, the levels are quite arbitrary, as in the Maslow ladder and the hierarchy for forming principles. These hierarchies could easily be put in other appropriate forms. However, in other cases, such as the hierarchy (biological tree) of organisms and the structure of inert matter, the levels have hardly any arbitrariness, and the dividing lines between the levels are for the most part clear and unambiguous. Moreover, any discussion of structure which omits hierarchy in some form is at best incomplete and at worst misleading. More specifically, as both Russell and Watzlawick illustrate in detail, complete avoidance of hierarchy makes clear communications difficult if not impossible. In physical systems no one could design a car, airplane, or computer without a very clear picture of the hierarchy of structure to be built into the system. As we have seen, there are at least four levels of hierarchy in human thought processes, and five levels of feedback modes.

In sum, we have seen that the typical structure of each of inert, naturally-occurring objects, of biological organisms, and of artifacts is hierarchical. Moreover, these are all the common kinds of material, corporeal objects in our world. We have also seen that communications, human needs, concepts, feedback modes, and the formation of "rules" typically have hierarchical structure; indeed, all five often demand the use of hierarchy to avoid confusions or paradox. Values often have hierarchical structure, but in this case the structures are typically more flexible from one individual to another and less easily given general form. The Linnaean "tree-chart" that organizes biology is a tree hierarchy. The Mendeleyev periodic table of the chemical elements, a foundation stone of chemistry, is a matrix hierarchy. Many other taxonomies indicate hierarchical structure. We need not go on. In sum, hierarchy is nearly ubiquitous as a structural form in our world. If we deny the existence of hierarchy in structure, we will end in confusing ourselves about how things are put together, how they work, and also about how we think, communicate, and use concepts.

For several reasons I have belabored the importance and near ubiquity of hierarchical structure beyond what is logically necessary. The full importance of hierarchical structures is not visible within many disciplines that treat a set of problems involving only one level of larger structures. The constraints that arise from the nature of hierarchical structure have been little studied and are not widely known but are critical for many questions in multidisciplinary discourse.

The Hierarchy of Constitution

Our next step will be to erect a "top-level" hierarchy to provide an understandable picture of the location of the major systems and the location of the disciplines of knowledge in relation both to each other and to our total knowledge. I call this "top-level" hierarchy of structure the "hierarchy of constitution." It is not new; it has sometimes been called the "system hierarchy." The hierarchy of constitution is shown in Figure 7-1.

The hierarchy of constitution is based primarily on physical size. The hierarchy of constitution shows the three major types of corporeal objects — biological, artifactual (human-made), and inert, naturally-occurring — in three separate columns for clarity. The numbers shown for the layers are merely for reference; they are wholly arbitrary.

There are thirteen levels of aggregation (or layers) in the hierarchy of constitution, not counting the unknown layers at the bottom and the top. Since all taxonomies are arbitrary, human-built models, one can make some changes in the layers, but most of the interfaces that delineate the layers shown in Figure 7-1 are quite clear and unambiguous. For example, we have no great difficulty in distinguishing molecules from rocks, nor planets from solar systems, and so on; these distinctions are natural and clear; they are part of reality as we now know it.

Figure 7-2 shows the location of some disciplines of knowledge in terms of the layers of the hierarchy of constitution from which they grow and to which they relate. The level numbers are the same as in Figure 7-1. Owing to space limitations, not all disciplines are shown, as indicated by five dots. However, anyone familiar with a discipline can readily place it in Figure 7-2.

There is a clustering of disciplines at the middle levels. This is not surprising, since these are the levels of primary human concern. The faraway levels are of interest to most of us primarily to the extent that they affect the middle levels. However, the absence of any single integrating discipline for the complete set of systems in these middle levels is surprising, and suggests a deficiency in our current scholarly arrangements.

Mere size does not indicate the complexity of the major features of the system: the most complex systems lie in the middle range of size in Figure 7-1, as you can see by referring to the values of the complexity index.

To put this differently, Figures 7-1 and 7-2 are not the real-world objects they depict; they are sysreps for one aspect of a complex set of levels which we believe, from data, exist in the world. Since they are sysreps we must expect that some parts of Figures 7-1 and 7-2 mirror reality more accurately than others; moreover, these figures represent only a small fraction of the real-world system, which is in its entirety far more complex. Once we recognize this, it becomes

Arbitrary number indicating the level of size	Biological forms	Human-made objects, systems	Natural physical objects
9			Unknown
8			Universe
7		Space probes, space communications	Galaxies
6			Solar systems
5	Global ecologies	Space systems, United Nations	Stars, planets
4	Marine ecologies	Large sociotechnical systems, systems of transport, national governments	Continents, oceans
3[a]	Local ecologies, forests	Sociotechnical systems (human-made ecologies)	Geologic features (mountains, valleys, etc.)
2[a]	Clans, herds, tribes	Large hardware (buildings, machines)	
1[a]	Families	Simple hardware (artifacts, hand tools, furniture)	
0[a]	Multicellular plants, animals	Materials (steel, semiconductors, etc.)	Aggregations of atoms and molecules
−1	Unicellular plants, animals		
−2	Organelles, macromolecules, proteins	Semiconductor circuits	Individual molecules
−3			Individual atoms
−4			Subatomic particles
−5			Unknown

Figure 7-1. The Hierarchy of Constitution: A Taxonomy of Objects Arranged by Size and Nature. Note that size does not correlate with complexity; see Chapter 4.

[a]Levels 0, 1, 2, and/or 3 are sometimes called the "classical level," referring to classical physics.

Size (as in Fig 7-1)	Representative objects from Fig. 7-1	Disciplines
9	Unknown	
8	Universe	Astrophysics
7	Galaxies	Astronomy
6	Solar systems	Astronomy
5	Stars, planets	Astronomy, astronautics
4	Continents, oceans	Oceanography, meteorology, geology, international relations, ...
3	Geologic features (mountains, valleys, etc., including human-made ecologies, nations)	Geology, ecology, navigation, seamanship, aeronautics, forestry, marine biology, agriculture, economics, political science, grad. business, public health, urban studies, law, engineering economic systems, operations research, history, geography, food research, public policy, ...
2	Groups of people, large hardware	Engineering (many branches), education, feminist studies, English, art, math, ethnology, sociology, humanities, computer science, communications, ...
1	Families, colonies, simple hardware	Psychology, ethnology, languages, linguistics, paleoanthropology, ...
0	Multicellular plants, animals	Zoology, botany, anatomy, psychology, biology, statistics, medicine (many branches), ...
−1	Unicellular plants, animals	Parasitology, biology
−2	Individual molecules	Materials science, chemistry, biochemistry
−3	Individual atoms	Atomic physics
−4	Subatomic particles	Subatomic physics
−5	Unknown	

Figure 7-2. The Hierarchy of Constitution, with the Location of a Number of Disciplines Indicated. Note that a number of disciplines also apply to the levels adjacent to those shown.

clear that the view that hierarchy cannot be a valid basis for analysis, because it is "man-made," as one formal reviewer of an earlier draft of this work wrote, is at bottom a confusion between **system** and sysrep. It is just this kind of confusion which makes the need for the distinction between **system** and sysrep critical for understanding. After all, Figures 7-1 and 7-2 are not rocks or organisms, or. . . . If seen literally, they are pieces of paper with markings on them.

Conclusions for Chapter 7

Hierarchy is a nearly ubiquitous structural feature of systems, concepts, communication, and thought. In order to understand the structure of inert systems, living systems, books, concepts, communications, and many other matters, we need the concept of hierarchy.

The overall hierarchy, called the hierarchy of constitution (Figure 7-1), is a useful framework for understanding the place of disciplines in our total knowledge and also their relations to each other, as Figure 7-2 illustrates.

CHAPTER 8

Interfaces of Mutual Constraint
and Levels of Control:
Polanyi's Principle

During the Middle Ages, Christendom gave a unified overview of the world to many Western communities. This unified overview was theologically based, and held that the world and all forms of knowledge about the world, its surroundings in the sky, and ourselves could be understood in terms of the Christian Scriptures as interpreted by the Church. Galileo, who is generally recognized as the transition figure from ancient to modern modes of scientific thought, took a different view. Galileo is said to have remarked, "Ultimately we must understand everything in terms of the motions of matter." It is well to remember that Galileo was oppressed and persecuted for his ideas by the Church, which threatened to burn him as a heretic for suggesting that the earth was not the center of the universe but instead revolved around the sun. The reaction to such oppression is often to take up the opposite view. Psychotherapists sometimes call this process a "reaction formation." However, reaction formations are often an overstatement from another direction.

So we can talk about these two views, I will call the theological view "synoptic" and Galileo's view "reductionist"; we will define each type more carefully below.

Since the time of Galileo, we have had both synoptic and reductionist views in Western societies, with the synoptic views gradually losing ground and the reductionist views gaining ground, as we have developed more and more knowledge via science particularly about the physical world. As noted by Tarnas (1991) and many others, by the late twentieth century, both these views had begun to lose persuasiveness for many people in Western cultures owing to many criticisms and much new knowledge.

Nevertheless, we have had no other widely accepted overviews to replace the synoptic and the reductionist views. And as we have seen (Chapter 3), we cannot think without some form of schemata, and thus we tend to go on using the schemata we have even when we believe that they are far from complete. Thus we have had only two contradictory, and often quarreling, overviews, each claiming to be a complete worldview. As a result, during the twentieth century some people have tended to take up one of five positions: synoptic; reductionist; a belief in the synoptic and the reductionist views, held as an existential paradox; explicit attempts to reconcile the two conflicting views; and abandonment of these attempts to form an overview (and thus live without any coherent view of our world).

We will use the phrase "some people" at a number of points, so we need to be clear about what the phrase implies. "Some people" will be used when we seem to have no data on how many individuals actually hold a given view about the domain of applicability of a given sysrep. Under these circumstances, it is hard to say what is the "common" or "dominant" belief or view.

In the case of overviews of the world, the proportion of people who hold the various views has shifted over time. What we can say is that some people have held each of the five positions, and thus it is worth investigating to see which view(s) are tenable for various kinds of problems (domains). Sociological data on the question of who holds what views on the appropriate domain of various overviews would be useful for several purposes, but I have not found any thus far. If such data exist, references will be appreciated.

We will not try to settle the 300-year-old quarrel about which of the two overviews is correct; we will instead approach the question from a different perspective. We will ask, Is either view sufficient to allow us to comprehend all matters of vital concern to humans? To put this differently, "Does Hypothesis III (the Absence of Universal Approaches) hold with regard to worldviews?"

Since the issue is so old and so important, we will explicate three independent reasons (in this and the two following chapters) why neither the reductionist nor the synoptic view can be a complete worldview. The various reasons will not only make the demonstration robust, but will also help us to see more clearly where the boundaries of the appropriate domains are for each of the reductionist and synoptic views. The increased clarity about those boundaries will help us understand various cases of how disciplines relate to each other, as well as which views we need in order to adequately comprehend complex systems.

We will first state the synoptic view and the reductionist view, each in a stark, simple, extreme form. I will call these extreme forms "radical." Many less extreme and more subtle versions exist; however, examining the radical forms will add clarity in our discussion.

In their radical forms each view claims priority over other views and is seen as a universal overview of our world. Each is also "one-directional" in that it suggests (or claims) that it is a starting point from which all else derives or can be found. Each intimates (or, in some particularly strong versions, declares) that human life is determined by non-human forces. Let's look at each one.

The synoptic view is ancient; it exists as far back as we have traced the ideas

of humans. It is embodied to some degree in many religions and ancient my-
thologies. The details of these views vary widely. The common feature is that the
appropriate view is "top-down" and states in essence that there are "higher
powers" that govern and determine the actions in all the lower layers of structure
in the world. I will call the idea that top-level views can be used to find all the
matters that humans need to understand "the synoptic program."

Radical synoptic views—for example, that of the medieval Roman Catholic
church—approach a total top-down determinism. Such views suggest that all
choices are decided by God, or fate, or Allah, or the ghosts of our ancestors,
depending on the culture. I include "Allah," even though it is another name for
"God," to emphasize that different cultures have quite different views of the
details of what God thinks and how she/he operates. The commonality is not in
the details but is the synoptic view. Since these views posit the existence of
unknowable higher powers, God(s), they are grounded in spiritual faith. Let me
repeat, I am not suggesting that synoptic views are either wrong or without value
to humans, for such views are important to societies and to individuals. I am
suggesting that as views for understanding our world they are seriously incomplete. We will see why.

The radical reductionist view is relatively "modern," roughly 300 years old.
In the late twentieth century, some (seemingly quite a few) people in the physical
sciences hold this view, but I repeat, I have no reliable statistics on how many
people do hold such a view. A particularly strong form was stated three centuries
after Galileo by the marquis de Laplace, who is said to have remarked, "Give me
the trajectories of the molecules, and I will predict the future." Since this view
posits that everything is determined by the state of the molecules at a given time,
it also denies all human free will, since the molecules by themselves are said to
contain and foretell the future. Like the radical synoptic view, this radical reductionist view implies a determinism owing to the "laws of physical science about
matter" and not to the actions of God(s). At points we will call this "bottom-up
determinism." This radical bottom-up view is still believed by some physical
scientists; the most recent published example I have seen is only 30 days old as I
am revising this chapter (see "Research News" in the April 19, 1993, issue of
Science, quoted in Chapter 16).

Like the radical synoptic view, the radical reductionist view is not wrong;
indeed, it has proven extremely powerful for many purposes; it is, however,
seriously incomplete as a worldview, for reasons we will see.

Since bottom-up determinism is based on a belief in the validity of empirical
observations, and top-down determinism is grounded in spiritual faith, there is
no shared basis for resolving differences that the two views can generate; they
remain irreconcilable so long as they are taken, together or separately, in an
extreme form. Thus the struggle between these two views, though often glossed
over, has remained a troubling presence in Western intellectual thought and
Western culture since the time of Galileo. A view that allowed both spiritual

values and empiricism to coexist without direct conflict would thus be a boon to members of Western cultures. Indeed, since Western views, particularly with regard to the physical sciences, have come to provide a dominant mode of approach to many problems in most parts of the world, alleviation of the conflict would be useful worldwide.

The view of bottom-up determinism makes two claims: (1) all material objects are made up of "particles" of matter; (2) one can therefore aggregate the sysreps for particles and thereby find (or derive) all the behaviors for all systems. The caveat is often added to claim 2 that this can be done "in principle," but has not been carried out because of "practical difficulties." The work of carrying out these claims is often called the "reductionist program," and we will use that shorter name here to refer explicitly to the claims stated above. Since the views within physics on what constitutes elementary "particles" (or waves) have shifted over time, for this discussion we will use the term "particles" for the smallest bits of matter needed for the problem under study. The reductionist view can thus include either a classical or a quantum description of matter.

When we examine the two claims of the bottom-up determinists, there appear to be few if any reasons to doubt claim 1. I will therefore accept claim 1 as correct for the present discussion.

However, claim 2 is totally false. We already saw one reason that strongly suggests that this claim cannot be correct: the principles for the bits of inert matter are invariant over time and space, but to a significant extent we make up the "rules" for social and sociotechnical systems as we go along. Human social and sociotechnical systems can, to a large extent, restructure themselves in ways that are not accessible to inert bits of matter. Thus there appears to be an inherent paradox in claim 2 of the reductionist program. We will now seek stronger demonstrations of why the reductionist program is impossible, even in principle.

To minimize misunderstanding, let me repeat one thing about my motivations. I have no wish to deny the power and the utility of the methods of science within their proper domain. These methods have proven in the past three centuries so powerful in examining and coming to understand the structure of ourselves and our world, it would be hard to overestimate either their theoretical or practical importance. They have revolutionized our understanding of our world and, at second hand, our ability to control that world. They are a necessary part of the knowledge needed to create our ability to fly through the air, live under water, communicate with each other in real time around the world, and build bombs powerful enough to destroy the planet, among the numerous powers of modern sociotechnical systems we all know. For many domains, the power created by these systems has made us the effective rulers of the planet. Most of the urgent questions that confront us in the late twentieth century concern how we will use those powers — for good or for evil. Thus the reductionist method has not lacked success; it is, rather, that some of us have overstretched it. The current problem, the one that will concern us here, can be seen as a matter of success overrunning itself. Having said that, we can turn to the first demonstration that the reductionist program is impossible to carry out.

Interfaces of Mutual Constraint

The first demonstration of the incompleteness of both the bottom-up (reductionist) view and the top-down (synoptic) view as a way to understand very complex hierarchical systems rests on the existence of interfaces of mutual constraint in many important classes of systems. The concept of interfaces of mutual constraint was developed by Michael Polanyi (1968). Polanyi's paper is very important but, unfortunately, does not seem to be widely known; it seems to be a case of everybody's business is nobody's business. We will review Polanyi's ideas and then extend them in several ways. Polanyi used the phrase "interface of dual-level control" for what we will call "interface of mutual constraint" (because it is both simpler and more descriptive). The concept of mutual constraint is not an easy idea. We will therefore begin with some examples. Let's look again at the hierarchy of human speech (given in Chapter 7) and think about the lowest two layers, noises and words. What can we say about human-made "noises" and "words" and about the relationship between them as they are used in speech? Examination of how these layers interact in speech leads to four observations.

Observation A. The principles of acoustics and the physiology of the human vocal apparatus constrain the list of the noises we can utter. The limits of our ears constrain the list of noises we can hear.

Comments

There is a literal infinity of possible noises, but we cannot make spoken words out of noises we cannot utter.

A sufficient list of "primary dimensions" for noises is mass, length, temperature, and time. This implies the complete operating space of acoustics can be made up from these four variables. (Definition of "primary dimensions" is given in Chapter 9.)

Observation B. In a given language, particular noises are understood to denote specific words by virtue of social consensus.

Comments

The social consensus may be informal, peculiar to a discipline or subculture, or generally accepted via a dictionary standard.

Not all the noises we can utter constitute words in a given language; there are some noises humans can make that are not words in any known language. Consider the sound of "Gliboofongtomas." We can make this awkward noise; it is not hard to vocalize, but it is not a word in any language I know. Thus the vocabulary (or dictionary) of a given language further constrains the total list of noises by defining which noises are words in that language.

The "dimensions" of words are "symbolic forms," meanings, if you like.

Nouns represent classes of objects, verbs classes of actions, adjectives qualities, and so on.

It is difficult to think of any matter that is more completely determined by social consensus than a word in a given language.

Observation C. The noises we can utter do not determine the words of a language; they only constrain the list of noises out of which we can make words.

Comment

The demonstration of assertion C is not difficult; there are something like 2,000 human languages on earth, and many more subvariants (or dialects). The languages are all constructed from "utterable" noises. It follows that we cannot derive a vocabulary from acoustics and/or the physiology of the human vocal apparatus. If we could, there would be only one language.

Observation D. We cannot derive the principles of how sound propagates through air (acoustics) from the vocabulary of a language (or of all languages).

Comment

Statement D can be seen to be true from either of two bases: first, the "dimensions" of a vocabulary do not include mass, length, time, and temperature. Nor does anything in a vocabulary hint at the nature of propagation of weak pressure waves in air, which is the essence of the sound of speech as a physical phenomenon. Second, there is a literal infinity of possible noises, and the words in all languages use only a finite number of "noises."

The four observations A, B, C, and D, when taken together, define the relationship of the two adjacent levels of noises and words as used in human speech: the adjacent levels mutually constrain each other, but neither level determines the other.

We now generalize this illustration into Part A of what I will call Polanyi's Principle:

Polanyi's Principle, Part A. In many hierarchically structured systems, adjacent levels mutually constrain, but do not determine, each other.

This is the general structural relation between adjacent layers of an interface of mutual constraint in a hierarchy of structure, as Polanyi noted.

An interface of mutual constraint is more than a statement that "A constrains B"; it is a statement that "Not only does A constrain B, but B constrains A." Thus it is a situation of mutual constraint. Polanyi also noted that the three other interfaces in human communications are also interfaces of mutual constraint. Since the concept of interfaces of mutual constraint is not familiar to many people, and will be important in what follows, you may want to check for yourself that the relations among the other adjacent levels of speech are also interfaces of mutual constraint, to see whether you have assimilated the concept.

We need to look carefully at what the existence of this kind of interface implies for multidisciplinary discourse. In the example of words and noises, we see that when an interface is one of mutual constraint, this implies, first, that we cannot add up (aggregate over) the principles of the lower level (here, acoustics and the biology of the human vocal apparatus) and obtain the next higher level (here, words); and second, that we cannot merely disaggregate the higher level (words) to derive the principles of the next lower level (acoustics). Both these statements are true because constraint, by definition, implies fewer known conditions than the total number of degrees of freedom; that is what we mean by constraint, as equation (5-6) shows.

For multidisciplinary discourse the important result is: When we have interfaces of mutual constraint in a hierarchically structured system, neither the reductionist nor the synoptic program can be carried out in the way advocates of those programs have suggested is possible. To move either upward or downward in level of aggregation within a given system with interfaces of mutual constraint, we must supply added information to what is inherent in each level for the particular system of interest. Let's look at this mathematically.

Suppose an upper level, U, of an interface of mutual constraint, has N total degrees of freedom. Suppose, further, there are M constraints on level U coming from the next lower level, L, where $M < N$. Physically, this implies the number of open degrees of freedom, O, in the level U is:

$$O = N - M > 0$$

Only if $M = N$ would the behavior of U be fixed (determined) by L. The same mathematics applies to a lower level L. When the next higher adjacent level only constrains some of the total degrees of freedom, there remain some open degrees of freedom in level L.

Let us take the mathematics one step farther. What can be called "the fundamental solution theorem of mathematics" says, "We need a number of equations or conditions equal to the number of unknown (dependent) variables we are trying to find in order to have a solution to our problem." There are some exceptions, but they are rare, and as we've done at other points, we will leave them to specialists. But when we have an interface of mutual constraint, a number of conditions or equations equal to the mutual or unknown variables is just what we lack. To put this differently, we have fewer conditions and equations than we have unknowns. Thus, neither integration (the mathematical process for aggregation) nor differentiation (the mathematical process for disaggregation) can be carried out, across an interface of mutual constraint, unless we add conditions or equations to the information that is inherent in the structure. In the example of words and noises, we cannot get a dictionary from acoustics, nor can we get acoustics from a dictionary. In each case we need additional information.

The existence of open degrees of freedom, not determined by other layers in the structure of hierarchical systems with interfaces of mutual constraint, tells us unequivocally that neither bottom-up nor top-down determinism is correct. If either were correct, then there would be no open degrees of freedom in these systems, and we could carry out the mathematical integrations implied by bottom-up determinisms, or the mathematical differentiations implied by top-down determinisms.

We can push this logic farther. No form of either the reductionist program or the synoptic program, radical or otherwise, can be carried out for systems with hierarchical structure and interfaces of mutual constraint. Since hierarchical systems with interfaces of mutual constraint are both common and important, no reductionist view, even in moderate forms, can supply a complete worldview. The same is true of synoptic views.

To investigate this more fully, let's examine how open degrees of freedom are used to generate words from noises in human speech.

Have the 2,000 or so known languages exhausted all the possibilities of either noises or words? Definitely not! The linguists have now identified all the basic sounds humans use in all known languages. Linguists call the individual noises used to make words in a given language the "phonemes" of that language. All words used can be made up from these phonemes in the language under study. No known language uses all of the phonemes utilized in all languages. English uses about 40 phonemes; many more are known (of the order of 100 to 200, depending on how finely the noises are parsed).

How about written language? Is it determined by the forms (letters) we use? English has a relatively rich vocabulary (at least five times that of Spanish, according to some observers). Nevertheless, English by no means uses up all the possible combinations of its 26 letters in forming words. The possible combinations of 26 letters in twos, threes, fours, and fives already vastly exceeds the approximately 550,000 words in standard English.

Thus, neither spoken nor written languages exhaust the possible list of words. Open possibilities exist for creating more words in both speech and writing. And, as we have noted, language varies from culture to culture. Moreover, languages often drift over time, with some words disappearing and new words being created. We need only read Chaucer to see how much English has drifted since his time.

Can we make about acoustics the kinds of statements we just made about languages? Acoustics is the same everywhere in the world. There is a well-developed science of acoustics, and it has Entire Invariant Paradigms that are the same at all times and places. The theory of acoustics works remarkably well for many simple geometries. We have an uncountable number of instances when we have compared the predictions of the theory of acoustics with data and have obtained agreement to within the residual uncertainty in the data. This is as far as we can test any physical theory. In the case of acoustics, these many tests assure the accuracy of the predictions well beyond what we need for most purposes.

Figure 8-1 illustrates not only how noises and words mutually constrain each other in a language but also how we use the open degrees of freedom in language to generate new words and thus changes in our languages. The results thus deny

Constraint or determinant

Current and historical social choices	List E: Words used in one given language	(≈550,000 in English) constructed from phonemes of the language
Sociocultural history	List D: Phonemes used in one given language	(≈40 in English)
Observations of known languages	List C: All phonemes used in all languages	(100–200)
Physiology of vocal cords and ears	List B: All single sounds humans can make and hear	
Physics of pressure waves in air	List A: All possible sounds (an infinite list)	to infinity →

Figure 8-1. The Relations of "Noises" to Words: How We Construct a Language Using Open Degrees of Freedom via Human Choices. Note that the length of boxes indicates relative number on the list; the boxes are not drawn to scale.

any kind of language determinism not only as a matter of principle, but also in terms of the details of how we create changes over time.

Let's now examine another example which will illustrate the second part of Polanyi's Principle. We will now discuss control from many levels, rather than just between adjacent levels.

Hierarchy of Automobile Transportation

Social System

Traffic Laws of the State (Social Controls)
Rules of the Road (Social Controls)
    Driver (human control)
        Automobile (autonomic controls)
            Major assemblies
            Steering, engine, ...
                Component parts
                Lower levels

What does the phrase "levels of control" denote? It denotes the levels that guide and "control" the system in order to carry out its objectives. Usually the levels of control are in the higher levels in the system. When we drive a car, the molecules in the engine do not tell us where to go; a human, as the driver, decides the destination. Operating the controls, the human makes the choices that lead where she or he wants to go. The choices of route are constrained, but not determined, by the laws of mechanics, the road layout, what our particular car will do, the social "rules" for driving in a given locality, and so forth. As we saw with regard to speech, various levels in the system mutually constrain, but do not determine, each other. However, there is another aspect implicit in what we denote by the driver controlling the car using human-control feedback modes. We will state this more generally as Part B of Polanyi's Principle.

Polanyi's Principle, Part B. In hierarchically structured systems, the levels of control (usually upper levels) "harness" the lower levels and cause them to carry out behaviors that the lower levels, left to themselves, would not do.

The phrase "left to themselves" denotes behaviors that would occur outside the hierarchical structure.

Does this mean that a hierarchical system with various levels of control violates the governing principles of physics or biology at the lower layers? Of course not! If the upper levels where the controls reside tried to make the lower layers violate these principles, the task would not get done. The system would not go, would die, explode, or fold, spindle, or mutilate itself in some other way. Designers all know this well. It is the inexorability of nature about the way physical processes work; it arises from the invariance of physical processes in inert objects. In the case of your car, an obvious violation is an attempt to run it without gas in the tank — you can turn on the starter, but the engine won't (can't) obey your control command.

We create complex devices with hierarchical structures, such as cars, specifically so that we can control them, get them to do what we want for one purpose or another. Carrying out the complete task usually requires embedding the devices in larger sociotechnical systems, here the complete system of auto transportation. Neither the design of the devices nor our goals (what we want to do) can be found solely from either a reductionist or a synoptic view. A reductionist view cannot by itself provide us with goals for all our endeavors. A synoptic view, by itself, cannot tell us what kind of structure is needed to carry out a given goal.

Are interfaces of mutual constraint and systems with multiple control levels common? Indeed they are! They are nearly ubiquitous in biological systems, human-designed systems, in communications, and thus also in sociotechnical systems.

We have seen an example in automobiles, but the same remarks apply to computers, airplanes, and on and on. Space does not permit exploration of the numerous important examples in living systems that embody interfaces of mutual constraint and multilevel control. However, the neuromuscular system of humans is an example of two layers of mutual constraint, as you can check for yourself. We also have seen in some detail why human speech has interfaces of mutual constraint. The example of speech alone would make this kind of interface important for our understanding. Humans also use controls derived from religious and cultural values. As systems, we have multiple levels of control.

The higher levels in living organisms harness the lower levels in order to carry out life functions. Animals carry out four necessary acts for survival of the species: feeding, fighting, fleeing, and reproducing. Plants typically do only two of these — feeding and reproducing — but they also typically use hierarchical structures with interfaces of mutual constraint.

By means of hierarchical structures with multiple levels of control, living systems utilize available energy in the combination of food, water, and air in order to function. During growth or repair of parts, living systems use this available energy to create order within their own structure. These actions in normal functioning and in growth and evolution in no way violate the "laws" of thermodynamics when those laws are expressed in the proper frame of reference — despite many decades of speculation based on inappropriate system definition. The term "available energy" above signifies that only some forms of energy, not all, can be used for these purposes. The concept of available energy was originated, but not fully explicated, by J. W. Gibbs; for a definitive technical description of the concept, see Keenan (1941).

We humans also do other things beyond the four functions needed for survival. For example, we make automobiles in sociotechnical systems of manufacture and diffuse them into sociotechnical systems of use (transportation systems) in order to move ourselves and other things about more rapidly and effectively. We make perfumes to titillate our erotic senses. We make atomic bombs and mount them on missiles in order to kill other humans, and thereby risk destruction of the planet. And these are only three out of many examples of how we humans use sociotechnical systems to control much of the world around us.

Most complex artifacts and the systems in which we embed them are hierarchical structures utilizing both interfaces of mutual constraint and multiple levels of control. They are not simply aggregations of molecules that bump into each other in random ways. If you doubt this, it will help to remember that a modern automobile has about 10,000 parts, and each part needs on the average, say, 10 instructions for its manufacture. Thus roughly 100,000 parameters must be set, appropriately, by knowledgeable humans, using human design processes, before the drawings are sent to production by the design engineers. Moreover, the workers on the production line must understand these instructions and how to carry them out, if the car is to operate successfully. A question will help illustrate the point. How long would we have to wait for the bumping together of molecules to design the next model of a Chevrolet or a Toyota or a Mercedes well enough so it would run? Cars are created by a human design of a hierarchical structure containing several levels of control in order to harness the molecules to perform human-desired tasks, tasks that the molecules left to themselves would not do.

These remarks apply even to simple tools. Who has seen a steel-shank hammer or garden spade created by nature alone? Human purposes (of some sort) are "built into" these tools. You may want to check for yourself that biological systems, human systems such as institutions, many human-made devices, and sociotechnical systems all commonly have hierarchical structure and often have both multiple levels of control and interfaces of mutual constraint.

In sum, systems that have hierarchical structure with multiple levels of control and levels that mutually constrain each other are common enough and important enough that we must have views that allow us to provide reasonable understanding of such systems in order to understand our world.

Conclusions for Chapter 8

In systems with hierarchical structure and interfaces of mutual constraint, we cannot find adjacent levels merely by aggregation to a higher level or by disaggregation to a lower level, because the adjacent levels only mutually constrain, and do not determine, each other.

It follows that neither the top-down synoptic view nor the bottom-up reductionist view can, by itself, supply reasonable understanding of systems with hierarchical structure incorporating interfaces of mutual constraint and multiple levels of control.

Many kinds of systems with hierarchical structure and interfaces of mutual constraint are important to human welfare, including the structure of humans. Thus both the radical reductionist view and the radical synoptic view are seriously incomplete as a route to understanding the totality of problems of vital concern to humans. Moreover, the two radical views are only illustrations. The arguments in this chapter show that no synoptic view alone, nor any reductionist view alone, is sufficient to understand our world. We will need to look and see if there is a different approach that can encompass all the things humans need to understand after we have looked at the two other demonstrations of why the synoptic and the reductionist views are necessarily seriously incomplete.

CHAPTER 9

The Theory of Dimensions

In this chapter, we will develop a second, independent demonstration of the impossibility of both the reductionist and the synoptic programs. In Chapter 10 we will develop a third independent demonstration of this result. Why is this task done three times over? There are several reasons. The existence of three independent demonstrations makes the result more robust than one. Each demonstration speaks more strongly to particular groups of scholars. Chapter 8 may be persuasive for biologists; this chapter for scientists, engineers, and mathematicians; and Chapter 10 for computer scientists and individuals concerned with brain functions. The demonstrations in Chapters 8 and 10 are structural and verbal; the demonstration in this chapter is mathematical and meets current standards of proof. Finally, the three demonstrations taken together provide more tools for use in multidisciplinary discourse than any one alone.

What is the theory of dimensions? It is a theory that insists on a particular kind of consistency in the formation of equations modeling physical reality. The basis for the theory of dimensions is nothing more than the familiar idea that it is an error to equate apples and oranges. As we saw, when we fail to make "needful" distinctions for a given situation, even between apples and oranges, we cannot understand that situation well. In mathematical sysreps we make this idea of "needful" distinctions precise by insisting that each separate term in the equations we use to describe physical systems have the same dimensions. This idea, the need for the same dimensions in each separate term of the equations we use as sysreps, is called "the Principle of Dimensional Homogeneity." The words "separate term" indicate any group of symbols following a plus or minus sign. For example, in the equation A B/C = D + E F, each of A B/C, D, and E F may be forces, but some cannot be forces and others temperatures.

Let us look first at how the Principle of Dimensional Homogeneity has been used in writing equations for representing inert, naturally-occurring systems.

The methods of the theory of dimensions have been used as a tool in constructing mathematical sysreps and finding and generalizing solutions for particular problems by many scientists and engineers since the nineteenth century and earlier. However, this seems to have been done ad hoc for various applications. A piece of formal theory about dimensions, called the Pi Theorem, was added by Earl Buckingham early in the twentieth century. The Pi Theorem is one method for reducing the number of parameters needed to describe a design space. The Pi Theorem thus allows us to work with equations of a lower complexity index than would otherwise be the case. At the same time, the Pi Theorem tells us how to generalize results from individual cases to classes of problems. The theory included in the Pi Theorem seems to have been first formally organized and recorded in a monograph with related materials by Bridgman (1921). Bridgman's work remains a classic. Several later books by Langhaar (1951), Huntley (1953) and others also describe the theory and further clarify a few aspects. Kline (1965, 1986) extended the theory to include two methods, in addition to the Pi Theorem, for finding information about a class of problems when a complete solution cannot be obtained. One of these methods is more powerful and more reliable than the Pi Theorem. This method often provides a good deal of information that is helpful in laying out research programs, in simplifying data taking, and for other purposes. Interested readers can find details in the references just given.

These works all agree on one point: all the variables and parameters that appear in the equations of the physical sciences, and all the solutions for inert systems of naturally-occurring objects at the classical level, can be written completely in terms of no more than six "primary dimensions." One common list of primary dimensions for the classical level is: mass (m), length (l), time (t), temperature (T), voltage (v), and electric charge (c). The words "classical level" here denote objects of roughly human size (see Figure 7-1).

What does the term "primary dimensions" denote? The primary dimensions are the building blocks for all the variables and parameters in the equations of interest. Each variable or parameter in equations representing the physical world has the character of one of the primary dimensions, or can be formed as a product and/or ratio of the primary dimensions. Thus the lengths of our rectangular room **system** (Chapter 4) are parameters with the dimension of length. The variable metering airplane speed is the variable velocity. Velocity as a physical quantity has the dimensions of length divided by time (l/t). Next consider density. Density has the dimensions of mass per unit volume (m/l^3). By definition, the density of, say, water can be measured as pounds (mass) divided by the volume of the given amount of water. From experience we know that the dimensions of any variable or parameter describing inert objects can be expressed in this way, as no more than the product and/or ratio of a few primary dimensions — for example, the list of six given above. This is both a surprising result and a keystone of the physical sciences. It is precisely this result which keeps the index of complexity low for inert, naturally-occurring objects. The classic discussion of this point is given by Bridgman (1921).

In thinking about dimensions of inert systems at the classical level, we do not need to consider dimensions at lower levels in the hierarchy of constitution. This is unnecessary because whatever the structure (and the dimensions) of the lower levels, when we aggregate over the lower levels, we must come out with the known descriptions at the classical level written in terms of the known primary dimensions at that level, and no more. If other dimensions exist at lower levels, they must merge into (and emerge as) no more than a list of six primary dimensions at the classical level. Moreover, the known results about dimensions at the classical level are empirically relatively well established. I say "relatively well established" because if there is an area where we have relatively high certainty about our ability to predict behaviors, it is classical physics, which describes inert, naturally-occurring objects of classical size. As we have seen, the complexity index for these systems is low, and the behaviors invariant. We have over the past few centuries built powerful sysreps for many systems in this class, and we have in most cases an uncountable number of independent checks of the reliability and low uncertainty of the results these sysreps produce. In many instances, sysreps for these simple systems appear to be Entire Invariant Paradigms in powerful mathematical forms. There seems to be no other class of **systems** about which we can make these same remarks.

Niels Bohr, often seen as the father of quantum mechanics, insisted that any acceptable theory of quantum mechanics must be consistent with classical physics for any solution or sysrep that emerged at the classical level. This idea is often called "the Bohr Correspondence Principle." Thus the physics community agrees with Bridgman's ideas concerning the sufficiency of six primary variables at the classical level.

The list of six primary dimensions given above (m, l, t, T, v, c) is sufficient to describe all inert, naturally-occurring objects, but it is neither unique nor always necessary. For example, we saw earlier that the first four dimensions in the list were enough to describe acoustics; we don't need the last two for this kind of system. Also, we can easily use other sets of primary dimensions if we choose. We can, for example, substitute force for mass and the list will still be complete. However, one sufficient list is enough for our purposes.

Let's see what the theory of dimensions tells us about the relations between various levels in the hierarchy of constitution. Suppose we have an equation, E, that is a sysrep for any class of inert, naturally-occurring systems, and this sysrep provides very accurate and reproducible predictions for the known behaviors of this class of systems at a level L in the hierarchy of constitution. Let's take L to be the level just below and adjacent to the classical level. This is the molecular level -2 (Figure 7-1). Then for inert, naturally-occurring objects we can think about aggregating over level L to find the next higher level. If we have a mathematical model, we can do this aggregation by integrating the equation E for level L to find results at an upper level U. We can write these ideas in functional form:

$$E = F_1(m_j^a, l_i^b, t^c, T^d, v^e, c^f) \tag{9-1}$$

where i = 1, 2, 3 (for 3 directions) and j denotes that there may be more than one kind of atom present. In equation (9-1), a, b, c, d, e, and f are real numbers.

As Bridgman (1921) showed, the functional equation (9-1) is adequate for all the equations of classical physical theory. If we complete the problem by providing sufficient information about the particular case (boundary and/or initial conditions), and integrate (mathematically) over time and space to "aggregate" the system at the upper level U, we obtain the integrated answer, I, in functional form as:

$$I = \int E dx_i dt = F_2(m_j^a, l_i^{b+3}, t^{c+1}, T^d, v^e, c^f) + \text{constant} \tag{9-2}$$

where i = 1, 2, 3 (for 3 directions) and j denotes that there may be more than one kind of atom present.

All that happens when we aggregate is that we raise the power of the exponent of length by three and time by one. Moreover, this result is entirely general within the theory of dimensions and the operations of mathematics. The step from equation (9-1) to equation (9-2) is mathematically rigorous.

To avoid confusion, I note that the verb "integrate" and the noun "integration" are each used in two distinct ways in this book. First, the word "integrations" denotes "things that are put together in a structure" (the lay meaning). Second is the mathematical usage and indicates a specific mathematical process of summing in a defined, precise way. The symbol $\int$ (integral sign) in equation (9-2) denotes this summing process. We integrate in this mathematical sense to find the area under a curve, the volume within a prescribed space, the distance a car has traveled when moving at various speeds over time, and so on. Integration in the mathematical sense is thus the operation we need to sum up the bits represented by equation (9-1) to get a description of a system at the next higher level of aggregation. To distinguish the two we will use the modifier "mathematical" when the math usage is intended.

What we need to notice for our discussion is that the integrated equation (9-2) for the upper level U has no dimensions not already present in equation (9-1) for the lower level L. And this will remain true no matter how many times we integrate, that is, how many levels we move up in the hierarchy of constitution by mathematical manipulation of the equations that constitute our sysrep. The important thing, for our purposes, is that:

No New Dimensions Arise From Integration.

Now we ask, Are the six dimensions (m, l, t, T, v, and c) sufficient to describe the behaviors of all systems in the world? No they are not! They are sufficient for classical physics (that is, for inert, naturally-occurring objects of classical size), but they are not sufficient for the world. Let's look at some counterexamples to be sure about this. The primary dimensions for many models in economics, in much the sense that primary dimensions are used in the physical sciences, are money and the interest rate; many mathematical models in economics are built up using those primary dimensions (as variables). The primary dimensions of political actions are followers or adherents — regardless of how the followers are obtained and retained. The primary dimensions characterizing the "glue" that holds together communities of intimate others are love, affection, trust, and belongingness. There are other examples, but we need not go on; the point is clear. It is not just that one of these types of dimensions of other fields cannot be obtained by integrating over lower level L, as various people have pointed out in qualitative arguments; it is, rather, that none of them can be obtained. Rigorous mathematics tells us this immediately, with no inputs other than the theory of dimensions as used in the physical sciences and engineering.

How reliable is the theory of dimensions? As all well-trained scientists and engineers know, no equation of any kind that is an appropriate sysrep for classical systems can violate the Principle of Dimensional Homogeneity. We can write equations that don't follow the Principle of Dimensional Homogeneity, but in no known case do they properly describe the physical world. And this underlying principle is all we need to ensure the validity of the theory of dimensions. To put this in different words, the theory of dimension is presuppositional to the entire edifice of classical physics. And from this presuppositional principle, it follows immediately that physics cannot supply a complete model of the world. This argument was published in Kline (1986), and thus far no meaningful objection has been raised against it. It seems, however, to have been largely ignored within the physical science communities, where a common belief still seems to be that the reductionist program is possible "in principle."

I have not seen another instance in which the theory of dimensions has been extended as far as we have just taken it. Is this extension of the theory justified? It seems to be. The extension of the theory follows from no more than the idea of dimensions and the concept of functional representation of hyperspaces (discussed in Chapter 5). More specifically, if the functional representation of the hyperspace for our sysrep does not include all the relevant variables and all the relevant dimensions, then no mathematical manipulations will produce the needed variables or dimensions. The extension of the theory of dimensions for use as a multidisciplinary tool thus seems to be on solid ground.

To put this differently, none of the dimensions listed above for the various areas of life are transmutable into each other. Moreover, we gave only a few examples. Thus when we look, we see that the dimensions in various levels of the hierarchy of constitution are typically exogenous to and incommensurate with each other. In a few cases adjacent levels have the same dimensions, but in most cases they do not. This is an important idea for understanding the relationship among various disciplines.

We have not exhausted the list of dimensions that cannot be obtained by integrating equations that contain only m, l, t, T, v, and c as primary dimensions. However, one counterexample is enough, and we already have several wide and significant classes of counterexamples. Moreover, these counterexamples include matters of primary concern to humans.

Could we extend the equations of physics so they include the other dimensions needed to cover all areas of concern to humans? If we intend the equations to be appropriate sysreps for physics, we cannot. The systems physics describes do not process information, as detailed in Figure 6-1. If we changed the equations of physics to include variables describing human information (for example, money, interest rate), they would be incorrect as sysreps for physics. The equations would predict that inert, naturally-occurring objects could do things we know such objects cannot.

What about the reverse process? What does the theory of dimensions tell us about finding a lower level L from a higher level U via mathematical differentiation? It tells us precisely the same things. More specifically, disaggregating (by mathematical process of differentiation) does not alter the list of primary dimensions in the equations any more than aggregation does, provided length and time are already in the equations. Thus only if the dimensions in the upper level match those in the adjacent lower level is there a possibility of finding the structure of a lower level from knowledge of a higher level in the hierarchy of constitution by itself, and often this is not the case. That is, the dimensions often differ from one level to another.

Since this idea will be used at later points, you may want to check the result for yourself. You can do this by looking at the disciplines of knowledge and where they are in the various levels of the hierarchy of constitution (Figure 7-2), and then asking yourself, What are the variables and parameters in the various levels, and what are the dimensions needed to make up these variables and parameters? I think you will quickly see that only in rare cases is there a possibility that models for higher levels in the hierarchy of constitution will yield details about lower levels. In general, it is no more possible to find the structure of lower level L from higher level U than the converse, to find U from L.

Let's make this point more fully by examples. If we fail to examine the structure of humans, then the basis of physiology and medicine largely disappear. If we fail to examine the structure of plants and animals, much of agriculture and agronomy and all of systematic biology disappear. If we fail to examine the structure of human-made products, much of engineering disappears. If we fail to study the effects of various types of human communications on interpersonal relations, then no theory of physics and no set of fixed rules from top-level values will provide what we need to know to create emotionally healthy families and institutions. In sum we cannot get any of these structures or processes from either top-level values alone or information about the underlying bits alone. Nor can we get them from inputs and outputs of the relevant systems alone. If you doubt this, look again at Figures 7-1 and 7-2. We must study the relevant systems where and as they exist for some forms of information that are vital to human welfare.

Conclusions for Chapter 9

This chapter provides a second independent demonstration of the impossibility of either the reductionist or the synoptic program, even in principle. It also demonstrates again that neither top-down nor bottom-up determinism can be true, but this time the demonstration is based on dimensional considerations rather than open degrees of freedom. Moreover, the demonstrations in this chapter are mathematically rigorous, and they rest only on assumptions about physical systems that are presuppositional to the entire edifice of classical physics.

CHAPTER 10

Integrated Control Information

We will use the phrase "integrated control information" to denote information used in a human-control feedback mode, as defined in Chapter 6. Integrated control information in this sense is a combination of incoming information with a preexisting schemata in the human mind. The integrated information is used to activate muscular responses in a given situation. As we have seen, schemata are relational repertoires that can tie stored chunks of data to solution patterns in the human memory. As a result, integrated control information can quickly activate learned neuromuscular responses in circumstances that may vary somewhat from case to case. Since this kind of information invokes schemata, it often employs deep networks of related information that pass beyond a collection of facts or even use of an explicit "rule." Moreover, the relational networks are different in each human.

In order to see in more detail what the use of integrated control information implies in the human **system**, let's think about what you do if a truck suddenly appears in front of your car. In reacting to the sudden appearance of the truck, you acquire information (Oops! Truck in the way); you integrate this information with your schemata for driving already stored in your brain (Process information); you bring up action patterns from a relevant schema; and you act using your muscles (Apply the brakes! Turn!) to cause the car to change speed and/or direction.

In the phrase "integrated control information," the modifier "control" reminds us that the information is used in a human-control feedback loop. The modifier "integrated" reminds us of two things: first, that information is acquired via sensing; and second, that the acquired information is integrated with preexisting schemata in the brain. It is the combination of the preexisting schemata with the new information, when put together into a new synthesis, that is the basis for action. Neither the new information nor the preexisting schemata alone is sufficient to deal with the sudden appearance of the truck in front of you on the road because the details will vary from incident to incident. We do not yet understand how the brain does these processing and comparison functions, but there is no doubt that the brain does do them in a relatively short time (some tens or hundreds of milliseconds). These processing functions are still in the state of Heaviside's breakfast. However, current work in the cognitive sciences now seems to be leading relatively rapidly toward better understanding. As we have seen, the brain does not do these functions via a set of fixed rules; true expertise lies several levels above any set of fixed rules, and it is far more adaptable to local needs. See particularly Dreyfus and Dreyfus (1986), de Groot (1946/1965), and the other references in Chapter 3.

Nor do we want to pause and think when confronted by a truck on the road. If we had to pause to think about rules, we would be much more likely to crash. The brain uses integrated control information (schemata plus new information hooked to muscles) much more rapidly than if we had to stop and think about what we are going to do. The same is true of actions in sports, playing a musical instrument, and so on. We do not stop and think about where a tennis ball is going, or how to hit it on the court; we start running for the spot and preparing the stroke we need. If necessary we adjust course as we go, using a feedback loop.

The existence of integrated control information, and its use in feedback loops in the control levels of hierarchical systems, forms a third independent reason why both the reductionist and synoptic programs are impossible in many important classes of systems. Let's look first at the relation to the reductionist program.

Integrated control information is not accessible via integration over the lower levels L of living systems. We will use humans to illustrate this point because we have some relevant characteristics that other organisms do not.

In humans there are three types of preexisting information that are used to process acquired information and close various feedback control loops. These are: DNA (genetic information); the cultural information of the "tribe" or society; and individual information acquired via individual life experiences (including skills). All three types are stored in the brain and/or neuromuscular system of a given individual. All three of these types of information come from the past — at a given moment, they preexist. History matters. Moreover, they involve quantities (information) not determined by the lower levels of physical structure, as we have seen at several earlier points. Also, we must not confuse information inherent in "rocks" with information in DNA or in animal brains (see Chapter 6).

Every human brain has a different set of stored schemata and therefore to some degree a different brain structure. We recall that the number of possible human brain configurations is of the order of $10^{8,000}$. The number of people on earth (currently a few billions) is an extremely small fraction of $10^{8,000}$. So the uniqueness of human brains does not contradict the constraints of human biological structure. Moreover, you know that human brains are unique from your own experience, even without the numbers. All you need do to recognize the differences in human brains is ruminate on the following question, Have you ever met two individual humans who had exactly the same personality, and who would react identically, in word and deed, to all possible circumstances? And beyond your thoughts on that question, ask yourself, What two individuals have precisely the same sets of experiences used in forming expertise and hence the basis for many of their schemata?

Without appropriate integrated control information, which depends on our individually learned schemata, we could not avoid the truck on the highway, nor could we walk, talk, or do much of anything in our daily lives. As documented by Spitz (1965), Konner (1983), Johnson (1985, 1987, 1991), Stern (1985), and many others, the human child's early experiences strongly affect the number and form of the physical connections in the brain, and each of us has a unique set of these experiences. As many psychiatrists have noted, each client is different. Even to visualize what we see, and make sense of it, requires learning; see Sacks (1993). To some degree each new client is a new problem for the psychotherapist, who must learn the new emotional patterns and intellectual beliefs of the client. See, for example, Carl Jung's autobiography, or Viscott (1972). Even Stephen Johnson, who has developed a relatively complete and usable taxonomy of the existential developmental "issues" that lead to psychopathology, says that a minority of individuals do not fit any of the common "issues," and no individual fits one of the six issues in his taxonomy in a totally pure form. The therapist must learn about each individual client.

Nor are these differences restricted to the psychological domain. Some of us learn to play tennis, others to swim, ride horseback, play football. Each of these develops different muscular competences. Playing the piano or the violin involves still other schemata and muscular competences. As we all know, these skills are not interchangeable; they are highly particularized. Moreover, this list of skills is far from exhaustive.

Can we find human integrated control information by doing what is called in computer notation a "bit-map" of a human brain so that we could decipher the structure of a human's schemata from the bits? Such a map is not feasible at present owing to limitation of instruments. But let's suppose for the moment that it is feasible so we can discuss the idea. Given a complete bit-map of a particular human brain, could we interpret it? Not unless we knew the language and the culture of the person inside whom the bits are encoded. A computer analogy will help us see this point.

In writing this chapter, I might be typing in any of a number of high-level word processor "languages" on my computer. Unless you knew which word processor I had used, which operating system was running in my computer, and also the human language I am writing in, you could make no sense of the bit-map of the data recorded here. Each of these three kinds of language (processor, operating system, English) is a necessary "interpreter" essential to transforming the bits into a comprehensible message. This is true of the bits in the computer's volatile memory and also on its storage disk. In either case, without all three "interpreters" the bit-map would just be a string of zeroes and ones with no meaning at all. The same is true for a bit-map of the brain; one would have to know the language and the culture of the individual plus at least something about the person's individual schemata to interpret it.

Humans use integrated control information (including schemata) as central parts of human-control feedback operations, and these schemata cannot be found from the principles of biology and physics, even taken together, because the interpreters needed are personal. If human structures were fully determined by biological principles, then we would all have precisely the same brain structure and would act in precisely the same ways. As noted before, physics and biology only constrain brain structure.

Inert, naturally-occurring systems lack the information and feedback modes vital to living systems. We can learn about feedback modes only by studying living systems and human-created systems. More important for this discussion is what this implies about the equations, the sysreps we use for describing inert, naturally-occurring systems. If the equations we wrote as sysreps for inert, naturally-occurring systems contained terms that described the acquisition or processing of information, the equations would be inappropriate for those systems. These equations would predict behaviors that inert, naturally-occurring **systems** cannot carry out. And as noted before, a sysrep that predicts that a system may do things it cannot do is just as much in error as one that does not predict behaviors that the system can carry out. We saw this same result based on different reasons (Chapter 9). Thus integration over the lower levels L will not find the critical feedback functions that living systems use because the equations we use as sysreps for inert, naturally-occurring systems do not and should not describe feedback loops. This remark applies not only to integration over inert molecules but also to integration over the information in DNA. The information needed for driving a car is not in our DNA. If it were, we would not need to learn how to drive, or take a licensing test to prove we have done so.

Let us turn now to synoptic views. What is the relation between the learned schemata of an individual human and the higher level values of his or her culture and religion? Synoptic values tend to constrain but do not determine how we drive a car. Each of us drives somewhat differently; many of us change our driving pattern when a police car is near. Choices, and hence open degrees of freedom, exist concerning how we drive. The nondeterministic words "tend to" are needed in describing the effect of cultural values on our actions, because there are deviants in every society studied by ethnologists, and a deviant is by definition a person who does not follow the norms of the cultural values. To use the example of driving again, we see drivers blatantly violating both the laws of the land and the unwritten rules of the road on the highway nearly anytime we drive. In sum, we cannot find the integrated control information of a given individual from the cultural values either. At most the cultural values act as a guide to help us understand individuals' behaviors.

Thus the existence of what we might call "human information" — that is, integrated control information, which includes schemata in the human brain — forms a region of knowledge that we cannot fully understand from a reductionist view alone, a synoptic view alone, or the two views taken together. This marks for us the boundary between what we can get from either reductionist views or synoptic views and what we cannot. Let's look at one more example.

Suppose we have in hand a block of pure, lustrous white marble. We intend to carve from it a statue. We can carve one of beauty — say, a replica of Michelangelo's David — or one that you think is particularly ugly. The equations that govern the behavior of the "particles" in marble are the same for the ugly and the beautiful statues. Classical mechanics constrains our choices of how we can shape the statue. Mechanics can tell us, for example, that if we make the arms too thin, they will break and fall off. It is the addition of human aesthetic preferences, human information about shape not contained in the equations for the particles, that makes the difference between the beautiful and the ugly statue. This is the case in most human-designed objects. It is the insertion of human purposes (aesthetic or other types) as information that forms an impassible barrier for the reductionist program.

Since many people within nearly every culture carve many different statues (some beautiful and some ugly), the top-level cultural values do not determine the beauty of statues either, although they often shape ideas about beauty. Thus the use of aesthetic preferences to decide between the beautiful and the ugly statue illustrates once more the existence of open degrees of freedom at some levels in the human organism. The lower levels constrain some choices, but do not determine all choices. Physics allows carving the ugly statue and the beautiful one. The higher-level values tend to constrain the choices (a given culture may or may not approve of nude statues), but do not fully determine the form, and individuals may, or may not, follow the dictates of the laws or the mores of society.

Thus when we see the use of integrated control information (schemata) by humans in designing or controlling a system, we know we are in a domain where neither the reductionist nor synoptic program, nor both together, can determine all we need to know. This discussion gives the same results as the two prior demonstrations, but adds clarity about where the boundaries lie beyond which neither program can provide understanding on matters of vital concern to humans.

We now have three demonstrations that neither of the two old views is adequate to understand our world. Both are important views; both are seriously incomplete as worldviews. One demonstration is based on Polanyi's ideas about hierarchical systems with interfaces of mutual constraint. The second is based on the theory of dimensions, which is presuppositional to the entire edifice of classical physics. The third is based on the existence and use of integrated control information (using learned schemata) in human-control and human-design feedback modes.

The obvious question becomes, Is there another process that is adequate that will allow us to understand complex systems? I use the word "process" rather than "view" because, as we will see, more than one view is required. We will answer the question by stating Hypothesis V.

Hypothesis V: *The Need for At Least Three Views. Part A.* At least three views are needed for a reasonably good understanding of hierarchically structured systems with interfaces of mutual constraint: (1) a synoptic overview; (2) a piecewise view of the parts; and (3) a structural view of how the parts connect with each other in order to create the whole.

Hypothesis V: *The Need for At Least Three Views. Part B.* Hierarchically structured systems with interfaces of mutual constraint are both common enough and significant enough so that all three views are necessary in order to understand the full range of situations and processes that are vital to humans.

Comments About the Words in Hypothesis V

Synoptic: We have already defined a synoptic view as one that delineates: the boundary of system; the ways the system can interact with its environment; and the goals of the system, if there are any.

Piecewise: A piecewise view will denote a view of the smallest relevant bits that make up the system. These smallest relevant bits may be parts for machines; cells or DNA for an organism; subatomic bits, if we are concerned with semiconductors. In sociology and psychology the bits are often individual people, groups, or institutions. The word "relevant" emphasizes that no one type of bit suffices; the relevant bit depends on the problem (and hence the **system**) under study. The piecewise view includes theory and other forms of accumulated knowledge about how the bits work. Within a given problem, piecewise views may be needed for more than one kind of bit, and the different bits may lie at different levels of aggregation. For example, both DNA (large molecules) and cells are important bits for many biological problems. In a machine the parts or the molecules of the materials or both may be considered the bits depending on the problems of concern. In some problems, we have to move back and forth between one kind of bit and another. This implies shifting from one sysrep to another in our design over time. This does not cause confusions so long as we are clear about what sysrep we are studying at each instant. For each kind of bit, we need empirical testing of our principles if we are to have relatively well-grounded theory and reliable predictive capacity. To put this in different words, we must have "traceability," which connects our words and mathematical symbols item by item to the things and processes they represent in the world. Lacking traceability, we lose the possibility to make our concepts operational, and when that happens, we lose the essential grounding supplied by empiricism, as Bridgman (1941) warned us. We then run the risk of creating grand illusions, which we will discuss in later chapters.

Structural: A structural view denotes how the pieces at each level of size in the system hook together to create the next higher level, all the way from the smallest relevant bits to the complete system. As we have seen, neither a synoptic view nor a reductionist view can by itself provide a picture of a hierarchical structure. To find the details of structure, we must examine an appropriate system.

Hypothesis V asserts not only that no one view will be enough but also that no two views are enough. For many systems we need all three views for even an adequate understanding. Hypothesis V does not say that three views will be enough. It may be that in some cases we will need more than three. I leave this question open until the next chapter.

Hypothesis V covers one portion of Hypothesis III: *The Absence of Universal Approaches.* However, it describes that portion in more detail and with more precision. Hypothesis V is a particularly useful theorem for our discussion on multidisciplinarity because it will allow us to see more clearly the relations among the disciplines both with regard to the paradigmatic systems the disciplines study and the sysreps they use for that study. In addition, Hypothesis V is simple enough so that it does not violate Miller's 7-Bit-Rule. Experience indicates that Hypothesis V can be taught to most undergraduate students without difficulty. Except for the writer's recent classes, we do not seem to have been teaching it to any, and this omission has contributed to the difficulties we will examine in Chapter 17.

Most hierarchically structured systems with interfaces of mutual constraint have heterogeneous aggregation. A system with heterogeneous aggregation incorporates qualitatively different parts wired up and hooked together within the structure. A large block of pure carbon (or any other element) is homogeneous in aggregation; that is, the properties of the block are the same in each part for all parts above single atoms. Homogeneous systems have no information capacities. In an automobile, there are mechanical parts, electrical parts, glass parts, and others. In a human, there are many kinds of tissues and organs that are structurally distinct from each other. Thus autos and humans (and most other complex systems) have heterogeneous aggregation. It seems that systems need heterogeneous aggregation in order to have information-processing capabilities, and systems may also need interfaces of mutual constraint. The question of how complex a system must be to process information seems in need of more study than we can give it here.

A question may have occurred to you at this point. Why can't we use one view that incorporates all of the synoptic, piecewise, and structural? I know of no theoretical bar to doing this. What makes at least three views necessary for complex systems is the limitations of the human mind. We can't hold enough information in our working memory to look at the bits, the structure, and the whole of a complex system simultaneously. As a result we must move back and forth between piecewise views, synoptic views, and structural views in order to form a complete understanding of complex systems. In many cases we may need to examine results at many levels, one by one, in the hierarchy of constitution of the system of concern. If you doubt this is a true limitation on the human mind, try to hold in your mind all the details, the purposes, and the structure of any complex system familiar to you — for example, an automobile, a company, a tree, or an air transport system. I think you will find that even if it is possible, at a minimum it is so difficult that there is little utility in trying to think about the bits, the structure, and the system goals all at one time.

CHAPTER 11

Disciplines at One Level

Disciplines and the Human Design Process

The demonstrations in preceding chapters show that neither of the two conflicting positions (or overviews) that have tended to dominate thought in Western culture since the time of Galileo (reductionist and synoptic) is sufficient. Neither is a wrong, both are important. However, both are seriously incomplete in the sense that neither is capable of generating the totality of information of vital concern to humans, despite many claims that each is complete or can be made complete. We have shown these results for hierarchically structured systems, but thus far we have said little about systems lying in the same level of the hierarchy of constitution. Nor have we examined how we design systems with many hierarchical levels.

Can we derive all the results we need at a given level in the hierarchy of constitution from one discipline that applies to that level? In some cases we can, but in others we cannot. The answer depends on the complexity of the systems in the level of concern and the way we have defined the domains of the relevant disciplines. Let's look at the details. The theory of dimensions can help clarify the question.

When the behaviors within a given level are fully described by the same set of variables and parameters in two or more fields (either as equations or in taking data and correlating), the answer to our current question normally is affirmative. There seems to be no bar to deriving results in one field from the other. For example, if we want to know about how atoms join to become molecules, atomic theory and correlations from lab data are sufficient. Thus we can derive important results in chemistry from our knowledge of physics. Even when the details of some problems are too complex to solve at a given instant, we can expect to do more and more problems within the domain of interest over time. For example,

Sizes (as in Fig. 7.1)	Name	Disciplines of Knowledge
7	Galaxies	Astronomy
6	Planets	Astronomy, geology meteorology, oceanography
5	Large sociotechnical systems	Economics, law, engineering, management, sociology, the humanities, plus many more
4	Ecologies without humans	Ecology
3	Humans	Physiology, medicine, psychology, psychiatry
2	Multicellular non-human life	Zoology, botany, ethology
1	One-cell life	Biology

Figure 11-1. The Lack of Study of Sociotechnical Systems as Complete Systems.

there has been a steady progression of results for more and more complex atoms from the theories of quantum mechanics, and this process has been accelerated by the arrival of large digital computers. This is often the case within the physical sciences, since the systems of concern are relatively simple, and we know how to write a sufficient list of dimensions to cover all known cases in those fields (see Chapter 9).

On the other hand, in levels that contain very complex systems — for example, sociotechnical systems — we usually divide the problems up into disciplines that employ different sets of variables and different dimensions. We don't do this because we think it is an ideal way to analyze sociotechnical systems; we do it because sociotechnical systems are so complex that we must break them down into sections so that the human mind can grasp the needed details. If you doubt this, consider the question, How much serious study have you seen on complete sociotechnical systems? This situation is illustrated by a caricature in Figure 11-1.

Does this situation create problems? Yes! It has and does because sociotechnical systems often have parts that are closely coupled to each other, so that changes in one sector influence significantly behaviors and results in other sectors.

Since the various sectors of sociotechnical systems are often studied by separate disciplines, they are discussed in separate communities that often lack adequate communications with each other. Furthermore, the disciplines that study various aspects of sociotechnical systems often use variables that are exogenous to each other. Thus each discipline may be a cut through the complete hyperspace needed to describe sociotechnical systems.

When two disciplines have exogenous dimensions, we cannot derive the results in either from the other. When the variables are totally exogenous between the two disciplines — that is, do not overlap — we cannot expect to find much of anything about one discipline from the other. When the variables overlap in part, we should expect to be able to find some results in one discipline from the other, but not all. These results follow from the theory of dimensions, which tells us that we cannot find out all about apples by studying oranges, even though they both are a kind of fruit. For example, both market behavior and ecologies affect and are affected by human sociotechnical systems, but the variables in the two disciplines that study markets and ecologies are nearly totally exogenous to each other.

The variables of ecologies are species and the biological conditions for survival. The equations of micro- and macro-economics ordinarily contain no variables that would tell us about viability of ecologies, only about inputs and outputs to our economic (that is, sociotechnical) systems and how efficiently we use the inputs. We cannot derive all the information we need about ecologies from economics, nor can we derive all we need to know about economics from the theories of ecologies, even though many systems are properly studied by both disciplines.

In many problems the results of the two disciplines of economics and ecology mutually constrain but do not determine each other. The situation is then similar to adjacent levels in a hierarchical structure with interfaces of mutual constraint.

Similar remarks apply to economics and sociology, as we normally construct those disciplines. Sociology deals with questions of fairness among humans and how humans react to specific forms of organization, and these variables are also, at least in part, exogenous to the variables of economics, which are often no more than money and the interest rate. Despite this, a leading economist in a recent interview insisted that there was no need for sociology, that all the results of sociology could be found from economics. When the interviewer asked if he meant what he had said, the economist not only said "Yes!" but proceeded to strengthen and elaborate his initial statement. This statement by the economist is clearly an overclaim in the language we have been using, as the theory of dimensions shows. This is not an isolated example. Because we have lacked maps of the complete intellectual terrain, the various territories (disciplines) have often claimed more than their rightful domains.

We can see this matter in a more general way by using the concept of hyperspaces (see Chapter 5). The dimensionality of a complete hyperspace for a sociotechnical system is of very high order. That is, to describe a complete sociotechnical system, even in functional form, typically requires many, many kinds of variables and parameters, so many that it is usually hard to delineate them. When we create models or equations that use only a few of these variables (and/or parameters), then no later mathematical manipulations will allow the resulting equations or models to fully explore the complete hyperspace, that is, to study adequately all the problems of concern.

When a discipline is isolated from other disciplines dealing with the same systems, and the discipline uses variables that do not cover the complete hyperspace of the system, it is possible for solutions created within that discipline to miss important aspects of problems for long periods of time. We will see examples where this has occurred. Does this imply that we should not use simple models with fewer variables than those needed for the full hyperspace of a sociotechnical system? Not at all! Given the limits of the human mind, we must use cuts through the complete hyperspace of complex systems. What the result does imply is that we need to examine more carefully what these simple models can and cannot do.

Two precautions seem to be particularly important. First, we need to bear in mind the primacy of data over prediction of incomplete theory when the two are contradictory. Second, we need to examine results from all the disciplines that are stakeholders, in the sense that they supply relevant information about the problem in hand, and not argue that one discipline or answer takes precedence or, worse, covers all the domain. When we have failed to do these things, we have sometimes created inappropriate results. For some examples, see Chapters 14, 16, and 17.

It will help us gain insight about this problem to look at the human design processes we use in creating artifacts. The process is illustrated in Figure 11-2. The particular illustration shown is our familiar artifact, the automobile.

We find the structure for the physical parts of the automobile at levels below those at which use of the automobile occurs; but we find the values, that is, the personal, social, and ecological effects of automobiles, at higher levels. Moreover, we do not design an automobile by merely integrating (mathematically), using the principles and equations of science. Nor do we design the automobile merely by using the values of the culture or the buyers of automobiles. If we are to create a successful design, we must carry out both the upward and the downward loops over and over (iteratively) until all the criteria are met at all the relevant levels. Only when all the necessary criteria are met at all the levels do we have an acceptable and possibly successful design. This process belies the often heard statement that engineering is merely applied science. Science says

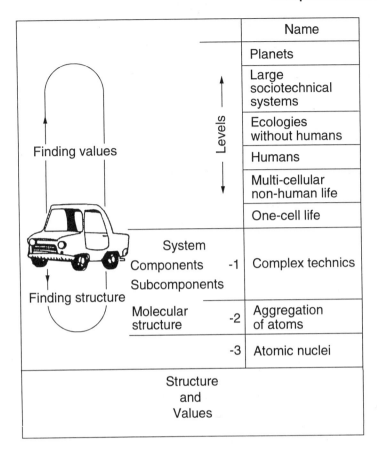

The figure contains the following labels:

	Name
	Planets
	Large sociotechnical systems
	Ecologies without humans
	Humans
	Multi-cellular non-human life
	One-cell life

Finding values

Levels

Finding structure

System Components Subcomponents	-1	Complex technics
Molecular structure	-2	Aggregation of atoms
	-3	Atomic nuclei

Structure
and
Values

Figure 11-2. The Two Loops of the Human Design Process: A Synthetic, Iterative Process and the Relations to Structure and to Values.

nothing about buyer preferences or cost targets. Nor do cultural values tell us anything about what structure will create the functions we desire from an automobile; the structural information must come from accumulated human design experiences with autos. Again we see that the barrier beyond which neither a reductionist nor a synoptic approach alone can pass is the interface where the use of human information becomes necessary.

There are some exceptions to the idea that values lie in higher levels. Most of these involve instances of designing a system to investigate some field of science, such as a particle collider for physics. We do not need the details; we note only that in any case we must iterate the human design process until all necessary criteria are met at all the levels of structure relevant to the system.

Another way to see this point is to consider the distinction between analysis on the one hand and human design on the other. Design requires ideas, often new ideas that originate within a human brain. As part of carrying out the design, we may do a number of analyses on components and criteria that link components. These analyses may be very sophisticated; they may use the most up-to-date science and computer capacities, but they are not the design. The analyses are verifications that parts of the design will do what we want. And what we want comes from human minds.

The two most important advances in the safety of automobiles in recent years are probably automatic braking systems (ABS, in the car ads) and air bags. We could have made such automatic braking systems decades ago, perhaps not as well or as cheaply, but we could have made them. We did not make them until an automobile designer thought up the idea and convinced the company he or she worked for to invest time and money in the design and development of this type of brakes. The same remarks apply to air bags. We could have made them decades ago, but did not until consumer groups and the government began to push safety standards for automobiles.

Conclusions for Chapter 11

When disciplines as formulated are cuts through a hyperspace of larger dimensions, it is critical that we bear in mind both the primacy of data and the need to examine results from all relevant disciplines. Appropriate solutions arise only when we satisfy all criteria for all the levels and disciplines that bear on a given problem or design.

Human design process, whether applied to hardware, systems, institutions, or interpersonal problems, is not mere analysis based on known science, although that may play an important part. Human design process is inherently synthetic, requires the human feedback mode, and often transcends the knowledge of any one discipline.

CHAPTER 12

Consistency as a Primary Criterion

The Limits of Reductionism and Synoptism

The results of Chapters 7 through 10 tell us that although both the reductionist and the synoptic views are important, neither view can tell us, by itself, all we need to know about matters of vital concern to humans. Both are incomplete as views of the world. This is useful information but leaves open several questions. The first of these questions is, *What are the limits of the domain of what we can learn from the reductionist and the synoptic views, respectively?*

To answer this question, we need to erect a taxonomy that includes all the major classes of systems of central concern to humans so that we can see what the reductionist and the synoptic views can each tell us about the various classes. Such a taxonomy is shown in Figure 12-1. It provides a suitable, but somewhat arbitrary, taxonomy of six major classes of systems. This taxonomy is not homogeneous, but contains several differing kinds of systems so that it covers both material systems and concepts. We have a new question and therefore take a new view and a taxonomy different from but not inconsistent with the hierarchy of constitution.

Before we can go farther, we must answer a question about the taxonomy in Figure 12-1, Do the six categories of systems cover all, or at least nearly all, of the matters of vital concern to humans? We can use the taxonomies of social philosophy and the careful taxonomy of Phenix (1964) as a check. This checking suggests that the six classes in Figure 12-1 cover, or nearly cover, all the matters of primary concern to humans, and that is all we need for this discussion. I hope you will check this against other lists and/or with your own experiences. If you find serious omissions, I would appreciate comments with specifics on what is not covered.

1. **Inert, Naturally-Occurring:**

Rocks, air, oceans, weather, atoms, molecules, ...

2. **Artifactual:**

Tools, machines, structures, synthetic materials,
sociotechnical systems

3. **Biological:**

Organisms, ecologies

4. **Human Systems:**

Social, political, economic, aesthetic, affectional

5. **Values**

6. **Communications**

Figure 12-1. Six Major Classes of Systems of Human Concern.

We are now ready to look at what each of the reductionist and the synoptic views can do. We will consider the reductionist view first.

The results we found earlier show that we cannot find everything we need by mere aggregation from the bottom up, that is, via the reductionist program, for four of the six classes of systems in Figure 7-1: communication systems; living systems; artifactual systems; human systems. This result follows from each of three independent reasons: first, important systems in all these classes have hierarchical structure and interfaces of mutual constraint; second, important systems in these four classes use integrated control information; and third, the dimensions in various levels of the four classes of systems are typically at least in part exogenous to each other and to the dimensions of particle or classical physics. Still a fourth reason exists, but it is suggestive rather than a formal demonstration. Human social and sociotechnical systems have feedback modes that do not exist in inert, naturally-occurring systems, and thus it is hard to see how any equations, or principles, that are appropriate sysreps for inert, naturally-occurring systems can by themselves properly model complete human social or sociotechnical systems.

Moreover, the bottom-up views, beginning from particles, tell us essentially nothing about a fifth class shown in Figure 12-1, values. This follows from the fact that assertions about "particles" have the character of "izzes." They say that physical nature behaves as it does; the processes are not altered by what humans desire or see as "good." Recall that we cannot get "oughts" from "izzes."

The only remaining class in Figure 7-1 is **systems** of inert, naturally-occurring objects. This ought not be a surprise; this is the class of systems that the principles and equations of the physical sciences were created to describe. And as we have seen, principles are general only in the sense that they are general remarks about particular classes of systems; we seem to have no universal principles that are adequate for all systems. Does this imply that the physical sciences tell us nothing about other classes of systems? No! Physics tells us quite a lot about nearly every level in the hierarchy of constitution. Indeed, physics seems to be the only discipline that has something, nearly always something important, to say about every level in the hierarchy of constitution. Physics just doesn't tell us all the important things we need to know except in the domain of physics itself.

Let us look more closely at the class of **systems** physics does describe completely. What we can do via the reductionist view within the class of systems physics has been created to describe? Suppose we take as the **system** a very large ball made of pure iron crystal or some water at room temperature and pressure. Either system will be homogeneous at all levels above that of atoms. In homogeneous systems there is no difficulty in finding properties by aggregation (mathematical integration) upward from the atomic level. Since every part of the system is a perfect model for every other part, all we have to do is understand one part, and then multiply the result throughout the whole system. But such systems are dull; they don't and can't do much. They seem to have few if any properties that we call emergent (or holistic). As we noted earlier, emergent properties are characteristics the whole system can exhibit which cannot be carried out by the pieces of the system in unassembled form. As we make a homogeneous system bigger nothing new happens unless the weight and pressure generated change the properties within the material or in the support structure beneath the system.

Thus it seems that we normally need heterogeneous systems if we are to see emergent properties. It appears that we need different kinds of parts in a system if we want the system to create more complex behaviors than the parts, each by itself, can exhibit. Living systems exhibit this heterogeneity over and over. Heterogeneity seems necessary for living systems. I have no proof for this idea about the need for heterogeneity to support life, but it seems right. There seem to be no data that disconfirm the idea.

Since there seems to be no theoretical bar for the reductionist program in the paradigmatic systems the physical sciences study, it is therefore not surprising that the prevailing view in the physical sciences seems to be reductionist. Thus a common belief in these fields seems to be not only that piecewise views are the most important but also that piecewise views are sufficient for all problems of human concern, at least in principle. Unfortunately, this is not so.

What, then, about top-down views and the synoptic program? What can we find from such views, and what can we not find? The situation is analogous to that of the reductionist view. Specifically, top-down views are necessary and sometimes sufficient for describing value systems, class 5 in the taxonomy of Figure 12-1. That is, synoptic views are relevant and appropriate for the class of systems they are intended to study or discuss. I say "sometimes sufficient" because the behaviors of humans are not invariant and are far more complex than the behaviors of the simple systems described by the physical sciences. As a result of this complexity, we have no easy way to check if a value system is complete, sufficient for all human purposes, or more desirable than another value system.

If we have hierarchical structure and levels of mutual constraint in a given system we cannot find lower levels from higher levels, as we have seen. Values do not determine the information contained in the skills (integrated control information) that each human possesses. Values do not have the same dimensions as those in the other classes of systems. And finally, some values are situational and hence not "derivable" from a set of fixed rules, as Whitbeck (1992) has pointed out. They require human design processes.

Thus, synoptic views tell us about values and about goals, the matters they study directly. Synoptic views cannot tell us the details of structure; the way inert, naturally-occurring systems behave; or all we need to know about communications systems, human social systems, or sociotechnical systems. Does this mean synoptic views have nothing to say about these systems? Not at all. Synoptic views are necessary to determine human goals and to design systems that we want in order to reach those goals and thus have something to say about many levels. Synoptic views are necessary to create an ethic for a viable future of humans and the planet Earth. They have a lot to say about four of the five other classes of systems besides values; they just don't tell us all we need to know about these other four classes.

Finally, synoptic views and values tell us essentially nothing about physical nature, naturally-occurring inert objects. These objects do what they do without regard for human values or desires. We might wish the tennis ball in the second-floor tennis-ball test would jump, spontaneously, back up to our hand so we would not have to fetch it, but our wishes won't make it happen.

Thus each of the radical synoptic and radical reductionist views gives us all or most of the information about the class of systems for which it is set up. Each tells us significant information about four other classes of systems in Figure 12-1. And, finally, neither tells us much if anything about the other.

Given this information, we can see not only that neither the reductionist nor the synoptic program is sufficient to study all problems of human concern but also that together they are insufficient, because we need still other information in order to study classes 2 through 5 in Figure 12-1. This is also evident from Hypothesis V, which states the need for structural views in addition to synoptic and piecewise views in order to understand many complex systems.

We are now ready to address a second residual question, What process will allow us to study all the questions of vital concern to humans? The answer to that question has already been suggested by the discussion of the human design process (Chapter 11).

When we are dealing with systems that involve more than one level in the hierarchy of constitution, or with systems that have within themselves hierarchical structure and interfaces of mutual constraint, we need to examine each level to find what we need at that level. In our automobile design example, we had to look at lower levels to find structure and at higher levels to find values. Moreover, we had to look at each level separately to understand the principles and constraints within each level.

As we have seen, there are some levels, mostly in inert objects, where more than one level follows the same principles. Nevertheless, dimensions, variables, parameters, behaviors, principles, and even the qualitative nature of principles can and commonly do change from level to level. When we look at the levels within the hierarchy of constitution one by one, we find that variations in the variables, the parameters, the dimensions, and the characteristic behaviors of systems from one level to another seem to be the common case, not the rare one. In many instances the feedback modes that systems can access and even the nature of the "rules" also vary between levels. Therefore, to be sure we can obtain all the information we need, we must start with the assumption that it is necessary to examine the dimensions, variables, parameters, behaviors, and principles at each level empirically. It is only in this way that we can study all the matters of vital concern to humans and place them on solid empirical foundations. The normal tenets of both science and ethics demand no less. Let us state this idea as a hypothesis.

Hypothesis VI: *Empiricism in Hierarchical Structure.* In order to provide an adequate empirical base, we must make observations at all levels of concern for the class of systems under study.

Hypothesis VI is not a single view; it is, rather, a process that will usually involve using several distinct views. Hypothesis VI demands that we adopt what we have been calling a multidisciplinary position. An illustration will help clarify the reasons why this is so.

Let us take as our **system** a medieval castle, more specifically the castle at Windsor. Our problem is to understand this castle and the lives that go on within it. Fortifications at the Windsor site go back some time in British history. The castle, in more or less its present outline, was built by William the Conqueror and thus dates from the late eleventh century. Suppose we consider the castle and the lives in it at 1100 A.D.

The castle wall winds along a curving ridge for a bit over 600 yards. Hence we cannot see its shape from any one point on the ground. We need to view the castle from several perspectives to understand its physical layout. No one earthbound view will do for even that simple purpose. But moving our view around in space is not enough to understand the physical structure of the castle. To understand the structure of the castle, we need to look at the foundation rocks, the materials of the walls and buildings, and how they were joined together. We have to move down in level of size. It is as if we used a zoom lens to move from a wide view to a narrow and magnified view in order to understand the physical structure. This is changing the view along a different dimension from the geographic. Beyond that, we would need to examine how the rooms related to each other and the purposes for which the rooms were used. To comprehend the room layout, we need an aerial view. To comprehend the uses of the rooms, we also need to understand the social structure, values, and communication systems of the people who lived in the castle in 1100 A.D. For that, we need a good bit of history both civil and military and also an understanding of the class structure of the times (sociology and political science). We would also need to understand the available technology in 1100 A.D. in Britain. This implies moving in still other dimensions. We need not prolong this example. The point is obvious. To understand a sociotechnical system such as Windsor Castle and its inhabitants requires many views along a number of dimensions. In short, the total characteristics of Windsor Castle form a hyperspace of high dimensionality. We need only add that compared to, say, Boeing, Fiat, Matsushita, or the international shipping industry, Windsor Castle at 1100 A.D. is a relatively simple sociotechnical system.

Let's now look at another question, What does Hypothesis VI tell us about the appropriate relations among the different levels in the hierarchy of constitution and in systems with hierarchical structure and interfaces of mutual constraint?

When we find a given behavior of a system from lower levels L (or higher levels U) and also by direct observation within a given level, then there is a logical demand that the two sets of results be consistent, that the results not contradict each other. However, there is no demand that results at either level be derived from the other. If we can derive one from the other, as we can in a few cases, that is certainly desirable, but it is not necessary in order to understand our world. It is only necessary that the results we find from varying sources be consistent with each other, a much less stringent condition.

Two circumstances can arise when we check to see if results from various levels are consistent for a given class of **system** which includes several levels in a hierarchy. This applies both to levels in the hierarchy of constitution and to levels in a single system with hierarchical structure. (1) If the results are consistent, there is no problem; we have merely cross-verified our answers, at least in part. We have thereby put our solutions on a solider basis. And (2) if the results found from two (or more) levels are not consistent, then we need to seek the source of the error.

Moreover, in the second case, we must not argue that either level determines (or governs or has priority over) the other level for any system in which there is hierarchical structure with interfaces of mutual constraint; or in which there are control levels for feedback functions that contain historically accumulated, integrated control information; or in which the levels contain some dimensions which are exogenous to each other. Moreover, at least one of these three conditions is very common in many important systems, and any one of the three is enough to prevent one level from determining the other.

This result carries an implicit requirement for multidisciplinary discourse about many problems. This in turn implies that workers in various disciplines need to talk with each other seriously, and not merely cede each other territory. As the remark by Gene Bouchard in Chapter 1 reminds us, for good interdisciplinary problem solution, we often need interpenetration of ideas from several disciplines. The previous paragraph also tells us if we study a given problem at the wrong level of aggregation, we will probably find misleading or even erroneous answers. This is not a new idea, but it seems to have lacked a basis other than experience in the past.

Thus far I have been able to identify five sources of possible errors that need to be checked when conflicts in results are found from two different hierarchical levels, U and L. These are (1) error in the principles or their application at level U; (2) error in the principles or their application at level L; (3) error in the transformation processes carrying results from level L to U or conversely; (4) unrecognized double definitions of single terms arising from different use of words in the different communities of scholars working at the different levels; (5) an assumption that the systems analyzed are the same when they are at least in part different at the two levels concerned. There may be others.

In cases in which the principles are well established, we particularly need to seek the errors in the last three sources, and this often has not been done. Since we have done much more work on the principles for given levels and fields of study than on the relations between them, the difficulties are more likely to lie in items 3, 4, and 5 rather than in the principles themselves. This focus has already been productive in several instances in which it has been tried. Some examples appear farther along in this book. A good example outside this book is the formation of what are now called "the cognitive sciences." In cognitive sciences, researchers draw on six formerly nearly independent fields in order to unify theory and data about one problem: the nature of the human brain. The six disciplines are psychology, ethnology, neurosciences, computer sciences, philosophy, and linguistics. These disciplines each concentrated on a different aspect of the problem in the past, involving both different levels of aggregation and differing aspects of the mind, and apparently as a result, some of the answers generated were oversimple. We have seen one oversimple answer, radical behaviorism (Chapter 6). For a history of cognitive science, see Gardner (1987). Since the human brain constitutes one class of systems, we ought not have six inconsistent pictures of it, since at least five of the pictures must be in partial error.

These ideas are of sufficient importance that they seem to warrant being embodied in an additional hypothesis. This can be stated in many ways; one follows.

Hypothesis VII: *The Principle of Consistency.* In systems with hierarchical structure and levels that mutually constrain one another, solutions must satisfy the principles and the data in all the relevant levels and fields of knowledge. The same is true for systems studied by more than one field when the dimensions of the various fields are exogenous to each other.

Hypothesis VII implies that a complete solution must include all the relevant dimensions in some way. This follows from the fact that a sysrep that omits variables of the complete hyperspace cannot fully examine the hyperspace of the system behaviors. Since it cannot fully examine the hyperspace, the solutions obtained from the sysrep are very unlikely to be complete. At best, they will be answers for some problems, but not others. At worst, the answers can be simplistic and/or misleading for all problems in the hyperspace.

Hypothesis VII, Corollary A. When solutions from more than one level in a hierarchical structure with interfaces of mutual constraint provide results for a given behavior in the same system, then the results must be consistent where they overlap. If the results are not consistent, then we must seek the source of error, and not argue that one level or one discipline governs (or has priority over) the other. The same remark applies when two disciplines give overlapping results and have some primary dimensions exogenous to each other.

We can elaborate these results more completely by looking at three cases.

First, systems with hierarchical structure and one or both of interfaces of mutual constraint between adjacent layers and use of integrated control information in feedback control loops. In this case, we cannot derive the complete principles or behavior of an upper level U from lower levels L, nor conversely.

Second, there is more than one relevant discipline of knowledge, and a discipline (D) involves some primary dimensions exogenous to the other disciplines. In this case, we cannot derive all of the behaviors or principles of discipline (D) from the other discipline(s).

Third, there is a hierarchical structure in the system, but no interfaces of mutual constraint and no use of integrated control information in feedback control loops. And, in addition, the same primary dimensions describe the behaviors at all levels. In this case, there is no known bar to derivation of behaviors and principles of upper levels U from lower levels L, nor conversely. However, this case occurs primarily in systems of inert, naturally-occurring objects — the domain of the physical sciences. It is not typical of biological, human, or artifactual systems nor of systems of concepts, communications, or values. Moreover, even within systems of inert, naturally-occurring objects it does not seem practical to try to solve all problems beginning from one level in many cases.

Before we end this chapter, it will be useful to look at one more question. Suppose we take a principle derived for one level in the hierarchy of constitution and transpose it to and use it blindly at another level. The word "blindly" in the previous sentence denotes "without checking the data base in the system to which the principle is transposed." Can this blind transposition create errors? Yes! It can and has. We will look next at two examples of a blind transposition of principles from one level to another that had unfortunate consequences both conceptual and behavioral.

These two examples are positivist philosophy and social Darwinism. Both had important impacts for decades. Both are now known as important scholarly aberrations.

Positivist philosophy is the idea that all of philosophy can be reduced to logical "rules," like those of Newtonian physics, and ultimately put into mathematical form. There were two schools of thought that pursued positivist ideas in philosophy, one in the United States in the early part of the twentieth century and the other in Vienna during the 1920's and 1930's. Positivist philosophy led to much simplistic dead-end work. It was not wrong, but it was seriously incomplete for reasons that are evident both in our discussions of the capacity of various systems for feedback modes that include self-reference (see Figure 6-1) and also in the more complete demonstrations in Chapters 8 through 10. Gödel's theorem rang the death knell on the idea that a positivist approach could supply a complete philosophy. And Gödel's theorem is closely related to complexity of the human design mode, since it centers on questions of self-reference. By 1990, most philosophers saw positivism as inadequate to be the basis for a complete philosophy.

However, in earlier decades, the ideas of positivist philosophy were sources of motivation for the researchers who pushed radical behaviorism, as those researchers stated. Thus an oversimple philosophy played a role in the difficulties arising from radical behaviorism. The ideas of positivist philosophy also reinforced bottom-up reductionist views in the physical sciences and endorsed them as worldviews. These reductionist ideas are seriously oversimple. In later chapters, we will see still further difficulties from this source.

Social Darwinism is the idea that survival of the fittest is a "rule" in human social intercourse. This "rule" denies the role of cooperation in families, institutions, and politics, where cooperation is often critical. Social Darwinism was used by Western employers in the early twentieth century to justify inhumane treatment of workers, thus rationalizing these abuses of power on the basis of inadequate scholarship. The details pass beyond what we need, but are well documented; see, for example, Gould (1981).

An able historian of technology who read a draft of this work, W. G. Vincenti, suggested that the idea of social Darwinism had still other evil consequences. Specifically, Vincenti suggested that some historians see the idea of social Darwinism as part of the roots of World War I. The leaders of some European nations apparently came to see survival of the fittest as a social imperative, and that they had to conquer and subjugate other peoples, those who are "less fit than we." Finally, some versions of social Darwinism incorporate an erroneous version of Darwin's ideas.

The two preceding paragraphs are not intended to suggest that competition is never desirable. Vibrant competition in the market is a key to economic productivity and rapid innovations; see, for example, Porter (1990). The point is, rather, that we need competition and cooperation in appropriate places. Our problem is to decide which is appropriate for given situations.

These two examples illustrate two of the ways through which difficulties have been created owing to the lack of a multidisciplinary discourse over the past several centuries. How did this occur? In positivist philosophy we see the transposition of methodology from systems where it is appropriate to systems where it is not appropriate. The results are not wrong; they are seriously incomplete. In social Darwinism we see the application of a principle for behavior correct in a few levels of the hierarchy of constitution (2, 3, 4, 5) to another level (human social systems) where it does not properly apply, where the principle is not only flawed but also led to pernicious results. These two examples by no means exhaust the list of significant difficulties created by blind transpositions of methods or "rules" from one level to another or from one class of systems to another. Some of these errors arising from blind transposition are now recognized, but others apparently are not. Some remain as erroneous views, often as overclaims, arising from specific disciplines. The sources of these difficulties have strong historical roots. For this reason, we will postpone more complete discussion of these difficulties until after we have looked at a brief history of the disciplines of knowledge.

Have difficulties arisen in the physical sciences and technology from lack of understanding that the proper criterion is consistency (not derivation)? Yes! A considerable number still exist. The difficulties are not well known and need some background we do not yet have, but we will come to some of them. In Chapter 14, we will see an example concerning innovation. A second example occurs in Chapter 16, in the discussion of the suggestions that quantum mechanics can be used as the basis for a worldview. A third is discussed in Appendix B, in the bet for physicists.

Are there examples where the criterion of consistency has been used with good results? Indeed there are. One example is the three different data methods (stratigraphic, magnetic, and fossils) used in geology. Another is the data methods used in paleoanthropology. Both these examples lie within a discipline and hence within a single area of discourse. Because we have lacked a multidisciplinary discourse, examples across fields are hard to find. One emerging example appears to be cognitive science, which has created a discourse about how the mind works from six formerly separate fields. Design of complex hardware usually demands consistency if the hardware is to function. There are many examples here, but they also lie in one professional discipline. References to success in using the criterion of consistency across two or more disciplines will be appreciated.

Figure 12-2 shows a caricature of the overclaiming disciplinary expert.

The fact that we must study each layer in the hierarchy of constitution in order to provide an adequate empirical basis for human knowledge leads to one more result. When we look at all the levels in the hierarchy of constitution, we see that some levels are at about human size and can be studied directly by the human senses while other levels are remote in size or cannot be studied by direct use of

View of the Insider

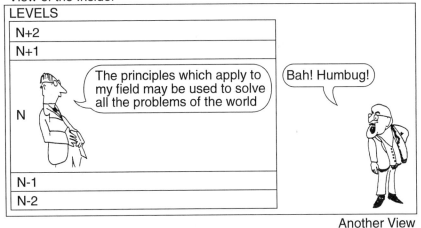

Another View

Figure 12-2. The View of the Insider (levels refer to hierarchy of constitution).

human senses. This leads to what we will call the "Guideline of Hierarchical Obscurity."

Guideline of Hierarchical Obscurity

The farther systems are from direct human observation in size, in speed, and/or in time, the more our observations become instrumentally bound and theoretically modulated, and the more difficult understanding the systems tend to be.

The phrase "instrumentally bound" denotes that we must use instruments to observe the phenomena, and this implies some degree of separation between the phenomena and what we can sense. The phrase "theoretically modulated" denotes that we must use theory in order even to plan experiments, since we cannot sense the phenomena directly.

It is not hard to see why the Guideline of Hierarchical Obscurity is usually correct. For objects and events of about human size and in present time, our senses can directly tell us a good deal about how they work. Thus a skilled mechanic will often come to have many of the basic ideas of theoretical mechanics inculcated by learning experiences and through disasters on the job, even though formal training is lacking. We all understand some of the basics of human communication from our uses of it. Instruments, lab tests, and theories deepen our understanding of such matters, but we always have recourse to direct observation, to check what the theories and instruments tell us. Given these direct checks, we are less apt to become "ungrounded" and to wander far off the track, and we are more apt to learn rapidly. For example, we find detailed pictures of fluid motions in Leonardo's sketchbook, though almost no instruments for measuring fluid motions were available in Leonardo's time. On the other hand, objects or events that are smaller than the eye can see are much harder to learn about. So are objects of very great size, such as galaxies beyond our own. Thus for the very small or the very large we must depend on instruments entirely, and our design and use of those instruments is essentially theory bound.

Similar remarks apply to events from the distant past (evolution of species) and to events that propagate at speeds too high for the eye to follow in detail (light). Events that occur in very small times also require use of instruments and lie outside learning by direct observation.

We can see this idea in another way by thinking about a few things earlier peoples could not comprehend. For example, there was no way for humans to know that micro-organisms are the sources of many human diseases, until microscopes of adequate quality became available in the nineteenth century. Nor was it possible to know of the existence of electromagnetic phenomena outside the frequency range of visible light, such as radio and TV broadcast signals. Ancient societies did not understand evolution, and even in the twentieth century we struggle to create an accurate picture of human biological evolution because so few remains of our biological ancestors have been found. These are only a few examples out of many.

For all these reasons, our ability to understand and interpret is different for different classes of systems. Thus it is not surprising that many matters that are common knowledge today were not understood by earlier peoples. We do not need to prolong discussion of this point. We only need to record it so we will have it available when we come to the discussion of the evolution of the disciplines over time and to quantum mechanics and its relationship with the philosophy of science.

It has been suggested by some people in the late twentieth century that all science has become theory bound, but this is a partial truth. It is an assertion that applies far more to some domains than to others. Many domains are accessible to scientists by direct human sensing, and when that is true we usually rely on direct sensing not only to study new problems but also to make sure we do not drift off course in our theories. Examples of fields that utilize direct observation include systematic biology, stratigraphic data in geology, and the motions of bodies we describe in classical mechanics.

Conclusions for Chapter 12

The central message of this chapter is: For many problems, a multidisciplinary position is mandatory. We have seen this result several times before. However, the materials of this chapter put this message on even firmer and more detailed bases. Moreover, what we have seen in Chapters 7 through 12 seems consistent with what we found in earlier chapters on a number of matters, including (1) the relation between sysreps and domains; (2) some systems are too complex for us to obtain solutions for the entire systems; (3) the boundary where both the reductionist and the synoptic programs are blocked is the interface at which human information, human choices, and/or human design processes begin to play a significant role in the problem of concern; (4) synoptic views cannot disclose the information we need about structure.

CHAPTER 13

Operational Procedures in Forming Sysreps for Complex Systems

The preceding chapters leave us with an important question. Does a multi-disciplinary position provide us with useful operational procedures for forming sysreps for very complex systems, particularly systems with hierarchical structure and interfaces of mutual constraint? The answer is emphatically affirmative. More specifically, when we combine what we have learned thus far, we can create a very useful agenda of questions for testing the validity of sysreps. I will call this combination of the relevant materials from Chapters 2 through 12 the "system/sysrep apparatus." Let's look first at what we can learn from applying the complexity index and the ideas about hyperspaces and dimensions to test for validity of sysreps. What questions does the system/sysrep apparatus suggest about the validity of "models" of the real world? At least four acute questions emerge:

- Do the dimensions of the sysrep match the dimensions of the system?
- Do the levels of feedback in the sysrep match the observed levels in the system?
- If there are interfaces of mutual constraint in the system, does the sysrep account for open degrees of freedom and the location of levels of control?
- Does the system require use of human integrated control information? If so, does the sysrep incorporate the need for this information and how it is to be learned and formed into well-assimilated schemata by the relevant workers?

Let's look briefly at the impact of each of these questions as they affect the foundations of disciplines.

Suppose we are studying problems that concern behavior in a sociotechnical system. Six human sciences (history, ethnology, sociology, psychology, economics, and political science) all deal with such systems in many of the problems they address. We have seen that sociotechnical systems are systems with many dimensions and usually contain significant open degrees of freedom.

If we create sysreps for sociotechnical systems which use only a few variables, we must then expect them to be less than fully adequate. Using only a few variables may capture some of the behaviors, but cannot explore the complete hyperspace and thus not all of the behaviors. A critical question will remain: How much of the variance can the constricted list of variables capture? This is the reason why correlation coefficients tend to be lower in value in the human than in the physical sciences.

If we make deterministic sysreps for sociotechnical systems we must expect not to be able to explain many things that occur over time, since the "rules" change.

How do these ideas affect various disciplines?

History and broader forms of ethnology have tended to discuss sociotechnical systems as wholes either by looking at specific time frames or by examining whole cultures. As a result, the scholarship in these fields has for the most part remained verbal rather than mathematical, and severely restricted "cuts" are less common than in some other fields. Some attempts to provide reductionist and deterministic theories in these fields have occurred — for example, techno-economic determinism in both ethnology and history. Deterministic causation based on the kinship system was also tried in ethnology. However, when these ideas were tested against a wide range of data, they have been seen to be inadequate. This is what we must expect to find, since there remain open degrees of freedom for human cultural choices in sociotechnical systems.

In psychology, as we have seen, radical behaviorism, a form of positivist psychology, provides some but not all of the ideas needed for understanding the human psyche because the feedback mode assumed did not match that of the real systems (humans). This is again what the system/sysrep apparatus suggests we should find.

Because of the problems they study, sociology, political science, and economics are particularly likely to encounter the difficulties that arise from using an overconstricted list of variables and omitting sufficiently complex feedback modes. In these fields, theories must nearly always be cuts through a hyperspace of higher dimensionality because we cannot understand nor model completely the full hyperspace if we use the viewpoints of these disciplines. It then seems to follow that we need to take more care than has sometimes been the case in two regards for these fields. First, we must view with caution predictions based on cuts through the hyperspace, and we must be sure that we do not claim that such theories override data, even secure barefoot data about the real-world systems. Second, we must accumulate data about the real systems and use them in an ongoing human-design feedback mode as the primary means for erecting, guiding, and improving sociotechnical systems. Theories based on severely constricted cuts through the hyperspace if used as the sole means of guidance are almost certain to mislead us, probably in important ways. Examples of where this has occurred are not difficult to find.

A field in which the role of human integrated control information needs particular attention is management. Models (sysreps) of management that suggest that any individual can manage any enterprise, if he or she is trained in management, neglect the need for understanding the schemata necessary to comprehend the implications of decisions. Neglect of the need for individuals within the organization to learn thoroughly the requisite integrated control information, both mental and neuromuscular, is also likely to create difficulties in the long run.

The short discussion of the questions that arise from the system/sysrep apparatus as it applies to disciplines only skims the surface and provides only a few examples. Nevertheless, this kind of discussion seems sufficient to point to the kind of questions that need to be asked about assumptions underlying various disciplines.

Questions of this type are only a first step for multidisciplinary discourse. Much further discussion of the system/sysrep apparatus as it applies to disciplines is needed. Indeed, in my own view, the application of the systems/sysrep apparatus to the model underlying disciplines is probably the least developed topic in this book. For some of the reasons why I believe this, see Appendix A.

Let us turn, then, to questions that arise from knowledge about hierarchical systems with interfaces of mutual constraint, since it is for these systems that the greatest confusions about reductionism and synoptism have occurred. There seem to be at least three essential questions one needs to ask about a hierarchical system with interfaces of mutual constraint which utilizes feedback controls and integrated control information:

1. How many levels are there in the system structure?

2. How many total degrees of freedom are there on each level?

3. Of these total degrees of freedom, on each level, how many are constrained by the levels below and the levels above in the **system** of concern? Or, to put this the other way around, how many degrees of freedom are left open for independent actions, thoughts, choices, and/or design options in a given level?

These three questions are minimum essentials for proper study of hierarchical systems with interfaces of mutual constraint; moreover, they are already sufficient to increase understanding in some ancient unresolved questions. We have often failed to ask these questions, instead attempting to derive results from an overnarrow basis or from one or another single discipline. This has led to many errors. (See examples in Chapter 17.)

In many cases it is also important to ask further questions about the nature of the "controls" in the system:

4. Which are the levels of control?
5. Are feedback loops autonomic, or do they involve human-control or human-design feedback modes?
6. Do the controls at higher levels have "jumpers" directly to lower levels?

The word "jumpers" denotes that control circuitry connects directly not to adjacent levels in the structure but to levels farther away. For a biological example of "jumpers," see van Essen, Anderson, and Fellemon (1992) on the structure of the primate eye. At the Hewlett Packard Corporation, they call jumpers in management processes "management by walking around." The top managers interact directly with employees at all levels, and do not restrict communications to individuals at the next lower level in the corporate hierarchy.

Questions 1 through 6 above are only a starter set for thinking about sysreps for hierarchical systems. Study of more examples is needed before the questions should be taken as an adequate basis. Nevertheless, they are enough to deal with some problems of importance which cannot be treated from single disciplines. We will look at three illustrations.

First, let's look at the question, How does one find structure and values for a hierarchical system with dual-level control and integrated control information? One looks at the lower levels of hierarchy within the system and also the higher levels in which the system is embedded. One finds structure by a downward loop from the level of the system to as low a level as needed for the question in hand, and then a return to the system level. One finds values by a loop, usually upward from the level where the system exists to the levels of use in the world and back again. This is precisely what we found in looking at the human design process for an automobile (and other artifacts) in Chapter 11. All I am adding here is that the process is general. The need for the two loops delineates clearly why "design" is an inherently different process from "analysis."

A moment's reflection about Figure 11-2 ought to tell us that we do not want to understand and take into account structure or values; rather, we *need* to understand and take into account structure and values. As Figure 11-2 shows, we need to use both the downward and the upward loops in the hierarchy of constitution. This applies not only to hardware but also to classes of systems studied by disciplines.

In short, not only is the multidisciplinary position practical. For many problems, it is necessary and therefore, in a sense, the only "practical" position.

In earlier chapters we found, from several different views, that there are open degrees of freedom at some levels in many complex, hierarchically structured systems. Given the operational questions we now have in hand, let's examine some examples of open degrees of freedom.

It will be useful to begin with the ancient question about whether humans have free will. This question has troubled some philosophers and many others for at least two millennia, and it remains subject to dispute. Let me suggest why the dispute has not closed. As posed, the problem asks an "en bloc" question about a hierarchical system. The question implicitly assumes that there is one answer that is the same at all the levels in the system. But this assumption is false; it implies a condition contrary to empirical observations. As a result of this false implicit assumption, the question as posed has no answer.

A simpler example may help us see the trouble more clearly. Suppose we ask, What is the temperature of an automobile? We know that inside a cylinder in the engine the temperature may be 3,000°F, in the front seat it may be 70°F, and on the outside surface of the car in cold winter weather it may be −40°F. There is no proper response because the question overconstrains the answer; there is no one temperature; the temperature is different in the different parts and at different levels of aggregation within an automobile system.

The classic formulation of the question of free will has a similar character. It assumes that the open degrees of freedom are the same in all levels of the hierarchical structure of the world and of humans, and that assumption is untrue. As we have seen, again and again, hierarchical structures with interfaces of mutual constraint typically have different variables and different open degrees of freedom in both number and kind in the different levels. Consequently, "en bloc" questions about such systems overconstrain the answer and therefore have no proper responses. Questions posed in this way tend to seduce us into generating two or more non-answers and quarreling over which is "right." This non-closing, endless dispute is just what seems to have occurred for two millennia regarding human free will.

Let us now pose the problem of free will differently. We ask questions 1, 2, and 3 listed above:

1. How many levels of structure exist in a human being?

Answer: Five physical levels and at least three levels of control in the brain. (We do not understand the brain well yet, but are rapidly learning more about its structure and functioning. Five levels of control is probably more accurate than three, but the situation is complicated, since the brain apparently has parallel as well as vertically arranged structure. See, for example, Dennett [1991] or Ornstein and Thompson [1984]. To make matters simple, let's take the lowest estimate of the number of levels in the brain, three, for discussion.)

2. How many degrees of freedom are there on each level?

Answer: So many we cannot count them on some levels (at least no one seems to have done so). The human body has hundreds of degrees of freedom in mechanical motions alone. You might ask yourself about the degrees of mechanical freedom in the human hand. I think you will find them hard to count. The human body has more than one thousand chemical feedback loops, according to some physicians I have asked. Some of the feedback loops are autonomic and "mind" the body. These automatic loops control digestion, keep our breathing going while we sleep, and so on. Others are operated by human-control feedback modes; we make choices. We can choose to hit at a baseball pitched toward us, or let it pass. We choose where and when we plan to walk and drive, and so on. The brain has a hundred billion or more neurons and a thousand or so possible connections from each of these to other nearby neurons. Moreover, since the brain "minds" the body, we must be careful where the control levels lie.

3. How many of these degrees of freedom in a human being are constrained from lower levels by the laws of physics, chemistry, and biology?

Answer: Of the total degrees of freedom in the human brain, only a handful are constrained by physics; a larger number is constrained by chemistry and biology. However, not nearly all of the total degrees of freedom are constrained by physics and biology, even taken together, either in the brain or in the muscle tissue. If they were, all humans would think and act alike — a condition grossly contradicted by our experiences almost every day. We cannot yet spell out all the constraints, but here also we are learning rapidly.

The lack of total determination of brain and muscle in the human individual is evident from numerous familiar barefoot data of the world. We can see open degrees of freedom that allow choices nearly wherever we look at the world about us. Let us look at a variety of examples sufficient to make the point redundantly clear because the question of human choices has been so long debated and is so important to our own future.

We create and alter cultures, languages, and, at a slower rate, values and religions. As we saw in Chapter 6, in human social and sociotechnical systems we alter behaviors over time so much that to a significant degree we make up the "rules" as we go along.

The rule across cultural systems is not invariance, but unimaginable variation, and many of the variations arise from human choices. The choices are constrained by history and values, by local ecological conditions, and by existing technology, but choices do remain in every documented case. This is indicated by the facts that all cultures studied change over time, and there are 2,000–3,000 cultures that seem to have evolved from a single small tribe. After tribes separated from each other, they made differing cultural choices even with regard to basic life-styles. They created different social forms and innovated different forms of hardware and systems. They created different forms of art and music.

In the area of artifacts, we design devices to suit the needs and desires of humans and human institutions. In the late twentieth century we do this almost at will, as discussed, for example, by Kash (1989). Let's look at an example in current societies. Automobile designs reflect the culture of designers and customers. The typical European car is small and corners tightly, reflecting the high price of gasoline and the ancient, hence often narrow, twisting roads. U.S. cars are typically larger and ride more softly, reflecting the vast distances and easy curves on U.S. freeways. A British writer on automotive matters described the Trabant as having a "farting little two-cycle engine which no gentleman would put on a lawn mower." What could describe more succinctly the economic incompetence of the former East German communist state? Many Swedish cars tend to be big and very sturdy, reflecting the hard driving conditions during the winters in Scandinavia. Upscale Italian cars are flashy and "macho" in appearance, representing the stereotypical Italian upper-class male values. Luxury Japanese cars cater to the comfort and ease of the driver and have quiet elegance, corresponding to Japanese cultural and artistic styles.

Are the designs of agricultural machines and trucks — both derivative from the auto industry — determined either by "fashion" in ways similar to cars or by science? No! In these types of hardware, the nature of what we want to do — cut wheat, crate bales, haul heavy or bulky materials, haul dangerous chemicals — must be decided before we can even begin the design process, and styling has little if any influence. Nevertheless, the character of these machines is created by human design choices, and varies from one machine to another.

The situation is similar for design of aircraft. Until we decide whether we are designing a commercial transport, a military fighter, or a light personal aircraft, we cannot even decide how large the plane should be or what kind of engine to use. The design constraints on an aircraft are very tight (if it is to fly); nevertheless, there are choices.

In the domain of art, the subject of a painting, the style in which it is rendered, the size of the canvas, and the materials used are all choices the artist makes. However, we cannot paint with materials that do not yet exist; there are constraints.

In music we have many styles and many instruments for creating music among which the composer can choose. However, we cannot play music with instruments we do not have. And our unaided ears cannot hear tones outside a known range of frequencies. Here also constraints exist. We may move these constraints by building new instruments and transducing frequencies to audible ranges, but the constraints are not likely to entirely disappear.

In the area of politics, we can choose a communistic bureaucratic state, a democracy, or a constitutional monarchy. These are collective human choices.

In economics we can choose a free market with some regulations or a partially state-run economy like that of Japan. Many countries have tried hierarchical economies under communism, but that no longer seems a viable modality. It is still a possible choice. We can imagine others.

In sports we can choose to train ourselves to play tennis, golf, soccer, or many other kinds of individual and team sports. Learning any of them well requires a choice to endure a long regimen of practice. However, in none of these sports can we exceed the energy output of the human system. We cannot merely flap our arms and fly downfield in soccer because we cannot in this way generate enough lift. We cannot broadjump 300 feet or run at 100 miles per hour or kick a ball 600 yards. There are constraints.

In science many humans once chose to believe that the earth was flat. Most of us no longer do. The basis for this choice is different from that in art and music. However, it is still a choice; we seem to have still some "flat earth" advocates.

In sum, examples of these kinds of choices are nearly endless. All these kinds of choices and others exist because there are open degrees of freedom at the levels of control in the human brain and also in human muscles. If the structure of the human animal were determined by the laws of physics and biology, choices would not be merely constrained by those laws, none of these kinds of choices would exist. This follows directly from equation (5-6). If there are choices, then the number of constraints is less than the number of total degrees of freedom. Moreover, in no case we know do the artifacts or our actions violate the "laws" of physics. The artifacts are designed within those laws. To put this differently, the laws of physics are constraints on what we can design and what we do, but by no means do they determine the design of our artifacts, our music, our art, or our values. In the same way our actions are constrained but not determined by the principles of biology. Our value systems also constrain our choices but in a "softer" way. Not only do values vary enormously from culture to culture, but also there are nearly always some deviants who do not follow the mainstream values even within a given culture.

Moreover, these choices exist whether or not a God the Creator exists. If we do not believe in a god, then we may, for example, choose to believe in Darwinian-Mendelian evolution as the source of the human species. If we believe in the Judeo-Christian God, we may believe that we were created in seven days by a male deity. If we are Hindu in our religion, we tend to believe a different idea about the origins of humans, and we worship both male and female gods. But in any case, what have been created are humans who have hierarchical structure with interfaces of mutual constraint, and this structure leaves open many degrees of freedom at several levels. We cannot make any possible choice, but within limits we can make a wide variety of choices. If we were created by a Creator, then he/she/it left us choices, and presumably he/she/it will decide on Judgment Day how well we have made those choices.

Thus the questions suggested by multidisciplinarity do not completely settle all questions about free will. However, they do give part of the answer immediately: There are some open degrees of freedom on some levels of the human structure; the higher levels of the environment within which humans live and the lower levels of our structure only constrain, and do not determine, the choices we can make, using our brains and our muscles.

Beyond this preliminary answer, the questions 1, 2, and 3 given above "unpack" the problem of "free will" and thus point the way toward a research agenda that can over time increase our knowledge of the answer. Perhaps even more important, this application of a multidisciplinary position illustrates how to stop trying to answer some kinds of unanswerable questions and quarreling among ourselves about the various non-answers. The illustration also demonstrates the utility of barefoot data in some problems.

The preceding discussion about free will and choices contains still another example of the importance of clarity in our concepts. If we do not have the appropriate concepts for a given problem, we cannot think clearly about it. In this case, we need three concepts: (1) the idea that human structure is hierarchical; (2) Polanyi's ideas about interfaces of mutual constraint; and (3) a clear grasp of the distinction between constraint and determination. We can then see that we ought not blame the ancients for a failure to parse the question of free will; they lacked concepts 1 and 2 entirely, and did not have enough mathematics to make concept 3 clear. This does not excuse those of us living in the late twentieth century for continuing to set the question improperly. All these concepts have been available for at least a generation.

Given the various results reached in earlier chapters, we are now in a position to approach another question that has long troubled Western culture. Perhaps we can provide a suggestion for how it can be handled better than it has been in the past. The question is, Can religion and science coexist peacefully, or must they remain in conflict?

Let's summarize what we have now said several times about worldviews. Synoptic views by themselves, including spiritual views, cannot tell us what we need to know about the fine-grain structure of systems. They do not provide a way to deal with the dimensions that we need in order to understand structure, and in their more deterministic forms synoptic views deny the opportunity for humans to make choices. However, we have just seen that many choices are possible in a wide variety of areas. Moreover, understanding structure is critical in biology, medicine, engineering, chemistry, and many other disciplines. Tibetan Buddhists suggest that the essential values are wisdom and compassion. Many of us favor those virtues. But we cannot understand the physical world from high-level values of this kind. The theory of dimensions (as extended in Chapter 9) tells us this unambiguously. To understand physics, we need to deal with variables such as mass, length, and so on, and neither compassion nor wisdom will lead us to such variables. Or, to put this differently, accepting Tibetan values will not help us much with bacteriology, geology, aerodynamics, or quantum mechanics.

Bottom-up views, like those often believed within the physical sciences, do not allow us to find anything relating to human values or human desires. They tell us nothing about compassion, and they only provide wisdom within the class of inert, naturally-occurring objects, which is far from all the wisdom humans need in either daily life or global affairs. Also science deals with "izzes," and we cannot get "oughts" from "izzes."

Let's look at this issue in terms of what we found in Chapter 12. Even if we use both the reductionist view and the synoptic view together, we cannot find all the knowledge that is critical for humans in four of the six classes shown in

Figure 12-1 (for example, organisms and ecologies; human systems; values that relate to the customs of an ethnic group; and appropriate communications between intimates).

What does this say about the relation of science and religion? It says, in several ways, that religion and science are essentially separate domains that do not intersect each other. They are both needed in many problems, but they say essentially nothing about each other. Indeed, a large open area of systems and problems exists between what each of the two domains tells us. Nor can either domain be derived from the other. Each domain embodies and is expressed in dimensions that are exogenous to the other. We thought that the two domains were in conflict only because some workers in each domain created "overclaims" about what their own special fields could do. Are these overclaims serious? History suggests that the overclaiming from each direction has created significant problems.

The Catholic church threatened to burn Galileo at the stake because he formulated a reductionist view. The decision of the Muslim clergy to override science and technology, from the synoptic view of the Koran, has cost those societies dearly over the past millennium.

Many physical scientists eschew all spiritual values because of this seeming conflict. Many psychotherapists, from Jung onward, have seen that living without spiritual values is at best a "hard way to live." My personal experience strongly supports Jung's view.

Governments run by clergy rarely have decent economies. In fact, I know of no nation or ethnic group that has created a society of abundance when run by the clergy. Nor do I know of an economy that has had a high growth rate under these conditions. Tibet has had a long and valuable spiritual tradition; many consider the Tibetan tradition an important source of spirituality even in the Western world. However, it has never had a society of abundance. Only the industrialized nations with free-market economies have created societies of abundance, thus far in history. The phrase "society of abundance" here denotes that at least 90 percent of the people are above level 2 on the Maslow ladder, in contrast with 10 percent or less who constitute a noble class. For a picture of the Maslow ladder, see Chapter 7. Prior to about 1960, no country that had a strong, dominant Roman Catholic church had created a society of abundance. Moreover, 10 percent is very high for an estimate of affluent people in agricultural societies. The Doomsday Book, the first census of England, was compiled at the order of William the Conqueror after he had ascended the throne. In those records, all the upper class, down to the lowest gentleman and including clergy, constituted far less than 1 percent of the population; most others lived at a bare survival level.

Furthermore, the only states that have been nominally godless, lacking a spiritual core, for as far back as we can trace history are the communist nations. These states lost track of the need for tolerating dissidents and creating fairness between the elite bureaucracy and the bulk of the people.

In short, history suggests that neither polar position (synoptic or reductionist) is desirable on purely pragmatic grounds. Moreover, the relevant systems are so complex that the Guideline for Complex Systems tells us a wide variety of data is the proper basis for decisions. Thus, there does seem to be a way to end the quarrels between science and religion, at least in part. It is simply for communities on each side of the 300-year-old argument to stop claiming that their community has a view that "owns" all the ideational territory of concern to humans. This suggestion is no more than a variation on the familiar statement of the Christian Bible: "Render therefore unto Caesar the things which are Caesar's; and unto God the things that are God's" (Matthew 22:21). This quotation and a multidisciplinary position essentially coincide on this issue. All we need do to reach this coincidence is update the biblical admonition to let things of the world include truth assertions about nature created by science. See Figure 13-1.

Science is a superb tool for understanding truth assertions, but truth assertions do not reach to things of the spirit, nor to values in general. Various spiritual paths, formal and informal, aid us in maintaining our sanity, our mutual obligations to each other, and our reverence for nature. Thus, spirituality is an essential foundation for a healthy community. Spirituality and science can supplement each other and live in peace, provided only that individuals primarily concerned with each view recognize the limits of "my" domain and stop claiming that "my" view owns all ideas and can therefore decide all behaviors appropriately. I have little doubt that some zealots on each side of this ancient argument will not choose to adopt the position suggested by multidisciplinarity. However, given what we have seen about the need for a multidisciplinary position, the road to a livable consensus seems open for individuals who want to take it.

It needs to be reiterated that all scholars or members of the general population have by no means held either a purely synoptic or a purely reductionist view. Enough individuals do seem to have held one view or the other, however, so that quarrels between the two camps, usually verbal but sometimes physical, have continued for more than three centuries in the Western world. One reads the effects of this quarrel, both mental and physically violent, day after day in the newspapers. I hope, over time, that a larger fraction of members of new generations will be more willing to take a position that does not allow any single viewpoint or method to be accepted as dominating or even as adequate for fully understanding our world and creating desirable human communities. Not only would this promote intellectual and spiritual peace, but it is the only logically tenable position for several independent reasons, as we have seen between Chapter 7 and this chapter.

We have come to a good point to end the discussion about structure. We will look at several more examples of applications in which a multidisciplinary position is necessary, in the next chapter. Before you read that chapter, you may want to use the six questions about complex systems to see if they aid your thinking in particular problems of interest to you. If you do so, I think you will find that the application of the multidisciplinary position to any broad problem of important

	Level	Name
The synoptist	6	Planets
The important things are up here	4	Large sociotechnical systems
	4	Ecologies without humans
	3	sociotechnical systems
	1	Families
"The culture gap"	0	Multi-cellular non-human life
The reductionist	-1	Unicellular plants and animals
	-2	Aggregation of atoms (molecules)
The important things are down here	-3	Atomic nuclei

Figure 13-1. The Important Things in Life.

scope in human affairs will seem familiar as a process — like the response of the person who asked an English teacher to explain the meaning of the word "rhetoric" and, on being told, exclaimed, "Why, I have been talking rhetoric all my life." Many of us have been using a multidisciplinary position for at least some problems for a long time because many problems demand it. We often had no choice if we wanted to see problems clearly. Many doctors and engineers are pushed strongly toward a multidisciplinary position by work experience. In fact, an M.D., Marsden Blois, from his direct observations about medicine, recently (1988) laid out the need for a multidisciplinary position regarding hierarchical structure. Nevertheless, we have lacked both a theoretical basis for multidisciplinarity and specific questions to help make the multidisciplinary position operational.

It is past time we gave up maintaining that either the synoptic view or the reductionist view can be a complete view of the world, and abandoned the three-century-old quarrel in which insistence on one view prevailing over the other has involved many of us who live in Western cultures. Each of the views is inadequate in five of the six major classes of systems of human concern; that is a major reason why the quarrel has not closed. A position of multidisciplinarity is not only logically necessary, but it offers us a more cooperative way to move toward increased understanding of ourselves and our world.

Before concluding this chapter, I'll describe one more example of the utility of the system/sysrep apparatus. Trends in mathematics and in some parts of theoretical physics have created sysreps that have moved farther and farther away from direct connections to systems in the real world. Have these trends caused difficulties? Recent unpublished work by M. R. Showalter suggests that they have. By looking closely at the connections between sophisticated mathematical sysreps and the systems they represent, Mr. Showalter has disclosed a difficulty in the way we have derived governing differential equations. Mr. Showalter also created a procedure for dealing with the difficulty. He used the new procedure to develop a very much improved sysrep for a critical part of the human brain (dendrites), the existing model for which had given results that were both quantitatively and qualitatively very far from observations. Other cases remain to be examined. The details of this work, both the dendrite model and the mathematical procedures, pass beyond the scope of this book and remain for the experts to evaluate. The relevant matter for this discussion arises from the fact that Mr. Showalter has read and made helpful comments on two earlier drafts of this book. He tells me that the system/sysrep apparatus, in the sense described in this chapter, was a critical basis for his work. More specifically, Mr. Showalter says, repeated applications of the kinds of questions posed in this chapter were crucial in moving the work forward when he was stuck at various times.

Mathematical representations of physical phenomena are one of the least likely places to encounter difficulties arising from the methods we use in creating sysreps. If difficulties have occurred in this area, and Mr. Showalter's results suggest that they have, there is an important need to improve the ways we formulate and test sysreps. This chapter forms a beginning for such improvements.

The result of the previous paragraph can be seen from a different view. Alfred Korzibski warned us that we need to be very careful not to confuse the map (sysrep) with the territory (system). P. W. Bridgman delineated the need for what he called "operationality." By operationality, Bridgman meant the ability to reproduce data "hands-on" in the laboratory. The essence of Bridgman's idea is what I call "traceability." I take traceability to denote the ability to trace the connections between each part of our sysrep and the corresponding part(s) in the system accurately item by item. When we loose traceability, we are essentially forced to take the map (sysrep) for the territory if we are to use the sysrep at all.

Is this loss of traceability, and the resulting confusion between sysrep (map) and system (territory), likely to cause significant difficulties? Indeed, it is. History illustrates the seriousness of the problem again and again and again. Let's look at a few examples. Consider, first, the myths about how the earth came to be and about how humans came to be which are held by the 2,000–3,000 ethnic groups on earth. No two of these myths agree, and yet each has been strongly believed in by a number of people at some point in time, and each is distinctly at odds not only with geological data now available about the age of the earth but also with paleoanthropological data about the lineage of human beings. The difference between the myths and the scientific data is not how strongly the beliefs are (or were) held, but whether or not there is traceability of the sysrep to the relevant parts of the system. Consider also the fundamental errors in the ancient Greek ideas about dynamics at the height of the Golden Age. Finally, consider the basic belief during the Elizabethan era that human health was governed by four "humors." We need not prolong these examples. In each case we see that when the sysrep is not traceable to the system item by item, the tendency of the human mind to prefer simplistic explanations to no explanation can and often has led us to egregious errors in our understanding of the world. Is there any reason to believe that the modern mind is any different in this sense than it was 3,000 years ago? No! There are neither biological reasons nor data. Evolution is too slow to have made much change in this matter. And there are data nearly everywhere showing the problem still exists; see examples in Chapter 2. I will give one more. The understanding of the entropy principle in some areas of science includes not just one but several severe errors. These errors have diffused into public awareness and have enormous impact on how we perceive the world. All of these errors rest on nothing more than a failure to define accurately the system under discussion.

In sum, when we lack traceability, we lose the foundation stone that differentiates ancient methods from those of science since the time of Galileo, and this is true even in mathematical modeling and in physics. Under these conditions, we need to be very cautious about what we come to accept as appropriate sysreps.

Conclusions for Chapter 13

The multidisciplinary position is not only necessary for appropriate study of many classes of systems, but it also leads us to ways that assist in several kinds of issues that are far more difficult, if not impossible, when approached from any single disciplinary view. Specifically, a multidisciplinary position helps us:

- Resolve the top-down versus bottom-up arguments, which have long plagued many fields of study;
- Brings forward a new "position," which allows us to study both values and structure instead of one or the other;
- Begins to unpack at least some seemingly intractable questions, and thus can establish a research agenda that may provide more complete answers;

- Suggests one way in which the 300-year-old war between science and religion can be at least partially resolved for anyone who desires to do so. The resolution merely requires that individuals stop overclaiming what any single viewpoint, method, or discipline of knowledge can do. This may well not satisfy specialists of the sort depicted in Figure 12-2, but it is a possible consensual view for anyone who chooses to adopt it. In this way, the use of a multidisciplinary position establishes a basis for study of complex systems which is inherently more cooperative than the old claims of priority of one level or structure over another, or one discipline over others, claims that in any event are false for at least four of the six major classes of systems of human concern.

Combining the ideas we have developed about complexity, structure, and hyperspaces with careful use of the system/sysrep idea provides us with an agenda of acute questions which can be used to test the validity of sysreps, even those underlying whole fields of study.

All these gains are possible only when we use the system/sysrep apparatus carefully to achieve traceability between the sysrep and the system and when we take into account the impact of the complexity of the system, the types of feedback accessible to the system, and the impact of open degrees of freedom arising from interfaces of mutual constraint in the structure of the system.

CHAPTER 14

Examples of
Multidisciplinary Analysis

We have now developed a number of tools and hypotheses for use in multi-disciplinary discourse. Let's see if we can gain new information by applying these tools and concepts in a few illustrations.

Sociotechnical Systems

We have already defined sociotechnical systems as systems that link people with human-made hardware to perform tasks that humans want done. Knowledge about sociotechnical systems inherently involves the physical, biological, and social sciences working together. Sociotechnical systems are an important arena for applications of multidisciplinary concepts and tools. Examination of the nature and the impact of sociotechnical systems can be seen as an overview of many disciplines from the perspective of applications.

Sociotechnical systems form the physical bases of all human societies both past and present. Thus the existence and the use of sociotechnical systems are an Entire Paradigm about human societies. An apparently sound basis for this assertion is the ethnological taxonomy of human societies. This taxonomy includes five types of societies: hunting and gathering; pastoral; horticultural; agricultural; and industrial. In the language of this discussion, the basis for the ethnological taxonomy is the general type of sociotechnical system used to secure the food base for the society. Since the ethnological taxonomy includes all known tribes on earth, the taxonomy in itself supports the assertions of the first two sentences of this paragraph. All known "tribes" use sociotechnical systems. See, for example, Cohen (1968).

When we look at past societies, we see that the assertion about sociotechnical systems can be made stronger. The stronger assertion rests on two facts: first, the long history of the use of such systems; and second, the purposes for which we use sociotechnical systems.

It was not Homo sapiens, our present species, that first began to use sociotechnical systems as a way of making a living on earth; it was our biological ancestors two species back in time, now often called Homo habilis. Homo habilis began to use simple forms of sociotechnical systems about 2 million years ago. This assertion is based on the compiled data of paleoanthropology. See, for example, Johanson and Maitland (1981). Note that there is still much controversy about descent from Homo habilis because the data are so sparse. I follow Johanson and Maitland here, as one widely accepted version.

The primary purpose of sociotechnical systems is to extend human powers both quantitatively and qualitatively. A secondary purpose is to reduce the amount of hard and unappealing labor that humans must do to survive. We use sociotechnical systems to extend our muscle powers, thinking powers, sensing powers, transport powers, and many other human capacities. Using sociotechnical systems we can "see" many kinds of things the unaided human eye cannot — for example, via X rays and infrared night-vision systems. And this is by no means the end of the list of the ways we extend our capacities by using sociotechnical systems. To some extent we even increase our ability to create aesthetic and erotic pleasures via paints and tools, musical instruments, oils for massage, perfumes, and so on.

Figure 14-1 shows the curves of the growth of ten important human powers, over the past 100,000 years. The growth in our powers has arisen almost entirely from human use of and human improvements in sociotechnical systems. The growth of human powers via sociotechnical systems shown by the curves in Figure 14-1 imply the existence and the use of the human-design feedback mode.

Each curve is formed by using the same kind of ratio. This ratio is the performance of the best system in wide use by humans at the given point in time divided by the unaided human power to accomplish the same function. For example, speed of travel on earth is taken as the fastest available transport system in wide use at the time shown, divided by unaided human walking speed (the Sierra Club estimate of 2.5 miles per hour for long distances). Other human capacities are normalized in a similar way. I call these ratios "technoextension factors." Figure 14-1 is reproduced from Kline (March 1977).

Several things about Figure 14-1 are surprising. The curves do not appear in any history book I have seen, even though they portray a vital part of human history. This absence again suggests the lack of study of sociotechnical systems as wholes, with the result that human technological powers are often seen as the work of individual humans and individual technical devices rather than as the output of complex systems integrating individuals, social arrangements, and technical devices.

Many of the increases in human powers created by use of sociotechnical

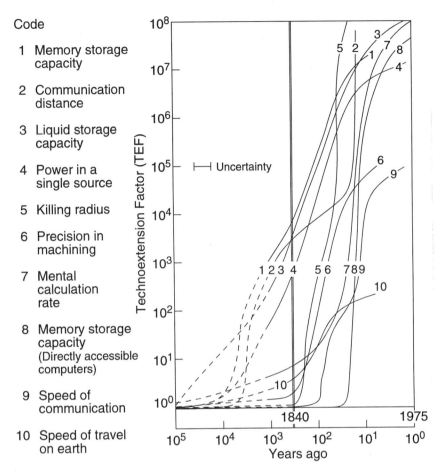

Figure 14-1. The Growth of Human Powers Over the Past 100,000 Years Plotted as Technoextension Factors (TEF).

systems have now reached beyond a billion times the values obtainable by a single human unaided by sociotechnical systems. The rate of increase in human powers over the past 100,000 years, when aided by sociotechnical systems, is astounding. Moreover, the rate of change has accelerated during most of the time shown in Figure 14-1.

When we examine the form of the curves, we see two things: first, each curve is doubly exponential in time (since each curve is still an exponential curve when plotted in log-log coordinates); and second, most of the rise in value in techno-extension factors has occurred since about 1840. This increase in the rate of growth of human powers since 1840 has been independently verified by Lienhard (1979), using a mathematical model of growth rates.

There appear to be two bases for this astounding rate of growth of human powers: (1) the rate of increase in the power of human systems has been roughly proportional to the power at the given time; this relation between value and growth leads to exponential behavior over time, as is well known; (2) the rate of innovations has decreased geometrically between each major period of time. For details, see Kline (1977). It is this billionfold increase in the more significant human powers that has made us, for many purposes, the Lords of the Planet.

The adoption of sociotechnical systems and their use in what I call the "basic pattern" created what appears to be an essential branch point where human evolution deviated from the evolutionary path of other animals. Let us look at what happened. Our biological ancestors, whomever we name them, about two million years ago, began to use two relatively simple forms of sociotechnical systems in a combined way. Specifically, they began to create tools and devices in sociotechnical systems of manufacture, and then they diffused the resulting tools and devices into sociotechnical systems of use in order to increase our inherent (that is, unaided) capacities. It is this combined use of sociotechnical systems of manufacture and use which I call the "basic pattern." Using the basic pattern, men began to make clubs, spears, and so on, which aided the hunt, and women began to make and utilize baskets and travois, which aided the gathering of foods. At a later time some of these tribes established a base camp and learned to ignite, control, and extinguish fire. We are not very sure about the details, but this rough outline is enough for this discussion.

Our biological ancestors of two million years ago already had brains evolved to the point at which they could make innovations that surpassed those of other animals. No other animal has learned to ignite, control, and extinguish fire even in the twentieth century. Using fire is a more complex technological task than using rocks or sticks as tools which some other animals do. What is even more important, the process of the basic pattern fed on itself in a positive feedback loop, which we now elaborate briefly.

The alterations in the way of life adopted by our ancestors, or at least by some of them, placed a premium on enlarged mental powers to improve not only tool making but also the social organization and skills needed in hunting animals and locating, gathering, and storing edible plants. The advantages of more elaborate language, of dextrous hands with an opposable thumb, and of enlarged memory and thinking powers in these tasks are considerable. As a result, evolutionary pressures led gradually, over about two million years, to a fourfold increase in the size of the human brain and an even greater increase in the complexity of our brains. This increased complexity led ultimately to human consciousness as we know it and to the ability to think of and visualize never-before-seen tools, processes, and systems of still greater complexity. The survival benefits created by use of the basic pattern also seem to have led to the increase in vocal powers (discussed in Chapter 8) and to the remarkable manual dexterity of humans. Regarding the brain, see Durham (1991); for the other powers, see, for example, Cohen (1968).

Without providing all the details, we can say in sum that the adoption of the basic pattern by our biological ancestors placed us on the evolutionary path that created the unusual thought, speech, and manual powers Homo sapiens came ultimately to have. Like all evolutionary processes, these changes took vast amounts of time, millions of years. The changes did not occur all at once. But this does not explain why the path diverged from that of other animals.

The divergence seems to have occurred because our ancestors gradually increased their powers to innovate what we called "human design capacities." And we already noted (in Chapter 6) that human design capacities constitute a more complex mode of feedback than any other animal seems capable of utilizing. The use of design capacities by one generation would not by itself have altered our evolutionary path. A second step was also required, the education of the young to perpetuate those innovations the community saw as desirable. This need for education still exists and has grown more urgent over time as our sociotechnical systems have grown more complex. As A. N. Whitehead (1959) told us, the human race stands only one generation from "barbarism." All we need to do to return to a "barbaric" state is to stop educating our children. Perhaps it would take two or three generations, but Whitehead's point is clear enough. From this point of view it is important to note what barbaric implies in this connotation. Barbaric does not imply a simpler value system, religious system, or social life. Hunting and gathering tribes routinely have very complex religious, value, and social systems. Barbaric does imply the use of cruder, less complex sociotechnical systems.

These evolving changes arose in part from the fact that the adoption of the basic pattern gradually altered the environments inside which our biological ancestors lived. The proto-human sociotechnical systems began, very slowly at first and then with accelerating speed, to alter the effective environment of humans and hence the evolutionary pressures and thus, finally, the evolutionary path of humans. To put this in different words, the adoption of the basic pattern set up a back-and-forth, iterating interaction between our biological structure and the environments our biological ancestors themselves created by use of the basic pattern. In this way, step by step during several million years, use of the basic pattern shaped us into who we are. An example of the idea occurs in Winston Churchill's memorable phrase when he discussed rebuilding Parliament after World War II, "First we build our buildings, and then they build us."

In the late twentieth century, nearly everything we do is bound up with use of sociotechnical systems. You might want to check the previous sentence for yourself by listing for one 24-hour period all the sociotechnical systems that you use or directly affect you, and then listing all the other sociotechnical systems needed to keep systems on the first list running. If you do this, I think you will see that our augmented capacities do not arise from the actions of any one person. The augmentation of human powers is a property of human communities, and this remains true even when gifted individuals initiate particularly large improvements in the systems. To put this differently, large complex tasks usually require many skills and many people working together in a large integrated sociotechnical system. It is the integrated systems, and not the bits and pieces nor the individual humans, that have allowed us to create the amazing curves in Figure 14-1.

It is thus fair to say that the use of sociotechnical systems is bred into our bones, our thought processes, and our emotional makeup. We are who we are because of the adoption of the basic pattern by our biological ancestors about two million years ago. In this sense, humans are the quintessential sociotechnical animals. This leads us to a final observation about sociotechnical systems.

Other animals use sociotechnical systems, but they do not purposefully innovate in those systems, as far as we have been able to observe. Beavers create beaver dams and ponds. Ants create anthills, bees create beehives, and so on. However, in each species except for humans, the sociotechnical systems look the same, generation after generation, for as long as we have records. If changes occur in the systems, they occur at the very slow pace allowed by biological evolution. This is not true for humans because our evolutionary path has carried us to the point at which our human design capacities, coupled with what we call "culture," allow us to do two things: first, we can envisage and make changes in our sociotechnical systems which we believe will improve the systems; and second, if when tried the changes seem to be improvements, we perpetuate them by education (both formal and informal) of the upcoming generation of children. We do this through what we call culture.

At the end of the nineteenth century, a few corporations learned how to purposefully create innovations of products on demand, and by 1940 this process had diffused widely. We call this process "research and development" (R and D). R and D does not always reach its goals, but it has done so often enough to create the astounding accelerations of the technoextension factors we see in Figure 14-1. These corporations have thus internalized and systematized innovation within their culture. Rothschild (1990) estimates that the evolution of human-made systems has, on the average, proceeded at roughly one million times the rate of evolutionary change. In the late twentieth century, the pace has been much faster than this average.

Thus, the use of innovation and perpetuation of innovations in the sociotechnical systems through culture distinguishes us from other animals in a qualitative way. The operative word is "qualitative," because such a distinction has long been sought by philosophers and other thinkers, but is elusive until we examine sociotechnical systems as wholes and the role they play in human history and human life.

In a widely read book, *An Essay on Man*, the German philosopher Cassirer reviews the literature on the differences between humans and other animals. Cassirer (1969) reaches two major conclusions. The first is that earlier suggestions concerning tool making, thought, and other capacities of single humans do not distinguish humans qualitatively from other animals. These capacities create only quantitative differences, since other animals use tools, think, use language, and so on. Other animals even have primitive cultures, as described in detail by Bonner (1980). Cassirer's second conclusion is that the important distinctions between humans and other animals are two and they are both quantitative:

(1) We use "symbolic forms" of far greater complexity than any other animal. What we called schemata in Chapter 3 are a good example of complex symbolic forms in Cassirer's sense. We saw in Chapter 8 that even relatively simple schemata for humans (use of verbs and nouns for classes of actions and objects) lie beyond what other animals seem to be able to do. Indeed, the remarks about speech drew heavily on Cassirer's work.

(2) When we choose to, humans can, by envisaging long-term goals, delay gratification far longer than other animals. Examples of the delay of gratification are all around us. It may take ten years or more to build a large dam or power plant. We create jigs to create tools that will be used to make components for products that will not be sold for years. And these are only a few examples. All these processes involve human design capacities and the ability of human cultures to educate our young to perpetuate innovations we see as desirable. Other animals do not do these things, as we just noted.

Thus, thinking about sociotechnical systems leads us to a long-sought qualitative distinction between humans and other animals.

For our discussion, it is also worth observing that this qualitative distinction between humans and other animals rests on use of the human-design feedback mode. As we saw in Chapter 6, only humans have the capacity to use this feedback mode. This observation adds two points to our discussion: first, it provides a basis for why the difference is qualitative; and second, it tends to confirm the idea that adoption of the basic pattern did branch the path of human evolution from that of other animals.

For our multidisciplinary discussion, it will be useful to ask, Why did many able and thorough scholars — for example, Cassirer — miss what they were seeking? Since the answer needs more knowledge about the mental states of Cassirer and other scholars than we can obtain, all we can do is recite the history and see what it suggests.

Studying the differences between humans and other animals, Cassirer investigated five areas of activity: science, art, myth and religion, language, and history. He looked at the literature and the practices in each of these areas thoroughly but separately. Cassirer did not consider sociotechnical systems or other systems that combine many human activities. What we see, then, is the following: long study of individual disciplines and literatures by many able scholars did not reveal a qualitative difference between humans and other animals. Study of sociotechnical systems does, rather quickly.

We have long suspected there is some kind of qualitative distinction between humans and other animals, but the nature of the difference does not seem to become clear until we begin to think about multidisciplinary, human-created systems rather than individual humans or individual disciplines. The history of this search for a qualitative distinction is a powerful, if anecdotal, argument for the importance of the multidisciplinary position and also for the importance to humans of sociotechnical systems.

Models of Innovation

Let us turn to another example, models of innovation for products in industrial societies. In this discussion, it is important to hold in mind that sociotechnical systems are not merely systems of hardware, nor are they merely economic systems, social systems, or legal systems. Particular sociotechnical systems are often all these things and more. Sociotechnical systems are thoroughly and inherently multidisciplinary. When we combine the highly multidisciplinary nature of sociotechnical systems with the many reasons why they are important to humans, the importance of sociotechnical systems for multidisciplinary discourse becomes evident. Sociotechnical systems are a primary arena within which the disciplines of knowledge must deal with problems of common interest.

Most current scholars concerned with economic competition in the increasingly global marketplace of the 1990's agree on one point. In many industries, particularly hi-tech industries, innovation is the key to long-term success of firms. This includes innovation not only in products but in other areas as well. In these industries, firms either innovate or, in the long run, they die. Moreover, "the long run" seems to come faster and faster as we reduce more and more the time needed to create innovations, as Figure 14-1 shows. One would think, then, that there would be agreement on at least two things: how to define innovation; how innovation proceeds, in at least a general way. However, there has been widespread and continuing disagreement on both questions.

As preparation for discussing innovation, it will be useful to summarize what we have seen at several earlier points about the uses of words and concepts. I will call this summary "Seneca's Dictum," since the idea comes from one of Seneca's letters. What Seneca said, in compressed form, can be stated, "When the words are confused, the mind is also." However, there are two levels of this kind of confusion. We will therefore state Seneca's Dictum formally in two parts.

Seneca's Dictum, Semantic Level. When we do not use words in a consistent way, our communications tend to become confused.

When we hold different ideas about the meaning of words, we often misunderstand each other, and such misunderstanding can lead to unending arguments. I will assume that readers in the late twentieth century understand semantic confusion, and not provide examples. However, the ideas of semantics do not contain the entire message in Seneca's statement. There is also a conceptual level inherent in Seneca's statement which does not seem to be as widely appreciated.

The conceptual level concerns what we called "schemata," and can be stated as follows:

Seneca's Dictum, Conceptual Level. When we do not have clear, appropriate schemata, we cannot think clearly.

Is this conceptual level important? A few examples will show us that it is very important. Consider the terms acceleration and evolution. Each of these terms was created in order to better understand a given area of study. Each is a powerful schema around which the human brain can organize an entire realm of knowledge. Newton used the word "acceleration" in order to provide the Entire Invariant Paradigms for gravity and classical mechanics we still use in most work. Darwin used the term "evolution" as it is still used in biology. Without these schemata, we cannot understand even reasonably well mechanics, gravity, or biology. The ancient Greeks, absent the concept of acceleration, had a view of mechanics we can only call "wrong" in the sense that it gives erroneous predictions. An editor of a biological journal, Futuyama (1983) wrote, "Without the concept of evolution, nothing in biology makes much sense."

Essentially similar remarks apply to many other key schemata, for example "culture" in ethnology; "relativity" in Einstein's sense; "genes" in the sense of Mendel; and "micro-organisms" in the sense of Pasteur. This list of important schemata that underlie a particular domain of twentieth-century knowledge is far from exhaustive, as you can check for yourself by thinking about nearly any field you know. We usually begin by tailoring the key concepts, and then we elaborate the field in terms of the frameworks we erect using these key concepts.

Particularly important for multidisciplinary discourse is an idea that follows from the conceptual level of Seneca's Dictum. Since we cannot think clearly without schemata, we tend to use the schemata we have. If we have only one set of schemata, and they come from one discipline, then our thinking tends to become discipline limited. This idea will become important in Chapter 18.

Given this background about the importance of clarity in words and concepts, let's return to the question of product innovation. The accepted definition of the word "innovation" has until recent years been that provided by the economics community: "An innovation is the introduction into the market of a new product." This definition sounds sensible, and it was long accepted. In a meeting in 1986 of several hundred leading engineers and economists discussing the intersection of technology and economics, this definition was used repeatedly, but was questioned by no one, including me. The proceedings of this meeting are published in Landau and Rosenberg (1986), so this is easily checked.

It was only a few years later that I realized that the accepted definition of product innovation was far too narrow; see Kline (1991a).

Why is the definition of product innovation too narrow? It excludes many matters that are vital to innovation. This becomes evident as soon as we realize that innovations do not occur only in hardware (that is, products) but, rather, in

all parts of our sociotechnical systems. Thus, the long-accepted economic definition excludes innovations of many kinds — for example, in manufacturing processes and machinery; social arrangements in the factory; the morale of workers;
the effectiveness of the relations between manufacturers and their suppliers and
customers; the quality of the product; and the range of functions the product can
perform. And each of these other matters is often important, sometimes critical,
in competitive use of innovations, as Porter (1990), among others, has documented. Hence I have suggested a broader definition of innovation as follows:
"Any improvement in the sociotechnical systems of manufacture and/or use
which increases performance as perceived by customers." Performance includes
not only cost but also quality of both products and services, range of functions
that can be accomplished, and so on. See Kline (1991a). Innovation in general
also includes other matters.

This failure to define product innovation broadly enough is not trivial. It
contributed to a long period after World War II during which the United States
neglected both the manufacturing process as an area for research and university
teaching. The Japanese did not; see Kline (1989).

What, then, about models of innovation? By 1985, models of innovation had
been created within six separate disciplines: economics, engineering, science, political science, sociology, and ethnology. The models are quite different from each
other. Six quite different models is surprising and implies no agreed-on model.
Even more surprisng is that workers in each field were largely, or even totally, un-
aware of the other five models. Ed Constant (1980), in what I consider one of the
best single books describing how a large technological revolution actually occurred, labels the political science, sociological, and ethnological models "simply wrong." Moreover, these models do not seem to have had wide influence. I
will therefore not discuss them. The other three models (from economics, engineering, and science) have each had wide influence. A brief discussion of them
will aid our multidisciplinary understanding.

The economics model borders on being a non-model; it is simply a black box
inside which things happen, but nothing is portrayed of how things happen inside
the box. Economists suggest that innovation occurs as the result of the spur of
competition between firms. It is as if we described medicine as a black box
needing no doctors, or nurses, or knowledge for its performance, but merely a
free market for medicine to spur competition. For some details, see Rosenberg
(1982). The economics model is caricatured in Figure 14-2.

What about the engineering model? Engineers are, and have been for about a
century, the primary actors in industrial innovations. Many of them get paid, as
professionals, to create innovations for companies in both products and processes; others do innovations through consulting or inventing. Many engineers
work wholly within what can be appropriately conceptualized as sociotechnical
systems of innovation, systems with the purpose of creating improved sociotechnical systems of manufacture and use. Nevertheless, the view within engi-

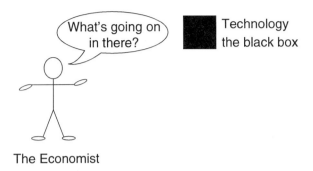

Figure 14-2. The Economist's View of Innovation.

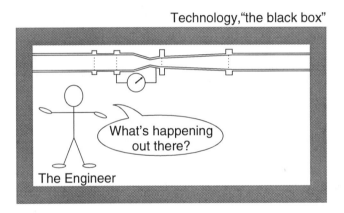

Figure 14-3. The Engineer's View of Innovation.

neering has also often been too narrow. It has often focused on the steps for developing hardware, and has omitted other aspects of innovations such as the social aspects of the sociotechnical systems. The engineering model is caricatured in Figure 14-3.

Why are both the economics and engineering models too narrow? Each represents one level of aggregation in the sociotechnical systems of manufacture, use, and innovation. The economists focused on the level of the firm, the market, and the customer. The engineers focused on the level of hardware. Both neglected, to a significant degree, the social aspects (and other factors) of the systems with which they were concerned. Neither seems to have seen the relevant sociotechnical systems as wholes, at least much of the time.

This failure to think about the whole system is far from trivial, since the competence of firms is not merely in the devices that occupy engineers, nor is it

Research
Development
Production
Marketing

Figure 14-4. The Science (Linear) Model of Innovation.

merely in the inputs and outputs, which occupy economists. The competence of firms resides in the community of people who constitute the firm and the machinery and systems they use to do their work. This result emerges clearly from the study of innovation systems in fifteen countries by Nelson and his colleagues (1993). It also emerges independently from the work of Rothschild on learning curves (1990). Rothschild provides credible data about how the cost of making a product declines as a function of the total number of units produced by the industry. This decline arises from learning within firms, and it usually follows a predictable form of curve on log-log coordinates. See also Abegglen and Stalk (1985) on how a number of Japanese firms have used this idea to win markets from Western competitors who did not use the idea until more recently.

What is the science model of innovation? In the literature it has sometimes been called the "linear model." The linear model is shown in Figure 14-4. It was the dominant model used in government science and technology policy in many Western countries after the end of World War II. It has been used by the federal government of the United States until the beginning of the Clinton administration in 1993. The linear model has not been used in Japan, however. See Kodama (1986). The linear model is still used as the basis of arguments by scientists for funding their work, but is often not made explicit. See, for example, the arguments about the purposes and the funding for the superconducting supercollider which went on for about a decade and were ended in 1994 only by congressional budget decisions. Like the old economic definition of innovation, the linear model looks reasonable but has many serious shortcomings. No less than six deficiencies, each serious, are listed in Kline (1991a). I mention only two. The linear model assumes that we use only this year's research in building new products. This is far from the mark. The idea that we use only this year's science in innovations, inherent in the linear model, is no more true than the idea that we live only in houses we have built this year. The knowledge we use in innovations includes not only all accepted science, old and new, but also both technological paradigms (last year's designs) and the skills embodied by long experience in the neuromuscular systems of technicians and craftsmen employed by the manufacturer and by the suppliers. In many cases the technological knowledge and the skills are more important than the science, but the details of these matters pass beyond what we need in this discussion. A second problem with the linear model is that it takes a rare source of innovations to be the only source of innovation, and omits the common sources. More specifically, most innovations come from human designs, not from science. Moreover, science at most enables innovations; it does not complete them. There are some advances through which science has directly enabled whole new industries — lasers and Hertzian waves are good examples. However, we have seen one of these radical advances only once or twice a decade even in the fast-paced growth of science in the twentieth century. An uncountable number of innovations occur each year from design and invention processes, sometimes with little or no science involved. See, for example, Vincenti (1989). Moreover, most careful observers agree that incremental innovations are more important on balance to competitiveness of firms over the long haul than the rare science-enabled innovations.

Is a better model of innovation available than the three we have discussed? Yes! It is the chain-linked model; see Kline (1985a, 1989, 1991a). The chain-linked model is shown in Figure 14-5.

This is more complex than the other models, but is nevertheless coming into use with remarkable speed worldwide in the 1990's. I have checked why the chain-linked model has diffused so rapidly with a number of innovators I consider wise. They almost all told me something like, "We knew the old (linear) model was very bad, but we had nothing better. Hence when we saw a better model we quickly adopted it." These answers lend support to two ideas we have seen at earlier points: we cannot think about complex matters without schemata; and when we lack appropriate schemata, we often use an available schema that is less than fully appropriate, and such use may distort our perceptions. We have not space here for a detailed discussion of the chain-linked model. For details, see references above. It will be useful to draw one conclusion from its history, however.

Since the chain-linked model is a schema I created, I have reflected several times on whether I could have created it without understanding that sociotechnical systems are the relevant systems, that is, without adopting a multidisciplinary position? As far as I can tell, the answer is No! The ideas needed for the chain-linked model came from two sources: first, personal experiences working on innovations in a number of industries; and second, the multidisciplinary position for thinking, which I had been developing for a decade and a half at the time the chain-linked model was written down.

Models of innovation thus provide an example of a significant problem that was not amenable to separate attack from six distinct disciplines, each approaching the problem separately. The words "not amenable" in the previous sentence denote results not appropriate for the full task in hand. None of the three older models we examined, which arose from a single discipline, can be called "wrong"; they each have something important to say about the problem area; all

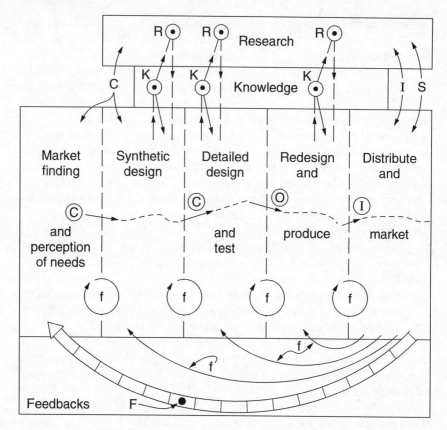

Figure 14-5. The Chain-Linked Model of Innovation. *Key:* f, F = Feedback information loops; C-C-O-I = Central chain of innovation; I = instruments for research and industrial use (two-way flow); S = Support of long-range research by industrial corporations; C = Enabling of designs by science and questions arising in science from problems in design; K, R = Links to existing knowledge and research output.

three are, however, seriously incomplete. Feedback on the chain-linked model from many sources since 1985 suggests that it is complete or at least nearly so. See, for example, Aoki and Rosenberg (1987). We also see that relevant experience, when combined with a multidisciplinary position, rather quickly produced an improved schema for the problem of concern.

Since economists are the primary workers concerned with the productivity of national economies, it will be useful to address the question, Can the conventional theory of economics properly address either the innovation of improvements in a company or the productivity of an economy? The words "properly address" in the previous sentence essentially ask, Can the theory, even in principle, deal with the problem adequately?

There exists what approaches an entire literature concerning the shortcomings of neoclassic economics as a predictive theory. See, for example, Burton Klein (1977), Nelson and Winter (1982), Porter (1990), Kuttner (1991), Rothschild (1990), and Dietrich (1991). We have neither the space nor the need to recapitulate all the arguments these and other authors present. What is relevant to this discussion is to ask whether we can see the bases for the difficulties in terms of the multidisciplinary concepts and tools we have developed in this book? Let's think first in terms of hyperspaces, as discussed in Chapter 5.

The industrial systems involved in innovation are typically sociotechnical systems. As we have seen, the dimensionality of sociotechnical systems is very high. Does economic theory model this high dimensionality, or on the contrary is it a cut through the hyperspace? The theory of economics deals with inputs and outputs to a firm and with market functions and customer preferences. When equations are set down, they often contain only two primary variables: the interest rate and money (in dollars or some other unit). In addition, the theory is one of static equilibrium. In neoclassic theory, time is not used as a variable except in terms of the time value of money (interest rates).

Economics is thus not only a cut through a hyperspace of much larger dimensionality, it is also a cut that severely constrains what can be explored and thus the range of answers that can be obtained. Are these limitations serious? In my view, they are indeed serious conceptually and have sometimes played a role in misconceptions about appropriate national policy in the area of innovations. See Porter (1990), Kuttner (1991), Brooks (1993). The oversimple linear model has also sometimes created misconceptions in U.S. decisions on innovation policy; see Kline and Kash (1992).

Economic theory stays at essentially one level of aggregation in the hierarchy of constitution, the level of firms, consumers, and markets. The theory consequently misses important matters at both higher and lower levels. At higher levels, it misses the importance of human social values, particularly equity in the social system; it also misses the importance of maintaining healthy ecologies. At lower levels, it lacks any concepts or variables that would answer the critical questions facing the workers who actually carry out innovations, that is, managers of research and development, inventors, research and development engineers, production engineers, and production supervisors. This is so because the theory contains no variables that can be used even to think about the question, How can we make innovations that will make the system more cost effective, produce higher-quality products with improved characteristics, and so on? The answers to these "how to" questions, in various sectors of the system, are at the core of innovations; increases in economic efficiency; increases in productivity; development of new products; and improvements in products and services. Unless these questions were being addressed, the learning curves delineated by Rothschild (1990) and the growth curves in Figure 14-1 would not have occurred. However, finding answers to these questions demands use of variables that are exogenous to economic theory. Economists call them "externalities."

The word "externality" to most of us denotes "external to the problem in hand." But this is not what economists mean when they use the word "externality" in communicating with each other; they mean "external to the market." And "the market" excludes all the factors that by definition answer the "how to" questions about innovations. The market also excludes social problems in the society and problems of the environment. We see, then, why economic theory has treated technology and innovation as a black box; the cut through the hyperspace of the complete problem used to define the domain of economic theory essentially forces this view.

Let us look at one more aspect to be sure that economics is a severely constrained cut through the hyperspace of complete sociotechnical systems. Economics in its classical form is an equilibrium theory that does not include time as a variable. But innovation by its very nature creates changes over time. This lack of an evolutionary component in economic theory has been noted by many scholars; see, for example, Burton Klein (1977), Nelson and Winter (1982), and Rothschild (1990). This constraint, the lack of a time variable, in itself ought to tell us that the theory cannot deal with change, and therefore with increases in productivity, which by definition require some change over time in our sociotechnical systems.

There is nothing wrong with taking a cut through the hyperspace, as economic theory does; we often need to make cuts of various sorts in order to create models the human mind can comprehend, as we have noted several times. Moreover, cuts through a hyperspace can tell us quite a lot. Indeed, economics has provided us many useful pieces of knowledge and understanding. For example, markets do work better for many functions than anything else we know, and it is useful for the economics community to keep reminding us of this important idea. What does cause difficulties, however, is a community's argument that a severely constraining cut through the hyperspace of the complete systems of interest provides theory that takes precedence over empirical observations, even when the theory becomes counterfactual. This is particularly true when the systems studied are very complex. As the Guideline for Complex Systems tells us, in such systems there is a primacy of data.

Despite all this, the economics community still seems to believe that it can deal with innovation and improving productivity via conventional economic theory. I do not agree, for the reasons given above (and a number of other reasons we have not space or need for). Nevertheless, if history is a guide, what I say is very unlikely to have significant impact within the economics community. Consequently, the issue needs public debate, which will include scholars beyond the economic community. In the hope of stirring public debate, I have offered a bet about the ability of economic theory to handle innovations appropriately (in Appendix B) at ten to one in favor of any economist who wants to take up the challenge.

The Nature/Nurture Issue

In recent decades we have had again very strong claims made for bottom-up biological determinisms emanating from the field called sociobiology. Are these claims correct? Do they violate some of the hypotheses we have been developing in this volume? Let us see what the sociobiologists have said, and compare that with the hypotheses of this volume. We can start with a quotation from E. O. Wilson, the founder of sociobiology. In his book (1975, 1980), Wilson says: "[Sociobiology is] the systematic study of the biological basis of all social behavior." The key word to note in this quotation is "all." Apparently owing to the controversy this book aroused, a later book (1981) by Lumsden and Wilson weakens the statement to: "Social behaviors are shaped by natural selection. . . . Those behaviors conferring the highest replacement rate in succeeding generations are expected to prevail throughout the local populations and hence ultimately to influence the statistical distribution of culture on a worldwide basis." The key word to note in this quotation is "shaped." If one reads "shaped" as "constrained by," there can be little argument with the quotation. If one reads "shaped" as "determined by," then it is equivalent to the quote from Wilson's 1980 work. Lumsden and Wilson seem not to have said which denotation they intended.

When we compare the quotes just given with Hypothesis V (the need for three views), we see there is a direct conflict. The quoted statements also conflict with Hypotheses III, VI, VII and Polanyi's Principle because human structure is hierarchical and has interfaces of mutual constraint. Either quote above implies that one level in the hierarchy of constitution (that of molecules in the form of DNA) is all we need in order to understand all the other levels, including those that contain human social behaviors. The claims of Wilson and Lumsden and the ideas of Hypotheses III, V, VI, VII and Polanyi's Principle cannot both be correct.

The nature/nurture problem has been so much discussed and is so controversial, there is not space here to even summarize the vast literature. It will be more useful as a test of multidisciplinary discourse to approach the problem anew and see what we can do, if anything, with the methods and results developed in prior chapters.

We can begin by using Hypothesis II, "In multidisciplinary work, we need to honor all credible data from wherever they arise." In this problem, Hypothesis II implies going beyond the bounds of biology, ethnology, and genetics to include barefoot data from everyday life, as well as scholarly results about childhood development, information theory, control theory, and other sources.

Let's begin with control theory, since we are talking about causation over time and hence control of the systems of concern is a critical element. I next state a proposition that seems to have no accepted name. It is the Central Presupposition of Control Theory.

The Central Presupposition of Control Theory. To control a given system of any kind, the control elements of the system, whether autonomic or human, must be able to effect changes in the system in times that are less than one-fourth (and preferably less than one-tenth) of the characteristic time of the change of the parts of the system that are to be controlled.

So, we have a short, memorable name for this presupposition, I will usually call it "Draper's Dictum," after C. Stark Draper, who was a major contributor to the theory and practice of control systems and widely regarded as the father of inertial guidance.

The words "effect changes" subsume all four elements of a feedback loop: sensing, processing, deciding, and acting.

As far as I know, workers concerned with control theory do not disagree with Draper's Dictum. The dictum can be demonstrated from theory, but this requires some exotic and sophisticated mathematics, and we will not examine these details. You can, however, understand the idea for yourself. To change the amplitude of the motion of a child's swing, you must observe the motion; process what you see; and move your hands in and out, all within a small fraction of the total time of one back-and-forth motion of the swing. If you cannot do that, you cannot control the motion of the swing.

What does Draper's Dictum say about the statements that imply biological determinism? It says that they are simply wrong. There is no possibility that biological evolution could have controlled the rate of changes shown in Figure 14-1. This impossibility has been true for the entire 100,000-year period shown. However, the idea of biological control (determination in any direct form) approaches the ridiculous when we look at the rates of change over the period 1840–1975 while holding in mind the Central Presupposition of Control Theory. As already noted, Rothschild (1990) estimated that human sociotechnical change, on the average, has gone about one million times faster over the past 35,000 years than biological changes in humans owing to evolution. If we accept Rothschild's estimate, then the control of evolution of human systems by genes is equivalent to an attempt to control the speed of an airplane propeller rotating at 10,000 rpm by a device that requires 100 minutes to perform one control action. And this is only for the average rate of change for 35,000 years; for the twentieth century the times of genetic changes are even farther from what is needed.

An even more forceful illustration is to think of yourself driving a car down a twisting mountain road at 30 miles per hour. As the "controller" of the car, you will need to turn the steering wheel through a significant arc every few seconds to follow the road. If you could turn the wheel only once per minute, you would surely wind up in a ditch rather quickly. If we accept Rothschild's estimate of technical change as one million times faster than evolutionary change, then we see that had we waited for genetic changes to steer the system, we would surely have wound up in the ditch of a failed species long ago.

Careful data by many observers on childhood development and by many researchers in psychology also show that biological determinisms cannot be true, but Draper's Dictum is perhaps the clearest and most forceful disconfirmation of the claims of sociobiology. There is no need to examine other reasons in detail. The apparent impermeability of disciplinary boundaries in the late twentieth century has allowed the creation of ideas on this question that not only violate well-established principles in other disciplines but also have led to prolonged sterile debate and thus much wasted effort of many able scholars.

Let's now turn the question over and ask, What can we justifiably say about the nature/nurture problem from a multidisciplinary position? A good place to start is what I will call "Durham's Hypothesis"; it summarizes the central hypothesis of Durham's *Coevolution* (1991).

Durham's Hypothesis. Genetic information and cultural information are two separate, interacting sources of human information; each evolves over time, but at different rates of change.

Addition (by author): Human skills form a third type of human information which interacts with the other two. Skills are necessary for maintenance of human societies over time. Skills are socially transmitted and evolve.

Durham makes the case for this hypothesis thoroughly. He posits the existence of five distinct modes of interaction between genetic and cultural information. He then documents the existence of each mode of interaction with a thorough case study. As we have noted before, one case is enough to establish existence. When we have clear examples in hand, we do not need a "theoretical proof" of existence. Durham's cases are done with care and thoroughness, and they confirm his hypothesis beyond much doubt. They make clear by examples that genetics and culture are independent streams of information, and that they do interact. Both streams of information evolve over time, but at very different rates of speed. Moreover, both the independence and the interactions are necessary to explain some beliefs and situations in actual human societies.

For our discussion, it needs noting that in every one of the five cases Durham studied, he employs a multidisciplinary position. That is, Durham looks at the data from many formal disciplines and other sources. For example, in one case Durham studies an unusual marriage custom in the Thongpa class in Tibet. In this class, two or even three brothers conventionally marry one woman. No other known ethnic group has this marriage pattern. To discover the underlying reasons for these unusual arrangements, Durham examines the structure of property and inheritance, the economic conditions, the environmental conditions, and the class structure. Durham also employs the concept of semiotic encoding developed in ethnology. In semiotic encoding, the real reasons for a custom of an ethnic group (usually an important custom) are hidden beneath the surface (often in religious dogma). All these elements are essential to understanding the marriage customs of the Thongpas.

More important for our purposes is that the Thongpa marriage customs are not the result of biology; they are, rather, the result of an unusual situation in the local ecology and social structures. This is clearly indicated by what occurred when many Thongpas emigrated to India after the Chinese invasion of Tibet. In the next generation, most of the Thongpas reverted to the more usual, one-man one-woman form of marriage, indicating the earlier custom was a social and not a genetic choice. The other cases each give strong support to Durham's Hypothesis. For details, see Durham (1991).

In his work, Durham uses the narrow definition of culture which seems to best suit the needs of ethnology. For our purposes, we will use a wider definition of culture. We once again need to pause briefly to clarify words. The narrow denotation of culture I will call "culture-N." Culture-N for ethnologists denotes all the shared ideas held by members of a tribe or a society. Culture-N thus includes the basic values of the tribe and also the mores and taboos that "everyone" is supposed to obey. The word "supposed" is needed, since all societies appear to have "deviants," individuals who do not follow the common cultural "rules," as we have noted several times before. To some degree, hardly anyone follows all the rules of his or her culture.

The broader denotation of culture I will call "culture-B." Culture-B denotes all the knowledge a society holds including all the knowledge for doing tasks needed for survival (and the skills for doing the task). It also includes the skills needed for art, music, and the craft-works the tribe members create. More generally, culture-B includes all the knowledge both theoretical and tacit that any member of the tribe holds which will be transmitted to the next generation.

The central distinction between culture-N and culture-B for our purposes is that all members of the tribe understand culture-N ideas while only some (or a few) members of the tribe have to understand many of the bits of knowledge needed for specific skills included in culture-B. Since many members of large societies hold information that others do not, culture-B is a much broader category of information than culture-N, particularly in the complex societies we now call industrial.

The division of labor implied in describing culture-B allows human societies to perform many tasks that would not be possible if all members of the tribe had to learn all the skills the society uses. This distinction seems to go back to the earliest use of the basic pattern, with the differentiation of knowledge and skills between men and women by our biological ancestors. One of the bases of our sociotechnical systems, and thus our extraordinary powers, is the division of labor. This implies that many skills need to be learned by only a small fraction of the population.

We are now ready to look at another way of thinking about genetic versus social controls which is instructive for multidisciplinary discussions. We can start by laying out five positions along the scale from pure nurture to pure nature as a causative factor in human life.

Assertion 1. The information carried in our DNA determines all of culture and all the individual human behaviors of each person.

Assertion 2. The information carried in our DNA determines the large preponderance of the behaviors in human cultures, and the individual human's socially learned behavior plays only a small part.

Assertion 3. Both genetically carried information and learned social behavior are major sources of behaviors for cultures and for individual humans. Both genetics and socially learned knowledge must be considered for many problems, and sometimes together.

Assertion 4. Socially learned behavior determines the large preponderance of cultures and individual human behaviors; genetic information plays only a small part.

Assertion 5. Social learning determines all behaviors of cultures and individual humans. Genetic inheritance plays no part in behavior; it only creates physical structure.

Please notice two things about Assertions 1 through 5. First, they use the verb "determine" (not "constrain"). Second, they cover the full spectrum from total genetic control at one end to total social control of behaviors at the other. Assertions 1 through 5 set five defined arbitrary, but definite, positions along the full spectrum so we can look with clarity at various points along the way.

Using the method of negative inference, we can easily find examples that disconfirm both Assertions 1 and 5.

Examples that disconfirm Assertion 5 include Down's syndrome, a genetic malfunction that occurs in a small fraction of all societies for which we have data. Down's syndrome has very large negative effects on the capacities of the individual affected. A second example is bipolar depression, in which a genetic component is now well verified. Treatments via talk therapy have been ineffective while the condition can often be controlled by chemical treatments; studies of identical twins raised separately have revealed a surprising range of similar behaviors. See, for example, Pennebaker (1990), who sorts and reviews the data in detail. One clear example would disconfirm Assertion 5 as an Entire Paradigm. We have just seen three. There are many others.

In a similar way, some examples that disconfirm Assertion 1 include marasmus, the severe retardation created in human infants who receive grossly inadequate loving attention from, and interaction with, adult humans; the resulting effects are severe. Lacking loving adult human interaction, 40 percent of the infants do not survive to two years of age even when they have ample food and shelter. The survivors almost all suffer severe emotional dysfunctions. See Spitz (1953, 1983). Indeed, the marasmus syndrome was described and labeled by Spitz, an M.D. And the phrase "Tender Loving Care" (TLC) was created by Spitz as a "prescription" for nurses caring for human infants in foundling homes in order to avoid the severe negative effects of marasmus. Although this summary is sufficient for this discussion, one needs to read the complete paper (1953) to get the full impact of such deficiency in human attention on the development of human children. The same need for affectionate attention from other members of the species is also true for our closest biological cousins, the Rhesus monkeys; see Harlow and Harlow (1962). Another example that disconfirms Assertion 1 is multiple personality disorder. In this severe psychiatric disorder, one brain seems to house two or more personalities who do not know of each other's existence, at least until psychiatric treatment rectifies the condition. The condition is somewhat like that of Dr. Jekyll and Mr. Hyde, but is not in the least fictional. The condition is not common, but probably is not as rare as we once thought. The cause of multiple personality disorder in the cases that have been studied is prolonged and severe early childhood abuse, usually sexual. See, for example, the summary by Dennett (1991, p. 420). A third example is skills of many kinds, including musical skills, sport skills, skills for running machine tools, professional skills. All these skills, and others, are learned. Each requires long dedicated learning and practice. Which of us is born with the skill to be a world competitor in any sport? We sometimes say we live in the steel age, but which of us is born with the skill and knowledge needed to make steel? Which of us is born knowing how to use a computer, or learns to use one without explicit, purposeful learning?

Thus we have not one but many examples that disconfirm Assertions 1 and 5. If we look at these same examples, we see that they also disconfirm Assertions 2 and 4. By elimination, negative inference, this leaves only Assertion 3 as a possible general statement. Assertion 3 is not wrong (as statements 1, 2, 4, and 5 are), but it is not a general statement, since it does not cover all aspects of human behaviors. We have already seen examples of particular human behaviors that are determined by genetics, and other particular behaviors that are determined by social learning. If we look, it is not hard to find behaviors that are primarily constrained by genetics but with a social component and other behaviors that are primarily constrained by social learning but have a genetic component. Since we cannot say that Assertion 3 is uniformly true for all human behaviors, we must conclude: no one position of the five given in Assertions 1 through 5 is correct for all cases. What we must have if we are to make sense of the nature/nurture issue, is an eclectic — that is, multidisciplinary — position. In this sense, the nature/nurture problem is like the free will problem; if we demand a single solution by asking, "Is it A or B?" we overconstrain the answer, and this tends toward non-closing arguments over two non-answers.

We need to address one more question before we end this illustration. We saw above that many skills of human adults are learned and not genetically transmitted. Are these skills important or merely trivial phenomena? If you examine a broad range of skills, I think you will quickly see that some are trivial from the view of human survival, but many are essential to maintaining the sociotechnical systems we use to survive. Some of our learned human skills are far from trivial.

Before we turn to conclusions for this chapter, it will be useful to summarize in the form of a guideline a point we have now seen several times.

Guideline for Scholarly Controversy

When two (or more) groups of empirically grounded scholars create conflicting solutions for a single problem, and this leads to back-and-forth arguments for decades, then it is likely that each group of scholars has some of the truth but not all of it.

Why is this so? If one group had all the truth, over time its solution would probably come to be the accepted answer, provided only that each group is grounding results in empirical observations. It is not hard to spell out the logic more fully, but this is the essence of it. A corollary follows.

Guideline for Scholarly Controversy, Corollary A

When two (or more) groups of empirically grounded scholars have a long-continued argument, an improved solution can often be found by reframing the problem to include the solidly grounded data underlying both sides of the argument.

More specifically, what seems useful is three steps: first, examine the problem from a broader perspective; second, examine what is correct in all the credible data in the relevant fields and from other sources; and third, attempt to reframe the results in a new and broader paradigm that does not violate any credible data. Hypotheses V, VI, and VII, which concern the need for at least three views and the need to examine all levels in the structure to be sure all the results are consistent, can often provide useful checklists in this process.

Conclusions for Chapter 14

The three illustrations in this chapter have one common feature. They all concern significant issues for which several approaches, each from a single discipline, have given simplistic answers, and for which a multidisciplinary position rather readily gives more complete and appropriate answers. The improved solutions do not come from merely bringing the concepts of the individual disciplines to bear one by one; they require one or both of two changes: (1) the conceptual interpenetration of the ideas and data from more than one discipline; (2) definition of a broader class of systems so that the full hyperspace can be explored. In sum, there are some significant problems that require a multidisciplinary position.

CHAPTER 15

The Evolution of Disciplines, 1500–1900

How have the disciplines as we know them in the late twentieth century taken on their present forms? We have detailed histories of the development of many particular disciplines, but the separate histories do not fully answer this question. We need in addition an overall description of the main intellectual trends since the time of Newton in order to see how the disciplines have interacted with each other.

From a historical view, dividing the part of scholarly knowledge which deals with truth assertions into a large number of separate disciplines is a recent development. Since it also is primarily a Western development, we can limit our overview to the period since about 1500 A.D. in the Western world. We begin with a very coarse overview and then expand some details that are relevant to our discussion.

During the Middle Ages in Christendom, in the dominant European cultures, scholarly knowledge was considered to be derived from theological origins. Not only ethical and spiritual values but also descriptions of how the world was formed and how it worked were seen as theological questions, decidable by reference to the Christian Scriptures and theological explanations by the Church. Thus, even though some parts of what many people believed were quite inaccurate sysreps, when measured by the twentieth-century norms of science, there was a unified, shared overview of the world. Peter Berger (1969), in an excellent book on the functions of religion, describes religion during the Middle Ages as a "sacred canopy." As Berger tells us, this canopy held aloft a unified picture of the world, reassured individuals in the face of the uncertainties and vicissitudes of life, and provided a shared belief system. It served important human functions.

This monopoly of thought held by the Church was shattered by Luther and others in the Reformation. The increased freedom for thought which resulted in Protestant and mixed Protestant/Catholic countries allowed development of other bases for understanding the world.

This opening to new thought led at the time of the Renaissance, about 1450–1500 A.D., to reclaiming within Western thought the ideas developed in ancient Greece. These Greek ideas, preserved largely within the Muslim societies, passed back into thinking in Christian societies when Muslim writings were recovered in Spain after their expulsion. These Greek ideas exalted rational thought, logic, and the life of the mind. For the most part, however, the ancient Greek thinkers did not use empirical evidence; they relied on thought and discussion, not only as the sources for knowledge, but also as the means for verification. In order to have a name for this kind of process, I will call it "dialectical," using the term in a broad sense and in contrast to empirically based data and principles.

Ancient Greek thought about the physical world had been summarized by Aristotle, and his writing was taken as an authoritative source regarding natural phenomena by many European scholars in the period during and following the Renaissance. This use of Aristotle as a source of "the truth" about the physical world was similar to the way the Scriptures had served during the Middle Ages. This view led to what was called "natural philosophy," which was taken to include all the scholarly knowledge that lay outside theological knowledge. For several centuries, natural philosophy was still seen as largely a single body of knowledge.

This unity of natural philosophy was still in vogue at the time of the Enlightenment, as evidenced by the attempt of the French encyclopedists in the 1740's to summarize all human knowledge of the world in a relatively compact set of treatises. Moreover, even in the eighteenth century, a large part of scholarly work still did not employ what we today call empirical methods. That is, scholars did not see the need for going out into the world and checking for themselves the results stated by sources taken as authorities. Francis Bacon had pointed to the importance of empirical evidence in his *Novum Organum* published in 1620. However, the idea only slowly diffused through the scholarly communities. For many purposes, Aristotle's views thus still reigned as the ultimate authority. During this period between the Renaissance and the rise of modern science, the primary role of philosophers with regard to natural science was not to question the content of what had been given by Aristotle, but, rather, to interpret the meaning of what Aristotle had said as it reflected onto the existential issues of human life, much as had been done earlier with the Scriptures.

Since the early eighteenth century, science, and hence the realm of truth assertions, has taken a quite different course in two ways. First, more and more specialized fields of knowledge dealing with truth assertions have arisen. Second, the specialized fields began to use empiricism as both the initial step in finding and the ultimate arbiter of truth assertions about nature. The turning point into the current era is often seen as beginning with Galileo, and as complete with the creation of two Entire Invariant Paradigms by Isaac Newton — one for classical mechanics and one for gravity. However, Newton's work was published in Latin, and it involved a new and relatively difficult mathematics (elementary calculus), which Newton erected and used to create the paradigms. As a result, they diffused but slowly. It was a number of decades before it began to be clear that Newton's two paradigms could be used to create accurate results in such areas as the strength of structures, the motions of fluids that are pervasive in the air and water around us and also in biological systems, and human-made devices.

However, the diffusion of Newton's paradigms accelerated over time. For more details of this acceleration, see de Solla Price (1962). This led to more and more specialized disciplines, each branching from natural philosophy and adopting empirical grounding. By the end of the nineteenth century, with a few exceptions the major disciplines that constitute departments in our large universities in the 1990's existed or were coming into being. During the first half of the twentieth century, further specialization proceeded rapidly, splitting these larger areas into still finer parts, and as we all know, this process still continues in the late twentieth century. Some of these finer parts now have a membership larger than the full community of scholars centuries ago.

In recent decades, however, a counter trend has begun. That is, some new disciplines have been formed by mergers at the interfaces of two or more previously existing disciplines (for example, geophysics, behavioral biology, biochemistry, and social psychology), and some instances of many disciplines working on common problems cooperatively are beginning to come into being. However, so far only a few of these multidisciplinary mergers creating new research programs have appeared, and they are often not accepted and supported as full partners with the older disciplines in our institutions of learning.

For the most part, the new disciplines that arose after 1700, and more rapidly as time progressed, adopted an empirical approach. However, adoption of empiricism as the key step in confirmation occurred at significantly different times in different disciplines. Also, because Newton's work had become so famous by the nineteenth century, nearly all the new disciplines attempted to create paradigms similar to those of Newton. More specifically, the objective became to create Entire Invariant Paradigms that were simple in form and used only a few variables.

The time when the empirical method was adopted can be seen as a historical branch point for each discipline. At its own branch point, each discipline broke away from "natural philosophy" to form a new empirically based domain of specialized knowledge. We don't need the details of how each discipline did this splitting off. It is enough to note that the branching was usually gradual. Philosophy, for the most part, has remained methodologically rooted in dialectical, verbal methods not based on observations. This remains true in the late twentieth century.

In the late twentieth century, a typical large university will have fifty or more departments. Each department will usually have three to ten subprograms that constitute largely separate disciplines or at least distinct research programs. In this way we have divided the world of knowledge into some hundreds of "pieces," and a large fraction of these "pieces" deals primarily with truth assertions over some domain.

As a part of this development of specialized disciplines, primarily since about 1850, the scholars and researchers in each field have become more and more professionalized in two senses. First, individuals are paid to be expert in a particular domain of knowledge. In the late twentieth century, the vast majority of specialists earn a living as experts. For the most part, they are no longer amateurs, and they no longer rely on the personal patronage of a king or a powerful noble. Prior to a century or so ago, that was distinctly not the case, as the record of science and scholarship of that time attests. This larger and less biased economic support for specialized experts has allowed the number of individuals doing research science and scholarly work of all sorts to multiply many times over.

Historically, the data suggest that a society first becomes abundant owing to increasing productivity and then begins to do significant amounts of science and scholarly work, not the other way around. This seems to be the reason why science and the modern disciplines dealing with truth assertions were primarily a story of Western men until well into the twentieth century. Before that time, most women were disenfranchised by cultural constraints, as were most men in other areas of the world by economic constraints.

In any case, these professional specialists soon began to communicate with each other about what they saw as their domain of expertise. They formed what sociologists have come to call "invisible colleges," communities of individuals with shared scholarly and research interests. The earliest of the professional societies in science date from the seventeenth century, but the rapid growth of many specialized societies began in the last half of the nineteenth century.

As both de Solla Price (1962) and Rothschild (1990) have documented at length, a necessary precondition for the existence and functioning of invisible colleges is sufficiently rapid, accurate, and inexpensive means for recording and transmitting information. As long as writing had to be laboriously copied by scribes, it was too expensive for use by most people and remained primarily in the hands of the Church and of monarchs. This was a major tool in maintaining privilege and power for a few people. The invention of relatively cheap printing by Gutenberg in 1455 broke this monopoly, setting the stage for the long process that led several centuries later to invisible colleges and the wider distribution of knowledge. These shifts thus arose out of shifts in the sociotechnical systems supporting society. This is not an isolated instance. Innovations in sociotechnical systems have been a primary engine of change in both economies and cultures (including values), as Mead (1972) noted in her final work and Rothschild (1990) documents from a different perspective.

In the late twentieth century, the allegiance of academic researchers to these invisible colleges is often stronger than to the particular university that pays them, for two reasons. First, promotion within the research universities usually requires that members of the relevant invisible college value their work. Second, the interests of researchers and scholars often align with those of other members of the invisible college more closely than with those of many scholars in other disciplines on the home campus. As a result, the individual disciplines have become more and more separate domains of discourse. In many cases they have become largely "walled off" from connections to and feedback from outsiders. Moreover, "outsiders" in this context include not only the general public but also workers in other specialized areas of knowledge.

The vessel that contains professional knowledge for solving problems and carries out tasks for society is seldom any one individual; it is nearly always the community of workers. The communities carry out the professional tasks, and this often requires combining talents of various sorts held by a number of individuals. The communities set standards of testability and of credibility for data. Through actions, they define the degree of "persuasiveness" which must be met before new knowledge is accepted. Members of the invisible college also publish journals and review and certify curricula. Up to the time of Newton, these functions were usually performed by the whole community of scholars. By the end of the twentieth century, these functions were nearly always left to specialized groups.

These specialized communities have increased the standards of acceptable knowledge in nearly every field. Sometimes the increases in standards have been gradual; in other cases a particular study or professional review has initiated jumps in standards.

Through these processes of specialization, professionalization, formation of invisible colleges, and improving scholarly standards, we have, collectively and during the past three centuries, multiplied what the human race knows with reasonable assurance about physical, biological, and social nature many, many times over. In nearly every case the relevant communities have used empirical grounding as a central basis and the system idea as a central underlying concept (although often not by that name). These processes of specialization and professionalization have been of overriding importance in the history of the human race. The work of these specialized communities underlies much, but not all, of what we saw about the acceleration of human powers in Figure 14-1.

At the same time, we have largely lost a unifying overview of any kind, a difficulty long lamented by many scholars, particularly by humanists. From the view of verifying knowledge and from the view of the social uses of the new knowledge, we have also lost nearly all of what the larger society and the larger community of scholars deem appropriate in various special research programs. To a great extent, each discipline has become an independent intellectual "dukedom" unconstrained by larger social units. This has led a few specialists to the extreme belief that their discipline has the right to support for its work uncoupled from any responsibility to the social order or to the priorities of the society.

Given this capsule and thus oversimple picture of what has occurred over the past few centuries, what have been the typical steps through which a modern discipline dealing with truth assertions is established and continues to develop, after it has branched from natural philosophy and formed a quasi-independent intellectual domain?

The typical steps through which disciplines dealing with truth assertions arise and mature are described, in what follows, as eight steps. The description is neither unique nor definitive; it only attempts to be relatively complete and characteristic so it can be used to examine the similarities and differences among the various fields and also to consider what particular disciplines can and cannot do.

Eight Steps in the Development of a Discipline Dealing with Truth Assertions

1. Selection of a class of systems with an associated set of problems. This defines a domain with which the discipline will deal and also therefore implicitly defines matters that lie outside the domain. This domain may be refined, contracted, or expanded over time, but it is rarely completely altered.

2. Observations of the behaviors within the class of systems. This almost always includes formation of words and concepts aimed at facilitating accurate descriptions and increasing understanding. In many cases, these concepts, and the variables through which they are described, are not initially obvious. Considerable sorting and rearranging has often been required to reach appropriate choices for both the concepts and the variables. In many fields, this process has not been done in one step, but has been iterated over time using the human-design feedback mode (described in Chapter 6). The process has often involved much argument, testing, and debate.

3. Organization of the observations into a taxonomy. This allows sorting of problems into subdomains: each of which has systems with sufficiently similar behaviors so that "rules" for the behaviors of each subdomain can be formulated. Over time the rules can sometimes be generalized to include a broader range of systems. Moreover, taxonomies are far more critical in some domains than others. However, an initial subdivision into an organized taxonomy has been essential in nearly every branch of science.

4. Formation of "rules" that describe the phenomena within the taxonomy either as a whole or for particular subdomains. The statement of the "rules" nearly always involves an inductive leap that goes from an assertion about

some cases to an assertion about all cases within a class, which is to say, a domain. The generalization implied therefore logically demands further empirical verification.

At this point in our discussion, we are still using the word "rules" to include principles, precepts, hypotheses, paradigms, guidelines, axioms, "laws," and so forth. As noted before, the "rules" can be expressed in words, in mathematical equations, or in pictures or diagrams, or any combination of these three modes.

5. Testing of the "rules" by observing if they are also valid in further cases that were not part of the data base used in forming the "rules." This often involves development of improved methods of testing and of evaluating data, and these, over time, improve both the instrumental and the methodological standards of the field and hence the accuracy and credibility of the data.

6. When necessary, reformulating the "rules" to provide increased accuracy as sysreps for a given domain of systems or to broaden (or narrow) the domain of systems, the domain to which the given "rules" apply. (This process often feeds back into reformulation of concepts, as also noted in step 2.)

7. As time goes on, in some cases, we accumulate more and more examples that demonstrate that the "rules" work for a given class of systems. We then become surer and surer of the "rules." The "rules" nevertheless remain human made, and since the process involves (in step 3) an inductive leap, many sophisticated workers in science in the late twentieth century hold all these "rules" subject to retesting and reformulation when needed, and not as "the final truth." Nevertheless, in some domains we find that the rules seem to be converging on an Entire Invariant Paradigm of great predictive power for the domain of concern. We saw some examples in Chapter 6. Note that "laws," when used for "rules" in this sense, is a misnomer. Mother Nature does not write laws; humans do.

8. In the late twentieth century, another stream of work has appeared, the use of very large digital computers both for processing volumes of data and for doing simulations of various phenomena. Simulations are manipulations of a sysrep in the computer. Simulations are particularly powerful when they can be based on difference equations formulated from Entire Invariant Paradigms (so long as the numerical work is adequately done, a distinctly non-trivial task). When simulations are based on inadequate models, they will far more often than not give inadequate results. To put this differently, numerical precision does nothing to guarantee the accuracy of a sysrep.

A number of comments about the eight steps will be useful in our discussion. The processes are not linear, a one-way street running from step 1 through step 8, as I have already tried to indicate by noting some particularly important feedback loops among the steps. The evolution of a discipline nearly always involves iteration of various steps, in various orders, over time. We will not deal with all those possibilities; there are too many cases, and we do not need them for our purposes. We only note this evolutionary process is more matrix-like than linear in nearly all disciplines, once the field has gone through the first stages of development. As I have long told research students, there are two speeds in research: slow and backwards. It is not the reality but the constraints of verbal forms that cause us to describe the evolution as a seriatim set of steps.

The sequence of steps 1 through 8 is typical, but by no means universal. Some disciplines cannot be developed through all the steps owing to the complexity of the systems studied, for reasons we saw in Chapters 4, 5, and 6. In some cases, we can find Entire Invariant Paradigms; in others, we cannot. In some cases, we can express the "rules" in mathematical forms; in others, we cannot now and may never be able to. To assume that we can and should do the same things and use the same methods and views in all disciplines is crippling; it can mislead us — and has, at times.

A particularly important distinction arises from the discussion in Chapter 4. For simple systems with invariant behaviors, we can often create what we can call "grand theory" and use the theory to make reliable analytic predictions. "Grand theory" hence denotes theory for a class of problems. We can often use "grand theory" in this way in physics and simple engineering analyses. On the other hand, for very complex systems that contain open degrees of freedom, we cannot create reliable "grand theory" and hence need to rely on data, incrementalism, and feedback (see Chapter 4).

This is an appropriate place to discuss necessary conditions for stating "rules" in mathematical form. We cannot use mathematics as a sysrep unless we can rank order one or more characteristics in terms of some metric (or measure). For example, we can state that A is longer than B because we can measure length in, say, meters. We have an ordered scale for short–long. We can thus use the value of length as a variable in mathematical equations. On the contrary, we have no metric for a scale of ugly–beautiful or for hate–love. We can usually tell the end points apart, but we cannot accurately associate ugly–beautiful or love–hate with a ranked set of numbers. Hence we cannot express beauty or love by mathematical equations. This does not make them less important, only different from length, mass, money, votes, and so on.

Many descriptions of the empirical process have omitted explicit statement of step 1 and/or step 3. However, both steps are essential, and both are particularly important for some aspects of multidisciplinary discourse.

Why are taxonomies important? There are in the world some millions of species of plants and animals. Arguments still continue over whether there are a few millions or a few tens of millions, but it is certainly a large number. The first step in making sense of biology was a taxonomy that organized this vast array of species into an understandable structure, or order. We can mark this point as 1736, when the great Swedish biologist Carl von Linné (usually known as Linnaeus) created a hierarchical "tree" for classification of species in his *Genera Plantarum*. Some encyclopedias call this the "starting point of systematic biology." Linnaeus' treatise appeared several decades after Newton published his "laws" in the *Principia*. Biology reached step 3 in its evolution afer some parts of physics had not only reached step 4 but had also achieved accurate mathematical expression of Entire Invariant Paradigms.

Chemistry was slower to reach the taxonomic stage. A taxonomy is vital to chemistry, since there are 96 natural atomic elements in nature (even when we do not count isotopic forms separately). We need a taxonomy to understand how the field can be organized in our thinking (recall Miller's 7-Bit-Rule for the mind). An arrangement of the chemical "elements" was achieved by the Russian scientist Dmitri Ivanovich Mendeleyev in 1869, and in 1871 he announced that there were three gaps in his table. This enormous scientific achievement is a hierarchical structure (the periodic table of elements) that relates the nature of each element to its atomic number. However, the periodic table is not a tree but a two-dimensional matrix-ladder in form. A surprising aspect of Mendeleyev's periodic table was its predictive power. The three holes noted by Mendeleyev were all filled (in 1875, 1879, and 1885). Moreover, the properties of these elements fitted into the series suggested by the periodic table. Mendeleyev's periodic table also provided the underlying structure needed for further exploration by physicists of the nature of atomic and subatomic structure. Mendeleyev's periodic table is very firm, in the sense of nonarbitrary, although one more series, the inert gases, was added after Mendeleyev's work. It is not a human-devised structure but a fundamental picture of nature disclosed by human investigation. It would be hard to find a more powerful illustration either of the importance of taxonomies (step 3 in the sequence above) or of the fact that many taxonomies have little if any arbitrariness introduced by human ideas in forming sysreps. Moreover, as we have seen, information inherent in the structure of matter differs from the information held by humans in their minds or that is present in DNA.

It is worth reiterating that those individuals who deny the existence of hierarchical structure and firm taxonomies, and some current humanists do, are denying the very basis of both modern chemistry and modern biology.

The importance of taxonomy is also dependent on the field. In physics, there is a long-standing taxonomy that is evident in the list of beginning courses, but it has only five or six areas, unlike the elaborate taxonomies of biology and chemistry.

The taxonomy of physics has another characteristic that we need to note: the subdomains described by the taxonomy are "nearly separable." "Nearly separable" here denotes that each subdomain (for example, electromagnetism or mechanics) can be used by itself to solve many important problems. Problems that require several domains to reach solutions are common, but they can usually be created by patching together knowledge from the subdomains in ways that are often known in advance. Taxonomies in the human sciences tend to be less obvious and, when erected, to have fuzzier boundaries. Since the human sciences often deal with a highly coupled system, the individual human, they are much harder to separate into distinct subdomains in a relatively clean way.

All the processes discussed above apply to creating truth assertions about what happens in the world within a given domain, not to the world at large. In this sense, a discipline is a sysrep for a class of problems, and the remarks in Chapters 3 and 13 about systems, sysreps, and domains are applicable, including the need for a clear definition of domain as an inherently necessary part of any truth assertion about nature.

Steps 1 through 8 do not apply to formal systems of logic, most notably mathematics. In formal systems of logic, one typically begins with the statement of a set of axioms, usually a few simple axioms, and then deduces numerous consequences within that closed system of logic. The whole process is deductive, once the axioms have been stated, and the need for feedback is much reduced. For example, in arithmetic we name and order the numbers, and set down the rules for addition, subtraction, and multiplication; everything else in arithmetic follows. In elementary algebra, one starts with the idea that an arbitrary number can be represented by a letter symbol, adds the commutative, permutative, and associative rules, and all the rest follows. Similar remarks apply to most branches of mathematics. It is particularly clear in Euclidean geometry because Euclid formally axiomatized the bases two millennia ago. The current name for these kinds of constructions is "formal systems," and we need to note immediately that some powerful theorems, including Gödel's, that apply to formal systems do not necessarily apply to the world as it exists, since the world of material entities and living creatures is not composed of human-made formal systems. More specifically, by construction, formal systems have no means for self-reference; many entities in the world do (see again Figure 6-1). Also, formal systems must not be self-conflicting; human ideas and actions often are.

We will call the process for creating formal systems "Cartesian axiomatization" (after René Descartes) to distinguish it from steps 1 and 2, which we will call "Baconian empiricism."

Armchair thinking about what might happen in the given class of systems or, far worse, about an undefined class of systems has historically led to erroneous ideas many times. For this reason, more and more disciplines since Newton start with the presupposition that the first two steps in forming truth assertions about nature, whether physical, biological, or social nature, is to define a domain and make systematic observations of systems in that domain. No matter what processes follow later, these must be the first steps if we are to call the results science in the twentieth-century sense of that word. As many writers have noted, it is this empirical grounding both at the beginning and through feedback loops which most clearly distinguishes modern from ancient study of truth assertions methodologically, just as the system concept distinguishes the two conceptually.

At the very beginning of modern scientific methods, Newton's inductive generalizations coupled empirical observations to Cartesian axiomatization in mathematical form for rapid further advances. At this moment, in the late seventeenth century, the method had become qualitatively more than empiricism alone. To describe science as "the empirical method" is thus seriously incomplete, even at that time.

When a discipline reaches this point, whether the theory is mathematized or left verbal, the full power of the system/sysrep approaches becomes available. Understanding how to use the apparatus only grows slowly, field by field. In some fields the full power of the apparatus is still not utilized, even in the late twentieth century. Moreover, Chapter 13 suggests that it would pay us to develop the apparatus more fully and carefully in many fields.

There has been considerable discussion in recent years about the way in which theory modulates and "colors" the kind of observations we make, but this cannot occur in a strong form during the first two steps at the beginning of a discipline because then we have no "rules" and no theory. Theory can only be invoked at a later stage. Moreover, theory is far more important in modulating experiments in some fields than in others owing to the effects of hierarchical obscurity (see Chapter 12).

Whenever we express the "rules" for a given discipline in mathematical form (step 4 in the sequence above), several important things happen, often implicitly.

• We link the knowledge in the field to a defined set of variables. Any phenomena that cannot be described by these variables then implicitly become exogenous to the sysrep as long as we use these equations. It does not necessarily follow that these phenomena are exogenous to the system, only to the sysrep. We saw an example of the importance of this distinction in the discussion of neoclassic economics (Chapter 14).

• Often many deductive consequences can be found because the relevant formal systems of mathematics come to apply. Since mathematicians have worked out many detailed and accurate deductive consequences for many formal systems, we often immediately have in hand a number of powerful tools for analyses and computations. Sometimes we even immediately have in hand complete solutions to problems because the specific forms of mathematics have already been worked through in detail for mathematically identical problems. However, if the form of Cartesian axiomatization (that is, the branch of math) used is inappropriate, we may wholly, formally, and deductively reach some erroneous conclusions. We saw one such example in d'Alembert's Paradox.

• Mathematization creates a potential for an iterative loop between Baconian empiricism and Cartesian axiomatization. It is this iterative loop that is the most powerful method we know for adding to the existing body of what we call science. And it is here that theory may begin to strongly modulate experiments. When we use this loop not only do we repeatedly ground results in empirical observations in the developments that follow, but we often also learn the type of empirical observations we ought to make and how to make them. That is, the theory suggests which experiments are most likely to be valuable for further gains in knowledge. A particularly good discussion of the effective mode of using this loop is given by Platt (1966). However, such a loop is more readily accessible in some fields than in others owing to the relative complexity or simplicity of the systems studied and to hierarchical obscurity. If the system is so complex that we cannot provide a theory for the entire system, then the full power of this method is not accessible. If the system is totally opaque to direct observations, we have far more difficulty in forming schemata that the human mind can readily grasp. This has been the case for both quantum mechanics and relativity.

In thinking about the history being described, we need to recognize that it was a branch of physics — specifically, classical mechanics (including gravity) in the hands of Galileo and Newton — that was the first instance of successful formation of rules following the steps all the way from 1 through 4. In addition, both paradigms describe a domain that concerns inert, naturally-occurring objects with a complexity index of 4 or less, and both domains exhibit deterministic invariant behaviors. Despite this, the process from step 1 through 4 took about three centuries from Copernicus through Kepler and Galileo to Newton. This again illustrates how much the increase in knowledge has accelerated in the nineteenth and twentieth centuries. Finally, the systems that Newton's "laws" describe are not of great variety, so that no significant taxonomic work needed to precede the inductive leap that Newton built on the work of Copernicus, Brahe, Kepler, and Galileo. To put this differently, Newton was able to largely bypass step 3 (taxonomy) because it was not critical for this particular area.

For the two major classes of systems Newton studied, his principles have over time been shown to be Entire Invariant Paradigms. By this I imply, as before, that we now have an uncountable number of observations in many qualitatively distinct situations in which Newton's "laws" have been used to make predictions that were later verified empirically with results as accurate as the uncertainty in the measurements allow. This has continued to be true as we have developed more and more precise instruments of measurement. We have come to believe that the principles are valid and accurate, within a well-understood domain.

Newton created what turned out to be an Entire Invariant Paradigm for two very significant domains; and those paradigms are expressible in simple mathematical principles that are functions of only a few "hard" variables (complexity index of 4 or less). These facts played an important role in later developments, as we will see below.

For roughly two centuries, it was believed by many scientists that Newton's paradigms applied to everything in the universe. In the twentieth century we have found that the domains for which Newton's "laws" are Entire Invariant Paradigms are not universal, although we still believe that the "laws" cover quite a lot of territory. To avoid misunderstanding, I note that I am aware that some philosophers now say, "Newton's laws have been overthrown." However, I do not agree with this statement, for reasons we will see in the next chapter.

Moreover, given steps 1 through 8 (described above), we must expect that the domain of applicability of "rules" will need to be broadened, narrowed, or both, in different ways as we test more examples because the initial leap to a principle or law is nearly always based on a relatively restricted class of data, as Newton's "laws" were. For multidisciplinary discourse, it is particularly important to be clear that modifying the domain differs qualitatively from modifying what the "rules" say about what occurs within the applicable domain.

Given this framework, let's look next at the order in which various disciplines branched from "natural philosophy," particularly when they moved to the taxonomic stage and to mathematization (when that has happened).

During the nineteenth century, all the major fields of classical physics were brought at least to step 4, the enunciation of Entire Invariant Paradigms in mathematical form. These domains developed largely in the order that would be suggested by two constraints: complexity of the systems and hierarchical obscurity. That is, mechanics of discrete bodies arose first, followed by extensions to continuous media. Next came the laws describing energy and the properties of substances (thermodynamics), which began in the 1820's and were completed by the 1860's. Extensions to chemical equilibrium appeared in the 1870's. Electromagnetism was complete well before the end of the nineteenth century. In essentially all these areas, understanding has been refined and improved pedagogical materials created, but none have gone through revolutions of the "rules" since that time; only some modifications of domain have occurred. Newton's paradigm for gravity was given a different interpretation by Einstein in his theory of relativity. However, with only a few exotic exceptions, special relativity and Newton's formulation give the same results. Einstein chose to make gravity as seen by Newton a limiting case of his theory.

Biology and medicine remained in taxonomic and descriptive modes until about the middle of the nineteenth century. Recognition of micro-organisms as the source of many diseases was accepted after much dispute in the third quarter of the nineteenth century. The bases of statistical genetics and the theory of evolution were each created in the last half of the nineteenth century, but their union did not arrive until the twentieth century. The detailed chemical bases of genetics were still being worked out at the end of the twentieth century. These dates support the idea that the general trend has been from less to the more complex systems and from the directly observable to the more and more hierarchically obscure.

Before we look at the origins of the human sciences, we need to look at the spirit of the times in nineteenth-century Europe, because it had a large effect on how some of these disciplines began, and these effects persist to some degree in the late twentieth century. Economic growth then was so rapid in Europe that there was a net monetary deflation over the entire nineteenth century. That is, a given amount of a particular currency would buy more goods in 1900 than it had in 1800 in the industrializing European nations. This is nearly unique in history; inflation has been rampant most of the time in money economies nearly everywhere else. Also, at this same time, the major fields of classical physics had been put in place and seemed toward the end of the nineteenth century to be providing "final truths" about how to understand the physical world and hence by extrapolation all problems. The ability of doctors to cure diseases was advancing rapidly. So were the techniques and productivity of agriculture, the industrial arts, and engineering. Simultaneously, the practice of democracy was spreading, following the political principles created in the U.S. Constitution, thus creating more liberties for many people. Finally, improved social and sanitary conditions for many sectors of society were being rapidly achieved. Death rates dropped dramatically, and longevity increased significantly. Many new services and amenities became available to the growing middle class.

As a result, the idea that progress was continuous and its sister idea that the human race is perfectible came to be held by many individuals in late-nineteenth-century Europe. The negative side-effects of pollution, overproduction, and harsh working conditions were largely glossed over in this period because the gains for many humans were so great. As far as science was concerned, these views led to two ideas: (A) "Good" science should be like what had been done by Newton; that is, it should express "iron laws" giving the final truth in terms of simple principles using only a few "hard" variables and parameters; and (B) Humans were "progressing" over time in some kind of steady, monotonic way.

We will need to look very carefully at idea (A), the use of the Galilean-Newtonian method as an ideal for the development of disciplines, since that has affected matters of central concern in this book. However, by the late twentieth century, idea (B) had been overtaken by events and largely debunked. We will not discuss it further.

With this background, we can turn to discussion of the human sciences. There are six fields that we can consider human sciences. Two go back to ancient times: history and political science. One dates from the eighteenth century as a specific domain of study: economics. There are also three newer human sciences: psychology, sociology, and anthropology.

We will not say much in this brief account about history and political science, noting only that they became professionalized in the late nineteenth century, and this raised scholarly standards. We have already discussed economics briefly and will add only a few remarks later. It is the three newer human sciences that need discussion at this point.

Anthropology, sociology, and psychology all began as formal disciplines of knowledge in the late nineteenth century in Europe. As a result, they were all affected at their roots by the spirit of the times.

All three of the behavioral sciences have important roots going back to the work of the French philosopher and social thinker Auguste Comte in his *Positivist Philosophy*, published in a series of lectures and papers between 1828 and

1842 in France. Comte's ideas need describing, since they had important later effects.

Comte coined the word "sociology" and announced that he intended to create a science of sociology comparable to the science of Newton. This is as far as I have been able to trace the origin of the idea that the social sciences should model themselves on physics, although others very probably had the same thought as early or at least not much later. Both the ideas that "sociology" should be a science and that it should mimic physics in its methods were endorsed by John Stuart Mill in the following decades, and Mill's prestige aided in diffusing both ideas widely in European thought.

Comte did not use the word "sociology" in the sense that it is used in the late twentieth century. Rather, he intended sociology to include the study of all forms of the behavior of humans, that is, the complete range of the "human sciences" (as we are using the phrase). Comte did not use the empirical method. Instead, he created a picture of a hierarchy of disciplines, and he suggested that "sociology" should descend from the other disciplines in a series of hierarchical steps but should nevertheless become a "master discipline." The hierarchy that Comte suggested went in descending order: math, astronomy, physics, chemistry, biology (including physiology), sociology. Comte saw each of the fields as increasing in specialization beginning from math. He also thought that each could be understood only with the aid of the preceding fields in the "descent." Comte's ideas contain three sources of confusion: first, they mix up levels in the hierarchy of constitution; second, they confound sysreps with systems; and third, they confound formal systems (which are "rule" bound) with systems of physical and biological entities (which are not "rule" bound). Because of this threefold confusion, Comte's ideas on hierarchical derivation of the social sciences were not possible of achievement (see Chapter 7). The hierarchical derivation part of Comte's ideas has therefore withered away. Nevertheless, Comte's hierarchy is worth noting because it delineates nearly the same order (with the exception of astronomy) as a common "pecking order" of prestige among the disciplines of science which still exists in some places in the late twentieth century. More specifically, some scholars consider the disciplines that use "hard" variables and produce Entire Invariant Paradigms as in some sense better than those that do not (as Thomas Kuhn was to say later, "mature" as opposed to "immature"). In some instances, scholars also put math at the top of the status order. I have seen no tracing of the origins of this pecking order. However, the fact that Comte already expressed this order indicates that the idea is not of recent origin. So we have a name for it, I will call this snobbish hierarchy "Comte's Pecking Order."

As already noted, Comte's Pecking Order among the disciplines puts formal systems at the top and then follows from simple systems to more and more complex systems. It exalts the simple and denigrates the complex. Moreover, the hierarchy is not grounded, in any sense I can find, in an inherent importance of the disciplines involved.

Let's restate the implicit assumptions underlying the beginnings of the three new human sciences as implied by Comte. Stated in stark, extreme form, these are (1) the study of human behaviors should be made into "sciences"; and (2) "sciences" should mimic physics, that is, create "iron laws" stating simple principles in terms of a small number of "hard" variables.

In the late nineteenth century, as psychology, sociology, and anthropology each adopted the empirical method and began to branch from natural philosophy, the founders nearly all began with those two ideas that seem to have come from Comte. Whether these ideas descended primarily from Comte, or had other roots as well, is not nearly so important as the fact that, at their beginnings, all the mainstream work in the newer human sciences adopted these two ideas. This is not a post hoc reading. There are nearly always dissenters in any discipline, but the dominant "founding fathers" in all these disciplines were quite explicit about the use of these twin ideas. For example, Sigmund Freud, in the area one would think most removed from the behavior of inert, naturally-occurring objects, the human psyche, tried to erect simple principles using only a few variables and announced he was doing so to be "scientific." Even in describing the unconscious for the first time, Freud used words taken from mechanics (energy, drive, impulse). Since this one example will have to serve to illustrate several areas, and in order to minimize bias, let me quote two researchers who are themselves within the Freudian tradition. Weiss and Sampson (1986) say,

> The method Freud recommended in the papers on technique reflects his wish to base his technique both on a scientific theory of the mind and a rational approach to the patient. In developing his theory of the mind, Freud was influenced by the physics of his day, which assumed that all phenomena in the physical world could be derived from a few simple elements governed by a few simple laws. Freud assumed that all or almost all mental functioning may be derived from a few simple mental elements, namely impulses and defenses, governed by a simple mental law, the pleasure principle (1926b, p. 265). Moreover, Freud assumed that impulses and defenses interact dynamically, much as do certain forces in the world.

The quotation is a complete paragraph without change; Weiss and Sampson cite Freud's *Psychoanalysis*, in *The Standard Edition* (1926), 20: 259–70, published in London by the Hogarth Press.

None of this discussion is intended to suggest that the methods adopted within physics have been unsuccessful. On the contrary, they have been unimaginably successful in creating relatively well-grounded understanding of the inert, naturally-occurring physical world, and at one remove, of enormous value in creating human-designed physical devices. As we have noted before, it is not an instance of failure but, rather, of success overrunning itself, thereby leading us to believe that certain ideas and methods can be used beyond where they are appropriate sysreps.

In sum, at the end of the nineteenth century the ideas that Newton's paradigms were "universal" became pervasive. Many thinkers took Newton's ideas as an adequate basis for a single view of the human world and all its concerns. More-over, a significant sector of the philosophy community endorsed this idea. Nor does there seem to have been widespread, important dissent from the idea that Newton's paradigms were sufficient for a worldview. Nietzsche seems to be nearly alone as an influential dissenter among nineteenth-century philosophers. However, as we have seen at several earlier points, physics by itself cannot be a complete sysrep for all matters of human concern. There are apparently impass-able conceptual barriers at two levels in the hierarchy of constitution. One arises at the edge of the domain of the physical sciences from the theory of dimensions; the other, at a higher level, from an inspection of what lies outside the domain of truth assertions.

We need to look now at a few things about the development of the profes-sional areas and their relationship to scientific knowledge since the time of Newton.

As we have seen, humans and our biological ancestors have, for something like two million years, been making innovations in the sociotechnical systems we use to secure our living. Science as we know it in the late twentieth century is about three centuries old. It must follow, as Ed Layton, a historian of technology, has noted, that we can make innovations without any science at all. Nevertheless, after World War II many people in the Western world came to believe the linear model of innovation, in which science is the sole input to innovation. This suggests that our understanding of the relations between science and large work-ing areas, such as medicine, engineering, agriculture, and psychotherapy, has been incomplete. We have not space for the details, but it is important for multidisciplinary discussion to note some general features.

All four of the working areas just mentioned use as much science as they can bring to bear, if not immediately, then diffusively over time. But this does not mean that any one of the four is "merely applied science," as we have sometimes been told. Each of these fields plays a symbiotic role in interacting with the relevant branches of science. The working areas in every case encompass far more than merely applied science, and the relations are matrix-like and involve many feedback links. The links are not a one-way street from science to those areas. Let us look at a few details in one case, engineering and the physical sciences, to be sure about this point.

Can engineering be appropriately described as merely applied physical sci-ence? The cases of engineering knowledge that is not science documented by Vincenti (1989) themselves give a sufficient answer. There is a vast range of knowledge needed in various branches of engineering which cannot appropri-ately be called science. There are also many areas in which the problems thrown up by the work within engineering led to scientific research, a mode of research I call "technology-induced science." In this mode the flow of information is back-wards from the picture of science setting off innovation; here innovation sets off science. Are such researches common or significant? Any brief scan of fields, such as aerodynamics, materials science, computer science, the theory of combustion, turbulence, and many others, will show that technology-induced science has been very common and very important in the history of science itself. Let me give two examples. In 1824 a young man in France asked himself the question, How efficient are the steam engines that I see altering the face of Europe? The result was the first statement of what we now call the second "law" of thermodynamics by Sadi Carnot. This is not the form of the "law" many scientists use, but it was the original form, and it is of particular value to engineers. In 1904, one year after the Wright brothers' first successful flight, Ludwig Prandtl was grappling with the problem of how aircraft wings create lift. He wanted to find out what had gone wrong with the work of d'Alembert (see Chapter 2). The resulting paper by Prandtl is accepted almost everywhere as the genesis of modern fluid mechanics. And, in addition, when the mathematicians looked at what Prandtl had done, they realized that the method needed study because it lay outside known mathematics. That study led to a whole branch of mathematics now called asymptotic perturbation theory. These are only a few examples of many.

Moreover, the eminent sociologist of science, de Solla Price, in his last paper argued that on balance technology had contributed more to science than science had to technology. Technology in a broad sense, as de Solla Price noted, had created the tools from which science was able to start: the telescope in physics and the microscope in many areas of biology, and this flow of instruments and methods from technology into science has continued down to the present time. But even all this is not the end of the story. The learned neuromuscular skills of mechanics, instrument makers, glass blowers, and machinists (to mention only a few) are critical in both science and technology. And these skills grew and continue to be maintained through crafts, not science.

We could say much more on this topic, but this is enough for the conclusion we need. The professional disciplines have benefited enormously from scientific information, and science has benefited enormously not only from the skills, instruments, and manufacturing capabilities in technology but also from the kinds of questions thrown up at the forefront of professional work in nearly every field. Working areas often deal with complete sociotechnical systems. Sciences are typically cuts through the hyperspace of such systems and are therefore not sufficient for all problems within the systems. It is seriously simplistic to consider medicine, engineering, agriculture, or psychotherapy as merely application of the related fields of science.

This brings our very brief summary to the end of the nineteenth century. We have here and there moved ahead of the story to maintain context and connect to later events. Nevertheless, the story as a whole seems clear.

Conclusions for Chapter 15

Disciplines of knowledge composed of professional workers are a very new kind of enterprise. Until the twentieth century, it is centrally a European story and a story of men. Women and members of other cultures are entirely capable of contributing, as we have seen in the twentieth century, but were for the most part disenfranchised in earlier times owing to economic and cultural constraints. History suggests that we get rich and then do high science, not the other way around. History also suggests that science flourishes only when excessive constraint on thought is not brought to bear by either the state or the church.

The essential methodological (not the conceptual) base of the vast increase in relatively well grounded human knowledge is the branching of fields, from the older philosophic methods of dialectic discourse and armchair thought, to the use of empiricism not only at the base but also by repeated use of feedback in the human-design and other feedback modes, including the system/sysrep concepts.

The disciplines developed in an order that roughly moved from the simple to the complex and from the directly observable to the hierarchically obscure.

The spirit of the times, in late-nineteenth-century Europe, combined with the particulars of the evolutionary processes of the disciplines, created a climate in which human progress was seen as continuous and the human being perfectible in a Newtonian-like universe of deterministic causes. This view has often been likened to a great clockwork. Moreover, the idea was circulating that if humans had not yet reached the goal of a return to the Garden of Eden, they were at least well along the path. This led all three of the newer human sciences to begin with the idea that they should ape both the methods and the models of physics, which was seen as the beau ideal of the world of scholarship. More specifically, the goal was to build simple paradigms expressed in terms of a few hard variables which would state the truth about human behaviors. Not all scholars agreed with these ideas. Also, I have stated the ideas very starkly for clarity. Nevertheless, they seem to have been the dominant ideas in the relevant communities of scholars in Europe in the late nineteenth century. We will have to see, in the next chapter, how this has worked out.

If we look back at the view underlying Adam Smith's great work in 1776, we see that it also used the idea of a great self-regulating clockwork, and expressed all of economics in terms of one simple principle — supply and demand. A century later Karl Marx based his economics on another single, simple idea — the role of class conflict.

In sum, four of the six human sciences were founded on the positivist ideas advocated by Comte and attempted to express all the behaviors in their particular domain by simple fixed values using a few hard variables.

Finally, the vessels that contain competence in large working areas are the communities that operate sociotechnical systems even in the most sophisticated professional areas, and the knowledge in each of these areas is far more than merely applied science.

CHAPTER 16

Relations Among the Disciplines in the Twentieth Century

Similarities and Differences

Two trends in the disciplines from the nineteenth century continued with growing strength in the first few decades of the twentieth century. The increasing wealth in a number of European nations allowed the professionalized communities of scholars to grow rapidly. These communities continued to use iterative feedback between predictive rules and empirically grounded data in the ways described in Chapter 15. The fact that these communities were now largely composed of professionals who formed "invisible colleges" also led in many fields to significant increases in every aspect of scholarly standards. David Potter's remarks (1954) about standards in history and the Flexner report regarding standards in medicine in the United States describe two examples among many.

As a result of these trends, explosive growth of knowledge occurred not only in depth of detail and in the number of areas studied but also in the assurance with which many results are known. The process of forming more and more specialized disciplines and subdisciplines allowed individuals to create more and more depth in their schemata about specific, relatively narrow domains. This has vastly increased our power to understand many specific areas of knowledge. At the same time, it has ramified the Tower of Babel formed by detailed schemata and jargon.

As a result, probably no one person, certainly not the writer, can create a balanced overview of what has happened to the content of what humans know collectively about ourselves and our world in the late twentieth century. However, an appropriate group of scholars could probably form far better overviews than we presently have; we will discuss how this might be done in Appendix A.

A new development in the twentieth century was the diffusion of leading research and scholarship in the disciplines dealing with truth assertions from Europe to the United States and, to a lesser extent, to many other areas of the world. In the case of the United States, the diffusion was speeded by two major factors: increasing wealth, and the arrival of many leading researchers and scholars from Europe. Their emigration to the United States owes much to the political strife and oppression of minorities in many European nations during the first half of the twentieth century. Leading scholars who were White Russians, Germans, and Jewish scholars of many nations emigrated to the United States, seeking a society more hospitable to research and scholarship and more tolerant of ethnic differences and also wealthy enough to support their efforts. Some of these émigrés were leading workers who brought with them established traditions for both research and the training of advanced students. Their work led to far more rapid advances in both knowledge and scholarly standards in many U.S. disciplinary communities than would otherwise have been possible.

In five of the six human sciences, many leading researchers continued to take the view that rigor and high standards implied being "physics-like," in the sense of expressing simple principles that stated "iron laws" in terms of a small number of variables. The exception among the human sciences was history, which continued to examine complete human systems. Specialization occurred via examining particular eras rather than by taking cuts through the hyperspace of social and sociotechnical systems. Ethnology began by looking for "the ultimate truth about human nature." However, the data accumulated showed so much variation in behaviors from one ethnic group to another, most workers shifted their view within a relatively short time. The other four human sciences continued for many decades to have strong elements of positivism in leading research programs.

The relatively pragmatic intellectual climate of the United States provided a particularly fertile soil for positivist ideas. We have already examined one notable example, that of "radical behaviorism." These programs grew stronger until at least the time of World War II, and positivist views still dominate programs in many university psychology departments in the United States as the twentieth century draws near a close.

However, during the early twentieth century, a paradoxical trend arose in the relations among the disciplines. In the same period when positivist views were becoming dominant in many research and scholarly programs in the human sciences, the model from which positivist views had grown, Newtonian physics, began to be questioned in the physics community. Within a few decades, roughly by 1930, the primary view of the physics community had shifted, and it was no longer Newtonian. We will need to examine these shifts, since the results have influenced not only widely accepted views of the world but also the relationships among a number of disciplines.

We cannot trace both these paths at once, since they diverge. I will trace the outcomes of positivism in the human sciences, and then turn back to what occurred in physics and the resulting relationships of physics to philosophy and other disciplines.

We will not use up much paper in describing the outcome of the positivist views in the human sciences because we already know what the outcome must be. As we have already seen, we cannot create "grand theory" for very complex systems that have open degrees of freedom. What we have taken to be grand theory has been some form of a cut through a hyperspace of much larger dimensionality. We must therefore expect positivist programs in the human sciences to provide some knowledge, often very important knowledge, but to remain seriously incomplete as sysreps of the domains they undertake to study. We saw why this is so in psychology (Chapter 6) and in economics (Chapter 14). We have also noted several times that the primary outcome of ethnographic studies has not been invariant "rules" providing "the final truth" about human behaviors; on the contrary, the collected ethnographic data gathered during the twentieth century show previously unimaginable variation across cultures to be the norm for many central forms of human behaviors. The same result—some important conclusions, but incomplete sysreps created by positivist formulations—has emerged in psychotherapy, in sociology, and in political science.

To put this differently, we do not seem to have found a single Entire Invariant Paradigm anywhere in the human sciences, and this remark seems to remain true in the late twentieth century. We have nevertheless learned a great deal of value about the human sciences; see, for example, the illustrations in Chapter 6 concerning communications and linguistics. These and many other results are very important for understanding humans and human societies, but they are not Invariant Paradigms. The Entire Paradigms of the human sciences tell us what will tend to happen or what may happen with given probabilities, but they do not say that "these details will occur every time." These results in the human sciences are not less important than results in physics, but they do have some quite different characteristics.

What, then, happened in physics? After 1900 the physics community began to move away from the Newtonian-Galilean view toward a quite different view as the result of developments in several new areas within physics, in particular, statistical mechanics, transport theory, relativity, and quantum mechanics. As these new subfields grew, a generation-long argument occurred within the physics community about "the proper fundamental view."

By the 1930's, the argument within the physics community was largely over; the dominant view, often called "modern physics," had come to be quantum mechanics. Einstein died without fully accepting the new (quantum) view. So, too, did other notable physicists, among them, Nobel laureate P. W. Bridgman. Some leading thinkers in physics have continued to contest some of the ideas, particularly the generality of what can be learned from the newer view. Nevertheless, over a period of two or three decades the physics community shifted from the Newtonian-Galilean paradigm to quantum mechanics as the basic view. This has occurred despite the fact that relativity and gravity still suggest a view, at bottom, other than current quantum mechanics.

For multidisciplinary discourse, the important point is that the dominant workers in the physics community thought of this new view not as one view among many, nor as a sysrep for a particular subdomain of physics, but as an improved basis from which everything else can be derived, at least in principle. An important part of this new view for our purposes can be summarized in this way: The world is not deterministic, as Newton and Galileo told us it is. Rather, the world should be viewed as "randomly probabilistic" and to some degree also as inherently "uncertain." The word "randomly" in the previous sentence denotes a model like that of statistical mechanics to differentiate it from other kinds of statistically describable but partially correlated behaviors, which are not "random." The added idea of uncertainty stems from the Heisenberg Uncertainty Principle, which affects some kinds of observations, but not all, at subatomic levels of matter.

The argument was again put forward by some members of the physics community that the smallest "particles" are an appropriate basis for a worldview because everything is made up of them. Thus, a common, seemingly dominant, current view within the physics community is that "in principle" one can derive all we need to know from quantum mechanics plus gravity.

Am I exaggerating? As long as we remember that we are speaking of only a significant (perhaps dominant) fraction of workers in the physics community, and not all, I don't think so. Only a few years ago one of the leading physicists of this generation wrote me, "Given quantum electrodynamics and gravity one can do all macroscopic problems on this earth." He expressed no qualifications of any kind. Moreover, arguments to the effect that further study of high-energy physics will lead to "the ultimate secrets of the universe" appear frequently in appeals for public funds for colliders and other devices desired for research. For example, in *Science* April 16, 1993, in an article titled "Research News," the following quotation appeared:

> Within the limits set by quantum mechanics, an omniscient superphysicist who cared to measure the velocity, momentum, and every other property of every other particle in the universe could predict the color of tomorrow's sunset, find out who killed JFK and how the dinosaurs died, and foresee when the world will end. All the information needed to build the universe at any moment in its history has always existed and will always exist, however mixed up it becomes.

We have not space in this chapter to discuss in detail all things that are wrong with the ideas in this quotation. However, the reader may want to ask himself or herself if the quotation mixes up the four inherently different meanings of the word "information" (see Chapter 4) and therefore runs afoul of Seneca's Dictum, When the words are confused, the mind is also. More specifically, ask yourself, Is the information bound into inert objects the same as information in human brains? And is the information in the structure of a human brain recallable after the death of an individual and the decay of the brain? Also remember that when we fail to make "needful" distinctions, we cannot understand our topic clearly.

If this assertion in *Science* represents the dominant view in the physics community, as it claims to, then at least some of the physics community still believes the statement of Laplace, "Give me the trajectories of the molecules, and I will predict the future." But they have now transmogrified the view into the concepts of modern physics and state the claim in terms of quantum mechanics.

However, if the ideas and explicit hypotheses we have been developing in this volume are correct, the claim that physics is a worldview cannot be appropriate, for several independent reasons. Such assertions about physics are what we have been calling "overclaims." More specifically, the ideas expressed by Laplace, by the leading physicists, and in the quotation from *Science*, are all in direct conflict with each of Hypotheses III, IV, V, VI, and VII in this volume and also with Polanyi's Principle. We must therefore look once again at the question, What is the domain of physics, in principle? Is it everything of concern to humans or less than that?

We have already seen that physics, even all of physics, cannot be a complete worldview nor a basis for one, for several reasons. Let's state two of these again. Such a result would be dimensionally improper in the sense that it violates an assumption that is presuppositional to all the equations of classical physics itself. We cannot get "oughts" from "izzes," and physics deals with "izzes" while the open degrees of freedom inherent in human social and sociotechnical systems make "oughts" of vital import to the human race and the planet. There are other reasons, but we have already explicated them, and this is enough. The materials we have developed force us to conclude that the assertion that physics is an appropriate basis for a complete worldview is a serious overclaim. It is serious because it has distorted worldviews and confused understanding of the relationships between the disciplines for many of us for a century or more. It has also blocked rapprochement between spiritual and scientific views, as Chapter 12 makes clear.

For this discussion, let us then accept the conclusion of the preceding paragraph — physics is not and cannot be a worldview — in order to move on to several other questions about the relations of physics to other disciplines. These questions include, What is the domain that quantum mechanics does describe appropriately, and what lies entirely outside that domain, if anything? What domain, if any, does classical physics describe appropriately? What has been the role of philosophy in these questions? Let's take these questions up one at a time.

What domain does quantum mechanics describe? It describes the domain it was made up to describe, the world of the subatomic. Physicists are the experts in this area, and there is no reason to doubt that quantum mechanics is the best model we have for this domain, even though we may in the future find a better model. We need not argue here whether quantum mechanics is a perfect sysrep for this domain, nor do we need to argue the precise upper limits of size of which quantum theory will give reasonable approximations. Those are questions for the physics community. From the view of the larger intellectual community we do need to insist that the physics community give us some basis for what they say about the limits of the domains of the various theories as they affect larger systems in the world. That is, we need something other than "It can be done in principle." History tells us that such an "in principle" assertion is a dangerous kind of claim, since it can neither be proved nor disproved and implies an unwarranted "projection" of a schema. More specifically, we cannot use the crucial system/sysrep apparatus on "in principle" statements. Accepting an "in principle" assertion (based on methods and views of physics) has twice seriously confused many scholars about worldviews in the past two centuries and thereby led to much misguided scholarship. If we are to understand ourselves and our world appropriately, we cannot afford to prolong or repeat this error.

We turn therefore to a more specific question, What classes of systems lie outside of what we can find from the "new" view of physics which was adopted about 1930?

Let's begin by pushing a little farther into the "meaning" of quantum mechanics as interpreted by the people in the field. In what seems to be the most widely accepted book on that subject, Herbert (1985) summarizes eight conflicting views within the physics community on the meaning of quantum mechanics within the physical world. The words "within the physical world" in the previous sentence denote inert, naturally-occurring objects. Herbert summarizes this extensive survey by saying, in effect, "none of the eight conflicting views seems to make much sense." Casti (1989) in an independent review of the meaning of quantum mechanics reaches similar conclusions, which we will not elaborate here. For our discussion, we do need to note several things. Eight views is equivalent to no generally accepted view. Eight conflicting views, none of which seems to make much sense, appear to be a remarkably poor basis from which to provide an explanation of the whole of our world and ourselves. Finally, neither Herbert nor Casti discusses any problem that has relevance to human social or sociotechnical systems, and thus the assertion that quantum mechanics is a worldview lacks any substantive demonstration or even a suggestion of a route to follow, once we pass beyond the inert, naturally-occurring world. Over and over in discussions in the physics community, we see a truly vast "semantic slippage" from knowledge of the "inert, naturally-occurring physical world" to the shorter but inaccurate phrases "of the world" or "of the universe." This omission of needful qualifying words misdefines the system by omitting critical descriptors. The result confounds our understanding (see Chapters 2, 3, and 4).

Given this picture, we can ask a more tightly framed question. Is quantum mechanics a good sysrep for the inert world we see daily around us, the classical world described, for example, by Newton, by Gibbs, by Maxwell, by our theories for structures such as buildings, and by the macroscopic "laws" of thermodynamics? A metaphor may help us see the situation without the need to examine sophisticated theories or advanced mathematics, which have long beclouded the issue for most of us.

The metaphor concerns the behaviors of cats and dogs. Cat lovers often say to dog lovers, "Please do not try to understand or explain the behavior of cats in terms of the behavior of dogs. Cats and dogs are both furry, four-legged, warm-blooded mammals; there are some important similarities. Nevertheless, the behaviors of cats are very different from those of dogs. Therefore one ought not map the behavior of dogs over onto cats. It leads to misunderstanding of cats."

If we accept the warning of cat lovers, as observations suggest we should, then logic impels the converse. That is, we ought not map the behaviors of cats over onto dogs either, because, as cat lovers told us, the behaviors of cats and dogs are very different. This is merely a metaphor; cats and dogs are not an accurate analog for quarks and tennis balls. However, the logic of the cat and dog metaphor applies to the question in hand. What the logic says is: Two classes of systems that are significantly different in behaviors ought not be described in terms of one another, in either direction. There are gray areas concerning what is a "significant difference" in this sense, but when there are clear, significant differences in behaviors, then the differences exist in both directions, not merely in one.

For decades, however, a view emanating from the physics community has been telling us two things:

1. Please be careful not to try to understand or explain behaviors at the quantum level of the very, very small by mapping over onto that domain what you observe of classical objects from everyday experiences. The two domains, objects of human size and the subatomic, are very different; mapping the behaviors of classical systems onto quantum systems is therefore misleading.

2. We ought to use the quantum view as the view of the entire world including objects of classical size and larger.

These two statements form a logical contradiction with each other, as the logic of the cat and dog metaphor tells us.

Given the logic of the cat and dog metaphor, we can now focus our question still more tightly. Several philosophers have told me in recent years that Newton's "laws" have been overthrown by quantum mechanics and relativity. Is this true? The barefoot data all around us answer this question. Modern physics does not invalidate Newton's "laws" as they apply to inert objects of ordinary size, moving at ordinary speeds. Our predictions about the tennis ball in the second-floor tennis-ball test come not from quantum mechanics but from Newton's "laws" of gravity and motion. As far as I know, we could not use quantum theory in its present form and make predictions for the falling tennis ball. If someone can do this, please let me know. For the falling tennis ball, relativity theory gives the same answer as Newton's "laws," but it is more complex to use and unnecessary. As we noted in Chapter 9, competent physicists know these things, since they insist that the Bohr Correspondence Principle be met; that is, no form of quantum mechanics is taken as appropriate in physics unless it gives results consistent with classical mechanics when we aggregate by mathematical integration.

Einstein's relativity theory gives the classical limit inherently; it reduces trivially to Newton's "laws" for the cases we see every day. Einstein designed his theory so it would do this purposefully. Hence we need no special "correspondence principle" for relativity.

Modern physics does, however, destroy the idea that Newton's "laws" are in any way "universal." Modern physics has shown that Newton's "laws" are "general" only for certain classes of systems. But this is just what Chapter 3 and also Corning (1983) indicate is the character of all known truth assertions. To put this differently, Newton's "laws" are not an exception to Hypothesis IV (particular "rules" apply to domains, not to everything).

What is important for our discussion is the following. The systems within the narrowed domain for which we believe Newton's "laws" are the governing "rules" not only exist, they are also very common and very important to human life. For these systems, Newton's "laws" form an Entire Invariant Paradigm with about as much assurance as anything humans know about the world. What some philosophers have told me about overthrowing Newton's "laws" is a failure to distinguish between the content of a "rule" within the domain to which the rule applies on the one hand, and the extent of the domain to which the "rule" applies on the other. Moreover, we must expect that the wider testing of a "rule," after its first statement, will often contract (or expand) our picture of the domain because the initial formulation is typically a conceptual leap from a few cases to a much broader class of cases (see Chapter 15). Since we have not been clear about the dangers of universalisms, it is not surprising that we have not been clear on this issue either.

As a result, the use of Newton's "laws" has not faded away, as the remark that they have been "overthrown" suggests they should have by now — half a century after the acceptance of the quantum mechanics view by the physics community. On the contrary, Newton's "laws" are almost certainly more widely used by more people in the design of more systems in the 1990's than ever before, simply because the number of engineers and others designing devices is larger than before. If you doubt this, ask any engineer from Boeing, Rolls Royce, Hitachi, or other such companies the following questions. Do you still use classical physics in designing your products? How much, if any, of your designs use ideas from quantum mechanics? Could you design your product beginning from quantum mechanics without classical physics?

Let's look at the question of the domain of "modern physics" (that is, quantum mechanics) from another perspective. We ask whether there are systems in the world which are not appropriately described as random probabilistic and uncertain. If we take the multidisciplinary position, including Hypothesis II (look at all the credible data, not just the data from labs or from one domain), then the answer is not hard to find. Barefoot data are all around us on this question. Even within the class of inert, naturally-occurring systems, the domain of the physical sciences, there are three different kinds of systems which mandate three different kinds of sysreps if we want appropriate descriptions for each kind. These three types of systems we usually call deterministic, random probabilistic, and chaotic. Some of these systems seem to have inherent uncertainty; some do not. The second-floor tennis-ball test describes one of innumerable inert physical systems that appear to have deterministic behaviors and only instrumental (not inherent) uncertainty. Appropriate sysreps for such systems therefore should have the same kind of characteristics. The way molecules bump into each other in a non-dense gas, and thus create emergent properties like temperature and pressure, seems to follow random probabilistic behaviors and thus needs a sysrep t hat has those characteristics (that is, statistical mechanics). Some of the behaviors we observe in the subatomic level of particles seem not only to be statistical in character but also to have inherent uncertainty, and therefore they seem to need sysreps describing this kind of behavior. However, this is difficult to interpret owing apparently to the limits of measuring methods and hierarchical obscurity. Perhaps these difficulties are part of what leads to eight conflicting views of the meaning of quantum mechanics, as noted by Herbert. The third class of systems, chaotic, is not as common as the other two in the inert physical world, and it was not explicitly recognized as a third class until well after World War II. However, such phenomena have long been known experientially; we merely lacked a name for them and clarity about their nature. For example, turbulent motions in fluids have been studied intensively for more than a century and have many important applications. These motions involve a high-order form of chaos, as we now understand the concept. Sysreps for many chaotic systems seem to need some kind of a mixture of deterministic and random probabilistic models, but we do not in the late twentieth century know how to form such sysreps very well. This is one reason why turbulence remains one of the most complex and important unsolved problems in classical physics, even though we have learned quite a lot about the processes of turbulence in the past few decades.

There is an obvious counterargument to the metaphor about cats and dogs which follows another line of reasoning. We now need to discuss this argument, since some physicists repeatedly use it in attempts to justify quantum physics as a worldview. They argue that quantum mechanics, when aggregated for larger systems, reproduces classical mechanics and thermodynamics, and therefore can be taken as the basis for more complex systems. There are three problems with this counterargument. First, the fact that a lower level aggregates to a higher level does not make the variables, the parameters, the behaviors, or even the "rules" in the operating spaces of the two levels the same. Indeed, in most cases, all these matters differ from one level to another in the hierarchy of constitution.

We do not expect a mob to act like an individual, even though individuals aggregate to a mob. Organisms are made up of cells, but the behaviors of cells are not those of humans, and so on.

Second, any assertion that all that humans need to know can be found from a theory about inert subatomic particles assumes implicitly that no emergent properties arise from: heterogeneity; feedback loops; or the nature of hierarchical systems with interfaces of mutual constraint. However, vast amounts of barefoot data show that each of these three kinds of structure in a system can by itself create an enormous array of emergent properties in both inert human-design and living systems.

Third, the assertion that the "laws" of mechanics and thermodynamics can be "derived" from statistical mechanics is unfounded. This issue needs careful discussion because these so-called derivations are a necessary link in the argument that the proper way to view all systems in the entire world is probabilistically and with an inherent uncertainty. If this assertion about "derivation" of the "laws" at the classical level is unfounded, the entire basis for taking modern physics as a worldview collapses. Let's begin with P. W. Bridgman's remarks about mechanics.

As Bridgman (1941) pointed out, the "laws" of classical mechanics apply to both the classical and molecular level. We know this from data. We can therefore put the classical "laws" into our theories at either the molecular level or the classical level, and then obtain the same "rules" at the other level by mathematical operations. If we found anything else, the analysis would be flawed because the data confirm that the "rules" of mechanics hold at both levels. This is consistent with what we found for systems of homogeneous aggregation (Chapter 9). We have consistent results for mechanics as long as we stay in the class of inert, naturally-occurring materials like gases, solids, and so on. However, even within these systems the best data we have confirming the "rules" of classical mechanics are at the classical level. It is not only circular but weakens the empirical basis to say that we "derive" classical mechanics from the "rules" at the molecular level. However, this is a minor logical difficulty.

The logical situation for hierarchical systems with heterogeneous aggregation and interfaces of mutual constraint contains a more serious difficulty. For these systems, Polanyi's Principle tells us that we cannot close the mathematics needed to do aggregations from one level to another. Moreover, from a vast amount of data we know that the "laws" of thermodynamics apply to such heterogeneous systems of classical size as wholes. Another, more detailed contradiction arises between the views of some of the physics community and the results of Chapters 8 through 12. The physics community seems to believe, almost without exception, that the "laws" of thermodynamics can be and have been "derived" from statistical mechanics. However, Polanyi's Principle tells us that "rules" for many important classes of systems to which thermodynamic "laws" apply cannot be found, in any way, from integration over lower levels in the hierarchy of constitution.

Which view is wrong? A careful examination of the logic shows that the so-called derivation of thermodynamics from statistical mechanics is an overclaim. More specifically, what has been shown by the so-called derivation in the accepted textbooks, such as Mayer and Mayer (1940), is the following. The results of statistical mechanics and thermodynamics are consistent for a few very special classes of systems, such as perfect gases and crystalline solids. Read as a derivation, the specific arguments of Mayer and Mayer contain not one but at least five types of logical errors. Read as a demonstration of consistency, which is all Hypothesis VII demands, the arguments like those by Mayer and Mayer are a highlight of human intellectual achievement. One only wishes that the results had not been overstated as a derivation. The details about the five types of logical errors in the so-called derivation are of necessity technical, and are therefore discussed in Appendix B.

Many members of the physics community are not willing to reconsider this issue; they regard it as closed, and the "derivation" in their view is done. Consequently, Appendix B offers a standing bet for any physicist, at ten to one, that he or she cannot produce a derivation of the second "law" of thermodynamics from statistical mechanics that is free from logical errors.

In sum, this more detailed examination of what can be found from physics gives two results: first, the paradigms have the nature that Chapter 3 suggests, that truth assertions apply to some but not all domains. Second, the limits of what we can obtain from physical theory lie essentially where Chapters 8, 9, 10, and 11 tells us they should. Let's review the results briefly.

Chapter 3 tells us that truth assertions about nature have reasonable assurance for the domain(s) over which we have verified the particular assertions empirically. Extensions beyond this domain are inherently questionable and must be checked by appropriate further empirical observations. If we assume that truth assertions are the same in a new domain by projection in Freud's sense, the basis is inadequate, and the projected "rules" may well give erroneous results. We have seen several examples of the errors this process has created, and will see more in Chapter 17. Thus, until we have checked the data for the new domains (particularly for new levels in a hierarchical system with interfaces of mutual constraint), we ought not accept projections of the view or the principles of any discipline onto larger domains. It is logically incorrect to do so. Consequently, any statement that results extend to an area beyond existing data "in principle" is at best very suspect. Indeed, in this instance the assumption that the microscopic "rules" hold at the macroscopic level in physics leads to a well-known apparent contradiction, the irreversibility paradox. Application of Hypotheses VI and VII along with Polanyi's Principle shows that the apparent contradiction is not physical; it arises from a misuse of sysreps of just the sort discussed in this paragraph. See Appendix B for details.

In the case of physical theory for the microscopic and subatomic, the limits of upward integration (mathematically) are seen on more detailed examination to be at the boundary where systems begin to have either inherently, or designed

Characteristics of the fields or typical systems	Physical sciences	Social sciences
Similarities		
1. Central concept delineating a modern field	Explicit system definition (by some name)	Explicit system definition (by some name)
2. Central methodology indicating a modern field	Empirically grounded (repeatedly)	Empirically grounded (repeatedly)
Differences		
3. Invariance of "rules" over time	Invariant	In part not invariant; can change
4. Invariance of "rules" over space	Invariant	Often not invariant (cultures)
5. Typical complexity index	Usually < 6	Usually $> 10^9$
6. Behaviors	Inherent, repeatable, often predictable; not changeable by humans; uncertainty due to measurement not behavior	Often under human control; often changeable; variation is the norm
7. Feedback modes	No feedback of any kind in naturally-occurring inert systems	Many kinds of feedback are critical to guidance of systems
8. Purposes, aims, desires	Seemingly not teleological; have no desires	Usually have goals, aims, needs, and desires
9. Learning capacities	None	Several levels in various classes of systems
10. Self-reflective capacity	None	A peculiar and important ability of humans (and perhaps other animals)
11. Customs, mores, etc.	Do not exist	Important in cultures
12. Emotionality	None	Important in many animals, including humans

Characteristics of the fields or typical systems	Physical sciences	Social sciences
	Differences (continued)	
13. Roles of groups	Rare	Important nearly everywhere for humans
14. Use of information	Systems cannot use information	Critical to most life
15. Causation	Often monocausal	Usually multi-causal in humans (feedback vitiates utility of idea of causation)
16. Effects of history	Rare, only in hysteresis	Inherent, often important
17. Aesthetic purposes	None	Normal, often source of actions
18. Communications	Only modes; radiation, diffusion, waves	Many modalities at many levels
19. Decomposability into domains	Usually easy and clear	Often very difficult, if possible at all
20. Recomposability from pieces	Usually straightforward	Often very difficult
21. Reliability of analytic a priori predictions	Often very reliable	Rarely reliable

Figure 16-1. Comparison of 21 Characteristics of the Physical and Human Sciences.

into them, significant amounts of "human information." That is, the limits lie where Chapters 8 through 12 indicate that they should. Physical theory is useful at higher levels in the hierarchy of constitution, and it gives us many important results; however, it is seriously incomplete at those higher levels. Physical theory (even if we had a totally complete physical theory) by itself is not a suitable basis for a worldview whether the theory is "classical" or "modern."

It will be instructive at this point to summarize many of the things we have seen about the differences between the physical and the human sciences by showing the characteristics of the two domains side by side. This is given in Figure 16-1.

Figure 16-1 shows two characteristics in common and nineteen characteristics that are quite different between the physical and the human sciences. Historically, we do not seem to have been clear enough about the differences. Figure 16-1 suggests why Comte's Pecking Order, and the positivist idea that we should search for simple "iron laws" expressed in terms of a few hard variables, has served us well in the physical sciences and badly on balance in the human sciences.

Given Figure 16-1, we can now discuss the nature of "rules" appropriately. Some of the "rules" we have called "laws" are Entire Invariant Paradigms; some are Entire Paradigms but not invariant; and some are guidelines that are useful but not always correct in terms of predictions. What have been missing in many cases are two things: first, a statement about the level of assurance of a given "rule"; and second, a semantics that reminds us of the level of assurance in the names we use to describe "rules." Missing such statements, we have sometimes created confusion by discussing dissimilar classes of theory as if they were the same. Newton's "laws" and Grimm's Law have very different characters.

In stating Grimm's Law, Greenberg gives us an example of what is needed. He says that the "law" states a mean value for rate of change in words over time in a language, and he reports the uncertainty in terms of a mean error. For Newton's "law" of gravity, the mean error of prediction for the proper domain is zero, as far as we can tell — that is, the scatter of the best available data lies within the uncertainty of measurements. Although it is not feasible or desirable to insist on uniform semantics everywhere, it would certainly improve our multidisciplinary dialogue if we routinely distinguished at least three types of "rules" from one another: Entire Invariant Paradigms, Entire Paradigms, and guidelines. I am not arguing for this particular semantics, only that we need some agreed-on semantics about "rules" if we are to understand each other even reasonably well. If we assume that all "laws," as we have used the term, are created equal, we are bound to end in confusion.

The Interactions of Philosophy and Physics

With the results of Figure 16-1 in hand, let us look at the reaction of the philosophy community to the knowledge that arose in the physical sciences after the time of Newton. Philosophy covers a larger domain than truth assertions alone. Dictionary definitions of philosophy say something like "Philosophy is the discipline that looks over the total terrain of human knowledge and helps us see how it goes together and what its meaning is." Has this task been appropriately fulfilled with regard to the interpretation of the physical sciences as they relate to worldviews? I regret to say, the task does not seem to have been done appropriately thus far. Why this task has been inappropriately done seems to me one of the most perplexing issues that this volume treats. Nevertheless, it seems to be so. Let us look at the outline of what has occurred.

In the late nineteenth century, a large sector of the philosophy community endorsed the idea of positivism. To put this differently, there was not general dissent within philosophy about the claim that the Newtonian view or positivist methods were appropriate either for the human sciences or as worldviews. There were always some influential dissenters — for example, Nietzsche — but the philosophy community at large did not seem to dissent. Indeed, in the early twentieth century two important schools of philosophy became explicitly positivist: Whitehead and Russell in the early decades in the United States, and the Vienna circle in the 1930's in Europe. In both cases, an attempt was made to bring all of philosophy onto an axiomatic, that is, positivist basis. Both attempts ultimately failed. The death knell for such approaches was tolled by the appearance of Gödel's Theorem, which shows that all formal systems remain incomplete in important ways.

But the failure of logical positivism as a basis for philosophy did not cause an about-face within the philosophy community regarding the use of physics as a worldview. Instead, after 1930, a major sector of the philosophy community gradually came to endorse the idea emanating from the physics community that "the proper fundamental view" was that of quantum mechanics and hence probabilistic and uncertain. In recent decades, courses have been given in philosophy departments which attempted to explain all phenomena of the world in these probabilistic and uncertain terms, in disregard of barefoot facts all around us which show that both deterministic and chaotic systems also exist, are common, and are important to human lives. I have heard a number of humanists in recent years say something like, "Human life is uncertain owing to the Heisenberg Uncertainty Principle." This statement is a fallacy; see Chapter 17. As we have seen in this volume, neither the quantum view nor the Newtonian view can provide a complete worldview. We will postpone to later chapters the question of why these difficulties occurred in the relationship of philosophy to science, because we need some of the ideas in Chapters 17 and 18 for the discussion. There is one part of the relation between philosophy and science which we do need to discuss at this point, however.

The philosophy community concerned with these issues did not seem to challenge the current view emanating from physics; instead, the philosophy community provided interpretations of why that view was correct from the perspective of "deeper layers of consciousness" as philosophers have understood those layers. To put this differently, parts of the philosophy community treated physics in much the same way philosophy had treated the Christian Scriptures during the Middle Ages. In this sense, science began to play part of the role that theology had played during the Middle Ages; science was taken as given, and in need of interpretation, even though many scientists themselves opposed that position.

What do deeper layers of consciousness denote in this context? Another way of looking at them is as higher levels of communication. Suppose I say, "The world is real," and you then say, "No, it isn't; it is just a recurring figment of your imagination." I can then move up a level in the hierarchy of communication and say, "On what basis do you claim the world is not real?" In return, you can move up another communication level and say, "On what basis are you questioning my beliefs?" This kind of dialectic can become an open-ended regress without any form of closure. See, for example, Watzlawick, Beavin, and Jackson (1967). And this is just the kind of open-ended dialogue that has occurred in philosophy on many problems. It seems to have occurred for two reasons: there appears to be no process for closure within philosophy as it has been practiced; there also seems to be little regard within the philosophy community for the importance of what we have been calling "domain." Parts of the philosophy community often seem to have sought universal truths sometimes about ill-defined or undefined systems rather than specific truths applicable to defined domains.

As a result, philosophy has contained a good many Hegelian swings in which thesis creates antithesis, then a new thesis is presented from still another direction, but no closure is reached. Science cannot proceed effectively in this way. Science, as we know it in the twentieth century, moves forward appropriately only when we periodically reach a tentative closure; we state a hypothesis and take it to be correct, subject to further empirical confirmation or disconfirmation; see Platt (1966). From time to time, we may overthrow top-level hypotheses (paradigms) in the physical sciences, but this is the rare case, not the common one. Few if any Hegelian-like swings have occurred in the physical sciences during the past century. What we typically see in the history of the physical sciences are modifications of domain or improvements of some parts of various fields, or "revolutions" in subsectors that are still within the top-level paradigms. In the domain of classical mechanics, there has been no revolution of content since Newton. In thermodynamics and in electromagnetism, there has been no revolution of top-level paradigms for more than a century. In all these and similar fields, we have had for many decades only elaboration of methods and breadth of problems, studied clarification of terms of reference and pedagogical improvements. We try hard in science to let nature, not dialectical discussion, be the arbiter and the means for successive, if tentative, closures. And as we saw in earlier chapters, this often leads us to a converging process regarding top-level paradigms in the physical sciences, but rarely if ever to Hegelian swings of ideas.

Even the largest "revolutions" in physics, biology, and geology typically have not involved as much difference between old and new paradigms as has been the case in philosophy. This difference will become important in Chapter 18. In this light, there seems to have been a mismatch in the interaction of philosophy and science because the philosophy community apparently did not look for empirical closure or use empirical checking. This apparent mismatch is a point that seems to need more multidisciplinary discussion.

Before we come to the end of this discussion of the relationships among the disciplines we need to note several trends that have begun, but only begun, in the late twentieth century.

Many scholars have begun to question whether the positivist view is appropriate within the human sciences. See, for example, Rabinow and Sullivan (1979, 1987). It is not that positivist approaches in the human sciences have entirely died away, but they have begun to be questioned more strongly and to lose the dominant role they played in many areas during the earlier part of the twentieth century. In a few cases this trend has swung too far. Some scholars have suggested that the paradigms of classical physics are relative and uncertain because they are socially constructed, as Ziman (1968) told us. But this is a confusion between the social processes in creating a sysrep on the one hand and the behaviors of nature on the other. The second-floor tennis-ball test tells us this clearly. Gravity does what it does, regardless of humans' descriptions of it. The behaviors are invariant. These scholars are thus overturning the error that troubled our thought for a century and creating another fallacy from the opposite position. They are in effect projecting what is correct in the human sciences onto the physical sciences, where the situation is different, as Figure 16-1 shows.

To put this in different words, sociotechnical systems have some components for which the "rules" come from the physical sciences and describe invariant behaviors, and these same systems have other components that follow the "rules" of the human sciences which do not describe invariant behaviors. Projecting either type of "rules" onto the entire behaviors of sociotechnical systems tends to create significant misunderstandings.

Since about 1965, there has been a growth within universities worldwide of a number of interdisciplinary programs. For example, human biology, urban studies, American studies, and science, technology, and society all study various aspects of human social and sociotechnical systems as wholes. Contrary to some views in conventional single disciplines, these interdisciplinary programs are not necessarily "soft" or "fuzzy" in the work they do. Some of these programs have produced more solid advances in knowledge than others, but that remark could be made about any discipline or set of disciplines over any significant time span. We have already described some significant results that emerge only from a multidisciplinary position (Chapter 14), and others are readily elaborated. Programs working on the interpenetration of knowledge from several disciplines need the results of multidisciplinary discourse to function optimally. If we have no clear idea about the relations between disciplines, unnecessary friction is nearly certain in interdisciplinary work.

Despite these developments, very few if any of our universities have institutionalized interdisciplinary programs well. No university I know has maintained ongoing multidisciplinary discourse. The curricula of our universities are still largely controlled by the departments that are organized along the lines of disciplines. This problem is not insoluble. However, proposed solutions have nearly always met resistance from existing power structures and traditions. As William Miller, former president of SRI International and a former Stanford provost, said in a meeting, "A solution requires only an act of administrative will." We have so far no clear, appropriate examples of such will in U.S. research universities, excepting perhaps Carnegie-Mellon University, which has chosen to create inter-disciplinary programs as a means for competing with other leading research universities.

Another recent development in the universities also supports the movement away from both positivism and the near total dominance of single disciplines as the only route to relatively well-founded knowledge; this is the creation, within the past decade or two, of a number of research programs and books that are truly multidisciplinary. The book by Corning (1983) regarding biology and larger systems and the work of Durham (1991) on coevolution have already been cited. A reintegration of the conflicting views toward psychology and psychotherapy, which have existed since the time of Pavlov and Freud, is being constructed in a series of books by S. M. Johnson. Four are now in print; see Johnson (1985, 1987, 1991, 1994). Johnson's work incorporates not only the ideas that have descended from Pavlov and Freud but also a dozen or so other twentieth-century schools of thought about the human psyche and also a great deal of new data about human development during early childhood. Johnson, who adopts both Hypothesis II and the Guideline for Scholarly Controversy, says explicitly in seminars, "We ought not select one set of credible data over another. We should instead look for a synthesis, a reframing, which is consistent with all the credible data." He says, for example, we ought not argue about whether Margaret Mahler or Daniel Stern is correct about the behaviors and the mental world of human infants. We should ask, "How do we account for both sets of data?" Some members of the psychotherapy community see Johnson's work as leading toward a better basis for working with clients.

In the realm of human consciousness, the results in linguistics (particularly the way infants learn language, noted by Chomsky) plus the results within computer science on the nature of intelligence led the research psychology community to understand that radical behaviorism was not the basis for a complete theory of psychology. They came to form a new consortium of six formerly independent disciplines to study the human mind (cognitive sciences). See Howard Gardner (1987), for the details of this coalition process. These illustrations by no means exhaust the list of highly interdisciplinary research programs.

In addition to these specific developments, it is worth noting, for our discussion, the nature of a number of major new disciplines which have arisen in the twentieth century: statistics, linguistics, communications as a study, feedback control theory, and computer science. These disciplines all concern, in one way or another, study of information and its processing. Some people have begun to call the twentieth century the "Age of Information." The name highlights the fact that little attention was paid to the nature of information as a subject in itself in the sciences that arose prior to 1900. This may help explain why some of us failed to understand two matters: first, human information is not and should not be described by the equations of physics; and second, there are qualitatively different kinds of information and feedback modes (see Chapters 4 and 6).

Modern view	Postmodern view
Rigid	Flexible
Mass production	Flexible production
Simple systems	Networks
Technical/rational monocausation	Pluralistic causation
Specialized work	Flexible work
Universalist	Local focus
Permanent	Flexible
Authority/totalization	Deconstruction/local control

Figure 16-2. The Modern View and the Postmodern, Compared.

Finally, in the past decade a movement has begun to occur in scholarship away from what has come to be called the "modern" view to another view, the "postmodern." "Modern" in this language is not well defined, but seems to imply something like what we have called "positivist" in this discussion. The postmodern view is more flexible. The whole subject is too new for clear delineation, but we can see its outlines if we compare a few characteristics (as in Figure 16-2).

The postmodern view moves in the direction of what we have been calling multidisciplinary discussion, and also takes into fuller account the differences between the physical and human sciences shown in Figure 16-1.

Conclusions for Chapter 16

The key shifts in the way humans accumulate knowledge about nature since the time of Newton have been: first, to a larger and larger number of communities of professional workers dealing with specialized domains of knowledge; and second, to utilization of iterative feedback loops between empirical observations and to formation of "rules" for domains defined by the system/sysrep apparatus. As we have seen, there are several reasons why none of these specialized domains contains the whole of human knowledge; nor can any one provide knowledge that can be used to derive the whole.

This process of specializing knowledge within communities of experts has simultaneously created many important gains and a few difficulties. The process has advanced human knowledge and facilitated humans' ability to create large societies of abundance. These societies of abundance provide the majority of their members with food, housing, economic security, and many amenities of life, the quality of which passes well beyond what could have been imagined even two centuries ago. See, for example, Schwartz (1983, 1985), Plumb (1973), and Bettman (1974). The changes have also created serious potential perils generated by humans themselves: for example, pollution, overpopulation, and nuclear arms. In the intellectual realm, the changes have left us with no overviews of the world or of human knowledge; there are also many overclaims arising from individual disciplines of knowledge. These two difficulties have seriously distorted our understanding of the whole.

As we might expect, we first succeeded within the empirically grounded disciplines in creating paradigms for quite simple systems that can be directly observed by humans. The increasingly specialized disciplines then moved, step by step, toward more complex systems and toward systems made more and more difficult for human understanding by hierarchical obscurity. As a result of this particular history, the idea long held sway that the methods and the type of principles created for simple systems were the ideal. In this way, the historical path created significant distortions in our worldviews, in our understanding of the relations among disciplines, and also in some subcommunities of the relative importance of various disciplines. These distortions do not seem to have been forcibly noted or significantly ameliorated by philosophy as it has existed since Newton. We seem to need a number of multidisciplinary views, what we have been calling a multidisciplinary position, in order to make significant improvements with regard to these distortions. To form a clearer picture of what these distortions entail, we will examine a number of overclaims in Chapter 17.

PART FOUR

Fallacies of Projection

Fallacies of Projection

Illustrations

Throughout this work, we have seen a number of difficulties in the powerful intellectual system we have developed in the past few centuries. Can we classify these difficulties and thus come to see their sources more clearly?

Most of these difficulties can be seen as what I will call "fallacies of projection." As the name suggests, fallacies of this type are projections of "ideas" that are appropriate in one domain onto another domain in which the same "ideas" are less appropriate or even totally erroneous. The word "ideas" in scare quotes is used in this chapter to imply any combination of principles, facts, methods, schemata, assumptions paradigms, and so forth — that is, any or all aspects of sysreps.

We will classify fallacies of projection into two subtypes, "projective errors" and "difficulties of incompleteness."

A projective error occurs when a single "idea" — for example, a principle — is carried over from its original domain to a domain in which it is not appropriate. Fallacies of incompleteness arise either from a sysrep that is a cut through a hyperspace of larger dimensionality, or from assuming a domain for a given body of knowledge which is larger than is appropriate — overclaims. In either case, the results obtained are usually not entirely wrong, but usually are seriously incomplete.

In order to examine these types of fallacies, we next compile a list of each subtype. The list includes examples we have already seen and others, so we can inspect the nature of the difficulties over a range of examples. None of the examples of fallacies of projection listed below are made up. Each of them has appeared in writing or in serious presentations by mature scholars. I will not always use the exact words of authors or speakers, but I have tried to be faithful to the meaning of the published or stated ideas while expressing the concepts clearly and concisely.

As I have already noted, there are no data I have been able to locate concerning what fraction of a given community believes or does not believe each of the fallacies listed below. The most we can say with reasonable assurance is that, in recent times, some serious scholars have believed each one.

Fallacies of Projection, Type I: Projective Errors

Fallacy I-a: Survival of the fittest applies to human social groups within given institutions (social Darwinism).

Mostly not true. This idea is now largely discredited, but did significant harm historically; see Chapter 12.

Fallacy I-b: We are in danger of "heat death" as a result of the entropy principle.

Not true. The error arises from application of the original statement to a domain where it is inappropriate. We are in no such danger for at least two billion years.

Fallacy I-c: The Heisenberg Uncertainty Principle explains why life is uncertain.

Not true. The principle does not apply to organisms (or many other systems).

Fallacy I-d: Entropy as defined in the technical world applies to social systems.

Not true; see the theory of dimensions (Chapter 9).

Fallacy I-e: All systems, including social systems and biological systems, tend toward (and not away from) disorder because of the entropy principle.

Not true for two reasons. (1) The entropy idea, when stated in this form, applies only to the system taken together with its surroundings. Inside themselves, nearly all living biological systems create order. Humans can and do create order locally, in both hardware and hardware-using systems. In both instances, entropy is created elsewhere (that is, outside the system considered). Nevertheless, there is a vast difference, philosophically and practically, between being able to create order locally and being unable to do so at all. The difference is what allows us to make the human-made world run; it is anything but trivial. (2) The entropy principle does not apply to ideas, it applies only to corporeal bodies of finite size. Hence the entropy principle is not a bar to human innovations or to diffusion of information more and more widely.

Fallacy I-f: "It is a general rule of logic that 'principles' are not to be multiplied beyond the necessary. Therefore, since interpretation in terms of energy has proved a general principle in the physical sciences, we must limit ourselves to it in psychology also" (Carl Jung, *Autobiography*).

Not true, for three reasons. (1) The idea of using the minimum number of principles is not a general rule; it is better considered a guideline, in the semantics of Chapter 16. (2) The term "energy" as used in psychology refers to something quite different from the denotation of "energy" in the physical sciences. Energy in the physical sciences has the dimensions of Force · Length. Energy in psychology is an elusive, undefined description of how much we feel like doing things, being active in contrast to being inactive. Energy in the physical sense is a conservative quantity; energy in the psychological sense is not. It is not that energy in the psychological sense is unimportant, only that it is both more elusive and quite different from energy in the physical sense. (3) Jung is projecting a principle from physics onto psychology, a quite different domain. He does not check the data in psychology. Jung's statement is an outright error of projection. I have included it to show that even great men have made such errors within the past century. We ought not blame Jung for this misconception, since he was only doing what nearly everyone else of his era did. The quoted statement is very much in keeping with the spirit of Jung's time; see the discussion in Chapter 15.

Fallacy I-g: The principles of the physical sciences are not invariant; they are only relative, since they are created by human consensus.

Not true. This confuses the social agreement about a sysrep with the behaviors of the **system** in the real world, as the second-floor tennis-ball test shows. This idea has been expressed primarily since about 1980. It does not seem to be widely held, but seems to be believed in a few small communities of scholars.

Inverse Fallacies, Type I

"Inverse" here denotes disbelief that a principle does not apply to a given domain, even though it is appropriate.

Fallacy I-h: The entropy concept does not apply to living systems (organisms).

Not true. When properly expressed, the entropy principle is a constraint on living organisms, but requires restatement in a different frame of reference from Clausius' original formulation. See, for example, Shapiro (1953). However, entropy, as defined by Clausius, does not tell us about the use of information in living systems, only about the matter.

Fallacies of Projection, Type II: Difficulties of Incompleteness

Fallacy II-a: "In principle," one can do all the macroscopic problems of the world starting from the principles and methods of physics.

Not true. See the review of this issue in Chapter 16; also Chapters 2, 7–12.

Fallacy II-b: Neoclassic economics is a sufficient basis for erecting a theory of innovation and hence for the growth of economic productivity.

Not true. See Chapter 14.

Fallacy II-c: Truth assertions are a sufficient basis for all human values.

Not true; see Chapter 1. Many physical scientists seem to believe this idea as an unstated presupposition. A few have firmly expressed it in writing. As many psychotherapists have noted, it is a hard way to live.

Fallacy II-d: The human brain can be fully simulated by a "rule-bound" computer or by any simple set of fixed "rules."

Neither statement is true. Open degrees of freedom exist in the human brain; see Chapters 4, 6, 7. We can continue to learn and alter our schemata as the world around us changes.

Fallacy II-e: The implied assertion in radical sociobiology that ultimately all human cultures and human behaviors are controlled by genetics.

Not true. See Chapter 14 and Durham (1991).

Fallacy II-f: All systems should be described in terms that are probabilistic and uncertain — as in quantum mechanics.

Not true. Even within inert, naturally-occurring systems, some behaviors are deterministic and some chaotic.

Fallacy II-g: Engineering is merely applied science.
    II-h: Medicine is merely applied biology.
    II-i: Agriculture is merely applied agronomy.
    II-j: Psychotherapy is merely applied experimental psychology.

Not true. Each of these four professions, in addition to science, involves not only a body of practice but knowledge for dealing with the real-world systems that are far more complex than systems tested in the lab. In all four cases, science is very important, but it does not supply the complete range of necessary professional knowledge or practice. See Chapter 15.

Fallacy II-k: A top-down (synoptic) view is sufficient by itself to understand all the problems of vital concern to humans.
    II-l: A bottom-up (piecewise) view is sufficient by itself to understand all the problems of vital concern to humans.

Neither statement is true. We need at least three views for many important classes of systems; see Hypothesis V, Chapter 10.

Fallacy II-m: Gödel's Theorem tells us that we cannot fully understand nature.

Not true. Gödel's Theorem applies only to formal systems such as mathematics. The theorem does not apply to systems that have self-reflective powers utilizing human-design feedback modes. See Figure 6-1 and Chapter 16.

Fallacy II-n: The household thermostat air-conditioner system is a good model for feedback in human communication systems.

Not wholly true. See Chapter 6. This difficulty arises from a source different from most others in this listing of fallacies. It relates to the modes of feedback "accessible" to the system.

Inverse Fallacies, Type II

The inversion for these fallacies involves the projection inward, within a discipline, of ideas from other disciplines.

Fallacy II-o: The idea that the newer human sciences ought to adopt the methods and viewpoints of classical (more specifically, Newtonian) physics.

On balance, this seems to have been an unfortunate idea. Comte's Pecking Order has not served us well.

Fallacy II-p: Logical positivism and logical empiricism.

Not true, as Gödel's Theorem tells us. This is related to Fallacy II-o, but it occurred in philosophy rather than in the human sciences.

Fallacy II-q: Disciplines that have not produced Entire Invariant Paradigms are "immature."

Not necessarily true. In a subtle way, this seems to be a subcategory of Fallacy II-o. It implies that all disciplines ought to be like physics. But see Figure 16-1 and Chapter 18.

Fallacy II-r: Data from study of non-human animals in environments controlled by the human experimenter are a sufficient basis for a complete human psychology.

Not true. The words "experiments on conditioning" can be substituted for the words "data from study of non-human animals in environments controlled by the human experimenter." In either case, the reference is to radical behaviorism. See Chapter 6.

Before we begin to examine what the difficulties just listed tell us, two comments are needed. First, as already noted, the subdivision of the total domain of truth assertions into a large number of empirically grounded specialties, each covering a defined set of systems, has on balance been of enormous benefit in terms of increasing human understanding of the world. It does not follow that our intellectual system is without flaws. Moreover, any vital system needs to examine its flaws as honestly as possible as a part of the processes of self-renewal and further advances. Second, we need to hold in mind the distinction between two similar-looking but fundamentally different processes. In one, we can try out ideas, principles, concepts, behaviors, methods, characteristics, and so forth, that have been observed within one domain to see if they work in another domain, and we give careful attention to data in the new domain. This process is nearly always provocative and is often a useful and important source of research ideas. In the other process, we assume, without checking relevant data within the new domain, that one or more "ideas" from another domain do apply to the new domain; this is the source of fallacies of projection. Guarding against fallacies of projection requires checking against sufficient data in the new domain. This is particularly important when we move our focus from one level to another in the hierarchy of constitution, because more often than not, new variables, new behaviors, and new principles exist in the new levels.

How widespread are fallacies of projection in our intellectual system of the late twentieth century? The listing above contains 26 fallacies of projection. The list is not exhaustive. It contains only some of the examples I have collected over the last decade or so as they came to my attention.

What would be required to make an exhaustive search? Probably a few dozen scholars from various disciplines who understood thoroughly the materials in Chapters 2 through at least Chapter 12 of this work. The task seems manageable, but does not seem to have been done.

To reinforce that the list is not complete, let's look at two more fallacies of projection that have occurred in very different kinds of communities, and then at three other fallacies of projection listed by another author.

Some pre-literate cultures believe the following fallacy:

Fallacy I-i: Forests, lakes, mountains, and/or features of inert physical nature can and do understand human actions and can reward or punish human actions.

Not true. As we saw in earlier chapters, inert, naturally-occurring objects have no capacity to read, process, or act on information. Fallacy I-i implies that such objects can do these things. These ideas have a common name, "anthropomorphism," which denotes carrying over (projecting) human attributes onto non-human systems that do not have those human attributes. An attribute projected in fallacy I-i is the use of information in control feedback loops.

Some interdisciplinary workers have recently suggested the following hypothesis:

Fallacy I-j: The total flow of energy per person through a society is a good measure of the advancement of the society.

Not true. Energy is a reasonable rough measure of the state of production of goods, but it tells us nothing about the state of social fairness, the spiritual health, or the political health of a society. Nazi Germany had a relatively high flow of energy per person.

Etzioni (1988) notes the following problems that seem to be based on fallacies of incompleteness:

1. Exchange theory in sociology;
2. Public choice theory in political science;
3. The idea that pre-literate tribes have economies that obey neoclassic economic theory.

Etzioni calls all of these theories "neo-classic," taking the term from economics. He also lists what we have been calling radical behaviorism and logical positivism as the same type of errors. Etzioni sees all these problems as arising from the idea that all theories should be like those of physics. Thus, Etzioni's term "neo-classic" expresses the same idea as "fallacy of projection." In addition, Etzioni says that the difficulties have occurred in sociology, political science, and ethnology, fields from which we have not drawn examples.

In sum, we have listed 31 examples of fallacies of projection, and they include examples in five of the six of the human sciences (excepting only history). It seems fair to say that fallacies of projection are not rare and have occurred widely in our intellectual system.

Conclusions for Chapter 17

What do the data of this chapter say about the patterns of fallacies of projection? Where are the ideas taken from and onto what domains are they projected? The 31 fallacies of projection listed break down as follows:

Taken from physics and applied to an area in the human sciences	8
Within the human sciences, arising from attempts to make principles physics-like	16
Taken from biology and applied to an area in the human sciences	2
Taken from the human sciences or humanities and applied to a physical science	2
Other sources	3

These data suggest that Comte's Pecking Order has played a significant role in our expectations about what "good" science ought to be.

The data also suggest a tendency to attempt explanations of very complex systems by oversimple sysreps. There are good reasons why the human mind tends to create and accept oversimple sysreps; see Chapter 3. The human mind seems to have a natural tendency to accept simple sysreps about complex systems. This does not make the sysreps appropriate; it does emphasize the importance of understanding the effects of the limitations of the human mind on our sysreps and guarding against certain natural tendencies (see Chapter 3).

Another aspect of the list of fallacies in this chapter is important for our multidisciplinary discourse. The inverse fallacies under category II projected inward into a discipline have over time nearly all been found to be fallacies and discarded by the bulk of workers in the relevant field. In the late twentieth century, logical positivism and logical empiricism seem to be in disrepute among the vast majority of philosophers. Radical behaviorism has lost favor in the research psychology community and will probably wither away over time. Social Darwinism has been widely criticized.

On the other hand, the ideas that have been projected outward onto the larger world by physicists, economists, humanists, and others have shown no obvious signs of abatement. Can we see the reason for this difference? We can see one reason immediately. When ideas are taken into a discipline, the ongoing discourse in the discipline, over time, tends to reveal their shortcomings. The processes of examination by a community are a central force in making the methods of science better than older methods as a means for creating, confirming, and disconfirming truth assertions, as Ziman (1968) explicated for us in detail. Within an active community of open-minded scholars, fallacies are apt to be recognized and eliminated over time. The opposite is true of projections outward onto the larger domain of the world. Here we have had no community and therefore no discourse among serious scholars that would tend to disconfirm the ideas. For example, there has been little if any dialogue between economists, engineers, and scientists that would have dispelled the difficulties in the models of innovation in all three areas (Chapter 14). Few of us are likely to argue that innovation is an unimportant topic in the late twentieth century, and hence such a discourse could have had useful results.

The previous two paragraphs constitute an additional argument for the importance of multidisciplinary discourse. They show that when we lack an ongoing discourse, we are far more apt to perpetuate certain kinds of intellectual difficulties than when we have a strong discourse that forces ideas from many sources to compete in an open forum of interested scholars.

Have fallacies of projection had significant negative effects in the twentieth century? The projections outward of the paradigms of a given discipline onto larger stages seem mostly to be "loose cannons" that have typically caused confusions but not serious difficulties. The absorption (introjection) of ideas into disciplines has, on the other hand, led to both weak theories and unfortunate actions. Let's look at a few examples.

Social Darwinism contributed to labor/management troubles in Western corporations for a long time, and to a lesser extent still does. Some scholars have suggested that social Darwinism was one of the causes of World War I and also the Holocaust.

Two projections of "ideas" seem to have had the most effects on our intellectual system. One is the idea that we ought to develop the human sciences on the model of Newtonian physics for both method and goals. The difficulties of logical positivism and logical empiricism in philosophy seem to have come from this same "idea." The founders of radical behaviorism in psychology stated that they had been strongly influenced by logical positivism. Radical behaviorism not only slowed the advent of an integrated psychology and comprehensive psychotherapy; it led to unfortunate advice to mothers which must have adversely affected many children (see Chapter 6).

The other "idea" that seems to have caused significant difficulties is the directly conflicting claim of reductionists and of synoptists to all the intellectual territory. Taken as worldviews, each is seriously incomplete for several reasons, as we saw in Chapters 7–12. The arguments between reductionists and synoptists have been so prolonged and have occupied so much attention on the stage of the discussion of larger concepts, they seem to have significantly obscured a proper understanding of the structure of complex systems. Even after Michael Polanyi pointed out central features of the structure of complex systems and documented their importance in 1968, few scholars in areas such as the physical sciences, philosophy, the human sciences, or genetics seem to have read Polanyi's paper or followed up on his ideas. Even Dennett in a seminal and important work, *Consciousness Explained*, seems to have missed Polanyi's work. This lends support to the idea that multidisciplinary discourse is important for discussing concepts that belong to many disciplines and have, therefore, until now belonged to none.

A comment about anthropomorphism, fallacy I-i, will be useful for our multidisciplinary discussion. When such beliefs exist in a pre-literate society, the beliefs are usually held by essentially all members of a given culture; this commonality is central to the idea of culture. Anthropomorphic beliefs have been very common in pre-literate societies. These beliefs provide illustrations indicating that a widespread community belief is not sufficient to give solid assurance for a truth assertion about nature. Empirical testing is the only method we have that provides relatively high assurance. Have anthropomorphic beliefs disappeared in industrial societies of the late twentieth century? Not entirely, it seems. For example, many people, usually not scientists, still seem to believe in astrology. If this were not so, it is hard to explain why we see horoscopes in many papers daily. Even self-destructive beliefs can be sustained in a small, relatively isolated community within industrial societies, as several tragedies of mass suicide within "cults" in recent years attest. Nor are these the only examples. In a recent letter to me (Williams [1994]), commenting on the manuscript, W. F. Williams makes two more points. First, the multidisciplinary position identifies desiderata and can test various disciplinary ideas against them. This can lead to raising important questions within the discipline considered. Second, cross-fertilization of ideas from various fields occurs over and over within multidisciplinary discourse.

The listing of fallacies of projection in this chapter lends strong support to the idea that we have overvalued the methods of physics (and the other physical sciences) and thereby in many instances tried to create principles in the human sciences which are invariant over time and space, and can be expressed as simple principles in terms of a few hard variables. As we have already noted several times, no such principles seem to exist in the human sciences. Nevertheless, as we have also noted, this is not a story of failure. It is, rather, a story of success overrunning itself; of successes convincing us that we can do more with certain methods than is possible. We also found outright errors of projection of the physical sciences being used like magic and thereby creating the same kinds of errors common in illiterate ethnic groups but in the opposite direction. Pre-literate people sometimes attribute some human characteristics to rocks. We have sometimes, since Comte, attributed some characteristics of rocks to humans.

CHAPTER 18

Fallacies of Projection

Possible Sources

In Chapter 17, we saw that there were two tendencies that have contributed to the difficulties in the powerful intellectual system we have created over the past three centuries for dealing with truth assertions. There has been a tendency to apply methods and viewpoints that are appropriate for one domain to other domains in which they are far less appropriate; the bulk of these projections have been applications of "ideas" from the physical sciences applied to the human sciences. Second, many of the sysreps we have created and used for very complex systems are oversimple; they are cuts through a hyperspace of larger dimensionality.

Both types of difficulties arise from inadequate or inappropriate use of human schemata. Since human schemata are for the most part learned, we need to ask two questions. What is it that creates overnarrow schemata in so many disciplinary experts? What can we do to alleviate the difficulties, if anything, via our educational systems?

Six sources seem important in creating the difficulties we have seen:

- The limitations of the human mind;
- The great complexity of many significant systems in the world;
- The seemingly strong desire of the human mind to "understand" itself and the world;
- The near total absence of multidisciplinary discourse;
- The near total independence of disciplines;
- The processes by which disciplinary experts are enculturated into their roles in society.

This list can be compiled in other forms, and there may be other sources, but let us begin our discussion by examining the effects of these six factors. We can start by looking at the combined effects of the first three.

The three limitations of the human mind appear important in the difficulties we are discussing: Miller's 7-Bit-Rule; the tendency of the mind to extrapolate (project) what is already known onto new problems and new domains, in the absence of contrary data; the need for well-learned schemata in order to think clearly about issues of any significant complexity. In addition, the human desire to know and understand, what Dennett (1991) calls our "epistemic hunger," pushes us toward accepting solutions even when they are oversimple.

Chapter 3 summarizes data showing that the human working memory can hold and manipulate 7 (plus or minus 2) uncorrelated bits of information, or about 4 chunks composed of several bits each. This means that we cannot think about all the details and the whole of a very complex system at the same time. We must scan the details serially, from several views, even for a system as simple as Windsor Castle at the time of William the Conqueror, as we have seen. After we have scanned the details, we must then think about how they go together and the system goals. To comprehend complex systems, we need at least three views: piecewise, structural, and synoptic. Of necessity, we must look at them serially. This creates a hazard that we will get stuck in one of the three views and not do the necessary breakdown, scanning, and reintegration.

Is epistemic hunger, the desire to understand the world, real for humans? I have seen no data on this issue. Much barefoot data suggest strongly that epistemic hunger is real, however. Consider the strong motivation of children to learn language and their enormous curiosity about the world, evidenced by the ubiquitous question, Why, Mommy (or Daddy)? We can use the criterion of behavioral biology as a way of checking further. We ask, Would epistemic hunger have had survival value for proto-humans? The answer seems clearly to be that it would have. Epistemic hunger is entirely consistent with and probably necessary for the path of human evolution that grew from using sociotechnical systems (Chapter 14).

When we combine the three ideas of the Miller's 7-Bit-Rule, the tendency to project known ideas, and epistemic hunger with the fact that many real-world systems are enormously complex, we can see that it is not only easy but also probably seductive for the human mind to be satisfied with oversimple solutions. Specifically, when we deal with the sociotechnical systems that are all around us and inherently have hyperspaces of very large dimensionality, we can easily mistake a cut through the hyperspace for a complete solution. This is consistent with the illustrations we saw in Chapter 17. It may help us to remember two ideas: All sysreps are not created equal; No known sysrep applies to all systems or problems.

Since the time of the Enlightenment, we have had no effective multidisciplinary discourse. This has led to a failure to create and attend to synoptic views of our intellectual system as a whole. We have, for example, failed to create wide understanding of the importance of domain, of the complexity of systems, and of the nature of systems with hierarchical structure and interfaces of mutual constraint. Even some of our brightest thinkers have failed to comprehend that there are no universal principles; there are only principles that are general for a given domain of problems. We have seen all these things several times, so we need not repeat the details in this chapter.

Also as a result of the lack of a synthetic intellectual system, each discipline has been largely an autonomous community working in isolation from other areas of study. The disciplines have been at risk from the effects of Acton's Dictum: "Power tends to corrupt, and absolute power corrupts absolutely."

We know many individuals who have held great political power who have become to some degree corrupted by it. But others seemingly have not. For example, Herbert Hoover, Harry Truman, and Dwight Eisenhower, who each held one of the most powerful positions on earth, showed little sign of corruption of their ethical underpinnings, whatever we may think of their particular political ideas. Acton's Dictum is not an Entire Invariant Paradigm; it is probably better seen as a guideline, in the semantics of Chapter 16. We seem to have seen more examples of this failure of power to corrupt in the United States and some other Western nations than in many other parts of the world. Why is this so? It will help our discussion to see what those nations have learned from the warning inherent in Acton's Dictum.

Acton's Dictum contains an important message: specifically, the warning that when a human mind lacks accurate feedback from the environment as a basis for ongoing calibration, it is apt to drift off course. Experiences in group psychotherapy reinforce this warning. However, it is in politics that an understanding of the warning has had the most attention. We can look at that experience to see what we can learn.

The creators of the U.S. form of government were well aware of the idea embodied in Acton's Dictum. Dietrich (1991) suggests that they may have even overreacted slightly to the warning and thereby created a system so stable that it tends toward what we have recently been calling "gridlock" in the federal government. What did the founding fathers do? They adopted, adapted, and created several social mechanisms in order to guard against the impact of Acton's Dictum. These include a government under laws, not men (the Constitution); guarantees of many individual rights of citizens in the Bill of Rights; the separation and balance of powers within the federal government; the provision that all powers not granted to the federal government remain in the hands of several states and the people. These ideas have been widely emulated since that time in other constitutions of organizations and countries. However, no similar set of checks and balances has existed within our intellectual system over the past century. The disciplines remain in a condition much like that of the thirteen American colonies during the decade between the end of the war of independence and the adoption of the Constitution. As a result, there has been no safe-guard against mass illusions even when the members of a given community of scholars consider themselves serious seekers after truth and do their best to adhere to that standard. If it is true that many (most?) human minds need accurate feedback from the environment for continuing recalibration, then, on balance, a total lack of external feedback to disciplines is not healthy even for the disciplines themselves. Has the lack of external checks and balances caused difficulties? Chapter 17 suggests that it has. And so do the barefoot data. Let's look at some ancient and some modern illustrations.

As noted earlier, pre-literate peoples often form schemata about cosmology and the origin of species which are mythical and magical. They may see the origin of the world in the upstream source of the river on which they live. They may see the rocks and streams and forests as gods; this implies that they project human feedback modes onto inanimate objects that do not possess these feedback modes. See nearly any summary of ethnology or Tuan (1974), for numerous examples.

Even in Hellenic times, our ancestors believed that there were gods for various human powers and also of particular places. Our ancestors also believed that there were four elements: earth, fire, water, and air. As a list of "elements," this can be seen as a mass illusion, since fire is a process and not an element (among other difficulties). Two millennia later, our ancestors believed that there was a mysterious fluid, "phlogiston," which explained chemical reactions; another mysterious fluid, "caloric," which explained heat flow; and a third, "ether," which explained how light propagated through space. Until just before 1500 A.D., many (probably most) Europeans believed that the earth was flat and if one voyaged far enough, the ship would sail off the end into an unknown void.

These earlier beliefs (schemata shared by given communities) illustrate that not only individuals but whole communities can share schemata in which they believe strongly but which are not in accord with empirical data. Most of us no longer believe the myths of ancient Western cultures because we have found more appropriate explanations. These newer explanations have in many cases strong empirical grounding. As a result, they allow us to make far more accurate predictions about the events that will and will not occur within our world. On balance, this appears, to me and many others, as a step forward in how we perceive the world. Does this mean that we have outgrown the danger of accepting oversimple schemata for complex systems? The data in Chapter 17 suggest that we have not, but the fallacies we have believed during the twentieth century are somewhat different in nature. Instead of being largely or wholly mythical, in the twentieth-century Western world they have primarily been incomplete or inappropriately projected schemata.

Edmund Burke reminded us centuries ago that "responsibility is the yoke of the free man." But we have not asked ourselves whether there are responsibilities that communities of scholars owe to the larger social system and to the intellectual system as a whole. And if so, are we educating scholars so that they understand these responsibilities, or are we providing them only with schemata that are too narrow for understanding broad questions within the world?

Enculturation within a community can create schemata that incorporate shared values, shared assumptions, and shared ideations. This fact is implicit in what ethnologists have found about cultures. As a result, when there is no feedback from outside, there are few if any safeguards against potential shared illusions within the community. This applies to disciplinary communities as much as others.

If there is no system for feedback from the outside to scholarly communities, mass illusions would be particularly likely when the schemata characteristic of a discipline merged with the self-interest of the community. Has this sort of thing happened? We saw several current examples of such illusions in Chapter 17. These included the long-continued overclaims by the physics community about what their discipline can do, and recent countervailing ideas that flip these statements over and create a mirror fallacy from the point of view of the social sciences. We also saw that communities of humanists and of theologians often take their own view, which is inherently silent with regard to structure, and claim it sufficient to understand our world. We have seen similar overclaims arising from economics (Chapter 14).

Many barefoot data tell us the same thing. When faced with a common problem about a sociotechnical system, lawyers tend to see the legal aspects of situation, engineers the hardware aspects, humanists the ethical problems, economists the market aspects, and physicists the aspects explicable via research and/or modern physics.

This is not a new idea. Decades ago, one of our broadest-thinking philosophers remarked:

> In questions of scientific methodology there can be no doubt that the scientists have been right. But we have to discriminate between the weight to be given to scientific opinion in the selection of its methods and its trustworthiness in formulating judgment of the understanding.
>
> The slightest scrutiny of the history of natural science shows that current scientific opinion is nearly infallible in the former case, and invariably wrong in the latter case.
>
> The man with a method good for purposes of his dominant interests, is a pathological case in respect to his wider judgment on the coordination of this method with a more complete experience.
>
> Priests, scientists, statesmen, and men of business, philosophers and mathematicians, are all alike in this respect.
>
> (Alfred North Whitehead [1959])

What Whitehead said can be put more succinctly, using the ideas in Chapter 3: Individuals think with the schemata they have, and not with schemata they don't have.

Our question can then be restated as, Do we enculturate disciplinary experts in ways that fail to guard against creation of overnarrow schemata that they apply to the world in ways that create oversimple sysreps because they have no other ways to think?

Let's list the steps by which we typically educate workers in a given discipline of knowledge, and then we can look in detail at this question.

1. Each discipline has an evolutionary history of ideas, methods, and views that arises mostly via descent with variations and to a lesser degree by large jumps in paradigms, that is, revolutions (see Kuhn [1962]).

2. The aspirant for membership in the discipline or profession must pass through a long and usually arduous time as a designated neophyte, a rite of passage (years of largely prescribed education).

3. Before the end of the time as a neophyte, the aspirant must pass certain tests. Performance on these tests will in part determine the esteem in which an individual is held by the community for some time.

4. This rite of passage often occurs in cohorts, as it does in many ethnic groups.

5. This group process, of neophytes passing through hazards together, often creates social bonding that lasts for a lifetime.

6. The tests involve the assimilation of much special knowledge and vocabulary that build shared understanding not easily accessible to "outsiders" (and outsiders here include other kinds of experts).

7. Often the vocabulary has hidden connotations that are sometimes semiotically encoded. This implies that many unspoken ideas are usually understood by members of the discipline, but not by others (this is also true in ethnic groups). As many ethnologists have noted, semiotic encoding into basic values (for example, in the religion of the tribe) is a stronger means for creating conformity than explicitly stated rules.

8. This semiotic encoding is often created by stories about how doctors, physicists, ethnologists, engineers, and biologists work. For example, the word "culture," and how one studies it, has taken on very large amounts of ideation, methodological implications, and meanings understood only by those knowledgeable in ethnology. The word "patient" in medicine carries similar connotations, as does the word "client" for a consulting engineer, and the words "phonemes" and "phonetics" play a similar role in linguistics. "Entropy" is a semiotic code-word in the sense that it carries many entailed implications that are well understood by competent scientists and engineers, but are confusing to others. And these are only a few of a great many examples in current disciplines.

9. The history of the discipline is often portrayed in largely mythic terms

conveyed through "stories" of "progenitive heroes" who are the intellectual "ancestors" of workers in the field. Moreover, each field has its own, essentially unique list of progenitive heroes, just as cultures normally do.

10. Attitudes toward the work of the field are also explicated and often inculcated. These attitudes differ from one field to another, particularly between the sciences, the professions, and the humanities.

11. All of what we have been describing in this section involves ideation that is shared, seen as very real by members of the discipline, and provides both prescriptions for actions and taboos (for example, "Do no harm to the patient" and "Report your data honestly and candidly"). These ideas, methods, views, and taboos form a systemic whole that is deployed to attack each discipline's paradigmatic problems in practice and at the frontiers of research.

The above description includes all five of the properties that Durham (1991, pp. 3–8) sees as an emerging consensus among ethnologists on the nature of the shared ideation of a culture. Paraphrasing Durham, I list these five properties: first, the values inculcated are "real" to the members of the culture; second, the values are socially transmitted; third, much of the meaning of the values is semiotically encoded; fourth, the values and taboos have systemic organization—they form a system of knowledge that is utilized as a whole to suggest behaviors and to approach problems; and fifth, the values have a social history, that is, they are the surviving variants of an evolutionary process.

Thus the idea that disciplines can be thought of as "subcultures" seems appropriate. We do need to note, however, that disciplines differ in two important ways from the culture of a small ethnic group. Disciplines do not provide a complete set of values or ideation. The disciplinary cultures cover only the work phase of a person's life, unlike culture in an isolated ethnic group in which no other views are present and the shared values cover essentially all of life. Outside of work, two members of the same disciplinary field can belong to quite different ethnic or family cultures. Second, since other values exist in other disciplines and in other areas of industrial societies, many disciplinary workers do not allow themselves to be totally enculturated by the views of their discipline. Rather, they maintain strong connections in two or more disciplines and/or pursue the development of broader views elsewhere in their lives. However, many "workaholics" do not. I have seen no good numbers on the fraction of scholars who are multidisciplinary in this sense; my impression is that the fraction is small, both in absolute terms and relative to the needs within the intellectual community and the academic community.

Moreover, the enculturation processes we have just delineated do not cease on completion of education. As the neophyte moves into an "adult" work phase within a corporation or a profession, he or she often needs to satisfy superiors and/or community leaders whose values come from the disciplinary culture.

Even within universities, successful young faculty often must pass muster with editors of journals who embody the disciplinary values in order to get the recognition demanded for promotions.

Are there any safeguards? There seem to be a few. In the first course that a student takes, in the area that will become her or his major discipline or profession, the assumptions of the field are normally laid out carefully (presuming the instructor is competent). This process includes a description of the domain of the discipline and, by implication, what therefore lies outside the discipline. However, after that class, the assumptions tend to disappear, to be taken for granted. Over time, the assumptions become the accepted ideation for the group as a whole, and they tend to drop from explicit thought. They are referred to primarily by means of semiotically encoded words (jargon). We also present to our students competing ideas and values in the courses we require for the breadth component of bachelor's degrees in most universities. However, these ideas are not later reinforced. In many instances these other views must in fact be subjugated to the values of the disciplinary major if the student is to satisfy his or her major professors and, later, employers.

Nor is all this the end of the story. Consider a practicing lawyer. Through his or her door, day after day, come legal problems. For the engineer the problems coming to him or her concern hardware. After years of such experience, it is seductive to believe all problems have a common character.

Given all this, what is surprising is not that disciplinary education and experience narrow the view of many disciplinary and professional workers, but that some of us manage to mostly avoid this narrowing.

To what extent are disciplinary experts, on the average, aware of this process of enculturation and of the fact that they work within what can be viewed as a culture? The answer, on the average, seems to be, Not much! A few years ago, a young woman approached a group of physicists working at a large research facility. She indicated that she wanted to study their activities from an ethnological view, as a culture. The physicists nearly without exception reacted by saying, "What culture? We aren't a culture. We are just dealing in the truth here." The dissertation, later published, revealed that the physicists were indeed a subculture, and some of the behaviors, values, and social arrangements of their "tribe" were, by ordinary standards, quite unexpected and unusual. I do not intend to single out physicists here; other disciplines are no different in this regard, as Whitehead noted.

If you still doubt these difficulties are real, ask yourself, How many times have you heard a disciplinary expert say anything resembling: "My field is rather narrow and of not much import, but another field called 'ABCD' is very broad and immensely important"?

As a result of all this, we cannot trust experts to be either clear or unbiased about the domain to which their field properly applies or to assess their own discipline in an unbiased way from a larger view. On this point, the historical data are clear. At present, the individual who has a detached view of his or her own discipline seems to be rare. If we use specialized domains to find relatively well-founded data about our world, and leave specialists to guard against over-simple sysreps, then an ancient aphorism surfaces: Who will guard the guards? We need some kind of larger intellectual system to form an outside view, as Williams (1994) noted in his letter to me.

Please do not interpret my remarks here in a pejorative or judgmental way; that is not the intent. The intent, rather, is to note that these kinds of difficulties are natural to the human mind and the human condition, and then to ask how we can guard against the difficulties.

It is not the role of the outside observer to propose solutions in detail for the problems that arise within disciplines. That task belongs to the workers in the discipline, and it must be left in their hands. An outside observer can sometimes focus problems and point them out, express concern about results that appear inappropriate, and ultimately express ideas that might be useful in alleviating the difficulties. Beyond that border, figuring out solutions must remain in the hands of the workers in the field because only they have the depth of expertise for the task. History tells us that when that border has been violated, we find episodes like the Soviet confusion in genetics over Lysenko's ideas. Those in the field will have to choose to address or ignore the problems. There is nevertheless an important role for outside observers.

Philosophy might have played the role of an outside observer of science. The definition in many encyclopedias and dictionaries suggests that it should have done so as a community obligation. Unfortunately, it does not seem to have done the task. Instead, segments of the philosophy community endorsed not once but twice the idea that physics was the ideal mode for science and so could be used as the basis for a worldview. Nor did the philosophy community seem to object after 1930 to the idea that all systems should be described probabilistically and contain inherent uncertainty; instead, the community seems to have endorsed the idea. Hence we need a further look at the relation between philosophy and science.

In the period after World War II, three disciplines dealt with the nature of science: the history, sociology, and philosophy of science. How have they dealt with the difficulties we have been examining?

The history and sociology of science have contributed a great deal to our understanding of the internal workings of science. We have already drawn on the work of de Solla Price (1962) and Ziman (1968) in the sociology of science and that of Kuhn (1962) in the history of science, and these are only a few of the more important works. However, in his seminal and justly famous study of scientific revolutions, Kuhn (1962) examines only cases from the physical sciences, not from biology or the human sciences. Kuhn also defines "maturity" in a science as the condition in which there exist Entire Invariant Paradigms that all but a few fringe workers in the field agree are correct, and from which everyone in the field starts analyses. This definition of "maturity" appears appropriate for the physical but not the human sciences. More specifically, the definition of "maturity" misses the point that there seem to be no Entire Invariant Paradigms in the human sciences, for reasons we have seen. By implication and apparently without intending to do so, Kuhn defines the human sciences pejoratively — as forever immature. It is little wonder that human scientists sometimes refuse Kuhn's central theses while workers in the physical sciences tend to endorse them.

The philosophy of science might have helped us see the broader features of the place of science in the larger intellectual world. Unfortunately, the philosophy of science seems to have done very little in this regard. This is not just my opinion, as the following two quotations indicate. "Very little of what is published on the philosophy of science is informed by first-hand encounter with laboratory investigation. [In contradistinction] a number of this volume's memoirs treat, more or less explicitly, the logic [and mathematics] of verification" (Joshua Lederberg, ed., *The Excitement and Fascination of Science: Reflections by Eminent Scientists*).

Early work in the history and philosophy of science focused on physics and essentially ignored the other branches of science. Since Lederberg is a geneticist, let's see what a leading physicist thinks.

Casti (1989) quotes Freeman Dyson, who organized at Princeton in 1979 the 100th anniversary celebration of Albert Einstein's birth. As a result of this experience, Dyson subsequently remarked that the Organizing Committee for the Einstein Centennial, collectively, knew all the physicists invited personally and at least knew the work of the historians of science who were invited. However, even collectively, they did not know a single person in the philosophy of science. Dyson then added, "There's a whole culture of philosophy [of science] out there with which we have no contacts at all. . . . There's really little contact between what we call science and what these people are doing — whatever that is." The fact that Dyson was accepted as the organizer for the Einstein Centennial speaks to the high esteem in which his colleagues hold him. Dyson has also been a contributor to cosmology and a number of problems in the intersection of science and public policy. Lederberg is not only a Nobel laureate in biology but also the editor of the volume cited, so he is intimately familiar with the work of eminent scientists in many fields.

If a highly respected biologist and a highly respected physicist do not recognize the literature of the philosophy of science as describing their subject, something has apparently gone wrong. Can we see what the problem is?

The philosophy of science in its methods has not followed several of the hypotheses of this volume. Let us see what this did to results and then we can examine some of the things that have transpired within the philosophy of science and also the validity and utility of the hypotheses of this volume.

The philosophy of science as it has existed seems to have ignored four ideas that this work indicates are important.

1. Empirical grounding by checking with workers in the field and being attentive to the resulting feedback have not been carried out. The remarks of Dyson and Lederberg make this clear. (As we have seen, iterative empirical grounding is the sine qua non for verification of truth assertions.)

2. Within the community of the philosophy of science until very late in the twentieth century, there seems to have been little if any recognition of the differences between the social and physical sciences, of the sort summarized in Figure 16-1. Workers in the philosophy of science have until recent years discussed science as if it were a single kind of "uni-bloc" endeavor with one method and one view good for all areas and branches of science and for all stages of a research program. This search for a universalism of method led to contradictions, and the community seems recently to have gone through a Hegelian swing and has been discussing the disunity of science. (To put this differently, the community seems not to have recognized the concept of Hypothesis III.)

3. At least some workers in the philosophy of science deny that the system concept is applicable to the human sciences or to their own field. When asked to define what they mean by science, some philosophers of science reply, "Some days we mean one thing and some days another." (A violation of Hypothesis IV.)

4. Some workers in the philosophy of science deny the validity of both hierarchy and taxonomy as concepts. They argue that both ideas are just the results of the human mind and therefore ought not be used in logical arguments or as a basis for study of the world. (As we have seen, barefoot data in an uncountable number of systems confirm the need for hierarchy as a structural feature, and taxonomy has been critical in essentially every field of science.) Without taxonomy biology, chemistry, and geology essentially disappear.

Item 1 above has resulted in a near total separation of the community of scholars in the philosophy of science from working scientists, as the quotations from Lederberg and Dyson show. The community in the philosophy of science has thus lacked the feedback it needs for affirming that results have not strayed offtrack. Such lack of feedback can lead to totally trivial results and even errors can go unrecognized.

Had trivial and erroneous results arisen in the philosophy of science as it stood in 1990? Yes, unfortunately, they had. Much of the literature of the philosophy of science is a discussion concerning what is *the* method and *the* view of science. "The" is emphasized to make clear that one method and one view were sought.

For example, Casti (1989) in his summary of the field notes that the philosophers of science have been debating two issues: which of three methods is the actual method used in science — Baconian empiricism, Cartesian axiomatization, or Popperian falsification (negative inference); and whether the proper view is Comtian realism, quantum instrumentalism, or Feyerabendian relativism. The word "or" is key in the two previous questions. It shows that logical "or"s have been used where logical "and"s were needed.

Is this a serious error? If one uses empirical data as a criterion, it surely is. It is easy to find many instances in the history of modern science in which a single research project, over a decade or two, has used all three of the methods the philosophers of science have been suggesting may be *the* method. Moreover, many of these research projects have used methods at one time or another which the philosophers of science seem not to have discussed at all. As we have seen, Newton already used two of the three methods (Baconian empiricism plus Cartesian axiomatization) at the origin of science as we know it in the twentieth century. To put this differently, two of the views that the philosophers of science have taken up serially as candidates for "the view" (Baconian empiricism and Popperian falsification) are both needed as the basis of verification of schemata in science sometimes even within one research program. Moreover, there are other methods that have been used in significant scientific research in addition to the three being argued about. If you look back at the description in Chapter 15 of how sciences dealing with truth assertions typically evolve, you will see that there are strong reasons why one needs each of these methods and views, and others as well, but often at different times within the evolution of particular sciences. In sum, the attempt to find a universalism of method and of view confused the discourse in the philosophy of science and led to non-closing arguments over several non-answers. Had the community in the philosophy of science maintained good feedback connections with working scientists, it seems improbable that this error would have occurred.

Let's look next at items 2 and 3 together. The result is a lack of adequate system definition and hence a confusion of comments about what are, at bottom, partly dissimilar **systems**. This has also led to non-closing arguments. Since the philosophers of science do not define their system at any particular point sufficiently (see Chapter 2), for a long time they tended to talk about science as if it had one method and one view. However, even a brief scan of Figure 16-1 shows that this is very far from true. The discourse, then, often has been confounded by unwittingly seeking single sysreps for systems with significant differences. As we have seen several times, when we ignore "needful" differences in a given topic, we cannot expect to understand the topic clearly.

What about the idea that the system concept does not apply to the human sciences? One need only read the work of Paul Watzlawick, who is widely accepted as a leading theorist in what is now called "family system therapies" and also "brief therapy modes," to see that the system concept is not only needed but also vital in those fields. Watzlawick emphasizes that the system concept is essential for getting things straight in his field of interest. As we saw (Chapter 3), it is a shift in system view (and no more) that leads from Freud's views on therapy to inclusion of other modes. There are numerous other examples.

What about item 4, the denial of the validity of all taxonomies and hierarchical sysreps as a basis for study. At least some humanists, apparently drawing on Wittgenstein's ideas about deeper meanings of reality, suggest that "hierarchy is an invention of the Western mind." (In case this sounds strange, let me add that I have that statement in writing, a serious review comment.) Some humanists have made similar comments about taxonomy. If accepted, this notion would destroy much of the bases of biology, chemistry, astronomy, geology, and other sciences at their very roots. Even physics, where the taxonomy is far simpler than in many other sciences, begins by dividing the total domain into about five subdomains (classical mechanics, electricity and magnetism, thermodynamics, quantum mechanics, and relativity). Farther along in the curriculum some of these may be combined or subdivided, but the initial empirical bases and introductions for students are typically based on some taxonomy of this sort.

Much of the literature of sociology focuses on problems of status and hierarchy, as does that of ethnology. No tribe has been discovered that does not have at least two levels of hierarchy in its social system. There are, of course, better and worse forms of social hierarchy. But discussion of that topic lies beyond the scope of this volume. Historians and political scientists sometimes remind us that a key to understanding historical events often is the question, Who holds the power? Power in this sense implies social hierarchy.

The basis for the design of airplanes, computers, automobiles, and all other complex devices is also destroyed the moment one rejects hierarchy of structure as either a concept or a reality. If you doubt this, ask a Boeing, IBM, or Hitachi engineer if they could design their products without explicit use of both hierarchical corporate structures and hierarchical control of designs.

If hierarchy is a Western invention, how do we account for the caste system in India or the imperial hierarchy of ancient China which existed for centuries before significant contact with Europe took place.

Are any of these difficulties in the current bases of the philosophy of science being repaired now? Only two, as far as I know. Some workers in the field have begun to broaden the study beyond physics to include biology and other sciences in the data base. Some workers in the history of science are beginning to insist that their advanced students study science via formal course work in depth, and some are beginning to have close ties to workers in science.

This is an unhappy set of conclusions about the work of a community. Hence, if I have missed some changes or made misinterpretations, I hope someone will supply references indicating what I have missed. One hopes the relatively new field of the philosophy of science will come onto stronger foundations. It is an area worthy of sound study. For that to happen, it does seem, however, that the community will need to reexamine long-held views about their own methods and assumptions and also forge strong feedback links with active workers in a number of fields of science.

What does this tell us for our multidisciplinary discourse? It reinforces the idea that we need multidisciplinary discourse in addition to disciplinary discourses so that we can maintain outside views and the feedback links from the larger world. The disciplines themselves need these links for their own benefit.

Before we leave the interaction of philosophy and science, we need to discuss one more set of remarks because they suggest a possible source for what seems to have gone wrong. In his lengthy and useful survey of the Western mind, Tarnas (1991) quotes Feyerabend's remark that "in an argument over paradigms, anything goes." Feyerabend's views of science are essentially nihilistic in that he sees no method as better than any other, and thus there is no basis for deciding what are appropriate versus inappropriate sysreps. But this idea seems strongly inconsistent with the enormous enlargement of relatively well-founded human knowledge that has come from science in the last three centuries. If any criterion is as good as another, how do we formulate the methods of verification to which Lederberg refers? Nevertheless, Tarnas not only quotes Feyerabend without dissenting, but then he asks, "What is the source of our human top-level paradigms?" Tarnas answers his own question by suggesting that top-level paradigms arise from the current collective unconscious of humans, in the sense of Carl Jung. If you ask psychologically sophisticated mathematicians whether Newton could have created calculus and mechanics out of the collective unconscious of seventeenth-century Britain, they are typically dumbfounded. The notion seems to them absurd, beyond serious consideration. If you ask physical scientists whether Gibbs's phase rule for the dimensionality of systems of substances or Maxwell's equations for electromagnetic phenomena could have arisen from anyone's unconscious, you get similar reactions. You may want to try this for yourself.

An even clearer example is the Entire Invariant Paradigm we call the Navier-Stokes equations for viscous compressible fluid motions. These equations are so complex that the full details cannot be held in working memory in their entirety, even by experts. We start analyses with a written form of the equations. These equations are not the sort of thing that arises from the formless, inchoate ideas of the unconscious; they are far too detailed, precise, complex, and extensive. Moreover, they involve far more than nine independent bits, and they must be written down to be elaborated and studied. Can we reconcile these different ideas? I believe so, if we pay attention to the levels of the concepts.

The collective unconscious, which we called the "spirit of the times," does seem to have influenced what we see as "good" science. To put this differently, the collective unconscious seems to have had a strong influence on the goals that all fields of science should seek. As we have seen, the "spirit of the times" was a source for creating positivist research programs in many human sciences. However, as soon as we look at the physical sciences or at more specific paradigms within given fields, we see that the influence of the collective unconscious diminishes or totally disappears.

Both Feyerabend and Tarnas also see the history of paradigms largely in terms of Hegelian swings. But Hegelian swings have been rare in the physical sciences, as we have already seen.

What, then, is the basis for the remarks by Feyerabend and Tarnas, both philosophers? Let's turn the situation around and ask two questions to see if they suggest an answer: What field has been most characterized by Hegelian swings of ideas? What field lacks closure criteria — and thus anything goes, in an argument over paradigms? The field that best fits both questions seems to be philosophy. This suggests but by no means establishes that these remarks by philosophers about science and scientific paradigms are projections of what they see in their own discipline onto disciplines in which the situation has been and is quite different. This in turn suggests that philosophers may be no more immune from the effects of the limitations and tendencies of the human mind than other experts.

Inferences from Chapter 18

Examination of the way we educate and professionalize experts in the various disciplines dealing with truth assertions shows they often undergo a strong process of enculturation. This enculturation creates and reinforces schemata in the minds of experts that can and often do act as distorting filters when applied to complex systems. At the same time, we provide disciplinary experts with no overviews that might act as countervailing "defiltering" schemata, and without such schemata, the human mind does not seem able to think clearly about the relevant problems.

The views of disciplines as we now teach them are not built on or connected with synoptic views of the world of ideas, or on the idea of obligations to the larger intellectual world. All problems outside the purview of the discipline are often implied or even stated to be of lesser importance. Nor is the need for checking theory iteratively against the real-world systems made sufficiently clear in some instances; this seems to be particularly true when data are needed most, for very complex systems. This process tends to be reinforced by the convergence of several characteristics of the human mind, including Miller's 7-Bit-Rule, our inability to think clearly without relevant schemata, our apparently strong desire to understand the world around us, and finally the tendency to extrapolate unless immediately contradictory data are present.

As a result of all this, we have seen many current examples of both overnarrow sysreps and overclaims arising from a number of disciplines. The effects we are discussing are not isolated; they have appeared at many points in our intellectual system. In a few extreme cases, we have even seen an insistence that theory derived from narrow cuts through a hyperspace of a system of very high dimensionality was more accurate than data on the systems under discussion. All too often, we seem willing to accept oversimple sysreps and believe what they tell us, sometimes even when the results are in obvious contradiction to many barefoot data in the world around us.

Once we recognize these frailties of the human mind, we can provide some safeguards to alleviate their effects. For example, we can present students with clearly stated synoptic views created through multidisciplinary discourse in addition to (not as a replacement for) disciplinary studies. We can point to the need for at least three views to understand complex systems: synoptic, piecewise, and structural. We can elucidate the nature of hierarchical systems with interfaces of mutual constraint. We can point to the lack of complete theory for entire systems of high complexity. We need not go on. We see what is needed — active teaching and discourse about multidisciplinary methods and results in addition to, not as a replacement for, instruction in specific disciplines.

Initially, recognition of the effect of limitations of the human mind on scholarship may appear frightening. On further consideration it has a strongly reassuring emotional aspect as well. Once we admit our limitations, we no longer need to chide ourselves for failing to do what we cannot do, thereby increasing our sense of self-worth. For example, once we know Miller's 7-Bit-Rule, we understand our need to write things down and file them, and we need not tell ourselves, "We *ought* to be aware of many problems or views all at once." This recognition is both programmatically useful and emotionally reassuring.

Should we blame scholars for the failure to create multidisciplinary discourse? Not at all. That will only aggravate the problems. What we need to do instead is to apply what I will call Deming's Dictum: "When an institution is not working, don't blame the workers, look at the structure." We will do that in Appendix B.

PART FIVE

Conclusions

CHAPTER 19

What Have We Learned?

A Summary of Results and Conclusions

This book has discussed multidisciplinary thinking as an explicit subject of study. It has been primarily concerned with those disciplines of knowledge which address truth assertions. It focuses on two central questions: (1) What are the appropriate relationships among the disciplines? and (2) What are the appropriate relationships between a discipline and overviews of the intellectual terrain or truth assertions? The discussion includes: three overviews that aid understanding of the connections between the disciplines; a number of tools for multidisciplinary study; examples of benefits from the use of a multidisciplinary position; a brief history of how the disciplines dealing with truth assertions have evolved and how that affected their development; illustrations of difficulties within our powerful but severely fragmented system of knowledge; and examination of possible sources of these difficulties in order to suggest what needs to be done to alleviate them.

Let us first recapitulate in broad outline what has been covered. The three overviews are based on: the system concept, and its relation to truth assertions and domains; a numerical index for the complexity of systems; and the structure of complex hierarchical systems with interfaces of mutual constraint. These three overviews overlap and reinforce each other.

Examples of the use of the multidisciplinary position have been given in order to illustrate that some problems cannot be properly treated by merely adding up models that arise from separate disciplines. The illustrations show appropriate treatment of some problems that require the interpenetration of ideas from various disciplines. They also show that we have misunderstood, in part, the "rules" for the relations of disciplines to each other.

The capsule history of how the disciplines evolved indicates that the disciplines, as largely independent areas of study carried on by a community of professional scholars, are quite new historically. The history makes clear the enormous benefits that the use of a large number of independent, empirically based disciplines operated by communities of professional scholars have brought us in understanding ourselves and our world. At the same time, the history shows that difficulties of two types have arisen: projections of schemata that belong within one discipline onto domains in which the schemata (or ideas) are either not appropriate or seriously incomplete; and the creation of many sysreps that are seriously incomplete. Examination of the sources of these difficulties suggests six contributing factors: the nature of the human mind; the way we enculturate experts in disciplines; excessive autonomy of the disciplines, which act as if outside feedback is less important than it is; the lack of synoptic views of the intellectual system; the great complexity of many common and important systems; and a lack of continuing multidisciplinary discourse.

Our discussion has made explicit not one but many reasons why there is no one method, no one set of principles, no one viewpoint, no one set of equations, no one discipline that is sufficient to understand all matters vital to human concern.

A considerable number of more specific ideas and results have also emerged from this exploratory discussion. A few of these results are virtual truisms, but many of them run counter to at least some common wisdom current in the intellectual world of the late twentieth century.

Let's now turn to a more detailed summary in which we will organize the results from previous chapters into five categories:

A. Systems and Their Mental Representations
B. Complexity and Its Implications
C. The Structure of Systems
D. Differences and Similarities Among Disciplines
E. Other Results Concerning Multidisciplinarity

All the statements that follow relate to the domain of truth assertions. Because the terrain is complex and interconnected, some of the statements of results overlap others in order to provide completeness.

At the end of each result in the summary below, the bases for the particular assertion are suggested, and an indication of the apparent firmness of the result is also usually given. In some instances, brief comments are also added concerning the stated results in order to clarify or amplify what we have already seen.

A. Systems and Their Mental Representations

A1. No truth assertion about physical, biological, or social nature is complete until the domain to which it applies has been appropriately and adequately defined (Hypothesis IV).

Basis. A vast amount of accumulated experience. Experientially, about as firm as anything the human race knows. Modern science and its many remarkable successes rest on use of the system concept (by whatever name).

Comments. The need for system definition does not apply only to the physical sciences and engineering. It applies at least as much to the human sciences. Indeed, because the paradigmatic systems studied are typically more complex and harder to define appropriately in the human sciences, on balance, the system concept may be more critical in those fields.

Appropriate and adequate definition of a system for a given class of problems is often neither trivial nor obvious; system definition frequently requires iterative improvements to achieve even a reasonably satisfactory condition.

At bottom, the system definition, whether stated or implied, strongly constrains what can be done, and what is missed, in a given field of study. Some system definitions make problems relatively easy, others make them relatively hard.

A2. When we confuse the map with the territory, the **system** with the sysrep, we are almost certain to end in confusion and perhaps in outright error (Korzibski's Dictum).

Basis. Very firm. Innumerable examples in many disciplines support this point.

Comment. In a given case, the confusion may or may not be serious, but a confusion of categories does exist. In pre-literate societies, these difficulties are often quite serious in their effect on behaviors. Nor have we totally surmounted these difficulties. We have seen several current examples in Chapter 17.

A3. The human mind thinks about matters, particularly complex matters, by associating them with previously constructed mental schemata. In this way we learn to do many things other animals cannot. However, when we lack appropriate schemata, we tend to project the schemata we have in our minds onto situations in which they may be inappropriate. Human construction of schemata via learning and experience is at once an enormous advantage possessed by humans (in comparison with many other animals) and also a source of risks that arise when we project schemata from one area of study onto other domains and new domains without rechecking the empirical grounding.

Basis. Chapter 3, including references.

Comment. Chapters 17 and 18 suggest that the implications of these mental processes for both understanding and misunderstanding are far greater than we seem to have recognized.

A4. Even within the domain of inert systems, including those designed by humans, we need at least three kinds of sysreps for effective analysis and understanding, that is, deterministic, probabilistic, and chaotic.

Basis. Chapter 14. The logic of the cat and dog metaphor (Chapter 16) plus much barefoot data.

Comment. Despite a century or more of claims by the physics community which contradict conclusion A4, the existence and importance of hierarchical systems with interfaces of mutual constraint supports this result unequivocally. An even tighter and independent demonstration needs only the theory of dimensions — a theory that is presuppositional to writing any of the equations of classical physics. Moreover, from the view of feasibility, we would currently need all three types of sysreps even if the need for all three classes were not theoretically supported.

A5. Scholarly workers on the opposite side of Snow's culture gap need to learn different lessons from the system concept. Non-technical people can use the system/sysrep apparatus (Chapter 13) as a particularly useful "window" for understanding the operation of science and technology. Many technical people need to be clearer that the system/sysrep apparatus and its handmaiden, rationality, are not sufficient to understand all problems of vital concern to humans.

A6. Because of limitations on the human mind, we need to break down complex systems into small "pieces" and study the pieces in order to understand the system. It does not follow that we can understand the complete systems from the "pieces" alone. We must not forget to reassemble the pieces and look at both the structure and the whole when we want to understand the complete system. Nor can we allow ourselves to forget emergent systemic characteristics.

Basis. Chapter 3; Hypothesis V; and Chapters 7–13.

A7. All known human societies, past and present, use sociotechnical systems as the physical basis for living. Use of sociotechnical systems by humans and our biological ancestors over the past two million years have:

- Branched human evolution from that of other animals, leading over time to ·our large brains and to our unusual power of speech and manual dexterity;

- Increased effective human powers millions (and, in some instances, billions) of times, thus making us, for many purposes, the Lords of the Planet;

- Sociotechnical systems are an arena in which many disciplines are needed and thus a place where multidisciplinary thinking can be explored.

A8. Study of sociotechnical systems and how we use them surfaces several important results:

- A long-sought but historically elusive qualitative distinction between humans and other animals;

- A much-improved model of innovation processes in industrial societies;

- Increased clarity about the nature/nurture issue;

- A demonstration that some conceptual problems demand use of a multi-disciplinary position, in contrast to merely "adding up" disciplinary views.

These results are examples and are not exhaustive.

B. Complexity and Its Implications

B1. There exist many important systems that are so complex that we do not have, nor can we expect to soon have, complete analyses or computer models describing all the details of the behavior of the entire system. For these systems we can only make complete analyses of some components. In such systems, we must create, operate, and/or innovate by human-design feedback mode in which we iteratively observe, perturb, and observe again. When we forget this, we confuse mathematical sophistication with accuracy and completeness, and we invite acceptance of oversimple ideas and oversimple solutions.

Basis. Follows directly from the values of the complexity index (Chapter 4).

Comment. The human-design feedback mode of research is not a less demanding mental activity than formal analysis. In very complex systems, research or innovation using human-design feedback often requires a very high order of judgment.

B2. Analytic or computer models of sociotechnical systems of any appreciable size inevitably represent only some features of the complete system (since they are cuts through a hyperspace of much larger dimensionality).

Basis. Chapters 4 and 5.

B3. In studying very complex systems, we can often reach better judgments about courses of action from experience and review of known behaviors of many similar systems than from formal theory based on a few variables. This creates a "primacy of data" over theory in studying, operating, and innovating in very complex systems (Guideline for Complex Systems).

Basis. A number of examples in sociotechnical systems.

Comment. This conclusion is tentative and leaves open a number of questions. For example, we seem to need further exploration and discussion concerning what forms of decision criteria are best for specific cases. This result taken with results B1 and B2 raises questions about the appropriate domain of mathematical decision theory and also about methodology for problems that cannot be set in mathematical form.

B4. If a sysrep takes some variables to be exogenous when observation of the **system** indicates that the variables are relevant, then the hyperspace of the sysrep is seriously incomplete. In such cases, it is dangerous to believe that the sysrep will provide adequate predictions for all relevant problems.

Basis. Chapter 4. The result is very firm; it is based on no more than an understanding of what we denote by variables and functions.

C. The Structure of Systems

C1. There are many complex systems for which even a reasonably complete understanding requires at least three perspectives: (1) a *synoptic* overview, including goals and connections to the environment; (2) a *piecewise* view of the smallest relevant components; and (3) a *structural* view of how the components aggregate to form the whole and allow functioning (Hypothesis V).

Basis. Ostensive. Many examples in many kinds of important situations illustrate the need for all three views. See also C2.

Comments. The words "complex systems" here denote specifically any system with hierarchical structure, interfaces of mutual constraint, and heterogeneous aggregation. Such systems are common and important, since they include both human beings and human-built sociotechnical systems.

Since this is true for systems, it must also be true for sysreps, if they are to be appropriate, and hence for the totality of knowledge in the disciplines.

C2. Each of B1, B2, and C1 shows that the reductionist program is impossible even in principle; and that no synoptic view, by itself, can provide the means for understanding either the pieces or the structure of complex systems.

Basis. Each of Chapters 4, 5, 6, and 8–12.

Comment. This is one of several reasons why the paradigms of the physical sciences are not and cannot be complete worldviews. The same is true of synoptic views in the humanities; they cannot reach to the details of structure and thus to biology and medicine, among other areas. This result illustrates the futility of arguments between supporters of each of two ancient but incomplete views (synoptic and reductionist) regarding which view owns all of the intellectual turf. Both views (and often more) are needed.

C3. The most we can expect to derive analytically when integrating or differentiating across hierarchical interfaces of mutual constraint is consistency (not derivation of the upper level from the lower or the lower from the upper).

Basis. Polanyi's Principle; see Chapter 8.

Comments. This result runs counter to much long-held disciplinary wisdom. Nevertheless, it is inescapable, since the relationship across such interfaces is constraint and not determination, and this fact, taken with the fundamental solution theorem of mathematics, impels the result.

It follows that the mathematical equations for either integrating or differentiating (mathematically) across an interface of mutual constraint cannot be closed until additional information is added. This added information can be found in at least two ways: by examining all levels in the structure of the system for the particular case; and by making human design choices in hardware or in sociotechnical systems.

C4. Normal adult humans possess the ability to use self-reference (at multiple levels) and to employ this ability in human communications. Humans also have the ability to envisage new, never-before-seen systems and then construct them (the human-design feedback mode). Finally, humans transfer the ideas needed for construction and operation of these complex systems by two systems of information (culture and skills) that are partially independent of and interact with genetic information.

Basis. Structure of systems (Chapters 5, 7, 9, 10, and 14); existence of cultures; the need for skills to maintain societies, particularly in industrial societies; language-learning in the human child; feedback modes discussed in Chapters 6 and 14. (See Durham [1991]; see also result D1.)

Comments. These bases seem firm, but need more study by many scholars in order to parse details. The relevant human capacities arise from the existence of residual open degrees of freedom in the human mind and in human behaviors.

No inert, naturally-occurring system has these capacities. Nor do other animals have all of them. As a result, humans have capacities that qualitatively transcend those of inert, naturally-occurring objects and other animals. (See Chapter 14.)

Attempts to model all human behavior via methods and/or behaviors of inert systems or other animals will therefore create a simplistic view of humans and their activities.

Simplistic models have been created in the past in many places, and these oversimple models have been the basis for many prolonged quarrels over turf between disciplines and, in some instances, for unfortunate actions in the world. (See Chapters 15–18; remarks on radical behaviorism in Chapter 6; remarks on economics in Chapter 14.)

C5. Because residual open degrees of freedom exist in human mental, social, and cultural systems, the systems usually evolve over time. As a result, over long time-spans, not only the behaviors, but also the "rules" describing the behaviors will sometimes change. To some extent, we make up the rules for human social and sociotechnical systems as we go along.

Basis. Chapters 4, 5, 6; many illustrations.

C6. The attempt to create "iron laws" (more precisely, Entire Invariant Paradigms) within human sciences using simple principles based on a few variables seems to have been a misguided expectation from the beginning. The attempt has created much new important knowledge, but it has also caused difficulties in many places for a century or more.

Basis. Conclusions B1, C2, C3; Chapters 5, 7, 10, 14–16.

C7. Hierarchy is a concept we must have, since it describes much (perhaps most) of the structure of many kinds of systems of importance.

Basis. Chapters 7 and 8.

Comment. This result seems obvious to most workers in systems theory, the physical sciences, engineering, political science, sociology, and other areas. It has nevertheless been challenged by some humanists, and is therefore stated in this list of results.

C8. Creation of taxonomies is a vital concept for creating many fields of science.

Basis. Chapters 15 and 16.

Comment. See comment, conclusion C7.

C9. The variables, parameters, behaviors, and the appropriate "rules" all typically vary between one level and others in hierarchical structures and in the hierarchy of constitution. As a result, transporting sysreps from one level to another by projection is likely to create errors. This is true even when we can connect the levels by mathematical aggregation.

D. Differences and Similarities Among Disciplines

D1. Residual open degrees of freedom are inherent in human mental, cultural, social, and sociotechnical systems. This makes the human sciences significantly different from the physical sciences.

Basis. Ostensive, many examples exist. See Figure 16-1.

Comments. The distinction between some constraints and complete determination is vital to understanding this result.

The existence of open degrees of freedom allowing change over time in human systems stands in sharp contrast to the physical sciences, in which vast amounts of data confirm the invariance of behaviors and principles over time and space.

A key difference between inert and living systems lies in the ability to use information. This presents to us an open question for further research, How is it that information arises, is stored, processed, and utilized as the bases for actions by living systems on the foundation of inert molecules that do not themselves possess these capabilities? Is it heterogeneity, structure, or some other feature? A related question is, How complex must a system be before it can acquire the capacity for various levels of processing and utilizing information?

D2. As a result of D1, normative choices cannot be avoided in human individual behaviors; in human social and sociotechnical systems; and in cultural evolution. This also implies important differences between the human sciences on the one hand and the physical sciences on the other.

Basis. Follows logically from D1 and the present power of humans.

Comments. Normative choices can be made on many qualitatively different bases — for example, spiritual, utilitarian, pragmatic, economic, affectional, combinations of these, and others. In many cases, avoiding an explicit basis for choice does not avoid the choice; it merely leaves the motivations implicit and tends to hide them.

Since humans have choices, and since for many purposes we have become the Lords of the Planet, some of the choices we make collectively will affect the future of the planet and our species.

D3. There seem to be no Entire Invariant Paradigms in the social or behavioral sciences (unlike the physical sciences).

Basis. Consistent with D1 and D2. See also Figure 16-1. This may be a firm result, but it needs further discussion and checking before we reach conclusions about the level of assurance.

Comments. A number of Entire Paradigms about cultures do exist, but they are not invariant in the way they play out in behaviors and values; they are, rather, enormously variable in terms of actual behaviors. (See Chapters 5, 10, 14.)

A useful metaphor is to think of the inert, naturally-occurring physical world as a set of rooms of fixed geometry which we can explore. This contrasts with the human sciences, in which we can, to a significant degree, design and reconstruct the rooms. There are constraints on the designs of the "rooms" of the human sciences, but the floor plan and many other features can and will be decided by human choices.

D4. Neither genetics nor culture nor the principles governing subatomic particles determine all human behaviors.

Basis. Each of C3, C4, D1, D2.

Comments. Genetics, culture, and physics only constrain human behaviors, for some matters tightly and for others loosely.

The fact that each of genetics, culture, and physics has been suggested as the determining factor governing human life (to various degrees, by various individuals) illustrates several points that emerge as results from our multidisciplinary discussion: views arising from one discipline are often too narrow for many problems; overclaims concerning domain have arisen from many disciplines; we have had no methods and no forum for resolving conflicting views concerning the same problem which arise from differing disciplines; and we have lacked synoptic views that would counterbalance overnarrow views and discourage intellectual overclaims (Guideline for Scholarly Controversy).

D5. The existence of many separate disciplines of knowledge dealing with truth assertions is very new from a historical perspective. The overall structure of the disciplines has grown in a largely ad hoc manner and with little external feedback and few constraints. On balance, the creation of separate, empirically based disciplines has been enormously fruitful. The result has been an exponential explosion of what humans know with a relatively high assurance in many areas. However, some difficulties have also arisen. These difficulties suggest the need for multidisciplinary discourse in addition to (not as a replacement for) the separate disciplines.

Basis. History of disciplines (Chapters 15, 16); existing difficulties in the intellectual system (Chapters 17, 18).

D6. The historical order of the development of the disciplines went from the simple to the complex and from the readily observable to matters that were more hidden from ready human observation (Index of Complexity, Guideline of Hierarchical Obscurity).

Basis. Chapters 15 and 16.

Comment. This history skewed the methodologies and goals in some fields for decades. To some extent it continues to distort those fields that study the most complex systems.

D7. The extent of the differences in character between the physical sciences on the one hand and the human sciences on the other has, on average, been underappreciated and understated for a century or more.

Basis. Chapters 4, 6, 7; Figure 16-1. More specifically, four sets of ideas developed in this book interlock and confirm each other in ways that show the importance and magnitude of the differences between the disciplines. These four sets of ideas are: the relation of truth assertions, systems, and domains; the structure of complex systems, including the incommensurate nature of dimensions in various disciplines and the nature of hierarchical structures with interfaces of mutual constraint; the extraordinary quantitative difference in the complexity of human systems and systems of inert, naturally-occurring objects; and the importance of sociotechnical systems in human evolution and in the physical bases of all human societies — sociotechnical systems cannot be fully comprehended as solely technical, economic, social, legal, or ecological.

E. Other Results Concerning Multidisciplinarity

E1. Science, in a broad sense, is the best means we have for discovering, creating, organizing, reformulating, confirming, and disconfirming truth assertions about nature. Science is not infallible, but it is far better for these purposes than any other method or set of methods we now know. At the same time, science is not sufficient to deal with all problems of vital concern to humans; in particular, science has little, often nothing, to say about questions that center on values and normative choices; aesthetics; human affectional relations; and matters of the human spirit.

Basis. Experientially firm, no logical proof.

Comments. We need to remember, particularly in academia, that to believe we can deal with all problems of concern rationally (that is, scientifically) is irrational.

We also need to remember that science is not one method but a complex of methods with many cross-links and feedbacks. The critical features of science seem to be: with regard to method — iterative empirical grounding; with regard to concepts — careful system definition; with regard to process — the need to convince a group of able peers. The system/sysrep apparatus (Chapter 13) can be a crucial element.

Within the domain of truth assertions, as some anonymous wag has noted, "Science tells the truth, nothing but the truth, but never the whole truth." Science does not tell the whole truth precisely because of Hypothesis IV (conclusion A1): Any one truth assertion relates to a finite domain, not to all possible systems.

E2. There exist problems in which the significant (that is to say, necessary) variables pass beyond those used in any single discipline. When this occurs, models based on single disciplines will nearly always be simplistic.

Basis. Chapter 10; discussion of innovation in Chapter 14. See conclusion B1. See also Durham (1991); Dennett (1991); and Howard Gardner (1987).

E3. No paradigm that is appropriate for the physical sciences can be a complete worldview.

Basis. A straightforward extension of the theory of dimensions, which is presuppositional to creation of all equations in the physical sciences themselves. See also conclusions A1, B1, C3, D1, D2, D3, and E1.

E4. No one of the human sciences, as they existed in 1990, is capable of treating all the problems of concern in human mental, social, and cultural systems.

Basis. Chapters 8–12.

Comment. The dimensions of the various fields are more often than not qualitatively distinct (incommensurate to each other). The single human is a particularly important example of the problem of representing complex systems by a few variables. There is only one system, the human animal. The hyperspace of variables needed to fully describe human behaviors has many variables, including some characteristics that cannot be rank-ordered and are thus not describable in mathematical terms (for example, love and affection, aesthetic preferences). Descriptions of the total hyperspace of human behaviors and systems by any few variables will therefore nearly always create models that are seriously incomplete; this incompleteness may or may not be important for a given problem, but it will exist.

E5. There are a number of explicit tools we can use for the study of multidisciplinary problems.

Basis. Illustrations in this volume.

Comments. Some particularly important conceptual tools for study of multidisciplinarity appear to be:

- The distinction between constraint and determination.
- The concept of residual open degrees of freedom as contrasted with the total number of types of variations possible for a given system.
- The distinction between necessary and sufficient conditions.
- The distinction between equilibrium and stability.
- The use of an extended form of the theory of dimensions as an aid to clarifying domains.
- The use of the concept of a hyperspace of all possible functional relations between inputs and outputs.
- The concept and importance of feedback, the existence of several levels of complexity of feedback and several distinct types of information.
- Recognition that an incomplete list of variables cannot give a complete picture of a complex system no matter how sophisticated the later mathematical manipulations on those variables.
- The Guidelines for Scholarly Controversy, of Hierarchical Obscurity, and for Very Complex Systems are useful ideas. They are only guidelines, not firm principles, but nevertheless seem to operate correctly a very large fraction of the time in multidisciplinary problems. They seem worth further study in various cases.

There seems to be a need for further discussion of three questions: What are the validity and the firmness of the various tools? What additional tools are useful for multidisciplinary discourse? Which should we teach students (some students? All students?)?

E6. We seem to need a better semantics for what we have called "rules" (principles, laws, paradigms, guidelines, and so forth).

Basis. Discussion in Chapter 16.

Comment. Unless we make clear the assurance level of a given "rule," we are not providing readers with vital information about our statement.

E7. The use of multidisciplinary discourse seems to at least partially resolve some old and unresolved issues.

Basis. See examples in Chapters 12 and 14. However, checking by many other scholars is needed.

E8. Overviews of the intellectual terrain of the late twentieth century are possible. They require suppression of excessive detail, but they are nevertheless important for understanding ourselves and our world.

CHAPTER 20

What Have We Learned?

Implications and Inferences

Chapter 19 lists 36 separate results. This is too many to hold in working memory. We need to formulate the results into coherent themes that can help us understand implications for the future. This chapter gathers the results we have found under six themes:

- The lack of any single approach to all the problems of human concern
- The complexity index
- Interfaces of mutual constraint
- Effects of the limitations of the human mind on scholarship
- The system/sysrep apparatus and its uses
- How important is multidisciplinary discourse?

Lack of a Universal Approach

We began this discussion with a hypothesis that there is no single method, view, discipline, set of principles, or equations sufficient to provide understanding of all problems of human concern. The results that we have seen confirm this hypothesis over and over.

In Chapter 1, we saw that the domain of truth assertions tells us little about beauty, values, or affectional relationships. What we know about the world provides background for ethical decisions but rarely makes final decisions for us about ethical, aesthetic, or affectional matters. Hence no one set of scientific principles or equations is sufficient.

Even for a system as simple as Windsor Castle in 1100 A.D., we need a number of views to understand its structure and uses. A few variables and/or parameters are not sufficient to describe important and common systems. For social and sociotechnical systems, there are open degrees of freedom which bear on significant issues. The choices we make using these open degrees of freedom will in large measure determine the well- (or ill-) being of the planet. The choices are great enough so that we humans make up some of the rules for social and sociotechnical systems as we go along. It follows not only that we will need to continue studying such systems but also that we cannot reach a final set of "rules" for them.

The two top-level views used in Western culture (synoptic and reductionist) for the past three centuries are each insufficient. The continued arguments between them are a quarrel over two non-answers. We need at least both these views and a third (structural) to understand very common and important classes of systems. It is interesting to think about how much useless argument and how many misleading conclusions we would have avoided had we for the past century taught students of this need for at least three kinds of views.

Some of the limitations that mandate more than one approach are fundamental. Social systems are different from systems of inert, naturally-occurring objects in many significant ways. Some domains of concern to humans have differing and exogenous dimensions. Other limitations arise because of the nature of the human working memory. Let us suppose, for thinking purposes, that there were no fundamental limitations, and we could find a theory not only for the forces of physics which explain some of the behavior of inert matter but also for the nature of life, the origin of complexity, the conditions needed for stable fair governments, and everything else. Could we use the theory? It is very improbable. Such a theory would almost certainly be so complex that it would not be comprehensible to the human mind nor "computable" in our largest computers.

Summing all this, we can now see a broader basis for Hypothesis III (no universal approaches). This result flows from nothing more than the variety and complexity or totality of systems of concern to humans. Some have invariant behaviors; some do not. For some we can create "grand theory"; for others we cannot. For some we need deterministic sysreps; for others we need probabilistic or chaotic sysreps — systems with heterogeneous, hierarchical structures differ in fundamental ways from one-level systems of homogeneous structure. It follows that we should not expect one research methodology to be good for all seasons. Given all these differences, it may seem strange that so many very able individuals created a "universalism" and that so many positivist theories were for decades claimed to be complete in fields where this cannot be so. However, when we look back at the reasons underlying the creation of fallacies of projection (Chapter 18), we see that these historical difficulties are not strange. They are not the result of malfeasance or lack of intelligence. They are the results of the limitations and tendencies of the human mind, taken with the way we have constructed our intellectual enterprise. As Deming's Dictum says: "When an institution is not working, don't blame the workers, look at the structure."

Implications of Complexity

The numerical values produced by the index of complexity for various classes of systems tell us we have often seriously underestimated the complexity of social and sociotechnical systems in comparison with systems of inert, naturally-occurring objects. As a result, we have often been misled by Comte's Pecking Order not only with regard to the status of various disciplines but also with regard to the kinds of principles we can expect to create for social and socio-technical systems. When we pass beyond a dimensionality of 3 or 4, the human mind is not capable of visualizing all the details in the complete system, and thus can easily overlook outcomes of importance in given systems. It is from neces-sity, not ignorance or stupidity, that we use cuts through the complete hyperspace to study social and sociotechnical systems. However, we do not seem to have paid enough attention to what such cuts imply about either predictive capacity or completeness of theoretical results. In some cases we have attempted to provide deterministic theories even when we cannot list with reasonable assurance all the variables and parameters of the system. In a number of fields we have tried to formulate simple fixed rules that spell out invariant behaviors, even though the "rules" for the relevant systems are in part subject to human choice and change over time. As a result, we have had many arguments over the assertions of the type "My cut is better than your cut." Since we cannot decide what lies beyond various cuts without a complete theory or an adequate set of data for the com-plete hyperspace, such arguments are usually sterile.

We do not have and are not likely to have complete theories or computer programs for all the details of very complex systems. We need to keep firmly in mind that we erect, operate, and improve very complex systems incrementally based on experience, judgment, and "guided" trials. When we attempt to erect or steer them by using oversimple theory, we are likely to make poor decisions. For these systems, there is a primacy of data, and we forget that only at our own peril.

Interfaces of Mutual Constraint

A particularly important source of misunderstandings has resulted from the failure to assimilate what Polanyi (1968) delineated for us about hierarchical systems with interfaces of mutual constraint. Because Polanyi's Principle lies in the domain of multidisciplinary analysis and outside the pure science disciplines as we have erected them, the principle has been neither widely understood nor taught. Again and again, we have had overclaims arising from particular disci-plines because we have not recognized that we cannot integrate or differentiate (mathematically) across interfaces of mutual constraint. The equations cannot be closed until we supply added conditions. Or, to put this the other way around, physics and biology constrain but do not determine social and sociotechnical systems.

These difficulties have been compounded by a lack of clarity on several other matters. We have failed to recognize that neither information nor feedback is a single category; each has several subcategories that need distinction from each other for many purposes. We have not used the theory of dimensions except in a few disciplines. It can be used in a rigorous extension of the simple idea that we ought not equate apples and oranges. Had we used that theory, many disciplinary overclaims would have been discovered almost immediately. A third difficulty, which has compounded the effects of the others, is the failure to recognize that not only the variables, parameters, and characteristics but also the appropriate "rules" usually vary from one level to the next in the hierarchy of constitution. As systems become larger and contain more types of components, new behaviors and characteristics often emerge and therefore require new rules. When we ignore these differences, attempting to derive one level from another without looking for new variables and parameters and behaviors, we are very apt to confuse ourselves. We have done so, many times in the past. We have been able to erect a reliable overall theory for some particular classes of problems. These usually lie in one level in the hierarchy of constitution. It does not follow that these principles extend to all systems in all levels of the hierarchy, since the variables, parameters, characteristics, and principles in some levels differ from those in others. We have also found a few principles that apply to many levels but do not give complete information about most of the levels, only some constraints.

The search for a unified theory, a single theory of everything (particularly a simple theory that is comfortable for the human mind), has led to confused thoughts at many times and places and sometimes to pernicious actions. Such universalism seems to be a holy grail, a chimera, not a realizable goal. A simplistic, unified theory of everything fits the desires and limits of the human mind, but not the messy, complex world we see around us. We need to inculcate this idea in our students. In many disciplines, what we have taught is nearly the opposite of this idea because of the way we educate and enculturate the upcoming generation of workers in "our" discipline. As we saw in Chapter 4, if we fail to make needful qualitative distinctions, we will be unable to understand the problems in which the distinctions are relevant.

We cannot expect to derive everything from any one view or set of principles. We must instead strive for consistency of results from different sources on a given problem.

Limits of the Mind

The human mind is at once the cutting edge of consciousness on the planet and an evolutionary "kludge" with severe limitations.

Since we can only retain 7 (plus or minus 2) bits in our working memory, we make up chunks, such as words, from a few bits and store the chunks in long-term memory. We then learn to connect these chunks into schemata for thinking about matters that concern and interest us. We cannot think clearly about anything of even moderate complexity when we lack an appropriate learned schema. The same is true for any kind of complex neuromuscular task. The human infant cannot see clearly, walk, talk, or understand sounds. We must learn schemata for even these foundation skills. When we lack the relevant schemata, we can neither think clearly nor perform muscular tasks well.

The mind also seems to project facts, views, feelings, and schemata into and onto unknown territory whenever there are no immediate strong contradictory data. These tendencies help us understand why there have been so many cases in which familiar schemata have been mapped into and onto domains where they are inappropriate.

Beyond these limitations, for which there are at least reasonably good data, there seems to be another tendency of the human mind. Our minds seem structured so that we strive to understand those things that concern us. As a result, the human mind seems to accept, nearly every time, simplistic explanations in preference to no explanation.

These limitations and tendencies of the human mind are not likely to go away. It follows that we ought to make students thoroughly aware of what they imply for scholarship. We do not seem to have done this.

The Mismatch of Mind and Complexity of Systems

When we combine the limits of the human mind with the numbers produced by the complexity index and also the existence of interfaces of mutual constraint, we see a serious mismatch between the human mind and the full complexity of important systems, one that we need to understand. We seem not to have perceived this mismatch clearly. We have sometimes seemed to proceed from an unstated idea that the human mind can understand whatever it chooses, anything at all, in a single bound. We thus sometimes ignore the need to assimilate bits into chunks and form schemata, as well as the slow but critical process of iteratively comparing sysrep and system.

All this forces attention on the need for grounding, on the enormous importance of traceability between our sysreps and our systems, and of iterative use of that traceability in the formulation of understanding, principles, and courses of action. Even apparently precise mathematical modeling of physical systems does not seem to be an exception to the vital need for both traceability and iterative comparison between sysrep and system. This iterative use of traceability is what most clearly distinguishes science from earlier methods of thought and understanding. Science, when it has worked particularly well, has usually involved this iterative loop (not just empiricism or theory formulation alone). When we abandon the iterative use of traceability between sysrep and system, or when we move into areas in which this iterative loop cannot be used, we are nearly as apt as our ancestors to create myths rather than a more accurate and complete understanding.

Even though we now possess far greater tools for thought and computation, there may in the end be limits to what humans can learn about things that are very small, very large, or very far removed from us in time. The Guideline of Hierarchical Obscurity makes clear that the farther we go in any of these directions the more we lose the ability to use traceability in the iterative loop between system and sysrep and the more we lose assurance about our knowledge.

The System/Sysrep Apparatus

Given what the preceding section tells us, it follows that we need to develop as fully and rigorously as we can the methodology of how we use the iterative loop between system and sysrep. The discussion in this book expands this methodology in two ways. First, fuller use has been made of the implications of complexity, hierarchical structure, the theory of dimensions, feedback control, and related ideas. Second, the relations between disciplines have been used to consider the "rules" needed in the overall intellectual terrain. This expanded usage has been called the system/sysrep apparatus. This apparatus brings together with the system concept the index of complexity; the limitations imposed by hierarchical systems with interfaces of mutual constraint; the existence of qualitatively distinct kinds of information and different feedback modes; the Central Presupposition of Control Theory; and other ideas developed in this volume. These added elements, singly or in combinations, help us sharpen and make more powerful the system concept. The system/sysrep apparatus provides operational tools that suggest directions in which to look for ways of moving problems forward. It suggests stronger tests for the adequacy of sysreps. It helps us see the limits of the domains of various disciplines, and hence the relationship between disciplines, more clearly.

Within disciplines the system concept is critical, for the elementary reason that we need to be clear about what we are discussing before we begin the discussion. The idea is, at bottom, a truism whenever clarity is important; nevertheless, "Be sure to define your system appropriately" is easy to say, but the realization is often difficult. The tools and the concepts (Chapter 12) help make the dictum more operational, more accurate, and more powerful not only for specific problems but also at the level of research programs and disciplines.

If we accept the idea that disciplines typically only constrain and do not determine each other, consensus on what is consistent becomes a central criterion for the intellectual world as a whole. The system concept plus the Guideline for Scholarly Controversy then suggest a route to consensus and away from unending feuds. In this sense, the system/sysrep apparatus can be an important tool for establishing appropriate relations among disciplines.

Is Multidisciplinary Discourse Important?

At the beginning of this volume, we put aside the question of the importance of multidisciplinary discourse so we could make an assessment after appropriate tools and results were available. Let's see what the tools and results tell us at this point.

We have seen that the human mind often projects known schemata onto domains for which they are inappropriate, and often accepts simplistic answers to broad, difficult questions. If we give the guardianship of our representations of truth assertions to disciplinary experts, who will sort out the projections of disciplinary results onto larger domains (overclaims)? Who will say, "That representation is seriously oversimple, and the resulting theory should not be used in preference to credible data as the basis for actions in the world?" Who will arbitrate conflicting results for the same problem which arise from different disciplines?

Are these questions best left to experts, as we have assumed, or do we need disinterested observers? We can answer this question by using the several acute questions we erected in Chapter 13. These questions concern the match of sysrep to system on such matters as: dimensions; levels of feedback; types of accessible information; number of levels of feedback; levels of control; open degrees of freedom; and variation or invariance of the "rules."

This does not look like an important change from current practice, but it is. Our current practice is to define a sysrep and ask, in a general way, "Is it adequate?" We have again and again been misled by this general examination in nearly every field of study simply because it is too general and does not check specifics. The seven preceding questions do look at specifics, and they look in just those places where we have seen errors. There are no doubt other specific questions, but this is a good starting list.

If the sysrep does not embody the same characteristics as the system on any of these several matters (and often others), then we cannot expect the sysrep to give us accurate answers. The addition or deletion of even one mode of feedback, for example, radically alters system behavior. But anyone can examine these questions and render judgment, expert or outsider, because the judgment does not require knowledge of internal details.

As we have seen (Chapter 18), the experts are biased by many factors. It seems, then, that we should look to unbiased outsiders to render judgments in preference to insiders, who are inevitably and understandably biased. It is this bias that leads to A. N. Whitehead's distinction between the details of "a method good for purposes of . . . dominant interests" on the one hand, and the application of that method to questions of "wider judgment" on the other, where the method is, in Whitehead's words, "invariably wrong." For our purposes the word "method" needs to be broadened to include paradigms and schemata, but the essence of Whitehead's idea keys the critical question: How can we maintain the independence of experts within their discipline while also making sure that the questions of wider judgment are made without bias and in the interest of all stakeholders involved?

Please notice that none of the seven characteristics listed above as needing matching between sysrep and system arise from the internal details of a particular discipline. They arise instead from the system concept plus observations about a wide variety of real systems. And all this repeats the basic warning that the answers will be appropriate only as long as we are sufficiently clear about the definition of the **system** under study, and that definition depends on the problem and on our purposes, not the rules of science per se. That is why we erected the questions in Chapter 13 and gave illustrations. They are acute tools that sharpen how we question the fit of sysrep to system. To avoid misunderstanding, it needs repeating that this refers to the total fit of the sysrep to the real-world systems, and not to the internal details of any given discipline.

This question of matching or mirroring of systems by sysrep is crucial to understanding multidisciplinary problems. It is an important reason why we defined the term "sysrep" (Chapter 2). Let's therefore examine how we should form judgment from several viewpoints which offer experience to guide considerations for complex systems.

In the Middle Ages, the Western world had a unified but authoritarian view based on faith. During the following centuries we have moved more and more to a severely fragmented set of empirically based but relatively narrow disciplines. In the late twentieth century, the fragmentation has become so great that communities of disciplinary experts sometimes act as if they owe no allegiance to and have no responsibility for larger social or intellectual wholes or other stakeholders in wider terrains to which they apply their results.

We can think of the situation in terms of the perennial question about the relative authority and responsibility of local communities in distinction with the total community — that is, the classic tension between "central" and "local." What can we say? The tension between central and local is an issue that cannot be fully resolved. It is not a question with a single "right" answer; it is, rather, a continuing tension between two legitimate desiderata. The most we can do in such a case is work at finding and maintaining an appropriate balance that works reasonably well for all the stakeholders in the relevant problem. Since we are dealing with two sets of very complex systems in the universities, one of ideas and one of institutions, we do not have a theory to guide us and must look at what experience tells us.

The relevant experience lies in large institutions, including governments. Much of what we have learned that is successful in such situations is embodied in the U.S. Constitution. Another successful example is the Japanese methods for forming consensus in order to operate what I have called "participatory hierarchies" (see Nakane [1971, 1973]; Kline [1989]). A third source of experience lies in the existing coalitions of disciplines for working on truly multidisciplinary problems — for example, the cognitive sciences on the nature and function of the human brain. What do these precedents tell us?

First, we need to teach students how their particular interests and disciplines connect to larger intellectual wholes and to the world. To do this we need to teach materials of the sort developed in this book and summarized in Chapter 19 and in the lists of hypotheses and guidelines at the end of this volume. I am not arguing that these materials are either unique or near optimal; as I have stressed, they are only a beginning discussion. I am suggesting that these are the sort of materials we need, and that we need to improve and expand the materials in the way scholars normally do over time. Then we need to inculcate into upcoming generations of students some of the more important warnings these materials embody about fallacies of projection and the other difficulties a severely fragmented system of disciplines tends to create, and to provide students with schemata that let them see how the pieces fit into the whole.

Can we do this when there is no forum or community that continues to address multidisciplinary problems? The answer seems to be that we cannot because communities of interacting scholars are the bearers and improvers of human knowledge. Communities are the vessels that hold and use human knowledge and transmit knowledge to the upcoming generation. As long as individual disciplines maintain the view that only "members of the club" understand the contents of "my" discipline, and hence the views of "outsiders" with respect to "my" discipline should be ignored (or at least severely discounted), the problem is not soluble. At the same time, we must not violate the important aspects of academic freedom. Is there a way to break through this apparent deadlock? I believe there is. If we add Whitehead's remark about where experts have nearly always been right (and where they have nearly always been wrong) to the Guideline for Scholarly Controversy, it suggests a possible route to follow. Specifically, disciplinary autonomy and authority are entirely appropriate for "internal" questions, but are not appropriate where other disciplines or larger world problems are significantly involved.

Let's put this once again in terms of the metaphor of the map of the 48 contiguous United States. Within some constraints, the fine-grained details of the territory inside each state belong to the mapmakers for that state, and only to them. Mapmakers for the country need to attend to the fit of the boundaries of all the states to each other. They also need to attend to the overall consistency of symbols, and hence to the views of the individual state mapmakers. The mapmakers for each state therefore need to attend to the consistency of their maps as they affect the map of the whole. For example, two states cannot both have sole ownership of a given bit of territory. They owe that consistency to the larger community of mapmakers and to the public. Consistency, not ownership of all the territory, is the proper criterion, as Hypothesis VII tells us.

For the intellectual system as a whole, what the map metaphor suggests is the need for consistency between synoptic views of the whole and the views within each discipline. The metaphor also implies that no one view of an argument between two or more disciplines is entitled to complete control of issues when interests overlap. Nor is withdrawing into one's own territory and ignoring the results of others a solution; it is part of the problem. A striving for consistency in the search for improved understanding is needed in many problem areas. Like the mapmakers for the states, the disciplinary experts owe this much to the larger intellectual community. These obligations to the larger community need not take up nearly as much time and effort as getting the internal details right. However, when the external obligations are totally ignored, we must expect difficulties in the map of the total intellectual territory. Thus far, this expectation has been fulfilled; we saw a score and more of examples of such difficulties (Chapter 17). In this section, we will see more about why this is so.

Are there examples of multidisciplinary work by individuals that has accomplished what is suggested above? Fortunately, excellent examples have appeared in recent years — among them, the work of Durham (1991), Dennett (1991), and Etzioni (1988). These three examples all have to do with areas where the index of complexity tells us multidisciplinary approaches are critical. This set of examples is far from exhaustive.

Let's also consider a wholly different and very large category of examples, design of complex hardware for human use. In Chapter 11, we found a need for two iterative loops to complete the process of human design appropriately. Each loop typically covers many areas that are regarded as separate disciplines. We need a downward loop with return to the level of the object in the hierarchy of constitution to understand the pieces and their connections to each other (structural picture). This loop may reach into fields as widespread as classical dynamics, optics, quantum mechanics, thermodynamics, structural mechanics, control theory, fluid mechanics, and electricity and magnetism, and also require know-how about particular production processes, markets, and other matters. We also need an upward loop with return to the level of the hardware in the hierarchy of constitution in order to understand the values involved and also the effects on social, political, and ecological systems, that is, other stakeholders. This upward loop may involve disciplines as disparate as economics, sociology, ethics, psychology, ecology, law, and others. When we treat such designs as wholly "scientific," wholly legal, wholly "economic," wholly "ethical," or wholly ecological we are not likely to find good long-range solutions.

To understand the total terrain, we need not only piecewise views but also synoptic and structural views, as we have seen again and again. To put this differently, the total intellectual terrain is a hierarchy with heterogeneous aggregation and interfaces of mutual constraint. Hypothesis V therefore applies. We need not one synoptic view but at least several, since there is no one view that can describe the full complexity of the problems of human concern in ways that are likely to be comprehensible to the human mind. We need piecewise views of many kinds. And we need to understand how the piecewise views join to create the whole. These structural views can rarely be derived from theory, and therefore need experience and ongoing study. Finally, we need to pay more attention to the differences compared with the similarities between disciplines. And this will also need piecewise, synoptic, and structural views.

A way to accomplish these tasks is not hard to see, once we look. We have already implied the answer several times. Many of the problems can be alleviated or even eliminated by adding multidisciplinary discourse to the ongoing discourses in the various disciplines.

Are there sound scholarly precedents for this action? Indeed there are! There is precise precedent in both linguistics and ethnology (and probably other areas).

From relatively early in ethnology, a central idea has been that the observations of a culture needed to be interpreted from the view of the insiders of the given culture. To put this in different words, the ethnologist was to do his or her best not to represent the view of his or her culture of origin. This idea was appropriate, and it has led to a great deal of learning about human cultures and human nature. However, when the ethnologists later approached the task of comparing and classifying the several thousand cultures they had documented, a new problem arose. The 2,000–3,000 cultures encompassed enormous variations in customs, beliefs, and behaviors. Thus the ethnologists realized that no one culture was a suitable reference frame for looking at all the others. Some different (outside) view had to be taken for comparative studies. They then named the insider's view "emic" (pronounced eemic) and the outside view "etic" (eh-tic).

The words emic and etic were taken from the last two syllables of the terms "phonemic" and "phonetic" as used by linguists who had encountered the same problem in studying languages. There are 100 or more phonemes used in human speech in all known languages. A phoneme is a distinguishable noise (see Chapter 8). However, no one language uses all known phonemes. Spoken English, for example, uses about 40 phonemes from the full list. Hence even the phonemes of any one language will not do as a basis for study of all languages. One must also have phonetics, the study of all the sounds from all the languages, from an "outside" or etic view.

This idea is not limited to linguistics and ethnology; it is necessary whenever we have variations between cases within a set of related instances. For example, in sports we cannot describe all sports in terms of, say, U.S. baseball, European soccer, or Afghani polo. Nevertheless, we can discuss the total domain of sports from at etic view and talk about the functions sports serve in human societies.

Since we have seen disciplines, including their ideas and their jargon, act in a very real sense as subcultures within a larger society, the need for an etic view also applies to our intellectual system. Workers within a particular discipline have an emic view of their own field, including its paradigms and schemata. They need such a view, and they are entitled to it. Without these emic views, we would have made little progress in creating relatively sound knowledge about our world. Moreover, this emic, insider's view should not be subject to outside tampering or authoritative dictates. History very clearly indicates the folly of such tampering.

Nevertheless, it is not only possible but very important, if we intend to create synoptic views of our total intellectual system, that we also have etic views that can overlook and connect the various "subcultures" to each other within the intellectual system. Such etic views are essential for at least two important tasks. First, they allow workers from many disciplines to speak to each other intelligibly. Second, to create a framework inside which our total intellectual culture can move toward consistency, a trend ethnologists have reported that essentially all successful cultures follow. We cannot expect to reach total consistency, but there is a continuing and important task of reducing inconsistencies within the total system of understanding. Striving for consistency seems no less important in a complete intellectual system than in a culture, although in both cases paradoxes will arise as part of the process and need to be tolerated for at least intermediate times.

Moreover, faculties in the universities have repeatedly reported that the wider judgments created by work in multidisciplinary programs have helped them understand their own discipline more fully. In the metaphor of the map, one understands the map of any one state better when it can be set properly within a map of the country.

Another name for an etic view of the domain of truth assertions is what we have been calling "multidisciplinary discourse." What we have shown in the preceding paragraphs is that the problem is not unique to the intellectual system as a whole. It arises whenever we need to compare a set of cases with common properties and also great variation of details from one member of the set to another. Moreover, when the strategy has been used, it has often succeeded. Given these ideas, we can return to calling the needed etic view "multidisciplinary discourse."

What does construction of satisfactory multidisciplinary views entail? What should the "balance of power" between central and local look like? It seems to me to entail several elements.

First, a willingness must exist within the community working with the etic views to cede the inside details to the insiders who rightly "own" them. Second, outsiders can and should ask the hard questions about the value and the validity of emic results from an etic view up to and including whether the emperor is wearing clothes. In this task the acute questions in Chapter 13 force the issues involved, as noted above. Outsiders can and should bring together conflicting results arising from various emic views and examine how such paradoxes can be resolved in a continual striving for consistency. Third, the pictures formed by the outsiders must not do violence to the concepts and results of emic materials as seen by insiders. Fourth, the insiders must concede the larger terrain encompassed by etic views of outsiders who rightly "own" the whole map.

Finally, we need to recognize that science in the late twentieth century is no longer in an infant stage in its ideas, its methods, its communities, its social status, or its freedom from persecution by higher authority. At the time of Galileo, the Roman Catholic church had the power to persecute and burn heretics, that is, anyone who disagreed with Church dogma. It no longer does. Heroic individuals, such as Luther, Galileo, Locke, Jefferson, Mill, and many others, took on and won for us the battle for our right to think and say what we please. That right was bound over into the right of free speech two centuries ago in the U.S. Constitution. The power has been taken from the hands of shamans and placed under civil law.

Some of our current religious leaders seem still to wish for the shamanistic power, but it is only a wish. That wish still troubles our world and no doubt will continue to do so into the indeterminate future. In democracies, however, that power no longer has the dictatorial force once given it by the pope and many other religious leaders in other times and places.

Science, in the sense of the international and local communities of workers who do science, is today a vital, powerful force worldwide. Science is respected, sometimes too much, by most individuals, governments, and companies. If this were not true, government funding of science could not exist in a democracy.

We need to put aside the fears spawned by the treatment of Galileo and replace them with a proper sense of obligation to our larger democratic communities that do not persecute us for our scientific views. Beyond the need for etic views, we have seen a number of other reasons why multidisciplinary discourse is important. Let's recap them.

- We need not one viewpoint but at least three (synoptic, piecewise, and structural) in order to understand almost any very complex system, and this applies with particular force to our complete intellectual system because it is extremely complex in all its elements. Even within the inert, naturally-occurring world, we need at least three kinds of representations to provide good models for all of the systems we observe: deterministic, probabilistic, and chaotic. Surely these are both ideas we need to teach all university students thoroughly. But we have not taught them for the obvious reason that few scholars have understood the ideas themselves, at least in explicit form. If you doubt this, you might look at Leff and Rex (1990), a volume published in the Princeton Physics series. In that volume it is routinely but invisibly assumed, without dissent, that the most elemental systems of physics, what I call "Gibbs simple systems," make up the whole world. These Gibbs simple systems have two degrees of freedom and a complexity index of three. They have no feedback modes. The world has systems with a complexity index as high as 10^{20} and critical feedback modes in many places. Nearly any scholar can judge the bad fit of 2 degrees of freedom to a system to a system with 10^{20} degrees of freedom with feedback loops. Thus Leff and Rex (1990) show that we have not finished with the difficulty which arises from asking only general questions about our sysreps.
- This beginning discussion has produced a surprising number of results.

More than a dozen seem to be new and in some measure iconoclastic. This strongly supports the idea that a significant area of discourse has been lacking. This lacuna has impaired our ability to present to our students a picture of the world that is both whole and comprehensible.

- The tools erected in this volume on multidisciplinary discourse are useful in many places within individual disciplines. Some of these tools, historically, have been treated only within the framework of disciplinary knowledge in ways that require considerable special knowledge. Some of these tools are contained in conventional courses on logic or mathematics; some are not. It seems that we need to teach a refined version of some of the tools illustrated in this volume — for example, the concept of hyperspaces, the distinction between constraint and determination, the elementary concepts of control theory, the theory of dimensions, and the index of complexity — to a much wider range of students.

- Two types of fallacies of projection have been common in our intellectual system for many decades. Chapter 18 suggests potential sources. Most of these difficulties have arisen from inadequate understanding of the limitations of particular disciplines, that is, the appropriate domains of particular sysreps. Underlying these difficulties seem to be several sources: the fragmentation of knowledge without the fragments being (or remaining) attached to synoptic views; the way we enculturate disciplinary experts; the nature of practice in disciplinary communities; the limitations of the human mind; the (apparently strong) human desire to understand; and the extreme complexity of many systems of importance in our world.

- In some cases, we have the components for solving broad conceptual problems, but they lie in separate areas of discourse, and we lack both the structure and a process to combine the concepts appropriately. See Chapter 14 for examples. In another example, many workers had by 1990 seen the lack of fixed rules in individual fields; no one seems to have seen the full scope or provided reasons why we should not expect to find fixed "rules" in many fields.

- A number of the results in this volume emerge from a three-step process: (1) build concepts; (2) discuss multidisciplinary topics (complexity, structure, etc.) using the concepts; (3) combine results of step 2 for further results. The emergent results at step 3 typically require the results of the preceding step. Thus, results of step 3 require the schemata created in step 2, and these schemata do not emerge from single disciplines. A good example of this kind of result is the merging of ideas about limits of the mind and the complexity of systems as a central basis for fallacies of projection. A second example is the principle of consistency, Hypothesis VII. Still another is our implicit assumption that a single human mind could leap from a single disciplinary context and its schemata to results in a wider context without forming the needed schemata for the new context. Unfortunately, the human mind seldom can make such a leap. This is why important conceptual results not accessible via individual disciplines can be found through multidisciplinary discourse.

- We live in an increasingly complex and interconnected world that contains more and more large complex systems. Operation of large complex systems requires teams of managers with good working relations and overlapping skills. To prepare students for such a world by enculturating them in emic disciplinary views with no countervailing overviews is mis-training.

- We elders have an obligation to provide the upcoming generation with overviews that are simultaneously understandable, realistic, forward-looking, and whole. I will call this the "obligation of the elders."

We can now put this section's discussion in a different way. We can say that the results of the formation of separate disciplines has been very powerful and successful, successful far beyond anyone's imagination two centuries ago. It has allowed us to increase our knowledge of essentially every sector of the domain of truth assertions and increase the assurance with which we know the results, many times over in less than three centuries. At the same time, it has left us with a severely fragmented system permeated with difficulties of several kinds. All these difficulties arise because we have not understood well the relationships among the disciplines; we have had no etic viewpoint, no perspective from which this could have been understood. Nor have we had a community that possessed the needed etic view and insisted on its validity and use.

As long as this remains true, we leave inherently etic decisions to individuals who have only emic schemata, and there will be no one to guard the guards. It must follow that we have no reasonable assurance, no safety, for our top-level concepts and results within the intellectual system because what we need to know lies buried in the assumptions underlying emic views and is hidden from public knowledge by jargon and unfamiliar concepts. Let's examine this further. Let's invert our perspective at this point and ask what will be inherently missing, what will we be unable to see and find, what will we lack, if we do not erect and maintain multidisciplinary discourse within an appropriate community of workers? At least the following:

- The means for assuring the accuracy of our knowledge base at the highest level, the assumptions underlying disciplines. We will have no safety in many of our most important concepts, ideas, and views.

- A disinterested umpire, a community with a forum to judge the proper distribution of research resources between competing disciplines. (Lack of such a community has resulted in the distortion of our post–World War II research funding, from any fair basis I can bring to bear.)

- A perspective from which we could judge what ought to be included in the non-disciplinary part of undergraduate education. As a result, we have compounded requirements out of existing disciplinary courses ad hoc. This extends even to the perspectives in the basic courses, which are often taught for those who will become experts in the field, and not the rest of us. Such an approach omits most cross-disciplinary and essentially all multi-disciplinary material, the materials that ought to be the glue that holds students' ideas together and forms the basis for their worldview when they reach graduation.

- A framework to facilitate solution of problems that require simultaneous application of more than one discipline.

- The ability to communicate with each other adequately, a lack that in turn inevitably makes it very difficult if not impossible to form the common goals and values that are essential ingredients for cooperative communities that can take effective action on our intellectual and educational problems.

- A community of scholars, whose concern is the intellectual enterprise as a whole. Such a group should lie at the core of our educational system in the university, but so far that has not been the case. We have not had, and do not have, anyone who will define the rights and the boundaries of the whole intellectual enterprise as stoutly as experts defend the rights and boundaries of their particular specialties.

- A community that can build the schemata needed for an etic view of our intellectual enterprise. Since the human mind cannot leap from an emic to an etic perspective, we continue to lack the schemata we need, and certain kinds of difficulties go unnoticed. It is as if we left our discussions of culture in the ethnological sense to the 2,000 or so separate tribes on earth. We would then know little of the great impact of culture on human life.

I will call these seven points "the list of gaps." Are the gaps important? Have the unfortunate expectations the list creates been true until now?

We have seen in this volume that we have been blind to the need for etic views of our knowledge base. We have created and far too often believed extremely simplistic concepts, models, and theories about complex systems in dozens of fields and research programs. Fallacies of projection, universalisms, and extreme disciplinary overclaims permeate our system. Knowledge that could easily solve important existing problems within disciplines has not been used because it remains locked behind the barrier of disciplinary pride on one side and the barrier of no interest to workers with other emic views on the other side. For example, the idea of Draper's Dictum could make real differences in a myriad of problems where it is not now known. So could the distinctions in types of information and feedback modes. The current state of knowledge of electrophysiology of the heart and brain misses core ideas of electrical engineering and

CONCLUSIONS

thereby remains primitive in some ways. And these are only a few of the serious results correctly foretold by the list of gaps.

On the other hand, in Chapter 14 we were able to see how to unlock some old apparent conundrums and deal with the paradoxes of many solutions to one problem — three examples were studied and a multidisciplinary approach used. The negative expectations that the list of gaps foretells have indeed been fulfilled in the past. We are now ready to state a final conclusion in two parts.

Final Conclusion

Part A. Multidisciplinary discourse is more than just important. We can have a complete intellectual system, one that covers all the necessary territory, only if we add multidisciplinary discourse to the knowledge within the disciplines. This is true not only in principle but also for strong pragmatic reasons. This will assure the safety of our more global ideas.

Part B. We senior faculty will be able to fulfill the obligation of the elders to present to our students worldviews that are simultaneously understandable, realistic, forward-looking, and whole, only if we construct and maintain a multidisciplinary discourse as an addition to the discourses in our separate disciplines.

I leave to Appendix A the question of how multidisciplinary discourse can be effectively adjoined to disciplinary work in universities by relatively small changes in structure. The disciplinary system at its beginnings was an idea of importance and power. However, in thinking about it now, we need to remember a short verse by James Russell Lowell:

> New occasions teach new duties; time makes ancient good uncouth;
> They must upward still, and onward, who would keep abreast of Truth.

This brings us back to our starting point, where it was emphasized that this is a beginning discourse that is far from complete. The discourse needs discussion by many others, and this needs a community for such a discussion. Building such a community for discussion of the issues raised by the list of gaps remains for the future.

Reference Matter

Implications for Education

Are there implications for undergraduate education from what we have seen in this volume? Several results bear directly on this question.

First, we need to supply our university students with overviews, a map of the intellectual country, in addition to, not as a replacement for, the 48 state maps of the individual disciplines. Without overviews, students lack schemata to understand our world. See Chapter 20.

Second, despite the common wisdom that we cannot construct overviews, we have seen several in this volume, and there is no obvious reason why others cannot be constructed.

Third, we have seen a number of tools and schemata for thinking about multidisciplinary issues. Teaching these tools and schemata to students would provide them with ways to think about the connections between their own disciplines and the world as a whole, which would be beneficial not only for the intellectual system as a whole but also for the individual disciplines. In other words, it is critical to provide students with ways to think about multidisciplinary issues in addition to key facts about multidisciplinary topics. If we taught students no more than the tools, hypotheses, and guidelines in this volume, we would have already moved some distance toward giving them useful schemata and methods for thinking about the intellectual world as a whole and how their discipline fits into that world.

Fourth, we have no body of scholars who are responsible for the task of creating, improving, and teaching multidisciplinary materials of the sort this volume begins to develop. It seems to be the lack of a community of scholars, and not impossibility, that has prevented creation of multidisciplinary materials.

Fifth, we think with the schemata we have, and we cannot think well, if at all, about areas in which we lack schemata. This topic cries out for study.

When we join these five ideas, we see that if we are to educate students in the non-major portion of their studies, we must have an effective ongoing multidisciplinary discourse among scholars dedicated to the task of creating and teaching multidisciplinary schemata. How can we create such a community of scholars? Our current academic arrangements do not support such a community. We need some structural changes. As Deming has said, "When an institution is not working, don't blame the people, look at the structure" (see Walton [1990]).

One way to obtain the needed changes would be to create what I will call a "Council of Senior Scholars" (the Council) within the university structure. The Council might consist of five to ten senior members of the faculty. The Council could be charged with two tasks: first, creating and carrying on a multidisciplinary discourse (within and without the university); and second, setting the requirements for the non-major part of undergraduate education via a consensual process.

A Possible Structure for a Council of Senior Scholars

Possible criteria for membership on the Council include

- Tenured status, with a strong reputation in at least one discipline of research and teaching;

- A strong interest in broad education;

- Perhaps most important, members of the Council need to have an attitude of humility about what they know and don't know, as well as a desire to learn about new areas;

- Members of the Council of Senior Scholars should be so selected that collectively they have a very wide range of expertise, including not only the scientific disciplines but also the humanities, social sciences, arts, and professional disciplines. The professional disciplines are important in the context of multidisciplinary discourse, since workers in those fields routinely confront highly multidisciplinary problems involving very complex systems;

- Each member of the Council might serve for a specified period of years (perhaps five to seven), with a fraction being replaced each year to ensure the steady flow of new ideas.

Powers of the Council

How can we provide for sufficient power for the Council of Senior Scholars and not abridge important aspects of disciplinary autonomy? The Council appears to need two different kinds of authority for two different types of courses.

Type 1: Courses taught within departments covering primarily disciplinary materials used for credit within the non-major part of undergraduate education.

For this type of course, the Council might have veto power on what is taught, but not directive power. The Council could say, "We do not believe that these materials are appropriate for non-majors." It could not say, "This is the way you must fix it." The Council might make suggestions for what might be useful in the "fixing" process, but the "fixing" would be left in the hands of the relevant disciplinary experts. This is a division of power that worked well in the creation of educational materials by the U.S. National Committee for Fluid Mechanics Films; these materials remain in use nearly everywhere 30 years after they were created. For Type 1, the Council might also have the power to audit courses to make sure that the spirit of multidisciplinary work is maintained and taught.

Type 2: Courses presenting materials that lie outside the purview of any single department but are necessary for creating the overviews that complete the intellectual system dealing with truth assertions and that relate the disciplines to larger intellectual wholes and to the world. For courses of Type 2, the Council might have the power to hire instructors and oversee the creation and teaching of the materials. For Type 2 courses, the Council would become, in effect, a department concerned with multidisciplinary materials per se. To avoid overexpansion of these courses, the governing body of the faculty could limit the number of courses that could be created and taught under the aegis of the Council.

Comments on the Work of the Council of Senior Scholars

What resources would be required to create and maintain a Council of Senior Scholars? An effort less than that for a small department should be sufficient.

Can we find individuals from among the 500–1,000 senior faculty of a research university who could serve as effective members of a Council of Senior Scholars? If my experience is a guide, we can. Every faculty knows such individuals among its members. Since the Council needs only a small number of members, the effect on the overall faculty structure would not be large; most faculty members could continue to concentrate on their particular areas of expertise.

Can materials like those developed in this volume be taught to undergraduates effectively? Limited experience suggests that they can and in a relatively short time. All the materials of this book have been covered (in improving drafts) in a three-unit course of ten weeks' duration in the Program in Values, Technology, Science and Society at Stanford during the years 1988–1992. Two lectures per week and two hours of section work in groups of fifteen or less have been adequate for a reasonable first treatment. Stanford undergraduates have responded to this class very well on the average. In the past few years the course covering the materials in this book typically has generated written comments on about 20 percent of the anonymous evaluation forms that say things like: "This course has broadened my entire outlook"; "This is one of the very few courses that has had an important impact on the way I view the world"; "This is

the kind of course I was looking for in my education, but had not found before."
Experience suggests that many first-year students are not ready for this kind of
material. Students seem to need as background at least a beginning toward a
major and a course or two in several other areas.

Is experience with multidisciplinary courses useful for faculty development?
Faculty participants in the Program in Values, Technology, Science and Society
at Stanford nearly all remarked to evaluators from the School of Education
something like, "The work in this program has broadened my perspectives on
my own discipline significantly." To the extent that this holds true in other
programs, members of the Council of Senior Scholars would move toward a
position from which they could help broaden the perspective of their own respec-
tive disciplines.

What status does the Council of Senior Scholars need? It needs to be respected by the faculty as working in a legitimate area of research and teaching
and also as having the authority to carry out its tasks. We might arrange this by
giving members of the Council of Senior Scholars significant status, say, "University Professor" rank and/or some significant pay augmentation (a 1 or 2
percent salary increase, or a fixed sum, like a prize). Given this status, with the
goals and the powers suggested above, what specific tasks might the Council of
Senior Scholars take up? For courses of Type 1, the Council might begin by
asking department heads and appropriate senior faculty questions like the following:

1. What materials in your discipline should every undergraduate learn, given
   the constraints on time arising from other requirements? Why?

2. Are these materials available in a form free from more than a minimum
   level of jargon? If so, where? If not, who in your department can be
   charged with developing and teaching them during the next few years?
   What resources would be needed to develop or significantly improve these
   materials from your discipline?

3. What are the limiting boundaries of the domain that can be treated within
   the current view and the current set of variables employed in your field?
   How do you justify these limits? Do you make these limits clear to students in your field?

4. Does the Guideline for Scholarly Controversy suggest ways within, or at
   the boundaries of, your field which might lead more rapidly to effective
   consensus for teaching overviews of the intellectual world or the connections of your discipline to others? If so, can the Council help in preparing
   such materials? What other kinds of experts are needed to prepare these
   materials?

5. What views, if any, in your field and its contexts will help connect the
   central core of knowledge in your discipline to the larger intellectual world
   and the domain of highly multidisciplinary problems?

6. What can your discipline do to help students understand themselves better in the context of recent gains in understanding human development and functioning? Are your students taught the limitations of the human mind and how they affect scholarly work? Do your students understand the all too human processes of denial and projection?

Given the answers to these questions, the Council of Senior Scholars could begin to construct an improved curriculum for the non-major part of undergraduate education by combining the results with work on Type 2 classes.

For courses of Type 2, this book might provide a starting place. The materials would need to be studied by a group of scholars, and improved and added to where necessary. This might require commissioning instructors to learn and teach the materials under the aegis of the Council. This is an area that needs a pilot study, since there are few precedents, but we know well many modes for developing course materials.

I would begin with a seminar format, with about half the time for discussion and half for presentations. I would use a consensual structure (or format) so that all members speak in each seminar and none can dominate. It is easy to create such structures. I will supply instructions, on request.

Need for Consensual Process

Questions 1 through 6 above are of considerable political delicacy in the academic world. The Council would therefore need to execute its work with special attention to the sensitivities of disciplinary specialists so that it begins by building a reputation for both cooperation and sound scholarship. For this purpose, a strong consensual decision process coupled to a flat structure in the Council, rather than a strong Chair structure, will probably be important. Building the case for strong scholarship might involve propagating ideas like those in this volume in various forms within the faculty, via the usual faculty organizations and communication systems, as items of discussion for some time before actions are taken. Finally, it might be required for each Council member to recuse (exclude) himself or herself regarding priorities of their original discipline within the curriculum. Why would recusion be important? Compare the questions What materials from your discipline do all students need to learn? and What materials should all students learn from disciplines outside your own? Question 1 tends to elicit biased responses. Question 2 does not. Question 2 also forces the thoughts of individuals toward the appropriate level and breadth. This idea was suggested by the results of F. Kodama in surveying Japanese industrial leaders about what technologies are important for the future. When Kodama asked a type-1 question, nearly everyone said, "My industry." When he asked a type-2 question, a useful consensus emerged.

Since we have little or no experience, the list of questions 1 through 6 is preliminary and would need modifications both for local conditions and over time. The Council of Senior Scholars might well start with one or two of the politically easier questions and limited objectives, and only later expand the list of questions and goals.

Since the idea is apparently a new one, and the systems are complex enough so that the Guideline for Complex Systems applies, the entire enterprise would need to be viewed as developmental and in need of learning from experiences over time. This would, I hope, include the sharing of experiences among many campuses via conferences plus journal and book presentations.

The answers to question 1 above from departments to the Council might usefully be compiled in a summary form and periodically updated. The replies of departments might be resurveyed every few years in some kind of rotating mode whereby each discipline is reprised every three to five years. In this way, the materials can be kept up to date and reassessed over time. The summaries would also supply a source book from which students could select materials of particular interest to them, based on more complete information than the usual catalog listings.

Let's now ask, Would processes within the Council of Senior Scholars be different enough from the way we have been designing curricula in conventional Committees on Undergraduate Education so that we could significantly improve the situation in the non-major part of undergraduate educations? I think so, for several reasons. First, the Council will stand outside the departmental structure; if it functions properly, the Council will create an etic view of the disciplines. Given the powers suggested above, the Council would have enough authority so that it could negotiate effectively with the departments. Since the members would be tenured, they could act independently from disciplinary biases without damage to their careers. Second, serious discussion of the questions listed above, coupled with absorption of the materials in this volume, will almost certainly change the nature of the discourse about the non-major part of undergraduate education. Third, faculty recognition that multidisciplinary discourse is a necessary, separate, important topic, not contained in the conventional disciplines, will go a long way toward alleviation of the difficulties we have seen in Chapters 17 and 18. Fourth, the requirement that members recuse themselves on matters of priority with respect to their own discipline will tend to block the kind of gerrymandering based on special interests that has too often influenced our decisions on the non-major part of undergraduate education. Finally, if the Council is given modest resources within the university structure to create new materials and hire young teachers interested in developing multidisciplinary materials, much can be accomplished within a decade or two, since up till now we have devoted little or no resources to this task.

A century ago, the research university was a brilliant institutional innovation. However, institutions need periodic reexamination and improvements if they are to remain appropriate to the times. We seem, in the late twentieth century, to have reached a point at which such reexamination is appropriate for our research universities as they structure and teach undergraduate education.

Two Standing Bets

The results of this book dispute overclaims that have long been seen as true by many disciplinary experts about what their particular discipline can do. Disciplinary experts have tended to dismiss, out of hand, comments from anyone who is not a "member of the club." This appendix therefore creates two standing bets, one for any interested physicist and one for any interested economist, in order to frame a public reconsideration of the relevant issues. These two communities are not the only ones that have made overclaims about the territory that their field of study can actually cover; that has occurred in many fields. Physics and economics were selected because the overclaims arising from these fields have had more effects in the twentieth-century world than those of some other disciplines.

In each bet the author offers $1,000.00 against $100.00 to any interested physicist for Bet A and to any interested economist for Bet B, as outlined below. The $1,000.00 for each bet will be escrowed, when the book is published, with the Wells Fargo Bank of California in a separate account. For each bet, a Judges Committee of three individuals will be appointed by the Publisher, Stanford University Press, in consultation with the author, but at the discretion of the Director of the Press. The Judges Committee, by majority vote, will decide in each instance whether the submitted materials meet or do not meet the requirements of the bet. Decisions of the Judges Committee will be final. Appeals of adverse decisions can be made by submission of an improved set of arguments with a new $100.00 ante. If $100.00 wagers are lost, the funds so created shall be utilized to support a fellowship in multidisciplinary study in Stanford's Science, Technology, and Society Program.

Each bet will stand either until some individual convinces the relevant Judges Committee that the author's views are wrong by submitting a proof of the question that is logically correct, according to a majority of the judges; or until midnight of December 31, 1999, whichever comes first.

Bet A—For Any Interested Physicist

The bet for physicists is that they cannot provide a logically correct derivation of the complete second law of thermodynamics from statistical mechanics. Some comments about this bet follow.

The author is well aware that many physicists believe that such a derivation has been given correctly in the standard books decades ago. It is this belief that is being challenged. The author of this book asserts that the most that can be shown is consistency in the statements of the entropy principle as they arise in the two domains (statistical mechanics and continuum thermodynamics) for limited classes of systems, not all systems. What is required to win this bet is a logically consistent derivation of the entirety of the second law of thermodynamics from statistical mechanics for the entire domain to which the second law is known to apply — that is, the entire macroscopic world, including human-made systems.

The author's view of this matter has two bases: first, the theory of structure of complex systems given in Chapters 7 through 13 of this book; and second, a reexamination in detail of the so-called derivation using the text of Mayer and Mayer (1940) as the specific basis for an analysis of the logic. I will call this "the demonstration."

In the view of the author of this book, the demonstration given by Mayer and Mayer, when read as a "derivation," contains five logical difficulties. What the demonstration establishes is consistency for a few special classes of systems which cover only a small domain relative to all the systems to which the second law of thermodynamics is known to apply. So that anyone taking up the bet knows the five major logical difficulties, they are listed below.

Logical Difficulties in the Demonstration

Logical Difficulty 1. The demonstration assumes that results that apply to a few very special classes of systems are correct for all possible classes of systems. More specifically, on this point the demonstration analyzes only homogeneous systems of particles of one kind (or a few kinds) at one level in the hierarchy of constitution (see Figure 7-1). The demonstration offers no proofs for systems of heterogeneous aggregation; systems with feedback loops; or systems with hierarchical structure with interfaces of mutual constraint. Each of the classes of the three systems has emergent properties that create behaviors and in some instances even "rules" which differ from those found in homogeneous systems of one pure substance. Moreover, systems of all three types are not only very common but also very important. Since all three types of systems are known to obey the macroscopic "laws" of thermodynamics, a complete derivation must show that these kinds of systems are included by the examples analyzed.

Logical Difficulty 2. Use of two different mathematical definitions of entropy without demonstration that the two are tautological to each other over the entire domain of interest. In particular, these are the Boltzmann definition (at the microscopic level) and the Clausius definition (at the macroscopic level). Agreement of one characteristic (an extremum value of a property at equilibrium for some **systems**) is taken as congruence for all systems.

Logical Difficulty 3. The proof assumes a principle that is known to be correct based on data at the classical (macroscopic) level, and uses the principle as part of the "derivation" from the microscopic level. This principle is sometimes called "the State Principle." In the demonstration, the applicable form of the State Principle is expressed for a Gibbs simple **system** as

$$s = s(e,v) \tag{B-1}$$

where s is the specific entropy, v the specific volume, and e the specific energy of the system.

Equation (B-1) states explicitly that specific entropy is a function of specific energy and specific volume, and no more. The word "specific" here denotes per unit mass. As J. W. Gibbs noted more than a century ago, equation (B-1) has eleven restrictions; he also noted that none of them is trivial. These assumptions are:

1. one pure substance;
2. sufficient mass to form a continuum;
3. system in equilibrium;
4. one phase of aggregation.

Plus the absence of the effects of seven kinds of physical phenomena:

5. gravity
6. motion
7. electricity
8. magnetism
9. capillarity
10. fluid shear
11. anisotropic stress in solids.

Gibbs did not assume that these processes were absent from the inert physical world; his only assumption was that, for the **systems** under study (the domain), these seven physical effects did not have a significant impact. In fact, in his third paper Gibbs showed explicitly that many of the effects specifically ruled out by equation (B-1) do have an important impact in some systems. Gibbs did this by relaxing some of the assumptions of equation (B-1) and examining the resulting new **systems**. The use of equation (B-1) thus in and of itself restricts the demonstration to a very small class of **systems**. An adequate demonstration would have to analyze **systems** in which all the restrictions implied by equation (B-1) were removed both singly and in combinations.

Logical Difficulty 4. Use of an assumption that bars disproof of a central conclusion. Specifically, the assumption that each particle can interact with all the others. In many macroscopic systems with heterogeneous aggregation of gaseous, liquid, and solid parts, this is untrue. We often specifically design systems to prevent some interactions between, say, a hot gas and combustible materials, but the macroscopic "laws" still apply, as far as we know.

Logical Difficulty 5. Circular reasoning with regard to the principles of conservation of mass, momentum, and energy as noted by P. W. Bridgman (1941). See below.

This completes the list of major logical difficulties that appear in the demonstration. However, there is an alternate line of argument that is sometimes used as the basis for suggesting that all systems in the world can and should be viewed as probabilistic. Studying this argument will allow us to check some of the ideas we have developed about hierarchical systems.

The argument is based on a "rule" called "microscopic reversibility" that applies to the molecular level in the hierarchy of constitution. The argument has two parts: first, since there is reversibility at the microscopic level, there should be reversibility at higher levels in the hierarchy of constitution because all material systems are made up of atoms or molecules; and second, if a system can reverse itself, then there is some probability, no matter how low, that it will do so. The argument leads to the idea that all systems can reverse themselves, in principle. This argument is a foundation stone for suggesting that the entire world should be viewed probabilistically.

However, physicists also know that systems at the classical level exhibit irreversibility; that is, at the classical level, processes occur which cannot be reversed completely. Indeed, we can readily delineate more than a half-dozen different kinds of well-known, elementary processes at the macroscopic level, each of which is inherently irreversible — for example, fluid friction or the shorting of a battery. In fact, if stated carefully, the existence of such inherently irreversible processes can be made into one possible statement (out of many) of the second law of thermodynamics. Moreover, the classical "rules" say that this inability to reverse many processes is not merely an improbability but, rather, an impossibility. We appear to have a paradox: the microscopic "rules" predict that any process can reverse itself at some level of probability; the classical "rules" state explicitly that it is impossible to reverse an uncountable number of processes at the classical level. This is called the "irreversibility paradox." It has persisted as a paradox in physics during the entire twentieth century. Do physicists believe that it is a true physical paradox? At the Rumford Centennial

Conference some years ago, Edward Teller said he did, clearly, firmly, and in emphatic bass tones. Is the irreversibility paradox a part of physical nature, or is it merely a confusion arising from the way we have used sysreps?

As we saw in Chapter 11, the primary requirement in hierarchical systems is that the results we get from two different levels about the same problem (or question) must not contradict each other; they must be consistent if our sysreps are to be appropriate. We stated further that when apparent contradictions are found, such as the irreversibility paradox, we ought not argue that one level "determines" the other, but seek the error (Hypotheses VI and VII). However, the irreversibility paradox does assume that the microscopic level "determines" the character of higher levels in the sense that it projects a microscopic "rule" onto the classical level. As we have seen again and again, such "projections" must be checked by data at the new level to which they are applied. We ought not assume that the character of different levels in the hierarchy of constitution is the same, because the variables, parameters, behaviors, and the "rules" frequently differ within the different levels. What do we see when we look at the classical level? What do the data tell us? We find that a number of independent processes are inherently irreversible. We must conclude that the "rule" of microscopic reversibility is inappropriate at the classical level. See Hypothesis VII of this book.

The remarks in the previous paragraph resolve the apparent paradox. There is no irreversibility paradox because the assumption that the "rules" are the same for the classical and the microscopic levels is wrong; the data, the appropriate arbiter, say the "rules" are not the same. The problem is not in the physics but in the way we have built and used sysreps in this problem. To be sure about this, let's look at the details more carefully.

As P. W. Bridgman pointed out decades ago, we often design ratchets into the devices we make at the classical level using the human design mode. But ratchets make nonsense of the notion of reversibility at the macroscopic level; ratchets are devices designed specifically to prevent "reversing" of a motion, and, when properly designed, they do so. Since many kinds of ratchets exist, their existence is barefoot data that tell us where the trouble has been. "Reversibility" is not a "rule" that applies to classical systems with heterogeneous aggregation. We are referring here not to "restorability" but to reversing the process in detail. That is what microscopic reversibility implies.

We can now refine our question. What about classical systems with homogeneous aggregation? Is there really a possibility of "reversing actions" in all such systems at some level of probability, or on the contrary is actually "reversing" an irreversible process truly impossible? Let's look at the often discussed case of a non-dense gas of one pure substance. I choose this example because it has often been used as a basis for arguing that all systems in the world can and should be represented probabilistically. For two generations, in some physics classes, students have been asked to calculate the probability of the reversal of an unrestrained expansion of a homogeneous gas. Let's call this example "the gas-in-a-box **system**" and examine it more carefully.

Suppose we do the classic gedanken experiment for the gas-in-a-box **system**. Let's be specific and take air at 1,000-atm pressure in a volume of 1 cubic meter held by walls within a corner of a cubic box 10 meters on each side. Let's also assume that the box is airtight, of constant volume, and a perfect insulator for both heat and electromagnetic radiations. At time zero we pull out the walls restraining the gas in the corner. The gas will expand and fill the room. After some bouncing back and forth of wave motions, involving highly irreversible processes (shock waves and friction), the gas will come to an equilibrium at 1-atm pressure everywhere in the box.

According to the argument for the probability view of the world, reversing this expansion process is very, very improbable, but not impossible. We do not see the reverse process, so the argument goes, because the probability is so low that we do not live long enough. Indeed, no one has ever reported seeing the reverse process in the gas-in-a-box system at any place over all time. The assertion that the reverse process can happen has no empirical foundation, and it rests only on a theory for a specific sysrep. If I am wrong about this, please let me know and cite the experimenter, protocols used, place, and date.

On the other hand, a calculation of the entropy increase owing to the unrestrained expansion of the gas into the room in the gas-in-a-box **system** shows a large increase in entropy in an isolated system. The second law of thermodynamics therefore tells us that this isolated system will never go back to its initial state; that is, the reverse process is impossible, not merely very improbable. This is a (perhaps the) classic example of the so-called irreversibility paradox.

If what the previous remarks say is correct, there is no paradox. The paradox only arises because we have projected the principle of molecular reversibility to a level where it no longer is appropriate, as we suggested above. Can we see why there is no paradox from a physical point of view?

Let's assume that the expansion process begins and ends at times t_1 and t_2. Let's assume further that we could somehow reverse all the trajectories of the molecules and let the process run from time t_2 to t_3 when, according to the probabilistic view, the molecules will be back in the one cubic meter within the corner from which they started. We don't know how to reverse the molecules, but let's assume for the argument we do.

Please don't tell me about Maxwell's demon. Using Maxwell's demon, we can produce as many violations of the second law as we desire. Logically, this implies that the demon is itself a violation of the second law. Hence it cannot be used as a model for a real macroscopic process.

Is this reversed process possible? If we start the reverse process, will it run to the end point of all the gas back in the corner from which it started before we pulled out the restraining walls? If not, what would alter the process? Even if the gas were a perfect hard-sphere ideal gas, the process is not possible on purely physical grounds as long as the walls are real solid walls, not some form of imaginary ideal walls. Why is this so? When we start the presumed reverse process at time t_2 the molecules will begin to move back along the incoming trajectories. As soon as some gas molecules begin to strike the wall, some of the local solid molecule(s) will be in a quantum state different from that in the earlier forward process. Therefore, a slight deviation in trajectory from the forward process for some molecules will soon occur. Such wall collisions will occur because nothing phase-locks the motions of the molecules in the air to the atomic states of the wall, and we are in a new time period. We cannot run time backward. Since many collisions with the wall are involved in the overall process, slight deviations in the trajectory of some molecules will occur early in the reverse process. Once one collision with the wall has occurred, altering the reverse trajectory a tiny amount from the path of the forward trajectory, the deviation will alter the process, so that it veers away from the reverse process and begins to move toward the equilibrium state. The normal arithmetic of statistical mechanics tells us this, since the probabilities of moving toward and not away from equilibrium are overwhelming. Thus the results of statistical mechanics forbid the reverse process beyond a few very early stages, as long as we are considering real vessels and not some ideal system that does not exist. In other words, there is a sixth difficulty with the conventional argument about reversing processes that leads to the claim that microscopic "rules" should be applied to classical systems. This added difficulty is not logical but, rather, physical. The demonstration depends on the existence of imaginary, ideal walls that differ in significant ways from all known real walls. And the differences resolve the irreversibility paradox in this paradigmatic example on physical grounds.

These are not the only objections to the possibility of the reverse process in the gas-in-a-box system and, hence, to the idea that all processes can be reversed. The imaginary reverse process also violates the momentum principle, but we do not need the details of why this is so. What we have explicated is enough to make the point we need for multidisciplinary discourse. The reverse process will not occur. That is why no one has ever seen it. Let's summarize the discussion so far.

What we have called the irreversibility paradox rests on an unstated assumption that is untrue. The seeming paradox arises because we have assumed (by projection) that a "rule" that applies to the molecular level applies everywhere. There is no paradox in the physics, only an error in the way we have used human-created sysreps. This ought not surprise us at this point. We have seen again and again that the behaviors, variables, and even the "rules" typically differ from level to level, and they do not usually remain the same. There is no irreversibility paradox; we only thought there was because we did not understand sufficiently the relations between levels in systems with hierarchical structure. This example thus gives further support to the remarks in Chapter 16 that it is not appropriate to describe all systems as probabilistic. Deterministic and chaotic systems also exist and need different kinds of descriptions (sysreps).

Bet B—For Any Interested Economist

In discussing innovation in Chapter 14, we saw a number of reasons why conventional economic theory cannot provide the "how to" information we must have to create innovations or increase productivity. In order to create a framework for testing this assertion, let us take the case of least complexity, the creation of a single product by a firm or an individual. To make the test meaningful, let's consider a major innovation. This suggests the bet that follows for economists (the conditions were stated above).

To win the bet, an economist must "postdict" from conventional economic theory the steps needed to achieve any one of the ten major innovations listed below, at the economist's choice. The term "postdiction" denotes a theoretical derivation of events that have already occurred. Here we ask for postdiction of the actual steps that were needed to create the innovation; the "how to"s required to get the job done. Conventional economic theory here denotes any form of static equilibrium theory carefully defined by the economist and including but not limited to neoclassic theory.

The list of inventions follows:

1. The radio
2. The turbojet engine for aircraft
3. The solid state amplifier (transistor)
4. The personal computer
5. The telephone
6. The automatic transmission for automobiles
7. The FAX machine
8. Nylon
9. Penicillin
10. The steam turbine

For the reader who is not an economist, it may be useful to add the following. Examples 1–10 are not the most complex cases. A number of very important product innovations have involved more complex systems and/or more difficult technical problems: the creation of the factory system in Great Britain, the U.S. creation of the "mass production" system in factories, or the recent creation of the Japanese system of manufacture (lean, flexible production); the atom bomb; radar; and the recent achievement of combined-cycle coal-gasification electric power plants with thermal efficiencies above 50 percent and extremely low levels of pollution. There are many other examples.

If we are to credit economists with the capability of predictive understanding of the innovation of products, and therefore also economic development and technology policy, in a global environment paced by innovations (which is the sort of environment we have in the late twentieth century), then someone must demonstrate that it is possible at least to take the first step, as given by this bet. If no economist can do that, then it becomes clear that we need to base advice about innovation, productivity, and technology policy on examination of as many cases as we can gather, and not on available economic theory (as the Guideline for Complex Systems indicates we should).

Finally I want to emphasize two things. First, the data suggest that economists are right regarding the critical importance of competition among firms and markets as free as we can make them while preventing abuses. Second, vibrant competition and essentially free markets are only a necessary condition; they are far from sufficient for creation of a viable economy or a reasonable degree of social equity. The purpose of this bet is to make clear the second point.

Hypotheses, Guidelines, Dicta, and Queries

Hypotheses

Hypothesis I: *The Possibility of Multidisciplinary Discourse.* Meaningful multidisciplinary discourse is possible.

Hypothesis II: *Honor All Credible Data.* In multidisciplinary work, we need to honor all credible data from wherever they arise. (This includes not only data from various disciplines and from our laboratories, but also from the world itself, since we have no labs from which we can obtain data for many important purposes.)

Hypothesis III: *The Absence of Universal Approaches.* There is no one view, no one methodology, no one discipline, no one set of principles, no one set of equations that provides understanding of all matters vital to human concerns.

Hypothesis IV: *The Necessity of System Definition.* Each particular truth assertion about nature applies only to some **systems** (and not to all).

Hypothesis IV, Corollary A. No truth assertion about nature is complete without a statement of the domain of applicability.

Hypothesis V: *The Need for at Least Three Views. Part A.* At least three views are needed for a reasonably good understanding of hierarchically structured systems with interfaces of mutual constraint: synoptic, piecewise, and structural.

Hypothesis V: *The Need for at Least Three Views. Part B.* Hierarchically structured systems with interfaces of mutual constraint are both common enough and significant enough so that all three views are necessary in order to understand the full range of situations and processes that are vital to humans.

Polanyi's Hypothesis, Part A. In many hierarchically structured systems, adjacent levels mutually constrain, but do not determine, each other.

Polanyi's Hypothesis, Part B. In hierarchically structured systems, the levels of control (usually upper levels) "harness" the lower levels and cause them to carry out behaviors that the lower levels, left to themselves, would not do.

Hypothesis VI: *Empiricism in Hierarchical Structure.* In order to provide an adequate empirical base, we must make observations at all levels of concern for the class of systems under study.

Hypothesis VII: *The Principle of Consistency.* In systems with hierarchical structure and levels that mutually constrain one another, solutions must satisfy the principles and the data in all the relevant levels and fields of knowledge. The same is true for systems studied by more than one field when the dimensions of the various fields are exogenous to each other.

Hypothesis VII, Corollary A. When solutions from more than one level in a hierarchical structure with interfaces of mutual constraint provide results for a given behavior in the same system, then the results must be consistent where they overlap. If the results are not consistent, then we must seek the source of the error, and not argue that one level or one discipline governs (or has priority over) the other. The same remark applies when two disciplines give overlapping results and have some primary dimensions exogenous to each other.

Durham's Hypothesis: Genetic information and cultural information are two separate, interacting sources of human information; each evolves over time, but at different rates of change.

Addition (*by author*): Human skills form a third type of human information which interacts with the other two. Skills are necessary for maintenance of human societies over time. Skills are socially transmitted and evolve.

Guidelines

For Complex Systems: In very complex systems, such as sociotechnical systems, we have no theory for entire systems, and must therefore create, operate, and improve such systems via feedback: that is, repeated cycles of human observations plus trials of envisaged improvements in the real systems. In such very complex systems, data from a wide variety of cases therefore become the primary basis for understanding and judgments, and should take precedence over results from theory based on cuts through the hyperspace (called "the primacy of data").

Of Hierarchical Obscurity: The farther systems are from direct human observation in size, in speed, and/or in time, the more our observations become instrumentally bound and theoretically modulated, and the more difficult understanding the systems tends to be.

For Scholarly Controversy: When two (or more) groups of empirically grounded scholars create conflicting solutions for a single problem, and this leads to back-and-forth arguments for decades, then it is likely that each group has some of the truth but not all of it.

For Scholarly Controversy, Corollary A: When two (or more) groups of empirically grounded scholars have a long-continued argument, an improved solution can often be found by reframing the problem to include the solidly grounded data underlying both sides of the argument.

Dicta and Queries

Acton's Dictum: Power corrupts, and absolute power corrupts absolutely. [Comment: Not invariably, but often.]

Burke's Dictum: Responsibility is the yoke of the free man.

Deming's Dictum: When an institution is not working, don't blame the workers, look at the structure.

Draper's Dictum: To control a given system of any kind, the control elements of the system, whether autonomic or human, must be able to effect changes in the system in times that are less than one-fourth (and preferably one-tenth) of the characteristic time of the change of the parts of the system that are to be controlled.

Heaviside's Query: Shall I refuse to eat my breakfast because I do not understand the process of digestion?

Juvenal's Query: Who will guard the guards? [Stated originally in a sexist context. Nevertheless, an important question whenever the self-interest of the guards conflicts strongly with their duties as guardians.]

Kelvin's Dictum: If I can make a mechanical model, then I can understand it; if I cannot make one, I do not understand. [Comment: Very useful in the physical sciences, but misleading in the human sciences.]

Kettering's Dictum: When you begin to think you know everything, all that proves is that the concrete in your head has begun to set.

Korzibski's Dictum: The map [sysrep] is not the territory [**system**]. [Comment: There is one important class of exceptions; in formal systems, such as mathematics, the system and the sysrep are identical by construction.]

Miller's 7-Bit-Rule: The human mind can only think about and retain in working memory 7 (plus or minus 2) uncorrelated bits of information. ["Uncorrelated" here denotes not a chunk or schema in the given mind.]

Russell's Dictum: Mixing concepts from different levels in a hierarchy of concepts usually creates paradox(es).
[Russell said "will create paradox."]

Seneca's Dictum: When the words are confused, the mind is also. There are two levels:

- When we do not use words in a consistent way, our communications tend to become confused.

- When we do not have clear, appropriate schemata, we cannot think clearly.
[From a letter by Seneca, summarized and extended.]

Whitehead's Dictum: In matters of method, the scientists have nearly always been right; in matters of wider judgment the scientists (and other individuals who are thoroughly enculturated into a single view) have nearly always been wrong.
[Restated.]

Yalom's Dictum: There is a strong correlation between the hardness of the variables and the triviality of the problem in my field (psychiatry).
[Restated.]

Glossary

Abundant society. A society in which at least 90 percent of the people are in a condition above Maslow level 2. *See* Maslow ladder, Chapter 7.

Autonomic. Designates a kind of feedback control that is built-in and rigid in the sense that it does the same thing every time. *See* Figure 6-1.

Barefoot data. Data that are credible owing to direct observation, without need for controlled experiments or laboratory tests — for example, existence of an animal or a plant species.

Bit. A piece of data storable as a single fact in the human brain, not the computer usage.

Chunk. A combination of several bits of data into a recognized arrangement within the human brain — for example, words.

Complexity, index of. A measure for the complexity of any system; defined and illustrated in Chapter 4.

Constraint. A condition that limits the scope of variables or parameters and thus the extent of possible variations within a system and/or in the design of a system. A critical distinction at many places is the difference between one or some constraints and complete determination. *See* Chapter 5, for discussion and illustrations.

Control. The guidance or periodic correction of a system so that it matches a desired set point, course, or goal, usually using feedback. There are at least three qualitatively distinct levels of complexity of control modes: autonomic (built-in); human-control (has a human in the feedback loop); human-design (reflects on the system from outside and designs improvements). *See* Figure 6-1.

Culture gap. A term coined by C. P. Snow to refer to the gap in beliefs and hence difficulties of understanding and communications between technical and literary people. Other such gaps exist in modern culture, for example, between engineers and environmentalists.

Cybernetic. Norbert Wiener's word for autonomic feedback control. *See* **Autonomic**; **Control**; **Feedback**.

Degrees of freedom. The number of different ways variations can occur in an operating space, a design space, or a hyperspace. *See also* **Open degrees of freedom.** Normally taken to be equal to the dimensionality of the relevant hyperspace. *See* **Hyperspace.**

Design space. The variations allowable in a design envisaged as a "space" with axes consisting of the parameters of the system under design. *See also* **Hyperspace**; **Operating space.**

Determination. Describes a totally fixed condition, not subject to change. *See also* **Constraint.**

Dialectical. A discussion seeking solution to problems without reference to empirical observations or data. (Hegelian dialectic is taken to be a special case.)

Dimensionality. The number of variables plus the number of parameters in a hyperspace. *See* **Dimensions**; **Hyperspace**; **Parameters.**

Dimensions. The nature of the variables needed to describe the system under study. *See also* **Primary dimensions**; Chapters 4, 5, and 9; Bridgman (1921).

Emergent properties. Properties exhibited by a complete (hooked-up) system that cannot be exhibited by the parts of the system in isolation. Also called "holism."

Emic. A view of a culture (or disciplinary knowledge) by a member of the culture (or the discipline); an insider's view. *See also* **Etic.**

Entire Paradigm. A principle that holds for all known examples in a class of systems, but occurs with differing details from case to case. *See also* **Entire Invariant Paradigm**; Chapter 6.

Entire Invariant Paradigm. A principle that not only holds for all known examples in a class of **systems** but also occurs with the same details in every case. *See* Chapter 6.

Entropy. A mathematically defined measure of the disorder in systems of inert parts. The entropy principle (second law of thermodynamics) has been widely misinterpreted owing to confusions about frames of reference, domains, and dimensions. *See* Chapter 17.

Etic. An outsider's view of a culture (or discipline of knowledge). *See also* **Emic.**

Feedback. A process used for control; normally has four steps: (1) sense information; (2) process information; (3) compare processed information with a desired state (set point); (4) if necessary, adjust system to match set point. There are several qualitatively distinct levels of complexity of feedback. *See* Figure 6-1.

Functional representation. A listing of the variables and parameters that determine the state of a system; defines the hyperspace of the system, but not the solution to the problem.

Guideline. A useful "rule" for a class of systems or problems that is usually but not necessarily correct.

Heterogeneous aggregation. A system that has qualitatively different kinds of parts hooked together.

Hierarchy, Hierarchical structure. A structure with distinct levels, or layers. Such structures are very common and have qualitatively different characteristics from systems that are all at one level. *See* Chapters 7–12; Polanyi's Principle; Hypotheses V, VI, and VII.

Holism. *See* **Emergent properties.**

Human-control feedback mode. A particular kind of feedback mode. *See* Figure 6-1.

Human-design feedback mode. A particular kind of feedback mode. See Figure 6-1.

Hyperspace, complete. The combination of a design space and an operating space for a given class of system. A metaphorical extension of the usual idea of "space." In a complete hyperspace the variables and parameters necessary to describe the class of system are visualized as axes in a space. When the parameters are fixed, the hyperspace reduces to the operating space. When the variables are fixed, the hyperspace reduces to the design space.

Inference. Used in the usual sense of logic. *See also* **Negative inference.**

Interface of mutual constraint. Interfaces between adjacent levels (in a hierarchical structure) that mutually constrain but do not determine each other. This type of interface has other important properties. *See* Polanyi's Principle; Chapter 8.

Magic. Used in the ethnological sense, that is, to denote an assumed causal connection that is incorrect.

Maslow ladder. A widely used ladder (hierarchy) of human needs. *See* Chapter 7.

Mirroring. The representation of a system by a sysrep; may be anything from very accurate to very incomplete, or even seriously distorting.

Negative inference. A process that seeks to discomfirm a hypothesis by means of counterexamples. A logic that closes, in contrast to inductive reasoning. *See* Chapter 1; Platt (1966).

Non-conscious processes. Processes in the human brain that are done more or less automatically without specific thought in working memory. Not the same as Freud's "unconscious," since items stored via non-conscious processes are subject to ready recall.

Open degreees of freedom. A number less than or equal to the total degrees of freedom. Usually the difference between the number of total degrees of freedom and the number of constraints. *See* **Constraint**; **Degrees of freedom**; Chapter 5.

Operating space. A "space" visualized as axes representing the independent variables of a system which can be altered during its operation. *See also* **Design space**; **Hyperspace, complete**.

Orthogonal variables. Variables that are perpendicular to each other in a generalized sense such that variation in one does not entail variation in the others.

Parameters. The axes along which designs can be varied in the design space for a **system**.

Piecewise view. A view of the smallest relevant bits in the system for a particular problem; the pieces may be individual people, machine parts, genes, quarks, atoms, or many other things.

Primary dimensions. A set of dimensions from which all the dimensions for a given domain of systems can be constructed as mathematical products and/or ratios. *See* Chapter 9; Bridgman (1921).

Projection. Used in this volume in Freud's sense, but extended, that is, the attribution to others of what we think, know, or feel, or the attribution of the qualities of familiar systems to unfamiliar systems.

"Rules" (in scare quotes). May be principles, paradigms, guidelines, or called "laws." *See* discussion in Chapter 16.

Schema (plural **schemata**). A human mental construct through which the human brain understands the world. May be strings of bits in memory. May be key ideas that underlie a field. May be a large relational repertoire about a given domain of interest, for instance, about chess, designing an airplane, or physiology. A given schema may be useful, or even essential, in a given domain, but distorting when carried over into other domains. Schemata are often transmitted via culture.

Science. As used in this work, science denotes a set of methods for finding, creating, confirming, disconfirming, reorganizing, generalizing, and disseminating truth assertions about physical, biological, and social nature.

Second-floor tennis-ball test. A test to illustrate the existence and the nature of deterministic systems.

Sociotechnical system. A system of combined social and technical parts. Used to create physical bases of all human societies past and present. A key arena in which the knowledge of various disciplines needs to interact. *See* Chapter 14.

Structural view. A description of how the system goes together for all the levels in a hierarchical structure.

Synoptic. A synthetic overview. Used in this work to denote an overview that (1) defines system boundaries; (2) defines what can go in and out of the system and other possible interactions between the system and the environment; and (3) states system goals, if there are any.

Sysrep. A representation — in pictures, words, or equations — of the **system** under study. The kinds of sysreps we form are limited in significant ways by the capacity of the human mind. *See* Chapters 2 and 3. In this volume, sysreps have special characteristics many models do not. The usual ideas are extended in Chapter 13.

System. An entity (process or whatever) in the world which is the object of study; system is defined by whoever is doing the study. *See also* **Sysrep**; Chapters 2, 13.

Technological paradigm. A device or piece of hardware that exists and serves as the basis for designing the next generation of the device.

"Tribe." Designates an ethnic group, usually a small band of pre-literate people, but sometimes used generally for a society.

Turbulence. A set of related chaotic phenomena observed in many fluid motions. Useful in multidisciplinary discourse as a rough boundary between **systems** that are simple enough to analyze completely and those that are too complex for us to form accurate sysreps for the entire system in the late twentieth century.

Uncertainty. The residual lack of knowledge about a measured value. Not the same as an error; rather, an estimate of what the probable measurement error might be.

Universalism. A truth assertion, method, or view that is claimed to be appropriate for all systems, but is appropriate only for some.

Variables. The quantities needed to describe the operating space of a system. *See* Chapter 5.

Variance. A statistical measure of variation equal to the square of the standard deviation of a variable.

Working memory. The part of the human mind that does active thinking. Also short-term memory, awareness, focus of attention; in computer language, the central processor, and other names.

References

Abegglen, James C., and George Stalk Jr. 1985. *Kaisha: The Japanese Corporation.* New York: Basic Books.

Airy, Sir George Biddell. 1879. *Theory of Errors of Observation.* London: Macmillan.

Allen, Thomas J. 1988. *Managing the Flow of Technology.* Cambridge, Mass.: MIT Press.

Aoki, Masahiko. 1988. *Information, Incentives and Bargaining in the Japanese Economy.* Cambridge, Eng.: Cambridge University Press.

Aoki, Masahiko, and Nathan Rosenberg. 1987. *The Japanese Firm as an Innovating Institution.* Center for Economic Policy Research, Stanford University Report, 106.

Axelrod, Robert. 1984. *The Evolution of Cooperation.* New York: Basic Books.

Ayer, Alfred Jules. 1959. *Logical Positivism.* New York: Free Press.

Bacon, Francis. 1773. *The Philosophical Works of Francis Bacon, Baron of Verulam, Viscount St. Albans, and Lord High Chancellor of England, Methodized and Made English, from the Originals, with Occasional Notes to Explain What Is Obscure.* London: J. J. and P. Knapton.

Barr, M. J. 1989. "Just-in-Time Manufacturing: Cummins Significant Benefits Report." In *Leading-Edge Manufacturing Strategies.* Proceedings of 5th European Conference, May 9–11, 1989.

Bateson, Gregory. 1972. *Steps to an Ecology of Mind.* San Francisco: Chandler.

Beavers, W. Robert. 1985. *Successful Marriage.* New York: W. W. Norton.

Benedict, Ruth. 1934. *Patterns of Culture.* Boston: Houghton Mifflin, Sentry edition paperback.

———. 1946. *The Chrysanthemum and the Sword.* Boston: Houghton Mifflin.

Berelson, Bernard. 1960. *Graduate Education in the United States.* New York: McGraw-Hill.

———. 1963. *The Behavioral Sciences Today.* New York: Basic Books.

Berger, Peter. 1969. *The Sacred Canopy: Elements of a Sociological Theory of Religion.* Garden City, N.Y.: Doubleday Anchor.

Bettman, Otto. 1974. *The Good Old Days—They Were Terrible.* New York: Random House.

Bijker, Wiebe E., Thomas P. Hughes, and Trevor Pinch. 1989. *The Social Construction of Technological Systems.* Cambridge, Mass.: MIT Press.

Blois, Marsden, M.D. 1988. "Medicine and the Nature of Vertical Reasoning." *New England Journal of Medicine* 318, no. 13.

Bonner, John Tyler. 1980. *The Evolution of Culture in Animals.* Princeton, N.J.: Princeton University Press.

Bono, Edward de. 1976. *Teaching Thinking.* Hammersmith, Eng.: Penguin Books.

Boulding, Kenneth E. 1969. *The Image.* Ann Arbor: University of Michigan Press.

Bower, G. S. 1981. "Mood and Memory." *American Psychologist* 36: 129–48.

Braybrooke, David, and Charles E. Lindblom. 1963. *A Strategy for Decision: Policy Evolution as a Social Process.* New York: Free Press.

Bridgman, P. W. 1921. *Dimensional Analysis.* Cambridge, Mass.: Harvard University Press.

———. 1941. *The Nature of Thermodynamics.* Cambridge, Mass.: Harvard University Press.

Briere, John. 1989. *Therapy for Adults Molested as Children: Beyond Survival.* New York: Springer.

Brooks, Harvey (Chair of Study). 1969. *Technology: Processes of Assessment and Choice.* Report of the National Academy of Science to U.S. House Committee on Science and Astronautics. Washington, D.C.: U.S. Government Printing Office.

Brooks, Harvey, with John Foster. 1993. *Mastering a New Role: Prospering in a Global Economy.* Report of the National Academy of Engineering Technology Policy Options in a Global Economy. Washington, D.C.: National Academy Press.

Browne, Lewis. 1925. *Stranger Than Fiction.* New York: Macmillan.

Bush, Vannevar. 1945. *Science, the Endless Frontier: A Report to the President.* Washington, D.C.: U.S. Government Printing Office.

Butterfield, Herbert. 1957. *The Origins of Modern Science.* New York: Free Press.

Campbell, Joseph. 1968. *The Hero with a Thousand Faces.* 2d ed. Princeton, N.J.: Princeton University Press.

Capra, Frithof. 1976. *The Tao of Physics.* New York: Bantam New Age Books.

Cardwell, D. S. L. 1971. *From Watt to Clausius: The Rise of Thermodynamics in the Early Industrial Age.* Ithaca, N.Y.: Cornell University Press.

Carson, Rachel. 1962. *Silent Spring.* Boston: Houghton Mifflin.

Cassirer, Ernst. 1969. *An Essay on Man.* New York: Bantam Books.

Casti, John L. 1989. *Paradigms Lost: Tackling the Unanswered Mysteries of Modern Science.* New York: Avon Books.

Chandler, Alfred D., Jr. 1977. *The Visible Hand: The Managerial Revolution in American Business.* Cambridge, Mass.: Belknap Press of Harvard University Press.

Chase, G. C., and H. A. Simon. 1973. "Perception in Chess." *Cognitive Psychology* 4: 55–81.

Clark, Mary E. 1989. *Ariadne's Thread: The Search for New Modes of Thinking.* New York: St. Martin's Press.

Cohen, Stephen S., and John Zysman. 1987. *Manufacturing Matters: The Myth of the Post-Industrial Society.* New York: Basic Books.

Cohen, Yehudi A. 1968. *Man in Adaptation.* 3 vols. Chicago: Aldine.

Comte, Auguste. 1842. *Positivist Philosophy.* Lectures and papers published from 1826 through 1842 in Paris. Available as *Le Monde Positive, en seize leçons.* Paris: Vigot Frères, 1917.

Conger, Stuart. 1973. *Social Inventions.* Report of Saskatchewan New Start, Inc. Saskatoon, Saskatchewan, Canada: Modern Press.

Constant, Edward W., II. 1980. *The Origins of the Turbojet Revolution.* Baltimore, Md.: Johns Hopkins University Press.

Corning, Peter A. 1983. *The Synergism Hypothesis.* New York: McGraw-Hill.

Critchfield, Richard. 1981. *Villages.* Garden City, N.Y.: Doubleday Anchor.

Dawkins, Richard. 1987. *The Blind Watchmaker.* New York: W. W. Norton.

de Groot, Adriaan. 1946. *Thought and Choice in Chess.* The Hague: Mouton. English translation, 1965.

Dennett, Daniel C. 1991. *Consciousness Explained.* Boston: Little, Brown.

Dertouzos, Michael, Richard K. Lester, and Robert M. Solow. 1990. *Made in America: Regaining the Productive Edge.* Cambridge, Mass.: MIT Press.

de Solla Price, Derek. 1962. *Science Since Babylon.* New Haven, Conn.: Yale University Press.

———. 1977. *Science, Technology and Society.* Beverly Hills, Calif.: Sage Publications.

———. 1986. *Little Science, Big Science and Beyond.* New York: Columbia University Press.

Dietrich, William S. 1991. *In the Shadow of the Rising Sun.* University Park: Pennsylvania State University Press.

Dolan, Edwin G. 1971. *Tanstaafl: The Economic Strategy for the Environmental Crisis.* New York: Holt, Rinehart and Winston.

Dore, Ronald. 1987. *Taking Japan Seriously.* Stanford, Calif.: Stanford University Press.

Drexler, Eric K. 1992. *Nanosystems.* New York: J. Wiley and Sons.

Dreyfus, Hubert, and Stuart Dreyfus. 1986. "Why Computers May Never Think Like People." *Technology Review* 89, no. 1: 42–61.

Drucker, Peter. 1985. *Innovation and Entrepreneurship.* New York: Harper and Row.

Durham, William. 1991. *Coevolution: Genes, Culture and Human Diversity.* Stanford, Calif.: Stanford University Press.

Edquist, Charles. 1988. *Technology Policy.* Stanford, Calif.: Stanford University Press.

Eiseley, Loren. 1961. *Darwin's Century: Evolution and the Men Who Discovered It.* Garden City, N.Y.: Doubleday Anchor.

Ellul, Jacques. 1964. "La Technique." Translated as *The Technological Society.* New York: Vintage Books.

Erikson, Erik H. 1950. *Childhood and Society.* New York: W. W. Norton.

Etzioni, Amitai. 1988. *The Moral Dimension: Toward a New Economics.* New York: Free Press.

Eysenck, Hans Jurgen. 1973. *The Experimental Study of Freudian Theories.* London: Methuen.

Farrell, Warren L. 1986. *Why Men Are the Way They Are.* New York: Berkeley Books.

Fenn, John B. 1982. *Engines, Energy and Entropy.* San Francisco: W. H. Freeman.

Ferkiss, Victor. 1969. *Technological Man.* New York: Braziller.

Flexner, A. 1925. *Medical Education.* New York: Macmillan.

Florida, Richard, and Martin Kenney. 1989. *The Breakthrough Illusion.* New York: Basic Books.

Forrester, Jay W. 1971. *World Dynamics.* Cambridge, Mass.: Wright-Allen Press.

Futuyama, Douglas J. 1983. *Science on Trial: The Case for Evolution.* New York: Pantheon.

Galbraith, John Kenneth. 1967. *The New Industrial State.* New York: New American Library.

Gardner, Howard. 1987. *The Mind's New Science: A History of Cognitive Revolution.* New York: Basic Books.

Gardner, John. 1968. *No Easy Victories.* New York: Harper and Row.

Gerstein, Dean R., R. Luce Duncan, Neil J. Smeiser, and Sonja Sperlich, eds. 1988. *The Behavioral and Social Sciences: Achievement and Opportunities.* Washington, D.C.: National Academy Press.

Gibbs, J. Willard. ca. 1872. *Collected Works.* New Haven, Conn.: Yale University Press, 1903, reprinted 1948.

Gilfillan, S. C. 1935. *The Sociology of Invention.* Chicago: Follett.

———. 1971. *Supplement to the Sociology of Invention.* San Francisco: San Francisco Press.

Good, Edwin M. 1982. *Giraffes, Black Dragons and Other Pianos: A Technological History from Christofori to the Modern Concert Grand.* Stanford, Calif.: Stanford University Press.

Goodenough, Ward Hunt. 1963. *Cooperation in Change.* New York: Russell Sage Foundation.

Gottman, J., C. Notarius, J. Gonson, and H. Markman. 1976. *A Couple's Guide to Communications.* Champagne, Ill.: Research Press.

Gould, Stephen Jay. 1981. *The Mismeasure of Man.* New York: W. W. Norton.

———. 1986. "Evolutions and the Triumph of Homology, or Why History Matters." *Scientific American* (Jan.–Feb.): 60–69.

Greenberg, Joseph. 1963. "Language and Linguistics." In Berelson 1963.

Harlow, H. F. 1959. "Love in Infant Monkeys." *Scientific American* (June).

———. 1963. "Animal Study." In Berelson 1963.

Harlow, H. F., and M. K. Harlow. 1962. "Social Deprivations in Monkeys." *Scientific American* (Nov.).

Harré, Rom. 1970. *The Principles of Scientific Thinking.* Chicago: University of Chicago Press.

Herbert, Nick. 1985. *Quantum Reality.* Garden City, N.Y.: Doubleday Anchor.

Herman, Judith Lewis, M.D. 1992. *Trauma and Recovery.* New York: Basic Books.

Heskett, John. 1980. *Industrial Design.* New York: Oxford University Press.

Hill, Christopher T. 1986. "The Nobel-Prize Awards as a Measure of National Strength in Science." Science Policy Report Study, Background Report no. 3. Washington, D.C.: U.S. Congressional Research Service.

Hirsch, E. D. 1988. *Cultural Literacy.* New York: Vintage Books.

Hofsteder, Geert. 1980. *Culture's Consequences.* Newbury Park, Calif.: Sage Publications. 5th ed. paperback.

Holton, Gerald. 1952. *Concepts and Theories in the Physical Sciences.* Cambridge, Mass.: Addison-Wesley.

Holton, Gerald, and Robert Morison, eds. 1978, 1979. *Limits of Scientific Inquiry.* New York: W. W. Norton.

Humphrey, N., and D. C. Dennett. 1989. "Speaking for Ourselves: An Assessment of Multiple Personality Disorder." *Raritan* 9: 68–98.

Huntley, H. E. 1953. *Dimensional Analysis.* London: McDonald and Co.

Inkeles, Alex. 1983. *Exploring Individual Modernity.* New York: Columbia University Press.

Inkeles, Alex, and David Horton Smith. 1974. *Becoming Modern.* Cambridge, Mass.: Harvard University Press.

Jacobs, Jane. 1961. *The Death and Life of Great American Cities.* New York: Vintage Books.

Johanson, Donald, and Edey Maitland. 1981. *Lucy.* New York: Warner Books.

Johnson, Stephen M. 1985. *Characterological Transformation: The Hard Work Miracle.* New York: W. W. Norton.

———. 1987. *Humanizing the Narcissistic Style.* New York: W. W. Norton.

———. 1991. *The Symbiotic Character.* New York: W. W. Norton.

———. 1994. *Character and Style.* New York: W. W. Norton.

Josephson, Mathew. 1959. *Edison: A Biography.* New York: McGraw-Hill.

Jung, C. G. 1965. *Memories, Dreams, and Recollections.* New York: Vintage Books.

Kaplan, David, and Robert A. Manners. 1972. *Culture Theory.* Englewood Cliffs, N.J.: Prentice Hall.

Kash, Don E. 1989. *Perpetual Innovation.* New York: Basic Books.

Keenan, Joseph H. 1941. *Thermodynamics.* New York: J. Wiley and Sons.

Kerr, Clark. 1964. *Industrialism and Industrial Man.* 2d ed. New York: Oxford University Press.

Klamer, Arjo. 1983. *Conversations with Economists.* Savage, Md.: Rowman and Little-field.

Klein, Burton. 1977. *Dynamic Economics.* Cambridge, Mass.: Harvard University Press.

Kline, Stephen J. 1965, 1986. *Similitude and Approximation Theory.* New York: McGraw-Hill; New York: Springer.

———. 1977. "Toward the Understanding of Technology in Society." Three articles. *Mechanical Engineering* (Mar., April, May).

———. 1985a. "Research Is Not a Linear Process." *Research Management* 28 (July-Aug.).

———. 1985b. "What Is Technology?" *Bulletin of Science, Technology, and Society* 5, no. 3: 215–18.

———. 1986. "The Logical Necessity of Multidisciplinarity: A Consistent View of the World." *Bulletin of Science, Technology, and Society* 6, nos. 2, 3.

———. 1989. "Innovation Styles in Japan and the United States: Cultural Bases and Implications for Competitiveness." 1989 ASME Thurston Lecture. Also available as Report INN-3B, Dept. of Mechanical Engineering, Stanford University, Stanford, Calif. 94305-3030; also in *Chemtech* (Aug.-Sept. and Nov. 1991); translation in Japanese available, Agne Shofu Publishing, Tokyo.

———. 1991a. "Models of Innovation and Their Policy Consequences." In *Proceedings 1st International NISTEP Conference on Science and Technology Policy Research, Shimoda City, Japan 1990,* edited by H. Inose, M. Kawasaki, and F. Kodama. Tokyo: Miwa Press. Also available as Report INN-4B, Dept. of Mechanical Engineering, Stanford University, Stanford, Calif.

———. 1991b. "A Numerical Index for Complexity of Systems: The Concept and Some Implications." In *Proceedings of the 1990 Association for Computing Machinery (ACM) Symposium on "Managing Complexity and Modeling Reality,"* edited by D. J. Frailey. New York: ACM Press.

Kline, Stephen J., and Don E. Kash. 1992. "Government Technology Policy: What Is It?" *The Bridge* 22, no. 1 (spring): 12–180.

Kline, Stephen J., and F. A. McClintock, 1953. "Describing Uncertainties in Single Sample Experiments." *Mechanical Engineering* (Jan.).

Kneebone, G. T. 1963. *Mathematical Logic and the Foundations of Mathematics.* London: D. Van Nostrand.

Kodama, Fumio. 1986. "The Innovation Spiral: A New Look at Recent Technological Advances." In *2nd U.S.-Japan Conference on High Technology and the International Environment, Kyoto, Japan, 9–11 Nov. 1986*, pp. 198–204. Washington, D.C.: National Academy of Sciences Press.

———. 1991. *Analyzing Japanese High Technology: The Techno-Paradigm Shift.* London: Pinter Publishers.

Konner, Mel. 1983. *The Tangled Wing: Biological Constraints on the Human Spirit.* New York: Harper Colophon Books.

Korzibski, Alfred. 1948. *Science and Sanity.* 3d ed. The International Non-Aristotelian Library.

Kroeber, A. L. 1917. "The Superorganic." *American Anthropologist,* n.s., 19: 163–214.

Kuhn, Thomas S. 1962. *The Structure of Scientific Revolutions.* Chicago: University of Chicago Press.

Kuttner, Robert. 1991. *The End of Laissez Faire.* New York: Knopf.

Landau, Ralph, and Nathan Rosenberg, eds. 1986. *The Positive Sum Strategy: Harnessing Technology for Economic Growth.* Washington, D.C.: National Academy Press.

Landes, David S. 1969. *The Unbound Prometheus.* Cambridge, Eng.: Cambridge University Press.

Langhaar, H. 1951. *Dimensional Analysis and Theory of Models.* New York: J. Wiley and Sons.

Larkin, Jill, J. McDermott, D. P. Simon, and H. A. Simon, 1980. "Expert and Novice Performance in Solving Physics Problems." *Science* (June): 1335–42.

Larson, Carl E., and Frank M. J. LaFasto. 1989. *Teamwork: What Must Go Right/What Can Go Wrong.* Newbury Park, Calif.: Sage Publications.

Lavender, Stephen J. 1981. *New Land for Old.* Bristol, Eng.: Adam Hilger.

Layton, Edwin T., Jr. 1992. "Escape from the Jail of Shape: Dimensionality and Engineering Science." In *Technological Development and Science in the Industrial Age,* edited by P. Kroes and M. Bakker, pp. 35–68. Kluuer Academic Publishers.

Leff, Harvey S., and Andrew F. Rex, eds. 1990. *Maxwell's Demon: Entropy, Information, Computing.* Princeton Physics Series. Princeton, N.J.: Princeton University Press.

Lienhard, John. 1979. "The Rate of Technological Improvements Before and After the 1830's." *Technology and Culture* 20, no. 3 (July).

Lumsden, Charles, and Edward O. Wilson. 1981. *Genes, Mind and Culture.* Cambridge, Mass.: Harvard University Press.

McGinn, R. E. 1991. *Science, Technology and Society.* Englewood Cliffs, N.J.: Prentice Hall.

McNeill, William H. 1963. *The Rise of the West: A History of the Human Community.* Chicago: University of Chicago Press.

———. 1976. *Plagues and People.* Garden City, N.Y.: Doubleday Anchor.

Mahler, M. S., F. Pine, and A. Bergman. 1968. *The Psychological Birth of the Human Infant.* New York: Basic Books.

Mandelbrot, Benoit. 1990. *Fractals in Physics.* Amsterdam: North Holland.

Mansfield, Edwin. 1988. "Industrial Innovation in Japan and the United States." *Science* 241 (Sept.): 1769–74.

Masterson, James. 1981. *The Narcissistic and Borderline Disorders.* New York: Bruner Mazel.

Mause, Lloyd de, ed. 1988. *The History of Childhood: The Untold Story of Child Abuse.* New York: Peter Bedrick Books.

Mayer, Joseph, and Maria Goeppert Mayer. 1940. *Statistical Mechanics.* New York: J. Wiley and Sons.

Mayr, Otto. 1979. *Origins of Feedback Control.* Cambridge, Mass.: MIT Press.

Mead, Margaret. 1949. *Male and Female.* New York: Morrow.

———. 1955. *Cultural Patterns and Technical Change.* New York: New American Library.

———. 1956. *New Lives for Old.* New York: Morrow.

———. 1963. *Sex and Temperament in Three Primitive Societies.* New York: Morrow.

———. 1972. *Blackberry Winter: My Earlier Years.* New York: Morrow.

Meadows, Donella, et al. 1972. *Limits to Growth.* New York: Universe Books. (But see also the 1973 study by the Science Policy Research Unit, *Models of Doom: A Critique of Limits to Growth.* London: Sussex University.)

Michener, James A. 1954. *The Floating World.* Honolulu: University of Hawaii Press.

Miller, Alice. 1983. *For Your Own Good: Hidden Cruelty in Child-Rearing and the Roots of Violence.* New York: Farrar, Straus and Giroux.

———. 1984. *Thou Shalt Not Be Aware.* New York: Farrar, Straus and Giroux.

Miller, George. 1956. "The Magical Number Seven, Plus or Minus Two." *Psychological Review* 63: 81–97.

———. 1963. "Thinking, Cognition and Learning." In Berelson 1963.

Mills, C. Wright. 1959. *The Sociological Imagination.* London: Oxford University Press.

Mishan, E. J. 1970. *Technology and Growth: The Price We Pay.* New York: Praeger.

Monden, Yasuhiro. 1983. *Toyota Production System: Practical Approach to Production Management.* Norcross, Ga.: Industrial and Management Press.

Morita, Akio. 1986. *Made in Japan.* New York: New American Library.

Mumford, Lewis. 1934. *Technics and Civilization.* New York: Harbinger Books.

Nakane, Chie. 1971, 1973. *Japanese Society.* Rev. ed. Harmondsworth, Middlesex, Eng.: Penguin Books.

Nayak, P. Ranganath, and John M. Ketteringham. 1986. *Breakthroughs.* New York: Rawson.

Nelson, Richard R., ed. 1993. *National Innovation Systems: A Comparative Analysis.* New York: Oxford University Press.

Nelson, Richard R., and Sydney G. Winter. 1982. *An Evolutionary Theory of Economic Change.* Cambridge, Mass.: Belknap Press of Harvard University Press.

Odum, Howard T. 1971. *Environment, Power and Society.* New York: Wiley Interscience.

Ogburn, W. F. 1922. *Social Change.* New York: B. W. Huesch.

Ogburn, W. F., and D. Thomas. 1922. "Are Inventions Inevitable?" *Political Science Quarterly* 37: 83–98.

Okimoto, Daniel I., and Thomas P. Rohlen. 1988. *Readings in the Japanese System.* Stanford, Calif.: Stanford University Press.

Ornstein, Robert, and Richard F. Thompson. 1984. *The Amazing Brain.* Boston: Houghton Mifflin.

Pacey, Arnold. 1975. *The Maze of Ingenuity: Ideals and Idealism in the Development of Technology.* New York: Holmes and Meier.

Pennebaker, James W. 1990. *Opening Up.* New York: Avon Books.

Peters, T. J. 1985. *In Search of Excellence: Lessons from America's Best Run Companies.* New York: Random House.

Phenix, Phillip H. 1964. *Realms of Meaning.* New York: McGraw-Hill.

Platt, John. 1966. *The Step to Man.* New York: J. Wiley and Sons.

Plumb, J. H. 1973. *In the Light of History.* New York: Houghton Mifflin.

Polanyi, Michael. 1958, 1962. *Personal Knowledge: Toward a Post Critical Philosophy.* Chicago: University of Chicago Press.

———. 1968. "Life's Irreducible Structure." *Science* 160 (June 21): 1308–11.

Porter, Michael. 1990. *The Competitive Advantage of Nations.* New York: Free Press.

Potter, David. 1954. *People of Plenty.* Chicago: University of Chicago Press.

Prandtl, Ludwig. 1904. "Boundary Layer Theory." In W. F. Durand, *Aerodynamic Theory.* Berlin: Springer, 1934.

Price. See de Solla Price.

Qin, Yulin, and H. A. Simon. 1990. "Laboratory Replication of Scientific Discovery Process." *Cognitive Science* 14: 281–312.

Rabinow, Paul, and William M. Sullivan. 1979, 1987. *Interpretive Social Science: A Second Look.* Berkeley: University of California Press.

Reich, Charles. 1970. *The Greening of America: How the Growth Revolution Is Trying to Make America Livable.* New York: Random House.

Reich, Leonard. 1985. *The Making of American Industrial Research: Science and Business at GE and Bell, 1876–1926.* Cambridge, Eng.: Cambridge University Press.

Reich, Robert. 1989. "The Quiet Path to Technological Preeminence." *Scientific American* (Oct.).

Reischauer, Edwin O. 1977, 1988. *The Japanese Today.* Cambridge, Mass.: Belknap Press of Harvard University Press.

Reiser, Stanley Joel. 1978. *Medicine and the Reign of Technology.* Cambridge, Eng.: Cambridge University Press.

Riley, John W. 1963. "Some Contributions of Behavioral Science to Contemporary Life." In Berelson 1963.

Rilke, Rainer Maria. 1934. *Letters to a Young Poet.* New York: W. W. Norton.

Rochlin, Gene I. 1959, and many later years. "Scientific Technology and Social Change." In *Readings from Scientific American.* San Francisco: W. H. Freeman.

Rosenberg, Nathan. 1976. *Perspectives on Technology.* Cambridge, Eng.: Cambridge University Press.

———. 1982. *Inside the Black Box: Technology and Economics.* Cambridge, Eng.: Cambridge University Press.

Rosenberg, Nathan, and L. E. Birdzell Jr., 1986. *How the West Grew Rich: The Economic Transformation of the Industrial World*. New York: Basic Books.

Rosenberg, Nathan, and Walter G. Vincenti. 1978. *The Britannia Bridge: The Generation and Diffusion of Technological Knowledge*. Cambridge, Mass.: MIT Press.

Ross, Ralph. 1970. *Obligation: A Social Theory*. Ann Arbor: University of Michigan Press.

Rothschild, Michael. 1990. *Bionomics: The Inevitability of Capitalism*. New York: Henry Holt.

Rousel, Philip A.; Kamal N. Saad; and Tamara Erikson. 1991. *Third Generation R & D*. Boston: Harvard Business School Press.

Roy, Ruston. 1981. *Experimenting with the Truth*. 1979 Hibbert Lectures. New York: Pergamon Press; University Park: Pennsylvania State University Press.

Sacks, Oliver. 1993 "To See and Not to See." *New Yorker* (May 10): 59–73.

Schlichting, H. 1968. *Boundary Layer Theory*. 6th ed. Translated by J. Kestin. New York: McGraw-Hill.

Schmookler, Jacob. 1966. *Invention and Economic Growth*. Cambridge, Mass.: Harvard University Press.

Schon, Donald. 1971. *Beyond the Stable State*. New York: W. W. Norton.

Schonberger, Richard J. 1982. *Japanese Manufacturing Techniques: Nine Hidden Lessons in Simplicity*. New York: Free Press.

Schumpeter, Joseph Alois. 1950. *Capitalism, Socialism and Democracy*. New York: Harper.

———. 1961. *The Theory of Economic Development*. Cambridge, Mass.: Harvard University Press.

Schwartz, Richard B. 1983, 1985. *Daily Life in Johnson's London*. Madison: University of Wisconsin Press.

Seneca. 1969. *Letters from a Stoic*. Harmondsworth, Middlesex, Eng.: Penguin Books.

Shapiro, A. H. 1953. *The Dynamics and Thermodynamics of Compressible Fluid Flow*. New York: Ronald Press.

Sharp, Lauren. 1967. "Steel Axes for Stone Age People." In Spicer 1967.

Siegel, S. 1957. "Level of Aspiration and Decision Making." *Psychological Review* 44 (July): 253–62.

Simmons, Robert H. 1981. *Achieving Humane Organization*. Malibu, Calif.: Daniel Spence Publishers.

Simon, H. A. 1955. "A Behavioral Model of Rational Choice." *Quarterly Journal of Economics* 46 (Feb.): 99–118. See also Siegel 1957.

Simon, Herbert. 1969. *The Sciences of the Artificial*. Cambridge, Mass.: MIT Press.

Snow, C. P. 1969. *The Two Cultures and a Second Look*. An expanded version of *Two Cultures and the Scientific Revolution*. Cambridge, Eng.: Cambridge University Press.

Spicer, Edward H. 1967. *Human Problems in Technological Change: A Casebook*. New York: J. Wiley and Sons.

Spitz, Rene Arpad. 1960. "Motherless Infants." In *Selected Readings in Marriage and the Family*, edited by F. Winch and Robert McGinnis, pp. 185–94. New York: Holt, Rhinehart and Winston.

———. 1965. *The First Year of Life*. New York: International Universities Press.

———. 1983. *Dialogues from Infancy*. New York: International Universities Press.

Squires, Arthur M. 1986. *The Tender Ship: Governmental Management of Technological Change.* Boston: Birkhauser.

Staudenmaier, S. J. 1985. *Technology's Storytellers: Reweaving the Human Fabric.* Cambridge, Mass.: MIT Press.

Steinem, Gloria. 1992. *The Revolution from Within.* Boston: Little, Brown.

Stern, Daniel N. 1985. *The Interpersonal World of the Infant.* New York: Basic Books.

Stone, Lawrence. 1977. *The Family, Sex and Marriage in England, 1500–1800.* Harmondsworth, Middlesex, Eng.: Penguin Books.

Sutton, O. G. 1949. *The Science of Flight.* Harmondsworth, Middlesex, Eng.: Pelican Books.

Tarnas, Richard. 1991. *The Passion of the Western Mind.* New York: Harmony Books.

Thouless, Robert H. 1974. *Straight and Crooked Thinking.* 17th ed. London: Pan Books.

Trevelyn, G. M. 1942. *English Social History.* Harmondsworth, Middlesex, Eng.: Pelican Books.

Tuan, Yi-Fu. 1974. *Topofilia: A Study of Environmental Perception, Attitudes, and Values.* Englewood Cliffs, N.J.: Prentice Hall.

Tushman, Michael L., and William L. Moore, eds. 1988. *Readings in the Management of Innovation.* 2d ed. New York: Ballinger.

van Essen, D. C., C. H. Anderson, and D. J. Fellemon. 1992. "Information Processing in the Primate Visual System: An Integrated Systems Perspective." *Science* 255 (Jan. 24): 419–23.

Varian, Hal R. 1987, 1990. *Intermediate Microeconomics: A Modern Approach.* 2d ed. New York: W. W. Norton.

Vierling, Jeffrey M. 1992. "Communitarianism in the Factory: Forming and Maintaining Cooperative Work Teams in U.S. Automobile Assembly Plants." Honors thesis, Stanford University. (Available from S. J. Kline on request.)

Vincenti, Walter G. 1989. *What Engineers Know and How They Know It.* Baltimore, Md.: Johns Hopkins University Press.

Viscott, David, M.D. 1972. *The Making of a Psychiatrist.* New York: Pocket Books.

Walton, Mary. 1990. *Deming Management at Work.* New York: G. P. Putnam's Sons.

Watson, James D., and Francis Crick. 1969. *The Double-Helix.* New York: New American Library.

Watson, John B. 1925. *Behaviorism.* New York: W. W. Norton.

Watzlawick, Paul. 1974. *Change: Principles of Problem Formation and Problem Resolution.* New York: W. W. Norton.

Watzlawick, P., J. H. Beavin, and D. D. Jackson. 1967. *The Pragmatics of Human Communications.* New York: W. W. Norton.

Weiss, Joseph, and Harold Sampson. 1986. *The Psychoanalytic Process.* New York: Guilford Press.

Whitbeck, Caroline. 1992. "The Trouble with Dilemmas: Rethinking Applied Ethics." *Professional Ethics* 1, nos. 1 and 2 (spring and summer).

White, Lynn. 1962. *Medieval Technology and Social Change.* London: Oxford University Press. Paperback reprint, 1970.

Whitehead, A. N. 1959. *The Aims of Education and Other Essays.* New York: Macmillan.

Whitfield, Charles L. 1989. *Healing the Child Within.* Deerfield, Fla.: Health Communications.

Wiener, Norbert. 1948. *Cybernetics.* New York: J. Wiley and Sons; Paris: Hermann.

Wilkes, K. V. 1988. *Real People.* New York: Oxford University Press.

Williams, William F. 1994. Private communication to S. J. Kline.

Wilson, E. O. 1975, 1980. *Sociobiology: The Abridged Edition.* Cambridge, Mass.: Belknap Press of Harvard University Press. (See also his *Sociobiology: The New Synthesis* [Cambridge, Mass.: Harvard University Press] for particularly sweeping claims about genetic determination.)

———. 1985. "Time to Revive Systematics." *Science* 230 (Dec. 13).

Womack, James P., Daniel T. Jones, and Daniel Roos. 1990. *The Machine That Changed the World.* New York: Rawson Associates; Toronto: Collier Macmillan.

Ziman, John. 1968. *Public Knowledge: An Essay Concerning the Social Dimension of Science.* Cambridge, Eng.: Cambridge University Press.

Zuboff, Shoshana. 1988. *In the Age of the Smart Machine: The Future of Work and Power.* New York: Basic Books.

Index

abundance, relation to science, 197
Acton's Dictum, 246
aesthetics, 8
Age of Information, 230
aggregation, may give emergent behavior, 222
agriculture, relation to science, 210, 238
airfoils, 24
Anderson, C. H. Robert, 26, 76, 91
anthropomorphism, as projection, 240
Aoki, Masahiko, 184
Aristotle, 195
auto, operation of and "rules," 40
automobiles, impact of culture on design of, 162
autonomic control, 90

Bacon, Francis, 195
Baconian empiricism, 203, 254
ballistic reactions, defined, 40
barbaric, meaning of, 175
barefoot data, 7, 38
barefoot empiricism, 63
basic pattern, as physical basis of human societies, 174
Bastille, fall of, 95
Beavin, Janet H., 105, 228
behaviorism, 94
Berelson, Bernard, 85
Berger, Peter, 194

bet: for physicists, 301–8; for economists, 308–9
Bill of Rights, 4, 87, 246
bit, defined, 33
Blois, Marsden, 167
Boas, Franz, 83
Bohr, Niels, 124
Bohr Correspondence Principle, 124, 220
Boston Tea Party, 95
bottom-up determinism, 113
Bouchard, Gene, 4, 149
Boulding, Kenneth, 30f
Bower, Gordon, 38
Bradshaw, Peter, 51
Braybrooke, David, 63, 65f
Bridgman, P. W., 123f, 168, 215, 222, 305
Briere, John, 38
Brooks, Harvey, 185
Buckingham, Earl, 123
Burke, Edmund, 247

caloric, 247
Campbell, Joseph, 84
Carnot, Sadi, 211
Carroll, Lewis, 17
Cartesian axiomatization, 203f
Cassirer, Ernst, 176f
Casti, John L., 218, 254
cat and dog metaphor, logic of, 219

Central Presupposition of Control Theory, 187
chaotic system, 221
Chase, William G., 32
Chomsky, Noam, 230
chunks: defined, 33; indexing of, 34; number of in the mind, 35
Churchill, Winston, 175
Clausius, 237
Clebsch, W. C., xiv
cognitive science, history of, 149
Cohen, Yehudi A., 82, 84, 171, 174
communications, levels of, 227
complexity: illustrated, 57; and its implications, summary of results, 267
complexity index, definition of, 49–51
complexity of humans, 58, 66–67
complex systems: understanding via three-step process, 42; operation of, 62
Comte, Auguste, 207
Comte's Pecking Order, 208, 226, 239, 241
Conger, Stuart, 93
consistency, principle of, illustrations, 152
Constant, Edward, 58, 180
constraint: illustrations, 78; relation to determination, 78
control: autonomic, 90; design-mode, 90; human-mode, 90; levels of, 118
control feedback loop, four steps in, 55
control theory, central presupposition of, 188f
Corning, Peter A., 93, 220, 230
Council of Senior Scholars, 296–99
criterion of consistency, illustrations of use, 152
culture gap, 15
culture-B, definition of, 190
culture-N, definition of, 190
cut through operating space, 73
cybernetic, 55, 93

d'Alembert, Jean, 24f, 211
Darwin, Charles, 179
data, primacy of in complex systems, 62, 74, 140
degrees of freedom, 75; and human choices, 79
de Groot, Adriaan, 32, 38, 94, 130; conclusions from test with chess players, 39
Deming's Dictum, 259
Dennett, Daniel C., 35, 44f, 192, 273
Descartes, René, 203

design, structured (not random) process, 120
design space, definition of, 50
de Solla Price, Derek, 54, 196f, 211, 252
determination, relation to constraint, 78
deterministic system, 221
development, necessity of for complex hardware, 62
Dietrich, William S., 185, 246
differences and similarities among disciplines, summary of results, 270
difficulties of incompleteness, 235
dimensional homogeneity: principle of, 122–23; presuppositional for equations of classical physics, 122–23, 126
dimensionality, defined by illustration, 71, 75
disciplinary boundary, 5
disciplines: denotation of the word, 3; as they relate to sociotechnical systems, 138; dealing with truth assertions, eight steps in development of, 199; professionalization of, 213; new in twentieth century, 230; as subcultures, 250
DNA, 202
domains and truth assertions, 20; three-part picture, 21
Down's syndrome, 191
Draper, C. Stark, 188
Draper's Dictum, 188f
Drexler, Eric, 64
Dreyfus, Herbert, 40, 63, 130
Dreyfus, Stuart, 40, 63, 130
Durham, William, 174, 189, 250, 273
Durham's hypothesis, 189
Dyson, Freeman, 253f

ecologies, complexity of, 60
economics, neo-classic theory of and innovation, 185–86
economists, bet for, 308–9
education, implications for, 295–300
Einstein, Albert, 215
Eisenhower, Dwight, 246
Elders, obligation of, 297–99
Emancipation Proclamation, 87
emergent properties, 2, 59
empiricism in hierarchical structures, 147
enculturation, into disciplines, 249
encyclopedists, French, 195
energy: in physics and psychology, 236; and society, 240
engineering, relation to science, 210, 238
Enlightenment, 195, 245

Entire and Invariant Paradigms, illustrations, 81
Entire Invariant Paradigm: definition of, 80, 85, 89, 179; lack of in the human sciences, 83, 85, 89
Entire Paradigm: definition of, 80; illustrations, 85
entropy, 236, 306
epistemic hunger, 245
ether, 22, 247
ethics, 8
ethnology in the nineteenth century, 83
ethnology, lack of "universal" behaviors of humans, 83
Etzioni, Amitai, 240
Euclid, 203
Euler, Leonhard, 24
Europe, spirit of in nineteenth century, 206
exogenous dimensions, in various disciplines, 139
experiments, effect of theory on, 204
expertise, 32; surpasses rules, 40

faculty, an obligation of, 297–99
fallacies of projection, 235; sources of, 244
family system work, 27
feedback: in biological systems, 56; five levels of, 89–95
feedback loops: definition of, 49–51; four steps in, 55; need for in science, 201
Fellemon, D. J., 76, 91
Feyerabendian relativism, 255, 257f
First Commandment of Academe, 5
formal systems, 18
free will, 159–61
Freud, Sigmund, 26, 38, 209, 230, 255
functional equations, illustrations of, 69–72, 125, 137
Futuyama, Douglas J., 179

Galileo, 82, 84, 110, 112, 137, 179, 195, 205, 216
Gardner, Howard, 149, 230, 273
gas-in-a-box system, 306f
Gibbs, J. W., 22f, 44, 59, 71, 75, 120, 218
Gibbs's phase rule, 257
Gibbs simple **system**, defined, 59, 72
God, and open degrees of freedom, 79, 163
Gödel's theorem, 151, 203, 227, 238f
Gottman, J., et al., 10, 105
Gould, Stephen, 151
grand theory, definition of, 201

Greek philosophers, ancient, 8, 10, 195
Greek science, elements in, 247
Greenberg, Joseph, 85
Grimm's Law, 85, 226
Guideline, definition of, 62
Gutenberg, 54, 197

hard variables, 86
Harlow, H. F., 95, 192
Harlow, M. K., 95, 192
heat death, 236
Heaviside, Sir Oliver, 7, 38
Heaviside's Query, 7, 32
Hegelian swings, 228
Heisenberg Uncertainty Principle, domain of, 227, 236
Herbert, Nick, 218, 221
hierarchical obscurity, guideline of, 153–54
hierarchical structures, key questions about, 158–59
hierarchy, examples of, 101–4; of constitution, 106–8; relation to disciplines, 108; variation of parameters and variables from level to level, 127
Hirsch, E. D., 41f
historians of science, 253
holism, 4
Homo habilis, 172
Hoover, Herbert, 246
human being: complexity of, 58; complexity of alternate estimate, 66; vocabulary of, number of chunks in the mind, 67; residual instincts of, 83; existential uncertainties of, 84; qualitatively different from other animals, 175f
human brain, number of possible configurations, 59
human communications, illustrated, 84
human control mode, 90; design process, 90; design process, two loops in, 141
human evolution, 175
human mind, some limits of, 35–45
human powers, acceleration of over past 100,000 years, 173
human sciences: definition of, 36; no known Entire Invariant Paradigms, 83, 215; ethnology, sociology, psychology, history, economics, and political science, 96, 207; search for "physics-like" principles, 214
Huntley, H. E., 123
hyperspace: explanation of, 70; cut through illustrated, 72, 74

ideal fluid flow, 25
implications of complexity, summary of, 278
inference, negative, 8, 20; strong, negative 19f
information: four types of, 52; genetic, 53; information in inert matter (rocks), 53; in humans, animals, 54
innovation: six simplistic models, 180–82; improved model, 183–85
instincts, residual, 83
integrate, two meanings of, 125
integrated control information, 129; illustration of use in driving a car, 129–30
interfaces of mutual constraint, 114–20; role of summarized, 278
inventions, social, 93
invisible colleges, 197
irreversibility paradox, 304, 307
iron laws, 93

Jackson, Don, 26, 105, 228
Johanson, Donald, 172
Johnson, Stephen M., 230
jumper connections, 90
Jung, Carl, 236

Kash, Don E., 161, 185
Keenan, Joseph H., 120
Keynes, John Maynard, 86
Klein, Burton, 185f
Kneebone, G. T., 104
Korzibski, Alfred, 18, 28, 43, 168
Korzibski's Dictum, 43
Kuhn, Thomas S., 249, 252
Kuttner, Robert, 185

Landau, Ralph, 179
Langhaar, H., 123
Laplace, marquis de, 112, 217
Laplace's equation, 25
Larkin, Jill, 32
Layton, Ed, 210
Leaning Tower of Pisa, 82
learning-by-doing, 63; by-using, 63
Lederberg, Joshua, 253f, 257
Lenin, 88
Leonardo's sketchbook, 153
levels of control, 118f
Lienhard, John, 173
limits of the mind, summary of, 279
Limits to Growth, 77

Lindblom, Charles E., 63, 65f
Linne, Carl von (Linnaeus), 202
logical positivism, 227
Lombardi, Vince, 9
Lowell, James Russell, 292
Luther, Martin, 195
Lysenko's ideas, 252

McNeill, William, 87
Magna Carta, 95
Mahler, Margaret, 230
Maitland, Edey, 172
map, metaphor of, 5f
marasmus, 192
Marx, Karl, 88, 212
Marxism, economics of, 88
mathematization, and feedback loops in science, 204
Maxwell, J. Clerk, 81, 218, 306
Maxwell demon, 306
Maxwell's equations, 257
Mayer, Joseph, 223
Mayer, Maria Goeppert, 223
Mead, Margaret, 92, 197
Meadows, Donella, 77
medicine, relation to science, 210, 238
Mendel, 179
Mendeleyev, periodic table of, 105, 202
messages, how the mind stores, 37
Mill, John Stuart, 208
Miller, Alice, 54
Miller, George (Miller's 7-Bit-Rule), 33, 35f, 202, 245, 283
Miller, William, 229
mind, limits of, 279
mirroring, of system by sysrep, 19, 283
mismatch of mind and complexity of systems, 280
modern physics, domain of, 220
modern view, compared to postmodern, 231
Morgan, J. P., 86
multidisciplinarity, summary of need for, 273
multidisciplinary discourse, 2, 281–92
mutual constraint, interfaces of, 114–20, 164

Nakane, Chie, 92, 283
natural philosophy, unity of thought in, 195
nature/nurture, five possible "positions," 191
Navier, M., 24

Navier-Stokes equations, 24
negative inference, process of, 8
Nelson, Richard R., 182, 185f
neurons, number in human brain, 58
Newton, Isaac, 75, 179, 196, 198, 205, 216, 218
Newton, Invariant Paradigms of, 196, 204f
Newtonian principles of classical mechanics, 81, 179, 226
Newton's laws, seen as worldview, 205, 210
Nietzsche, Friedrich, 210, 227

obligation of the elders, 292
open degrees of freedom: relation to constraints, 77–79; in speech, 116–18; in human brain, in artifacts, in cultures, in art, in music, in sports, 161–63, 238
operant conditioning, 94
operating space, definition of, 50, 69
orthogonal, defined, 51
oughts, relation to "izzes," 9
overclaiming, by disciplinary experts, 152
overviews, current lack of, 199

Paradigms, Entire and Entire Invariant, 80–86
parameters, definition of, 49–51
Pasteur, 179
Pavlov, 230
Pennebaker, James W., 191
Phenix, Phillip H., 8, 9, 143
philosophy, Hegelian swings in, 258
philosophy and physics, interactions of, 226–29
philosophy, lack of closure method in, 228; of science, difficulties in, 253
phlogiston, 247
physical sciences, characteristics compared with social sciences, 224–25
physicists, bet for, 301–8
physics, 127, 215–17
piecewise view, defined, 134
Pi Theorem (of dimensional analysis), 123
Planck, Max, 22, 23
Planck and Gibbs, 23
Plato's cave, xv
Platt, John, 19, 205, 228
Polanyi, Michael, 114, 164
Polanyi's Principle, 115, 119, 187, 222f; illustrated by structure of speech, 114–15
Popperian falsification, 255
Porter, Michael, 151, 185

positivism in the human sciences, 214
positivism, in United States, 214
positivism, outcome in twentieth century, 215, 217
positivist philosophy, 151, 207
postmodern view, compared to modern, 231
post-traumatic stress syndrome, 37
Prandtl, Ludwig, 25
presuppositions of author, xv
primacy of data in complex systems, 62, 74, 140
primary dimensions, illustration of, 122–24
principle of consistency, 149
probability view of the world, 306
Procrustean process, 73
Procter and Gamble, 86
projection, 44, 223
projective errors, 235
properties, emergent, 3
psychology, relation to science, 210
psychotherapy, relation to science, 238

quantum mechanics, 215
Qin, Yulin, 32

Rabinow, Paul, 229
radical behaviorism, 94
Rashomon, 41
rectangular room system, 73
reductionist view, definition of, 110, 277; limit of domain, 143–47
Reformation, 195
relativity theory, 219
religion, some functions of, 194–95
religion and science, relation between, 164–66
Renaissance, 195
research and development (R and D), 176
Rhinelander, P., xiv
Riley, John W., 37, 84f
Rilke, R. M., 10
Rosenberg, Nathan, 179, 184
Rothschild, Michael, 91, 176, 182, 185f, 197
Royal Society of London, 9
"rules": in social systems, 86; shift in Muslim societies, 87; semantics of, 201, 226
Russell, Bertrand, 104f, 227

Sacks, Oliver, 42
sacred canopy, 194
Sampson, Harold, 209

schemata, 31, 37, 41
Schlichting, H., 25
scholarly controversy, guideline for, 193, 230
science: defined by its goals, 9; and truth assertions, 21; errors in ancient Greek views of, 169; history of, 195–99; goals of, 272
sciences, order of development historically, 206; branching from natural philosophy, 209
Science, Technology and Society (STS), as a field, xv
second-floor tennis-ball test, 82
Seneca's Dictum, conceptual level, 178f, 216
set-point value, illustration, 91
Shakespeare, 59
Shapiro, A. H., 237
Showalter, M. R., 168
Simmons, Robert H., 10
Simon, Herbert A., 32, 34, 39
Skinner, B. F., 94
Skinner box, 94
skunk works, 4
Snow, C. P., 15
Snow's culture gap, 266
social Darwinism, 151–52, 236, 241f
social inventions, 93
social sciences, compared with physical sciences, 224–25
social systems, complexity of, 59
sociobiology, 187
sociology, origin of, 208
sociotechnical systems, 171–78
sociotechnical systems: complexity of, 60; lack of study of, 138; as basis for human societies, 171–72; purposes of, 171–72; of other animals, 176
solutions: disagreements among disciplines, 149; "blind" transposition to other levels, 150
"some people," usage in this book, 111
Spitz, Rene Arpad, 54, 95, 191
Stalin, 88
statistical mechanics, relation to thermodynamics, 224–25
Stentor, 91
Stern, Daniel, 54, 230
Stokes, G. G., 24
structural view, defined, 135
Sullivan, Harry Stack, 26

Sullivan, William M., 229
sufficient list of dimensions for inert physical systems, 123
supreme being, existence of, xvi
surplus value, theory of, 88
symbolic forms, 177
synoptic view, 110, 134, 277; limit of domain, 143–47
sysreps: concept of, 17; and mathematics, 168; in physics, need three kinds, 221
system concept, 15; limits of, 27; and culture gap, 29
system: definition of, 16; necessity of definition of, 20, 27
systems, formal, 18; six major classes of, 144; and their mental representations, summary of results, 264; structure of, summary of results, 268
system/sysrep apparatus, questions arising from, 156; summary of, 281

Tarnas, Richard, 257f
taxonomies, importance of, 201–3
Teller, Edward, 305
temperature, control of by four-step feedback loop, 56
theory, general, 20
thermodynamics, principles of, xx
Thongpas, 189
thought, tools of, 274
three views, need for (synoptic, piecewise, structural), 134–35
Truman, Harry, 246
truth, relation to "the good" and to beauty, 9
truth assertions: denotation, 7; domain of, 7; and intimate relations, 10
Tuan, Y.-F., 82, 84, 247
turbulent flow, complexity of, 57

uncertainty, in experiments, 85
uncertainty principle, domain of, 227
universal approach, lack of, 276
universalisms, 28, 31
U.S. Constitution, 4, 87, 246

van Essen, D. C., 76, 91
variables, definition of, 49–51
Vienna circle, 227
Vincenti, Walter, xiv, 58, 151, 210
von Neumann, architecture for computers, 64

Watson, J. B., 95
Watzlawick, Paul, 105, 228, 255
Weiss, Joseph, 209
Whitbeck, Caroline, 64
Whitehead, Alfred North, 175, 227, 248, 282
Wiener, Norbert, 55, 91
Williams, William F., 252
Wilson, E. O., 187
Windsor castle, illustration of need for at least three views, 147, 245
Winter, Stanley G., 185f

Wittgenstein's ideas, 256
women, historical disenfranchisement of, 197
women's suffrage, 87
words: human use of, 31; ambiguity of, 43
working memory: defined, 33; speed of, 35
world, reality of, xv
Wright brothers, 25

Yir Yoront, study by Sharp, 84

Ziman, John, 229, 252

Library of Congress Cataloging-in-Publication Data

Kline, S. J. (Stephen Jay), 1922–
  Conceptual foundations for multidisciplinary thinking /
Stephen Jay Kline.
    p. cm.
Includes bibliographical references (p.   ) and index.
ISBN 0-8047-2409-1 (cloth : alk. paper) :
1. Interdisciplinary approach to knowledge. I. Title.
BD255.K547 1995
001 — dc20
94-44008   CIP

⊗ This book is printed on acid-free, recycled paper.
It has been typeset in 10/12 Times by
Keystone Typesetting, Inc.

Original printing 1995

Last figure below indicates year of this printing:

04 03 02 01 00 99 98 97 96